COUNSELING:
THEORY AND PROCESS

James C. Hansen

State University of New York at Buffalo

Richard R. Stevic

State University of New York at Buffalo

Richard W. Warner, Jr.

Pennsylvania State University

Allyn and Bacon, Inc.   *BOSTON*

To Our Parents

BERNARD AND LUCILLE HANSEN

WAYNE AND ELEANOR STEVIC

RICHARD AND EMILY WARNER

Library of Congress Catalog Card Number: 74–183210

Contents

Preface

Counseling is a process that assists an individual in learning about himself, his environment, and methods for handling his roles and relationships. Although individuals experience problems, counseling is not necessarily remedial. The counselor may assist an individual with the decision-making process in educational and vocational matters as well as resolving interpersonal concerns. Counseling is an applied field in which the counselor uses behavioral knowledge to help the client. Theory is helpful in understanding the development of behavior patterns, the manner and extent of undesirable behavior, and the development of procedures for changing client behavior.

    The purpose of this book is to provide a base from which the aspiring counselor or the counselor in the field can build his own personal theory of counseling—hopefully a theory that he will use to guide his own practice. We realize that no one text can do justice to all the theories in the field of counseling. Our attempt is not to present an exhaustive treatment of each theory, but rather to provide the tools and general background to enable an individual to build his own counseling theory. In order to meet this objective, we begin with a general discussion of theory and theory development. The next three chapters deal with an overview of the contributions to counseling from self-theory, psychoanalytic theory, and learning theory. Chapter 5 is devoted to assessing the present status in counsel-

Preface

ing theory. The last chapter in Part I focuses on the counselor as a person.

Part II moves from the theoretical base to focus on the process of counseling. The section begins with a chapter on initiating counseling and a chapter on the diagnostic process. Chapters 9 and 10 present counseling as a relationship between the counselor and client and also examine the various stages and dimensions that occur in the process. Later chapters are concerned with specific topics in counseling such as decision-making, the use of tests, and vocational counseling. Some case material and interview typescripts are presented to illustrate the process. Obviously a professor's use of tape recordings and films as illustrations is an excellent method for making counseling come alive.

A book of this nature is not a project in creative writing nor is it basically our original concepts and experiences. We have drawn from the resources of theories and research by many writers in the field of counseling. We also acknowledge the stimulation of our colleagues and students as an important contribution to the completion of the book. Mr. Alan Hoffman and Mrs. Lois Warner provided editorial assistance; Mrs. Betty Blazer, Miss Margie Conaway, Miss Louis Gettig, and Mrs. Gail Hofmann assisted in typing the manuscript. We pay special thanks to Mrs. Ruth Bryant for the preparation of the manuscript.

JCH
RRS
RWW

PART ONE

COUNSELING

AND

THEORY

1

Counseling
Theory

While the profession of counseling traces its roots to the early 1900's and
the first work of Parsons, it was in the decade of the sixties that the field
of counseling experienced its most rapid period of growth. The influx of
Federal monies into the preparation and training of counselors created not
only more counselors, but also more and generally better counselor preparation programs. As a result, counselors graduating from today's educational institutions are generally considered to be better prepared to fulfill
their functions than were those who graduated a scant ten years ago. Further, this emphasis on counseling during the decade of the sixties has led to
the recognition that counseling services are a necessary and integral part
of social services.

While this period of growth has produced positive results, it is also true
that many of today's counselors seem to flail about, without a real notion
of where they are going or what they hope to accomplish. It is becoming
increasingly apparent that experienced counselors, as well as those just
entering the field, need to develop a more systematic approach to the profession of counseling. Both those counselors already in the field and those
about to enter must develop for themselves a set of guidelines they can use
to organize and make purposeful their behavior in interaction with clients.
In short, counselors need to develop a theoretical base from which they can
operate in meaningful ways. This chapter will deal with the topic of *theory*.

3

The first section of the chapter defines what a theory is and what it can and cannot do. It also describes how a theory is developed, on what it is based, and what are the elements of a good theory. The second section of this chapter will deal with the need for and the development of theory within the field of counseling, as well as its applicability for the man on the firing line, the practicing counselor.

THEORY

WHAT IS A THEORY?

If each of us possessed a photographic memory or the ability for total recall of our past events, we might not have the need for theories. All we would need to do to solve a particular problem would be to recall some facts from the past. Unfortunately, we know our memories are often very fallible. As each of us is confronted with vast arrays of information, we need some structure to organize that information. If one has a problem to solve plus a great deal of applicable information, but no plan of attack to solve the problem, it is extremely likely that the problem will go on unresolved. In effect, a theory is a plan of attack. It is the structure upon which the information central to a solution of a problem can be placed. This structure enables us to place the various kinds of data in their proper place, and to develop a sense of the relationship between each of the bits of data. Hall and Lindzey (1957) have quite succinctly defined a theory as a cluster of relevant assumptions that are systematically related to each other and to a set of empirical definitions. Thus, one should not assume that a theory can be just thrown together; rather, it grows out of a systematic analysis of past events.

As Stefflre and Matheny (1960) suggest, another way to conceive of theory is to consider it a model: a model around which the theorist attempts to blend the reality of his experiences with his notions about the plausible explanations for these experiences. In a real sense, the theorist attempts to make sense out of life through the construction of a framework or model that allows him to explain events in a logical and reasonable manner. In simple and plain language, a theory is an explanation of events. Further, it is an explanation that can be tested.

WHAT GOOD IS A THEORY?

Having discussed the question of what a theory is, we need to consider the related question of the why of theory. The question often asked is, "What good is it?" The answer lies in a theory's ability to help us understand what we are doing; that is, it gives us a structure against which we can judge how much progress we are making toward a desired outcome. Implicit in this is the assumption that a theory should influence what is being done. If, indeed, a theory does not influence what is being done, then the theory is useless. To try to function without theory is to try to function in chaos for, without placing events in some order, it is impossible to function in a meaningful manner. Those who claim that they can operate without theory are generally operating on some vague and implicit assumptions about the nature of events; that is, in reality they are working from a theoretical frame of reference. The danger in this approach is that an implicit or hidden theory is subject to the interjection of personal biases into an individual's interpretation of experience. To state a theory in explicit terms, while it runs the risk of being dogmatic, tends to minimize the problem of personal biases.

In summary, then, a theory is an explanation for events which can be tested. It is useful only to the extent that it influences behavior and, finally, it is better stated in explicit terms than in implicit terms.

How Does a Theory Develop?

How then does a theory develop? If it is a structure, then we must assume that this structure is based on some smaller pieces of information drawn from experience. It may be helpful to think of theory building in terms of a pyramid. At the base of the pyramid we start with the simple observation of a series of events or behaviors. Having made careful observations over a period of time, we then begin to make inferences about what we have observed. That is, we begin to try to relate some of these events or behaviors with one another. Hence, if we observe that every time a certain child is to take a test in math he is absent from school, then we might make an inference about the relationship between the two events. If we observe these events over some time, our inferences may become a hypothesis. The child is afraid of failure. In effect, at this point we have made a statement of what we believe to be the relationship between these two events. If we observe the behavior of this child in several situations, we are likely to see several different kinds of events and may make several further inferences about the relationship between these events. We may observe that this same child does come to school to take tests in other subjects. Further, we may see that the math teacher is extremely intolerant of students who fail, while the other teachers are much more tolerant and encouraging. As many of these events are observed and several inferences made, a series of separate but related hypotheses may be formed. These related hypotheses are the bases upon which a structure for a theory about the child's behavior can be established. Thus, in this example, as in all theory development, we started with observable events; inferences about the relationship between these events were made and over a period of time became hypotheses; assumptions about the relation of these hypotheses were then made and the structure for a theory was formed. Hence, the pinnacle of the pyramid has been reached.

A word of caution is needed here since it is often assumed that this is where the process is stopped. If indeed it is stopped here, the tendency is to think of the theory as a law, which it is not. A theory is always in the process of being formulated; it is not static or stable. As new observations of events are made, new inferences and hypotheses may be developed that will affect or change the basic structure of the theory. A true theory is only a provisional formulation of a position or interpretation, which is then subject to some form of verification and testing, and then followed by reformulation of the theory (Williamson, 1965). Hence, while a theory is based on observations of events, there is a need for continuing observations to either verify our assumptions and hypotheses or generate new hypotheses when the original ones cannot be verified.

A theory then is based on inferences and hypotheses made about the plausible relationships between a series of events. A theory, however, is not generated in a vacuum. It is generated by people in a certain culture at a particular point in time. Hence, as Stefflre and Matheny (1968) point out, a theory is derived from bases that are personal, historical, sociological and philosophical. Seldom is it truly scientific because the individual theorist's personal needs plus the societal needs tend to dictate the particular questions asked and the answers that are acceptable.

The element of personal need is present in both theory adoption and theory construction. Shoben (1962) suggests that it is our own psychological need structure and not what research tells us that dictates what theory we will adopt as our own. It would seem that both the theory builder and the person who is about to adopt a theory should look closely at their own need structure in order to determine the real reasons for choosing one theory over another.

The development of theory is also tied to the period of time in which it is developed. A theory too far ahead of its time in history is next to useless because it does not fit the requirements of the times. The times as much as anything else dictate the answers to problems that will be considered at least as plausible. History is full of examples of theorists who were far ahead of their times and thus found few people who would even listen to them, let alone try to implement the theory. The troubles of men like Columbus and the Wright brothers or the early space scientists are prime examples of this phenomenon.

As time affects the development of theory, likewise do the sociological or cultural elements that surround a theorist. The American society is one that is based on order, yet continually strives for the concept of man's unique individuality. Hence, we strive to find order in all things so that we can understand events and behavior but, at the same time, we want to feel that each person has some freedom of choice. Thus, in the development of most of our personality theories we try to blend these two sometimes contradictory feelings. We want order, but not to the extent that we accept a completely deterministic view of man.

In the American culture we are also very concerned with what works. We are generally not interested in theories that dwell in the past, for we are very concerned about what is happening now. We are a pragmatic people, and our theories are expected to deal with and give plausible reasons for events and behaviors as they occur in today's world.

Finally, to a great extent, the development and adoption of particular theories is influenced by the philosophical realm. The prevailing philosophy of the time or the place in which the theorist works or where the theory is to be applied dictates to some degree the kind of theory to be used or developed. It is, in part, philosophy that defines the goals for which men should be striving. It is philosophy that defines what is the good life or what are the acceptable kinds of answers. What in one place and time is considered the good life may not be the same in another time or place. Hence, the theory that is developed or used during these times will tend to reflect the dominant philosophy of the time.

In summary, then, we need to realize that theories do not grow in isolation. They are rarely completely scientific because of all the factors that impinge on their development. They are in fact a product of their time and place. In order to understand why certain theories are developed and used, we must know something about the personal needs of the theorists and of those who adopt the theory for use. We must know something about the historical time during which the theory was developed. We need to pay particular attention to the sociological and cultural factors that might have affected the theory, and finally we need to examine the philosophy of the times. In short, we can only understand the development of a theory if we fully understand under what conditions the theory was developed. This implies that the theory is tied to the period in which it was developed and thus is limited in usefulness. This, however, need not be so, for if we are truly concerned with theory and not law, then the theory is always evolving. If it is a good theory it is continually receptive to the formulation of new

hypotheses based on observation of new events. So while the basic structure of a theory may have evolved at a particular point in time, and we
should understand the effects of that time, a good theory will continue to
evolve in order to explain present events.

The basic premise upon which any good theory is built is the assumption that the theory is always in the process of evolving. When treated as
some absolute truth, the theory becomes dogma—not theory. There are,
however, other requirements a theory must meet in order to be considered
a "good" theory.

What Are the Requirements of a Good Theory?

The first requirement is that a theory must be clear. It must be easily understood and communicable. The assumptions or hypotheses contained in
the theory must be stated in such a way as not to contradict one another.
More often than not, a theory is difficult to understand not because the concepts themselves are so difficult, but rather because those concepts have not
been carefully and thoughtfully related or connected.

Secondly, a good theory is one that is comprehensive. It should not deal
with the exception or isolated cases, but rather should be so designed as to
explain a great many events in various situations. The utility of any theory
depends, in large part, on its comprehensiveness. In short, to be of any
value a theory must supply plausible explanations for a variety of phenomena in a variety of situations.

A good theory also needs to be heuristic in nature. A theory needs to be
stated in terms that are exlicit enough to generate research. It cannot be a
vague accumulation of thoughts that do not lend themselves to testable hypotheses. It needs to be so designed that it can be subjected to the rigors of
scientific inquiry.

A good theory should relate means to the desired outcomes. In effect,
the theory establishes certain techniques having some relationship with the
end product. These techniques must be shown to have some relationship
with the outcomes, for merely to define what outcomes are desirous without
stating the means to arrive at these outcomes is not theory, but rather a
mere statement of objectives (Williamson, 1965).

A final point concerning a good theory needs to be made. That is, a
good theory does not simply exist, rather it is something to be used. The
extent of its use will depend on the manner in which it was generated and
for whom. To the scientist, the best theory is one that can be subjected to
experimental testing, while to the person in an applied field the best theory

will be one that supplies adequate guidelines for the use of particular techniques. In a large sense then, a good theory can be defined as one that proves the most helpful to the individual who is using it.

In summary, a "good" theory is one that is clear and is stated in explicit terms. It is heuristic in nature and is subject to the rigors of scientific investigation. A good theory is like a good road map, which is always in the process of being filled in, and the final test of its worth depends on how helpful it is (Stefflre, 1965).

SUMMARY

In this section of our discussion of theory we have attempted to deal with the concept of theory apart from any one discipline; that is, we have attempted to build a general conception of what we mean by the word *theory*. It seems useful to end this section by summarizing the major functions of a theory. Shertzer and Stone (1968) have delineated four major functions of theory:

1. A theory serves to summarize and generalize a particular body of knowledge. It brings together a body of related knowledge and, in shorthand fashion, attempts to put the separate findings into a meaningful and useful package.

2. A theory serves to increase the understanding of a particular body of knowledge. It attempts to order data and to demonstrate those pieces of the puzzle that are the most important.

3. A theory provides the tools by which predictions may be made. It is like a diagram that depicts the various points and what may be expected to occur at these points. For the practitioner it acts as a guide to the particular pathways that are possible and what may result if certain routes are followed. It points out the relationship between means and ends.

4. A theory serves to encourage further research into the area. It makes no difference whether the theory is proved correct or incorrect; the importance of the theory is that it stimulates further investigations into the particular phenomena with which it is concerned. This is the point to which we refer when we state that a theory is always in the process of becoming. As new research evidence is accumulated, the theory is substantiated, revised, or simply rejected.

THEORY IN COUNSELING

Now that we have discussed the term *theory*, we need to turn to our principal concern. How does this concept fit within the realm of counseling? What do we mean when we talk about counseling theory or theories? Where do these theories come from? How are these theories developed? Of what value are they to the practitioner? In what ways does a counselor decide which of the vast array of theories he will adopt for his own, or how does he develop his own theory of counseling?

WHAT IS COUNSELING?

It would seem that in order to answer these questions we need first to decide on what it is we mean by the term *counseling*. As Tyler (1953) points out, counseling is a word that everyone seems to understand, but it is also quite apparent that no two people understand it in exactly the same way. The word has long been a part of our language, but the rapid growth of the professional field of counseling has only served to confuse the issue of what is meant by the term. Part of the confusion may stem from the fact that counseling as we now know it had its basic beginnings in related but separate fields.

One of the origins of the professional counselor was the vocational guidance movement. The founding of this movement is generally attributed to Frank Parsons and his publication in 1906 of the book, *Choosing a Vocation*. From this movement came the idea of a vocational counselor, a person who helped individuals understand the facts about the world and themselves and then tried to help them fit these two patterns of information together in some meaningful fashion. Here then was the beginning of a particular specialist called a counselor.

At about the same time, 1908, there began to emerge another field that would eventually combine with the vocational guidance movement to form what today we basically call counseling. In 1908, Clifford Beers published his book, *The Mind That Found Itself*. The book called attention to the problem of mental illness in our country. This, coupled with the emergence of the field of psychoanalysis, led to an increased interest in both the concept of mental illness and how people might be "cured" or helped. Out of this movement came rapid expansion in the fields of psychiatry and clinical psychology. Many of these people referred to what they were doing as counseling, just as did the people in the vocational guidance movement.

As both of these fields expanded, it became apparent to people in both fields that a combination of the two was needed. The vocational counselor found he was involved in personal and social counseling, and the clinical psychologists and psychiatrists found that they needed to consider some of the knowledge in the vocational field. This blending and overlapping of function has only further confused the use of the term *counseling*. One has only to peruse the literature in the field to sense this confusion and disagreement over what is and what is not rightfully called counseling.

COUNSELING VS. PSYCHOTHERAPY

Most of this confusion seems to stem from the attempt to define counseling as something different from psychotherapy. Writers such as Patterson (1966) suggest that it is impossible to make any clear distinction between the fields of counseling and psychotherapy. His contention is that the definitions of counseling apply equally well to the concept of psychotherapy and vice-versa. Other writers such as Tyler (1953) attempt to make a clear and defined statement about the differences between counseling and psychotherapy. She states that the aim of psychotherapy is generally considered to be some kind of personality change. Counseling, on the other hand, is considered to be primarily concerned with helping individuals utilize their full potential. We might classify psychotherapy as personality reorganization while counseling is concerned with the building of personal competencies in order for individuals to cope better with their life situation. Even while attempting to delineate between the two services, Tyler talks about a continuum, with counseling at one end and psychotherapy at the other.

Most writers in the field, while attempting to differentiate between psychotherapy and counseling, eventually talk about a continuum of services. Vance and Volsky (1962) suggest that counseling deals with the so-called "normal" individual whose problems are developmental in nature, while psychotherapy is concerned with individuals who are deficient in some respect. Their continuum is based on the kind of people with whom the two services work. A similar notion of the continuum is expressed by Brammer and Shostrom (1960). They suggest that counseling is largely concerned with the "normal" individual, and is characterized by terms such as conscious awareness, problem solving, educative, supportive, and situational. On the other hand, psychotherapy is concerned with reconstruction, depth emphasis, analysis, and focus on the unconscious with emphasis on neurotic and emotional problems.

Division 17 of the American Psychological Association in attempting to define counseling, suggested that counseling is concerned with helping individuals plan for a productive role in their social environments. "Whether the person being helped with such planning is sick or well, abnormal or normal, is really irrelevant. The focus is on assets, skills, strengths and possibilities for further development. Personality difficulties are dealt with only when they constitute obstacles to the individual's forward progress." (APA Report, 1961, p. 6). Hence, while Division 17 of the APA appears to be talking about a continuum, the focus of the continuum is not the individual but rather the manner in which the counselor or the psychotherapist works with his respective clients.

Wolberg (1954) attempted to differentiate between counseling and psychotherapy by defining three kinds of approaches: supportive, insight-reeducative, and insight-reconstructive. He sees the first two approaches as appropriate for counselors, while the latter should be left to psychotherapists. The supportive approach simply involves the counselor aiding the client in the development of an emotional balance such that the individual can function in a normal and productive manner. In the approach titled insight-reeducative, Wolberg sees the counselor as helping the client modify some of his behavior patterns; that is, he helps the client learn new and better ways of coping with himself and his environment. Finally, the insight-reconstructive approach involves a psychotherapist helping his client work toward an understanding of unconscious conflicts with the aim of helping the client reform his personality structure. As with the other attempts at the delineation of function, Wolberg appears to be discussing a continuum between counseling and psychotherapy.

It should be clear to the reader at this point that there is a great deal of difficulty in distinguishing between counseling and psychotherapy. English and English (1958, p. 127) aptly sum up the dilemma when they suggest that counseling "while usually applied to help normal counselee, it merges by imperceptible degrees into psychotherapy."

In examining this situation let us concede that, indeed, there is a continuum between what is counseling and what is psychotherapy. While they appear at opposite ends of the continuum, they are not dichotomous or mutually exclusive ways of helping people in need. Further, we can concede that the psychotherapist is occasionally involved in the kinds of things that counselors do most of the time and that the counselor may occasionally be involved in the kinds of things that psychotherapists do most of the time. Nevertheless, the counselor and the psychotherapist generally operate at different ends of that somewhat mystical continuum. The task here is to try to define that continuum to at least some degree.

As we examine the continuum, we need first to consider the reasons for the existence of counseling and psychotherapy. Our complex technological society has placed many demands on the individual, demands that involve the roles one is expected to play in society. These demands produce difficulty for everyone as they make transitions from role to role. In some cases this transition from the demands of one role to the demands of another causes intrapersonal difficulties for the individual. The individual is experiencing value conflicts within his own personality. In other cases, the difficulty surrounds the nature of the roles themselves. Here the individual is having some difficulty in placing himself into a particular role. Using these two interrelated but somewhat different problem areas, we can begin to construct the continuum we are seeking. To the left of the continuum we can place the intrapersonal conflicts an individual may be incurring and at the right we can place those conflicts that involve role definitions.

Intra-Personal Problem 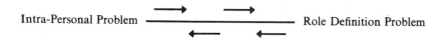 Role Definition Problem

FIGURE 1-1. The New York Academy of Sciences, 1953. Reprinted by permission.

This dimension recognizes that an individual's difficulty may occur in the development of personality, in the destruction of the personality through role demands, in role transition, in role choice, in conflicts among roles, or in contradictions between values and role expectations (Perry, 1955). It is in these cases that either psychotherapy or counseling can become useful to the individual.

As we examine this problem dimension, we can state that problems at either end of the continuum will vary in intensity and often will be related. However, an individual can have very serious role problems without any disturbance at the intrapersonal end of the continuum. Likewise an individual can have an intense intrapersonal conflict completely independent of the role demands. In large part, the individual's ability to deal with any problems that arise at the role conflict end of the continuum is related to the degree of any intrapersonal conflict. An individual who is experiencing intense intrapersonal difficulties will not be able to deal with any role-related concerns. Thus, in considering the type of assistance along this continuum that can best serve a particular individual, we need to consider the added dimension of the degree to which an individual suffers from some internal disturbance. That is, we can assume that the smaller the degree of internal disturbance the more able the individual will be to deal with difficulties surrounding role. In effect, the individual with minimal internal disturbance will be more apt to respond to shorter-term direct guidance types of experiences (Perry, 1955).

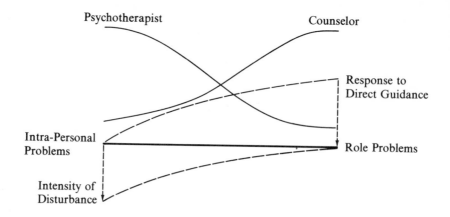

FIGURE 1-2. The New York Academy of Sciences, 1953. Reprinted by permission.

While this individual still needs to understand his personality, he will not need to examine it in terms of a complete restructuring in order to deal with the problems in the role area of the continuum. He does not need to restructure his personality in order to make a vocational choice or to deal with a problem in his marriage. At the other end of the continuum, however, an individual with an intense intrapersonal conflict will not be able to deal with problems created by role. What is called for here is an intense therapeutic relationship over an extended period of time, an experience designed to restructure the personality of the individual.

As one examines the continuum shown in Figure 1-2, it is in the area of intrapersonal conflict of high intensity that the psychotherapist does most of his work. The counselor does most of his work at the other end of that continuum with people who are more likely to respond to shorter, more direct kinds of learning experiences. This difference can be expressed by stating that counseling works toward the understanding and development of an individual's personality in relation to specific role problems. Psychotherapy looks toward the reorganization of the personality through interaction with a therapist.

As further clarification of the differences between counseling and psychotherapy, the diagram shown in Figure 1-3 may be helpful. In psychotherapy the problem is within the individual, while in counseling the problem is outside the individual. In psychotherapy the interaction is between therapist and client; in counseling the interaction is a 3-way interaction between client, counselor, and the problem.

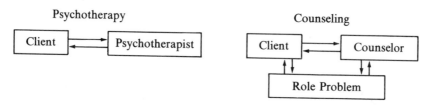

Psychotherapy   Counseling

FIGURE 1-3

What then is counseling as we define it? Counseling is concerned with helping individuals learn new ways of dealing with and adjusting to life situations. It is a process through which individuals are helped to develop sound decision-making processes in either an individual or group setting. This, in turn, will enable them to make the fullest possible use of their inherent potential and become fully functioning individuals. It does not attempt to restructure personality, but rather to develop what is already there. It is chiefly concerned with individuals' adjustment to themselves, the significant others in their life, and the cultural environment in which they find themselves.

COUNSELING THEORY

We have discussed theory as a plan of action, a model to be followed, or as a structure that provides guidelines for action. Likewise, counseling theory is a model around which plans of action are developed. Certainly a counselor cannot hope to help a counselee resolve his difficulties unless he can determine what is wrong with the present behavior. The counselor needs some model that enables him to determine what is normal or rational behavior from what is not normal or irrational. Further, he must understand the possible causes of behavior that is atypical and damaging to the client. If a client is having problems with interpersonal relations, it is important that the counselor have some frame of reference that enables him to understand the possible causes of such difficulty.

This is not to say that the counselor will have a definitive set of answers for each of the problems his clients bring to him, or that all clients with similar problems will have the identical causes of such behavior. Rather, the contention here is that the counselor needs to have some working assumptions about the probable causes of such behavior. While each individual case may be somewhat different, a theory enables the counselor to make some assumptions about the general causes of such behavior. If, for example, the counselor concludes that the client's interpersonal difficulties are caused by some events that happened in early childhood, the counselor may attempt to help the client gain insight into how these early childhood events are affecting his present behavior, and through this process of insight the counselor will assume that the present behavior will be changed. On the other hand, the counselor may view the client's problem as being caused by the learning of inappropriate responses to the situation and will attempt to help the client learn more appropriate ways of behaving. In either case the counselor has made some assumptions about the causes of the behavior and, based on those assumptions, has attempted to help the client. In speaking of counselors and theory, Schwebel (1962, p. 328) stated that "What we listen for here and respond to . . . depends in part on us as persons and part on our orientation, that is on a theory which has made particular assumptions about the causes of problems and the methods of treatment."

Whether the counselor's theory is implicit or explicit, the fact is that some theory does exist. As soon as a counselor begins to counsel with a client, he is making some assumptions about what kinds of behavior are maladaptive and some assumptions about how this behavior can be corrected. Hence, he is operating out of some theoretical position; whether he acknowledges the theoretical position or not is another question. A counselor who operates without asking what is happening, without some model of action, or without some assumptions about counseling is not only an unscientific counselor; he is a counselor who is very likely to flail about with little chance of success with his clients. He may in fact be operating from the dangerous assumption that whatever he does with the client will somehow do some good. Such a counselor is likely to do more harm than good to his client.

Counseling theories, then, provide a means of organizing what people have learned about the process of counseling. They are designed to serve as guides to indicate possible causes of a client's difficulties, to indicate what are the possible courses of action, and to indicate the desired counselor behavior in the counseling process. The theories themselves grow out of what is conceived to be the nature of man, what man should be, and assumptions about how the behavior of man is changed in desired directions.

THE BASES OF COUNSELING THEORY

Implicit in what has been said is that a counseling theory needs to be based on or in some way derived from a theory of personality. A counselor must have some knowledge of the manner and means of personality development from its infant forms to elaborated and more complex adult forms (Williamson, 1965). He must have some knowledge of not only the development of the normal personality, but he must also understand how maladaptive behavior is developed. Only as he understands the development of both behavior that is adaptive and behavior that is nonadaptive can a counselor hope to understand ways to help his clients. This requires the counselor to have some conception of the nature of man. If the counselor views man as basically evil, he will likely counsel from one perspective; if his view of man is that he is basically good, he will likely counsel from a completely different frame of reference.

A counseling theory also needs to have some conception of how man's behavior is changed. Most counseling theories agree that counseling is really a learning experience. The differences in the theories occur when the process of how this learning takes place is discussed. Some theorists argue that it is the nature of the counseling relationship itself that causes client learning to take place; other theorists argue that client learning takes place because the counselor uses reinforcement techniques. Hence, these two theoretical positions view the process of change differently, but they both include a process for change within their theoretical structures.

A counseling theory must also have some idea of what the end product should look like. Every society, even though societies may be different, develops ways of attempting to change undesirable behaviors and methods to encourage the desired behaviors. That is, the society determines what is the "good life." Likewise a good counseling theory includes some notions about what the "good life" is. In essence it places in some order a hierarchy of values toward which the counseling process is aimed. It is this hierarchy of values that ultimately becomes the goals of counseling. As Stefflre (1965) indicates, the specific goals for different theories may be somewhat different, but "implicit in all theories is the concept that the function of counseling is aiding students to desire to strive to achieve full human potentiality" (Williamson, 1965, p. 168).

Finally, a counseling theory must include some notions about the appropriate role the counselor should play. In large part it is the theoretical frame of reference from which the counselor works that determines his behavior in the counseling process. It will determine, for example, how personally involved the counselor will become in the process, and how much control of the interview he will undertake. The counselor's frame of reference will determine how much faith he puts in testing and other diagnostic devices. It will determine the extent to which the counselor uses directive techniques and interpretative statements. Perhaps most importantly, the theory from which the counselor works will determine his position on techniques such as acceptance interpretation, advice, and clarification. In short, a prime function of counseling theory is that it gives the counselor a way to rationalize his behavior (Shoben, 1962). A counselor's theory gives him a structure through which he can operate in the counseling process.

Counseling theory, then, must be based on knowledge that has been gained in the more basic areas of human development and personality. From these areas a counseling theory must derive some belief about the nature of man and how man learns. While counseling theory needs to be rooted in these more basic areas, it is an applied field and, as such, has no need to establish principles of behavior. The task of counselors and counseling theory is to define how behavior change is brought about and, more importantly, how this change is brought about in the counseling context.

This last statement implies that the counselor's role or his behavior in counseling is in large part determined by theoretical orientation. This theory may not indeed be very elaborate or complex but may be a series of very simple statements, or even one statement. A statement such as "My job is to get all my students into college," while not an example of a very good theory, could be a useful one. While the counselor's theory in large part dictates his role, it should be remembered that each counselor needs to seek and evolve his own particular theory.

THEORY AND PRACTICE

One prime criterion for a good theory is that it has to be useful. Yet, many practicing counselors and counselors-to-be seem to question the efficacy of using theory in their day-to-day work. The reasons for this situation may lie in the fact that many of the presently constructed theories of counseling are not useful; it may be that many of our theories are nothing more than descriptive in nature with no real plans for action, or it may be that counselors have simply not understood the theories as presented.

The point is that, whatever the reasons, there are a great many counselors who counsel from the seat of their pants, and the day is rapidly approaching when this method of operation will not satisfy our various publics. Counselors must begin to ask some very pertinent questions of themselves. First, they must ask: What is the basic purpose of what I am doing? What is our place in the entire educational picture? Once we have determined the answers to the first question, we need to ask: "What are the means to reach those goals and how are these means different from what other people do?" In determining these means we need to know what assumptions we are making about human nature and its development. It should be apparent that in answering these questions we are in fact in the process of theory development, and that this development is vital to the very existence of counseling.

As Brammer and Shostrum (1968) indicate, a counselor who does not have a solid foundation in the current thinking and research in the field, as well as a solid set of assumptions upon which to base his counseling, is doing nothing more than applying cookbook techniques to help clients solve their problems. Ford and Urban (1963) echo this point when they suggest that a counselor who does not have a systematic point of view is not only likely to be extremely inefficient in his work with clients, but may also do more harm than good. This situation tends to occur when a counselor works from some implicit rather than explicit theory. That is, in effect, he is never really sure from what assumptions he is working. When a theory is made explicit, a counselor has a better opportunity to test and evolve his theory based on his experiences and perhaps some of his own research efforts. As Shoben (1962) has indicated, a counseling theory is most useful when it has been tested in some degree by controlled experience.

If we can accept the suggestion of John Dewey (1959) that creative thinking is essentially a matter of seeing events and concepts in a unique or new pattern, then we can make the further assumption that every counselor has the potential for developing his own counseling theory. We would go further than this and suggest that every counselor must develop his own theory. It is of course to be expected that in this process one first investigates the present theoretical presentation in the literature. In developing a personal theory, the logical place to begin is with a theory that has already made some assumptions about the nature of counseling and hopefully been submitted to some empirical testing. This theory can then be submitted to the fires of experience in counseling, and out of this process should grow new hypotheses and assumptions or verification of the previously held assumptions. The original theory used is helpful to the extent that it gives the counselor a base from which to explore his world and an opportunity to develop his own tenuous theory which, in turn, gives some meaning and direction to his counseling.

As stated earlier many counselors seem to think of theory as somehow different from practice, as something that is concocted in an intellectual's mind at a university, as being somehow impractical, remote, and above all idealistic. Yet, it in fact goes very much hand in hand with practice. As a problem is confronted, theory can be employed to enlarge the number of events to which attention needs to be paid in order to derive an adequate solution (Shertzer and Stone, 1968). In essence, the theory is practical because of, not in spite of, its heuristic nature. In other words, theory enables the counselor to make systematic observations about his counseling experiences, it encourages the bringing together of various concepts in counseling, and it helps the counselor in the areas of prediction, evaluation of performance, and the improvement of outcomes (Brammer and Shostrum, 1960).

A useful way to conceptualize the relationship between theory and practice has been presented by Ford and Urban (1963). While the model they propose is designed for psychotherapy, it can be very useful for the field of counseling, and has been so adapted. Figure 1-4 presents the schematic design of this model.

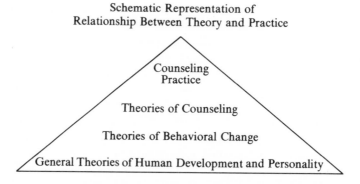

Schematic Representation of
Relationship Between Theory and Practice

Counseling
Practice

Theories of Counseling

Theories of Behavioral Change

General Theories of Human Development and Personality

FIGURE 1-4. *Schematic Representation of Relationships Among Theories.* By permission of John Wiley and Sons, Inc.

Figure 1-4 demonstrates our contention that there is and should be some relationship between theory and practice. Neither practice nor theory can stand alone, for one does depend on the other. At the base of the pyramid in Figure 1-4 are what we term general theories of human development and personality. These general theories most probably do not grow out of the counseling field, but out of such fields as psychology, sociology and anthropology. We could rightfully refer to this portion of the pyramid as consisting of abstract ideas, concepts, and assumptions. At this level, if we were using learning theory, an appropriate statement would be that both normal and maladaptive behaviors are learned by an individual through his interaction with his environment. At the second level we are still dealing with abstractions, but they are less broadly conceived than at the first level. At this level an appropriate statement would be that man learns new behaviors as these behaviors are rewarded in his daily life.

As we move toward the third level of the pyramid and deal specifically with counseling theory, the concepts are even less abstract. Very appropriate here is the statement: Positive verbal reinforcement used by a counselor can help a counselee change his behavior in the desired direction. This, of course, brings us to the top of the pyramid, counseling practice. Now it becomes a matter of implementing the reinforcement in the counseling situation; that is, the counselor using positive verbal reinforcement to help a client achieve a mutually agreed-upon behavior.

It should be noted that as shown in Figure 1-4, the whole process of moving from general theories of human development and personality to counseling practice is interdependent, and information flows in both directions. This is the whole process of evolving theory and practice. While one starts with some very general assumptions, it is to be expected that the outcomes of actual practice will modify or completely change the theoretical assumptions.

It is this model in Figure 1-4 that we would suggest counselors follow in their attempts to build a personal theory of counseling. Through this type of model they can begin with some general assumptions about personality, move to some general assumptions about how behavior changes, and then to a theory of counseling they can attempt to implement. As stated earlier, the logical place to begin this process is by learning what are the present theories in the field, and what the recent thinking and research have to say about these theories. Once this has been accomplished, it then becomes necessary for the counselor to try these theories in his own practice and research and to modify, reformulate, or discard them based on his own experiences. Without such procedures, counselors cannot hope to know where they are going with their clients, if they are indeed going anywhere.

In summary, perhaps the most salient point to remember is that as soon as a counselor begins to counsel, he does so on the basis of some assumptions, in terms of some frame of reference. By simple implication he is using a structure or model of some kind. The difference between counselors is not that they do not have a theory, but rather the degree to which that theory has been elaborated and made explicit. What is most vital is the encouragement to each counselor to develop for himself a theory that is explicitly formulated, regularly evaluated, and subsequently subjected to modification (Ford and Urban, 1963).

Rotter (1954) aptly summarized the principal values of theories in clinical work and his summary is equally useful to the field of counseling. He suggested that theories act as the basis for the construction of new instruments and methods as well as for testing the old methods. In addition, theories act as a means by which counseling techniques can be evaluated, as encouragement for the development of consistent assumptions, as evaluation devices for ideas and problems in counseling practice, and as an aid to help the counselor recognize and resolve the contradictions in the theory and inconsistencies between theory and practice. Only as counselors recognize the need for and the value of counseling theory will the field make strides forward. We need to know what it is we are about.

RESEARCH

In the discussion thus far we have emphasized the need for each counselor to develop his own theory and to make that theory an explicit one. The reader may well ask at this juncture, Does it make any difference in terms of practice which theory is used? For example, does it make any difference whether the counselor believes that behavior disorders grow out of early childhood experiences, or that instead they are caused by the environmental influences impinging on the individual? In terms of techniques, does it make any difference whether the counselor uses diagnosis and other analytic techniques or whether he uses relationship techniques? Some theorists say the counselor must be active in the counseling relationship, while others contend that the counselor should play a passive role. The list of differences over what are considered by different theorists as necessary for the counseling relationship can go on and on, but the question of whether in fact these variations make any difference in actual practice still remains.

The early work of Fiedler in this area has often been pointed to as an indication that one's theoretical position did not influence counselor behavior. Fiedler (1950a, 1950b) concluded that there was little difference in the way counselors operated, regardless of the differences in the theoretical orientations of the counselors. He suggested that it was not the theoretical orientation that affected counselor behavior, but that it was the counselor's experiences that had the most effect on his behavior. From this frame of reference it would seem that theory really does not affect actual practice, a point quite different from the one we have been stressing in this chapter.

More recent research in this area has found that a counselor's theoretical orientation does affect his practice. Sundland and Barker (1962) classified 139 therapists into three groups—Freudians, Sullivanians, and Rogerians—and they found that there were significant differences between those groups. Wallach and Strupp (1964) found that the theoretical orientation of the therapist affected the personal distance he kept from the client. McNair and Lorr (1964) in a study of 265 therapists also found that differences between the therapists could be attributed to their different theoretical positions. In another study reported by Strupp (1964) it was found that client-centered counselors and analytically oriented counselors responded to a filmed interview quite differently. The client-centered counselors were less inclined to develop a plan of treatment or to establish goals and were more favorable in their prognosis. Hence, it would seem that with the advent of more refined research techniques there is a growing body of evidence that theory does indeed affect practice.

Despite the apparent differences in theory and practice cited above, it is also apparent that most counseling theories have in common the belief that the counselor's intervention in the life of the client is for the purpose of bringing about change in the client. While there are differences, this may be what we should expect at this stage of development in counseling theory. As research efforts are continued, it may be that some theories will fall by the wayside and others will take their place, or that someday we will have a single unified approach to counseling. We may also discover that different kinds of problems and different kinds of people do require that counselors use different theoretical orientations.

It would seem then that in this embryonic stage in which counseling finds itself, it is extremely important for counselors to seek out answers to the effectiveness of various theories. They need to challenge what has been previously developed, and through this challenge to modify, drop, or develop new theories of counseling. Williamson (1965) suggests that a good theory is one that is *developed* by a counselor, not one that is adopted. Of course, this process calls for a counselor to adopt a proposed theory on a provisional basis, but then he should subject that theory to the test in counseling practice. Only through this process can a counselor develop a model that is meaningful and useful for him in his counseling practice.

CONCLUSION

In this chapter we have discussed the general topic of theory. We have considered how it is developed, why it is developed, the necessary ingredients for a good theory, and the functions that theory can serve. We have also considered the meaning of the word *counseling* and how it differs from *psychotherapy*. We concluded by saying that counseling is chiefly concerned with the individual's adjustment to himself, the significant others in his life, and the cultural environment in which he finds himself.

We next considered what we meant by counseling theory and how the theory should relate to actual practice. That is, counseling theory provides a structure to the counselor from which he can work in meaningful ways. Counseling theory by itself has no meaning. It has meaning only as it is useful in practice. Finally, we discussed the need for counselors to develop their own theory of counseling, based on a study of present theory, but modified and developed through their own counseling experiences and research. To help the reader begin this process, we can now turn to an examination of some theoretical contributions to counseling theory.

REFERENCES

Brammer, Lawrence M., and Shostrom, Everett L. *Therapeutic Psychology.* Englewood Cliffs, New Jersey: Prentice-Hall, 1960.

"Creative inquiry. John Dewey Centennial." *Saturday Review* 42:22–23.

English, Horace B., and English, Ava Champney. *A Comprehensive Dictionary of Psychological and Psychiatric Terms.* New York: McKay, 1958.

Fiedler, Fred E. "The Concept of an Ideal Therapeutic Relationship." *Journal of Consulting Psychology* 14:239–245.

Fiedler, Fred E. "A Comparison of Therapeutic Relationships in Psychoanalytic Non-directive and Adlerian Therapy." *Journal of Consulting Psychology* 14:436–445.

Ford, Donald H., and Urban, Hugh B. *System of Psychotherapy: A Comparative Study.* New York: John Wiley and Sons, Inc., 1963.

Hall, Calvin S., and Lindzey, Gardner. *Theories of Personality.* New York: John Wiley and Sons, Inc., 1957.

McNair, D. M., and Lorr, M. "An Analysis of Professed Psychotherapeutic Techniques." *Journal of Consulting Psychology* 28:265–271.

Patterson, C. H. *Theories of Counseling and Psychotherapy.* New York: Harper and Row, 1966.

Perry, William G. "The Finding of the Commission in Counseling and Guidance on the Relation of Psychotherapy and Counseling." In *Annals of New York Academy of Sciences,* Volume 63, Article 3, pp. 396–407, November 7, 1955.

Rotter, J. B. *Social Learning and Clinical Psychology.* Englewood Cliffs, New Jersey: Prentice-Hall, Inc., 1954.

Schwebel, Milton. "Some Missing Links in Counseling Theory and Research." *Personnel and Guidance Journal* 41:328.

Shertzer, Bruce, and Stone, Shelley C. *Fundamentals of Counseling.* Boston: Houghton Mifflin Company, 1968.

Shoben, Edward J., Jr. "New Frontiers in Theory." *Personnel and Guidance Journal* 32:80–83.

Shoben, Edward J., Jr. "Guidance: Remedial Function or Social Reconstruction?" *Harvard Educational Review* 32:431–443.

Shoben, Edward Joseph, Jr. "The Counselor's Theory as a Personal Trait." *Personnel and Guidance Journal* 40:617–621.

Stefflre, Buford (Ed.). *Theories of Counseling.* New York: McGraw-Hill Book Company, 1965.

Stefflre, Buford, and Matheny, Kenneth (Eds). *The Function of Counseling Theory.* Guidance Monograph Series. Boston: Houghton Mifflin Company, 1968.

Strupp, H. H. "The Psychotherapist's Contribution to the Treatment Process." *Behavioral Science* 3:34–67.

Sundland, D. M., and Barker, E N. "The Orientations of Psychotherapists." *Journal of Consulting Psychology* 26:201–212.

"The Current Status on Counseling Psychology." *A Report of a Special Committee of the Division 17 of Counseling Psychology of the American Psychology Association,* 1961.

Tyler, Leona. *The Work of the Counselor.* New York: Appleton, 1953.

Vance, Forrest L., and Volsky, Theodore C., Jr., "Counseling and Psychotherapy: Split Personalities or Siamese Twins." *American Psychologist* 17:565–570.

Wallach, M. S., and Strupp, H. H. "Dimensions of Psychotherapists' Activity." *Journal of Consulting Psychology* 28:120–125.

Williamson, E. G. *Vocational Counseling: Some Historical, Philosophical and Theoretical Perspectives.* New York: McGraw-Hill Book Company, 1965.

Wolberg, Lewis R. *The Technique of Psychotherapy.* New York: Grune and Stratton, 1954.

2

Psychoanalytic Contributions to Counseling

The psychoanalytic approach to counseling is probably the most widely known theory of counseling, and no text on theories of counseling would be complete without a section devoted to psychoanalytic theory. Since Sigmund Freud first introduced his theoretical thoughts to the world, they have been both increasingly accepted and yet subject to bitter controversy. Freud, like all great thinkers, continued to work on and evolve his theory of psychoanalysis and personality until his death. Despite this continual evolution on the part of Freud, several of his early followers—Adler, Rank, and Jung, among others—broke away from Freudian psychoanalytic theory and became leaders of their own branches of the psychoanalytic movement. This branching process has continued until today there are various schools of psychoanalysis both as a personality theory and as a method of treatment.

A chapter based on psychoanalytic thought is included in this text because of its profound influence on the activities of those helping professions, such as psychiatrists, psychologists, counselors, and social workers. As the field of psychology and counseling has matured, many of the concepts and practices used in psychoanalytic theory have taken on more importance for the field of counseling. Perhaps the most important outgrowth of psychoanalytic thought for counseling is the work of the Neo-Analysts. Of particular importance to the field of counseling is the work of the Adlerians and the work of a group known as the ego-analysts.

While Alfred Adler was the first individual to break away from classical Freudian thought, it has only been in recent years that his theory as a system of treatment has gained any widespread acceptance in the field of counseling. Most accounts of Adler attribute this to his rather unsystematic writing, which made it difficult for people to put his thinking into some form or system. At the same time there is little question that many of the concepts first stated by Adler can be found in many of our current theories of counseling. Such terms as empathy and respect for the client, for example, were first used by Adler. Thus, it is probable that Adler has had a greater impact on counseling than is usually realized. It is for this reason that a section of this chapter will be devoted to a brief discussion of Adlerian thinking.

In the discussion devoted to ego-counseling it will be clear to the reader that in some respects there is only a very fine line of difference between classical psychoanalytic theory and ego-psychology. It is this fine line of difference, however, that makes ego-psychology more applicable to the counseling situation than is classical psychoanalytic theory. The backbone of ego-psychology is the belief in building upon the client's strengths and assets without drawing out deeply repressed conflicts within the individual. The emphasis is on the role the ego plays in the control and development of each individual. Despite this difference, ego-psychology is based largely on psychoanalytic theory, with many of the leading writers in the field of ego-psychology, such as Hartman, being heavily steeped in psychoanalytic thought.

Because both the position of Adler and, most particularly, the position of the ego-psychologists have grown out of classical psychoanalytic thought, we should first consider some of the basic assumptions of classical psychoanalytic theory before moving to a consideration of the fields of ego-psychology and Adlerian theory and their relevance for the field of counseling. Because the ego-analytic position is closer to classical Freudian thinking than to the Adlerian position, we will follow the discussion of Freudian thought with the ego-analytic position and then turn to a discussion of the Adlerian position.

CLASSICAL PSYCHOANALYTIC THEORY

Freud was first of all a practitioner, and his theories grew out of his practice with people having psychosomatic illnesses. Freud's observations led him to conclude that man was, by nature, basically amoral, selfish, and irrational. Much of classical psychoanalytic theory is based on three major assumptions about the nature of man. The first of these is that the first five years of an individual's development are the most crucial and largely determine the adult behavior of an individual regardless of whether that behavior is considered normal or abnormal. Secondly, the sexual impulses of an individual act as key determinants of behavior. Sexual impulses are generally interpreted to mean the need for each individual to gratify all bodily pleasures. A third assumption is that much of an individual's behavior is controlled by unconscious determinants.

Freud believed that an individual's present behavior was determined by past emotional experiences. He referred to this assumption as *psychic determinism*. In short, man, as seen by classical psychoanalytic theory, is not a master of his own destiny. His behavior is directed by the need to gratify his basic biological needs and instincts. His behavior does not happen by chance but is determined, and if we knew enough about the unconscious part of the individual, all behavior could be explained.

LEVELS OF AWARENESS

In order to understand Freud's concept of personality development, we need to examine his distinctions between man's different levels of awareness. At any one point in time an individual can be aware or conscious of only a very limited number of things. A particular thought, idea, or feeling may occupy the conscious only for a limited time but, while it is there, we are unaware of other stimuli around us. The man who focuses attention upon a particular task while a vast array of events are occurring around him is an example of this phenomena. The man so intent on a football game that he doesn't hear his wife talking to him is a good example.

The second level of awareness described by Freud is the preconscious. Many ideas or thoughts, while not a part of the conscious, can be brought to a conscious state by the individual. When we are asked to recall a past meeting or event, we are calling into consciousness some ideas or events not in the preconscious.

The third level of awareness as described by Freud is the unconscious. It is this level of awareness that receives most of his attention and is one of his most significant contributions to the field of psychology. This is the portion of the mind that Freud believed largely determined the behavior of man. The individual is not aware of the mental activity that occurs in this part of the mind, nor can he bring into consciousness these activities. In fact, the individual unknowingly resists bringing these activities into consciousness. The traditional example of this concept is the man who hates his mother while not being aware that he has these feelings. The real importance of these unconscious feelings in psychoanalytic theory is that they constantly strive to become conscious and the individual must expend energy to keep them in the unconscious. Thus, Freud sees man in a constant state of internal conflict of which he is not aware.

Structure of the Personality

It was Freud's later work which today forms the basis of the psychoanalytic theory of personality. In his later conceptualization of the structure of the personality, Freud retained his concept of conscious, preconscious and unconscious while seeing an individual as made up of three subsystems: the id, ego, and superego. These three subsystems interact to such an extent that it is difficult to measure their separate effects on an individual's behavior. One of the subsystems seldom operates independently from the other two; rather an individual's behavior should be considered as the result of interaction among the id, ego, and superego.

Id

Freud saw the id as the original system of the personality. In the classic psychoanalytic sense a newborn infant is all id. That is, the id consists of the constitution of the infant—all he brings into the world with him. The ego and the superego will develop in the individual during infancy and early childhood and their forms will depend largely on the early experiences of the child.

It is within the concept of the id that Freud included man's instincts, the two most important of which are sex and aggression. The basic function of the id is to maintain the organism in a comfortable or low-tension state. Thus, when a child is hungry during infancy and demands to be fed, the id seeks immediate gratification of the hunger need in order to return the organism to a comfortable state.

Freud referred to the phenomenon as the "pleasure principle," and it is this principle that continues to govern the id into adult life. Most of the id processes occur at the unconscious level and influence overt behavior without the individual being aware of it. If we go back to our earlier illustration of the man who hated his mother, we can see an example of the id in operation. His feelings toward his mother may affect his relationship with the opposite sex though he may be unaware of this influence on his behavior. Generally, id impulses come into consciousness only when the ego is in a weakened state.

Ego

In the early stages of individual development the infant cannot distinguish between objects. Hence, when a baby is hungry he will put anything he touches into his mouth. At this stage of development there is no sense of the reality of the world. The infant must learn to discriminate between images in his mind and the objective reality. He soon learns that to form an image in his mind will not satisfy his need; therefore he is forced to begin to differentiate himself from the outer world. In effect, he must learn to find something in the outer world that fits with his mind's image and will satisfy his need. This matching process is referred to as "identification" and is one of the most important concepts in psychoanalytic theory. It is this identification process that separates the id from the ego.

The reader will remember that the primary function of the id is to satisfy the needs of the organism without regard to the realities of the world. The ego develops out of the id because of the organism's need to deal with the realities of the world. The object of the ego is to mediate between the pleasure principle by which the id operates and the outer world. The ego then operates on the reality principle and attempts to hold the discharge of energy until there is an appropriate object in the external world to satisfy the need. If we return to the example of the hungry child, we can see how the development of the ego alters the behavior of the infant. As the child learns to identify objects in the outer world that will satisfy his hunger, he ceases putting everything in his mouth. The ego then is the organized part of the id and is often referred to as the executive of the individual's personality.

Superego

As the process of identification is important in the development of the ego, it is likewise important in the development of the superego. The earliest objects in the external world that satisfy the infant's needs are his parents. Early in his development the child learns that direct expression of his impulses are likely to be looked upon with disfavor by those important others. That is, the parents act as disciplinary agents and, through a process of rewards and punishments of varying degrees, the child learns what is acceptable and what is unacceptable behavior. As this process continues through the child's early development, not only are the parents' values and customs adopted by the superego, but also the accepted values, traditions, and customs of the society become a part of the superego.

The superego is a form of internal control within the individual. When a child's behavior is appropriate, even when no one else is there to watch him, we can say that the superego has emerged. Freud considered the superego to be made up of two subsystems: the conscience and the ego-ideal. The conscience is that part of the superego that represents those things the individual believes he should not do. The ego-ideal represents those things that the individual would like to be. Either one of these subsystems often finds itself in conflict with the id impulses.

The superego can be considered, then, as a built-in control mechanism within the individual whose principle function is to control the primitive impulses of the id, which would not lead to accepted behavior. It is important to emphasize that this controlling occurs largely in the unconscious part of the mind, therefore not in the individual's awareness. In effect, the superego represents that which is ideal within the individual and thus strives for perfection.

In Freud's view the dynamics of personality are centered in the interaction between the id, ego, and superego. He described psychoanalytic theory as "a dynamic conception which reduces mental life to the interplay of reciprocally urging and checking forces" (1910b, p. 107). The id operates on the pleasure principle and constantly seeks gratification of needs, while the energy of the ego and superego are used both to meet the needs of the individual and to hold in check some of the impulses of the id. The ego must not only interact with the real world, but also must be able to control both the id and the superego. An individual who is dominated by his id will tend to be impulsive in his behavior, and a person who is dominated by his superego will be overly moralistic. Hence, one can see the importance of the ego as the executor of the personality. The individual's behavior is a compromise between the differing demands of the subsystems that make up the personality.

PERSONALITY DEVELOPMENT

Freud contended that an individual's personality was basically formed during the first five years of his childhood. He saw personality development as resulting from the individual's attempts to learn new ways of reducing tension, tension that emanated from four basic sources; physiological growth processes, frustrations, conflicts, and threats (Hall and Lindzey, 1957). The principal methods by which the individual deals with tension are identification, displacement, and his defense mechanisms.

In an earlier section we dealt with identification as the process whereby the ego and the superego were developed. In this section we are referring to identification as a process very similar to imitation. It is the process whereby an individual, in an attempt to reach a certain goal (e.g., reduction of some tension), incorporates the characteristics of another person into his own personality. Most of this process takes place at an unconscious level and is a process of trial and error. Thus, if the behavior taken on by the individual reduces the tension then the behavior is retained; if the new behavior is not successful in reducing tension then the behavior is discarded. While the first and usually most important people for the individual to identify with are the parents, the individual's adult personality comprises numerous identifications made throughout his development.

One of the unique individual characteristics of man is his ability to change the goal of psychological energy from one object to another. If an object that served to satisfy tension reduction is no longer available or loses some of its power, another object can and will take its place. This process of redirecting energy from one object to another object is called displacement. To a great extent the development of personality depends on this process of energy displacement or object substitution. As the new object is not likely to satisfy the need for tension reduction as well as the original object, the individual is constantly seeking new and better methods of reducing tension. This accounts for the constant striving of man and for the variability in his behavior.

A particular form of displacement, which Freud felt was most significant in the development of civilization, is sublimation. Sublimation is the process whereby the individual modifies the expression of a primitive impulse to conform with behavior that is socially acceptable. Sublimations usually take the form of channeling aggressive or sexual energy into intellectual, humanitarian, cultural, and artistic pursuits. Hence, as an individual matures, he sublimates or displaces his energy to objects that not only give him satisfaction but also aid the society in its development.

One of the most important roles the ego has to play is that of dealing with events that arouse anxiety within the individual. The ego may approach this problem by realistic problem-solving behavior, or it may attempt to use methods that deny, falsify, or distort reality. If the ego approaches the problem realistically, then the individual's personality stands to be enhanced; however, if the latter choice is made, then the development of personality is impeded. These methods are referred to as defense mechanisms. All defense mechanisms have in common the tendency to deny, falsify, or distort reality—and they operate unconsciously. While these defense mechanisms may operate effectively for the individual, the more they are used the more rigid becomes the individual's personality.

In the early stages of development the threats to the self that create anxiety come from outside the individual (e.g., people who are physically larger and who have complete control over the individual, such as parents). As the superego comes into existence, threats to the self can also occur from within; that is, the individual fears that his primitive impulses will get away from him and he therefore experiences a great deal of anxiety. Hence, the defense mechanisms are designed to cope with threats from within and from external sources.

It is important at this point to re-emphasize that these defense mechanisms take place primarily at the unconscious level. We will now turn to a brief description of the most prominent defense mechanism and will examine how these methods affect personality development.

One of the earliest concepts developed by Freud was that of repression. Repression is said to occur when the individual forces from his consciousness an impulse that causes anxiety. He attempts to do away with the impulse by simply refusing to acknowledge its existence. In such cases an individual may not see an object that is in plain sight, or the repression may actually affect him physically. A man may be so afraid of the sexual impulse that he becomes impotent. Although repression is necessary for normal personality development and is used to some degree by everyone, some people become overly dependent on repression as a defense. Such people tend to withdraw from contacts with the world and are generally tense and rigid in prsonality. In these cases the superego is said to be more prominent than the ego; that is, the ego has lost some of its controlling power to the superego.

In order to deal with a repressed impulse, the individual must believe that the impulse is no longer a danger to him. A child who represses his sexual impulses during adolescence may find that as an adult his ego can cope with these impulses and the repression will be lifted. In many cases, however, the individual never learns that his repression is no longer necessary. This explains why it is said that most people exist with a lot of childish fears, which no longer have a basis in reality.

Anxiety external to the individual is easier to deal with than is anxiety that comes from the id impulses. Hence, if the individual can attribute his anxiety to an object in the external world, he is likely to feel some relief. This form of defense against anxiety is called projection. It consists of first not recognizing a characteristic within oneself and secondly of attributing that characteristic to another person. Instead of saying "I hate my brother," the person using projection would say "My brother hates me."

Projection is a favorite defense of those people trying to enhance their self-esteem. The individual not only attempts to make himself look good; at the same time he tries to downgrade others. Thus, he lifts himself up at the expense of others.

When an individual has an impulse that produces anxiety, the ego may attempt to deal with the impulse by concentrating upon its direct opposite. If an individual feels hatred for another person, the ego may attempt to deal with the hate impulses by showing great outward signs of love toward the person. This form of defense is referred to as reaction-formation. Extreme forms of any behavior can usually be attributed to reaction formation. A phobia is also an example of reaction formation.

In Freud's view normal personality development occurs over a series of well-defined stages, which he refers to as the psychosexual development of the individual. As the individual moves from one stage to another, there is a great deal of frustration and anxiety-producing situations. If this anxiety becomes too great, the normal pattern of psychological growth may be halted, at least temporarily. In short, the individual may become fixated at a certain stage of his development because he is afraid to move on to the next stage. In such cases the individual does not want to give up a behavior pattern that has been satisfying for him and adopt new behaviors that he is not sure will provide the necessary satisfaction.

Similar to the defense of fixation is the defense mechanism known as regression. That is, a person may revert to an earlier phase of development instead of moving forward to another stage. This usually occurs when the individual is faced with a severe threat. A little child may revert to infant behavior in the face of a situation in which he feels threatened by a loss of love. A man may withdraw from heterosexual activities because he feels inadequate, and through withdrawal from these activities he avoids the situation that causes him anxiety. It is generally believed that when an individual regresses he returns to a stage of development at which he was once fixated.

It is important to remember that in both the case of regression and the case of fixation, their occurrence is relative in degree. Rarely does a fixation at a particular stage of development become complete; likewise a regression to an earlier stage of development is rarely total.

PSYCHOSEXUAL STAGES OF DEVELOPMENT

Based on his clinical work Freud felt that the development of personality, including the various defense mechanisms an individual uses, was largely dependent on the course of the individual's psychosexual development. Before discussing the various stages of the individual, it is important that we consider several key aspects of this theory. First, much of the process occurs during the first five years of life, after which there is a period of relative calm for six years, then during adolescence the process becomes very active once again. A second major assumption is that, at any one point in time in a person's development, one body area predominates as a source of pleasure to the individual. In normal development a person moves through an orderly sequence in which one body area gives way to another, and the order of this sequence is the same for everyone. The third major assumption concerns the failure of one body area to replace another one. Thus, there will be serious personality implications for a person who stops at one stage in the sequence and does not progress through the normal chain of events.

Freud believed that the first three stages of development took place during the first five years of life and he labeled them the pregenital stages. These three stages are the oral, anal, and phallic stages.

Oral Stage

Freud believed that the infant sucks not just to take in food, but also because it gives the infant a pleasurable sensation. This stage of development usually lasts through the first year of an individual's life. Because the child is very dependent on others during this stage, the prime personality characteristic developed during this stage is dependency.

Anal Stage

During the second year of the child's life, the source of body pleasure shifts to the anal zone of the body. It is during this stage that the manner in which toilet training is conducted is extremely important. A child who is dealt with very strictly during this stage may develop into a very retentive personality type. A person who is cruel, obstinate, or stingy is said to have been fixated at the anal stage.

Phallic Stage

During the period from age 3 to 5 or 6 the child is in the phallic stage of development. Freud asserted that during this period the child received pleasure chiefly through self-manipulation. As the importance of the genital areas increases, several psychological developments take place. It is during this stage that castration anxiety, penis envy, and the famous Oedipus complex develop.

Castration anxiety arises out of a boy's fear that he may lose his penis. His parents, in an attempt to stop him from masturbating, may make him fear the loss of his penis, particularly when a boy has an opportunity to see a girl who lacks a penis. He may conclude that he will be punished just as she has been punished. Similarly, a girl may develop a feeling of penis envy when she observes her lack of a penis. She may feel that hers has been removed because of some wrongful act on her part. In either the case of the male or the female, serious complications for personality development may be attributed to these developments.

The last development during the phallic stage is what Freud refers to as the Oedipus or Electra complex. Freud considered the identification of this process as one of his most important, and it is exceedingly complex. Briefly, the Oedipus complex concerns the boy's desire to possess his mother and remove his father from the scene. The Electra complex is the desire of the girl to possess her father and remove the mother from the scene. Since this relationship cannot be consummated, the resolution of this conflict is extremely important for later personality development. The child must abandon the parent object and become sexually motivated toward others. Later attitudes toward people of the opposite sex and toward those in authority are largely determined by the individual's success in working out the Oedipal complex.

Latency Stage

Toward the end of the fifth or sixth year of life until the age of adolescence Freud believed that the child is in a stage of latency; that is, a stage during which the child spends time developing skills not related to sexual implications.

Genital Stage

While the first three stages of development can be characterized as narcissistic in nature, during the genital stage this self-love begins to change into love of others. With the beginning of puberty the child enters a stage of development that hopefully will culminate in mature heterosexual behavior. The individual becomes transformed from a self-loving individual into a socialized adult. In this ultimate stage of development, the normal individual does not get pleasure from oral, anal, or autoerotic activities, and he is not bothered by castration anxiety or an unresolved Oedipus complex. Rather, he receives his greatest pleasure from a relationship with a member of the opposite sex.

In summary, Freud believed that personality developed as a result of two major factors. The first of these is the maturation of the individual as he moves through a natural growth pattern, and the second is the individual's learning to overcome tension and anxiety resulting from conflicts, frustration, and threats he experiences. The personality develops as the individual learns to form identifications, displacements, and defenses. All of these mechanisms are designed to rechannel the original impulses into more accessible and acceptable sources or objects. This development of personality takes place in an orderly manner and is related to the areas of the body from which the individual derives pleasure. Further, Freud's model of personality is a dynamic one in which the constant interaction of the id, ego, and superego is responsible for the way in which the personality develops.

ABNORMAL PERSONALITY DEVELOPMENT

As with the development of the normal personality, classical psychoanalytic theory views the causes of abnormal personality as being rooted within the individual; that is, a behavioral disorder is caused by some disturbance in the functioning of the individual. Much of the blame for this situation belongs to the ego, which for some reason has failed in its role as an executor of the organism. Instead of serving an integrative function, the ego allows the individual to overuse the defense mechanisms. This overuse, primarily regression, begins in early childhood. The child uses repression to deal with impulses that cause him anxiety, thus pushing them into his unconscious. There, these impulses remain, only to arise at later stages of development to cause the individual increased difficulty. If the ego had been able to deal with these impulses when they originally developed, a healthy personality would have resulted. In short, most behavior disorders are caused by a breakdown of the functioning of the ego.

In Freud's view the nature of a neurosis or a psychosis is largely due to the kinds of defense mechanisms used by the individual to defend himself against tension. It is also related to the stage of psychosexual development at which the individual was fixated, or to which the individual regresses. After attempting to cope with a situation and failing, the individual resorts to regression to satisfy his needs. This regression brings forth earlier anxieties and tensions that have been repressed by the individual. Neurotic behavior then develops in an attempt to deal with this tension. This behavior requires increasing amounts of energy from the organism in order to deal with the anxiety, hence the individual has less and less energy left over to deal with the realities of the world. Thus, a vicious cycle is established.

GOALS OF THERAPY

The major goal of the psychoanalytic method is to bring into the consciousness those repressed impulses that are causing the individual anxiety. These are the impulses of the id with which the ego has not been able to deal successfully. In the atmosphere of the therapy situation the individual is given a chance to face situations with which he has been unable to cope. The therapist establishes a situation that is threat free, and the individual learns that he can express his thoughts without the danger of being condemned. This freedom allows the individual to explore the appropriateness or inappropriateness of his present behavior and to consider new behaviors.

The basic techniques used in the therapy situation are free association, transference, and interpretation. Free association is simply the practice of letting the individual and, indeed, making the individual verbalize whatever is on his mind. The transference phenomenon is quite complex, but for our purposes an oversimplified explanation will suffice. Transference consists of the individual directing his emotional feelings toward the therapist as though he were the original object that caused the feelings. Interpretation is used by the therapist to help the individual intellectualize and to replace superego functions with ego functions. In short, interpretation is designed to bring the patient step by step back to the world of reality.

Despite its impact on the field of psychiatry and counseling, classical psychoanalytic theory is in need of more concrete formulations as to the manner in which behaviors are acquired and modified. Its impact on the study of human behavior and its modification could be even greater if all the concepts and propositions thus far developed could be developed into a full theory of human behavior (Ford and Urban, 1967). There have been many theorists, often referred to as Neo-Analysts, who have attempted to build upon the work started by Freud. Theorists such as Adler, Horney, Jung, Rank, Sullivan, and Fromm would be included in this group. Each of the theories postulated by these writers has a significant relationship to classical Freudian thought, but they are also complete enough in themselves to warrant separate consideration. It is impossible to include all of these theories in a book of this kind. Instead, it has been our attempt to present the reader with an overview of classical Freudian thought. Let us now turn to a consideration of the counseling theories that grew out of psychoanalytic thought and which we feel hold the most applicability for the field of counseling: ego-counseling and Adlerian counseling.

EGO–COUNSELING

While there is a wide diversity among the ego-analysts regarding the degree to which they accept Freudian thought, most of them do find it a strong basis for their thinking. Their concepts are, however, an extension of psychoanalytic thought with a major emphasis on the functions of the ego. Their concerns center on the autonomy of the ego, the development of the reality principle in children, the integrative function of the ego, the defenses of the ego, and the ego processes of perceiving, remembering, thinking, and acting (Hall and Lindzey, 1957, p. 65). In effect, they are concerned ". . . with the ego as organization—with ego-strength . . ." (Hummel, 1962, p. 464). Unlike Freud's belief that the individual's ego is formed out of the energy of the id, the ego-analysts believe that the ego is a completely separate system with its own course of development.

The ego is seen as not being dependent on the impulses of the id; rather it is viewed as a rational institution, which is responsible for an individual's intellectual and social accomplishments. The ego not only has its own source of energy, apart from the id, but also has its own motives, interests, and objectives.

The major emphasis of the ego-analysts is the study of what they term normal or healthy behavior. Their contention is that most of Freud's thoughts about normal personality development were based on his work with the abnormal personality. Hence, they question the validity of Freud's assumptions about normal behavior. Further, the ego-analysts believe that the antecedents of behavior are more complex and varied than the simple instinctual drives of classic psychoanalytic theory. In their view, man is not simply subject to his own innate drives, but is also subject to the situational events with which he comes in contact.

Hartmann, one of the leading exponents of ego-analytic theory, sees a place for learning in the development of the individual. He sees the ego as being composed of inherited ego characteristics, instinctual drives, and the influences of outer reality (1964). Ford and Urban (1967) have pointed out that what the ego-analysts essentially have done is to develop Freudian psychoanalytic theory into a broader, more adequate theory of psychology. Hence, the ego-analysts, while not making major revisions in classical psychoanalytic theory, do give more importance to the effects of environmental events and learned responses than do the classical psychoanalysts. It is important to remember that, while they acknowledge the importance of situational events, they are equally concerned with the role played by the psychological energy of the ego.

PERSONALITY DEVELOPMENT

Freud's view of man was that he was basically an animal driven by instinctual urges; that is, all behavior is determined and controlled by an innate psychological energy. The ego-analysts maintain that man is not simply an animal, driven by innate energy, but that there is much of a man's behavior that is independent of his innate drives. Hence, in their view man comes into the world with the capability to respond to different kinds of stimuli, only part of which can be attributed to innate energy. In early infancy the individual does respond in an instinctual manner, to satisfy his needs, e.g., hunger. These response patterns soon all but disappear and the individual begins to develop response patterns based on his environment. Hence, an individual's behavior is related to the manner in which he responds to situational events; it is learned, not instinctual. It is to the study of these learned behaviors through which the individual controls his own behavior that the ego-analysts have devoted most of their attention. Hence, the ego-analysts stress the importance of a healthy ego development within the individual, while still acknowledging the existence and importance of the id and the superego.

Of initial importance in the development of the individual's ego is the infant's relationship with its mother. It is through this relationship that the infant begins to develop a sense of ego and non-ego; a concept of what is self and what is outside of self or, as we would call it, the environment. If the child is frustrated in this relationship, then further development of the ego may be impaired because the infant is fearful of those things outside of the self. If, as is usually the case, this relationship is a good one, the individual's interest in those things outside of himself is increased and the chances for further normal development of the ego are enhanced. This then is the beginning stage for the development of the ego functions. It is important to remember that according to the ego-analysts, the ego develops from its own energy source and thus is not dependent on energy from the id as in the classic psychoanalytic model.

As the child develops an awareness of ego and non-ego in a non-frustrating atmosphere, he will begin to explore his outer world. It is during this period that trial and error learning first appears as the individual attempts different types of coping behavior for the situations he finds in his environment. Hartman (1964) places a great deal of importance on this period, for it is during this stage of development that physical maturity allows the child to manipulate things within the environment as well as himself. This development in turn causes the individual to come in contact with more stimulation, to which the child must learn to respond.

It is the ego-analysts' contention that most of an individual's behaviors are consciously focused toward specific objectives. Hartman (1961) contends that the individual derives pleasure or satisfaction not only from fulfilling innate drives, but also from developing mastery over problems presented by the environment. The child learning to manipulate a particular toy receives satisfaction not because he satisfied some inner need, but rather because of his success in accomplishing a particular task. As Ford and Urban (1967) indicate, it is this attention to behavior initiated through thoughtful, conscious planning that separates the ego-analysts from the classical psychoanalysts. The ego-analysts acknowledge that some behavior is caused by events of which the individual is not aware, but they also acknowledge that some behavior is caused by events in the individual's environment.

One of the most important events in the development of the normal ego is the development of communication skills by the child. It is this development that allows the child to deal in abstractions. The child learns to differentiate between the symbol for apple and the actual apple itself. He learns that the latter will satisfy his need for food, while the symbol itself will not. The development of this skill allows the child to think about events in his world without actually trying the event. Hence, the individual can experience in his mind a trip to the moon without actually facing the dangers of such a trip.

The development of language skills also gives the individual increased ability to differentiate between objects within his environment. As King and Neal (1967) point out, the child now has the power to understand that when he is bitten by a dog he should not assume that all dogs will bite him. Hence, he avoids the over-generalization that all dogs are bad. If the individual cannot make these abstractions subsequent to the event of being bitten by a dog, all dogs will cause fear in the individual.

Equally important to the development of thinking in abstractions is the development of the ability to delay termination or satisfaction of some behavior elicitor. As Erikson (1946) points out, it is the individual's ability to retain habitual patterns of behavior to bring satisfaction that provides one with an identity. In the face of depravation of satisfaction the individual must be able to recall times when he was satisfied after a similar period of depravation and, following that, learn to anticipate a future event that will lead to satisfaction. This calls for the development of individual control over one's drives. If the individual continually seeks immediate gratification of his needs, he will constantly be subjected to situations that cause him tension and anxiety.

One of the major influences on the development of the ego and its functions are those significant others with which the individual comes into contact. Hartman (1946) states that it is from these individuals the child learns certain ways to cope with and solve problems. Fromm (1947) suggests that the personality of the individual is developed through the process of relating himself to the world. He does this through the process of acquiring and assimilating things from the world in order to satisfy his needs, and by his relations with other people. While we have already discussed how the individual learns to assimilate things from his environment to satisfy his needs, we now need to consider this process of identification with other people in the environment or, as Fromm (1947) calls it, the process of socialization. It is this process of socialization that begins with the child-rearing practices of the parents and then is extended to others with whom the child comes into contact that will influence his particular life style. The importance of this process is that it provides the individual with a pattern of behaviors that will allow him to operate within the society (Fromm, 1947).

Thus, the ego-analysts tend not to emphasize the negative effects of society on the individual as did Freud, but place equal concern with the positive effects of society on the individual. This emphasis on the importance of the society in shaping behavior allows the ego-analysts to be more optimistic about modifying behavior later in life. They accept the fact that the basic patterns of behaving are established during the first six years of an individual's life, but they see these behaviors as only a base upon which new behaviors are built. The key to the development of normal personality is this ability to develop new patterns of behavior to cope with the new demands of a situation. As Kubie points out, the development of a normal personality involves . . .

> flexibility, the freedom to learn through experience, the freedom to change with changing internal and external circumstances, to be influenced by reasonable argument, admonitions, exhortations, and the appeal to emotions; the freedom to respond appropriately to the stimulus of reward and punishment, and especially the freedom to cease when satisfied (Kubie, 1958).

If the individual does not have this flexibility, then behavior development will cease or the individual will regress to earlier patterns of behavior in his hierarchy. Either way, the individual can then be said to be behaving in an abnormal manner.

What is implied from the preceding discussion is that the individual, through conscious effort, learns new patterns of behaving. Hence, the individual selects those ways of behaving that seem appropriate to him. Unlike classical Freudian beliefs, the individual is not solely subject to behavior elicitors outside of his awareness, but is instead an active agent in choosing and directing his behavior. These behaviors, if used often enough, will become automatic and will not require conscious thought. For instance, the child learning the complicated behavior pattern of hitting a baseball with a bat at first must think about what he is doing, but as he becomes increasingly proficient at the task, he no longer gives conscious thought to all the procedures required to hit the ball. He may then give conscious thought to where he wants to hit the ball, but this too with repetition will become an automatic behavior. Hence, patterns of behavior build one upon the other in a related network or system of behavior (Rapaport, 1951). Ford and Urban (1967) point out that these patterns of behavior may become quite independent of the original reason for their existence. A behavior originally used to respond to a physiological need may subsequently become a behavior used to respond to a situational event that is quite independent of the original need.

EGO-FUNCTIONS

Classical psychoanalytic theory tends to see the functions of the ego in a rather limited negative sense. That is, the ego deals with the demands of reality through the use of defense mechanisms. The ego-analysts tend to view the functions of the ego in a broader, more positive manner. In the classical view the ego functions involve the use of repression, projection, and other Freudian defense mechanisms that emphasized protective or regressive behavior. In the ego-analytic view the ego functions are used to cope with the environment through the use of reasoning and conscious thought processes. The former processes look to the past, while the latter processes look toward the future. Kroeber describes the defensive functions of the ego as being dominated by rigidity and the distortion of present reality while the conscious coping functions of the ego are dominated by the reality of the situation and are flexible (Kroeber, 1964). The latter approach emphasizes the individual's ability to deal with the environment and his own needs in a positive sense, instead of resorting to the use of defensive behavior.

It may be useful here to examine three categories of ego functions established by Kroeber (1964): impulse economics, cognitive functions, and controlling functions.

Impulse Economics

Impulse economics concerns the individual's ability not only to control his impulses, but to channel them into more acceptable and usable behavior. In the classical psychoanalytic theory, impulses are dealt with by displacement repression, or reaction formation, which amounts to the impulse being denied. If, instead of these behaviors, the individual chooses to deal with his impulses in a more positive sense, he will accept the impulse but will cope with it by redirecting its expression or by simply delaying the satisfaction of the impulse until a more appropriate time. An example is a male who delays sexual gratification with a woman until marriage.

Cognitive Function

As with the impulse economics function, the cognitive function of the ego can be used either in a negative, defensive manner or in a positive, coping manner. If one uses the cognitive functions in a defensive manner, the individual is once again distorting reality through such defensive mechanisms as intellectualization and rationalization. If the individual chooses to deal with his feelings, then he is coping with the situation through the development of objectivity. In this sense the individual is able to deal with the situation through his ability to analyze it and logically think through his solution as to how he will deal with it (Kroeber, 1964).

Controlling Functions

The controlling functions of the ego allow the individual to develop the ability to concentrate on the current task without being bothered by some of his feelings. It allows him to develop flexible behavior rather than regressing to past behaviors, and also allows him to be aware of other's feelings. If, on the other hand, the controlling functions are used in a defensive manner, the individual will subscribe his feelings to others, he will regress to former ways of behaving when he is confronted by a difficult situation, and he will simply deny to awareness those feelings that are painful to him.

The key to understanding the ego-analysts' position toward personality development and the use of ego functions is to realize the importance the ego-analysts give to the individual's ability to respond not only to needs generated within the individual, but also to respond to the situation. That is, behavior is not only elicited from within, but is also elicited by other people. Further, the manner in which the individual responds to the behavior elicitors is often under the conscious control of the individual. In the ego-analysts' view, man is not just an automated animal that responds in prescribed ways, but he often directs his own behavior. In the Freudian view, the ego responds in a negative fashion through the use of defense mechanisms while, in the ego-analytic view, man responds either in a rigid defensive manner or in a more positive coping manner. In short, the ego-analysts see the character of the individual as composed of a series or pattern of behavior interrelated with a network of independent systems. Some of these patterns are developed in response to innate psychological needs. As the individual matures, more and more of them are developed through his conscious thought processes as he responds to new environmental situations.

The Development of Abnormal Behavior

In an earlier section of this chapter it was pointed out that the ego-analysts have tended to emphasize the growth of the normal personality and have spent relatively little time discussing the growth of abnormal behavior. Nevertheless, we should attempt to understand their position in relation to abnormal behavior.

It will be recalled that in an individual with a normal pattern of behavior the ego functions act to establish patterns of behavior that successfully cope with the demands of environmental situations. Further, these patterns of behavior build one upon the other into a behavioral network, which we can call the person's life style. These behaviors are increasingly under the conscious, thoughtful control of the individual. When a situation or series of situations cause the individual to lose this self-control, we have a behavioral breakdown. That is, when an individual becomes threatened or overwhelmed by a situation and his behavior moves from conscious control to unconscious control, we have the seeds for the behavioral disorder (Rapaport, 1958). When this situation occurs, the ego-analysts believe that the functions of the ego have not been strong enough to cope with the demands and the control of behavior therefore moves from the ego functions to the id. Hence, in their view, abnormal behavior can be attributed to some breakdown or inadequate development on the part of the ego functions.

It is important to note here that a breakdown in one of the ego functions or the manner in which the ego deals with a particular kind of situation does not necessarily mean that there is a total breakdown of the ego. Some of the individual's behavior patterns may still operate in a very normal fashion but, because all patterns of behavior are related, it is necessary to understand the whole system of behaviors (Hartmann, 1953). One cannot understand the cause of the malfunction of one pattern of behaviors in response to a particular situation without understanding the entire system of behaviors. For example, one man will react to the stress of battle in an abnormal manner, while another will not. This difference in reaction to the stress is attributed to the different patterns of stable behavior that these individuals have developed.

The question now is, what causes an individual to lose control over his behavior? What happens that causes the ego to be unable to deal with situations that were adequately handled in earlier times? Rapaport (1958) believes that a particular pattern of behavior can be maintained only as long as that behavior receives some kind of reward. All of us are aware of the different kinds of language and behavior we use at home as opposed to the social settings. In both cases different patterns of behavior receive rewards in one situation and not in another.

Abnormal patterns of behavior then are generated when the individual loses conscious control over his behavior. This may happen because previously adequate behavior has not been reinforced and thus the pattern of behavior is no longer usable. As Ford and Urban (1967) point out, this is what occurs when a person is placed in a situation of stimulation deprivation for a period of time. Or the individual may lose control because his present patterns of behavior are inadequate to meet the demands of the situation. Rapaport cites the emergency of puberty as an example of a new situation arising over which the individual has not built an adequate pattern of behavior. In this case the sexual urge will dominate the individual until patterns of behavior are learned that will bring the sexual urge under conscious control.

In the ego-analytic view, then, abnormal behavior is caused by some breakdown in a functioning of the ego. As was pointed out earlier, this does not mean a total failure of the ego but rather a breakdown in a particular pattern of behavior. The normal individual can be thought of as having an ego that is flexible and capable of changing with the demands of the environment as well as the demands of his internal drives. The abnormal individual is considered as having patterns of behavior that do not change with the changing demands of the environment or the individual's internal demands. Further, in the ego-analytic view it is necessary to examine the whole system of behaviors within the individual before the cause of the abnormal behavior can be determined.

In the main, the ego-analysts differ from the Freudian viewpoint in the amount of importance they give to the functions of the ego. They attribute more conscious control of behavior to the individual than do the Freudians. Further, the ego-analysts are more concerned about the power that situational events have to elicit and effect the behavior of the individual. Hence, in their view the behavior of the individual and, indeed, his personality, are affected not only by his early childhood experiences, as in the Freudian view, but also by the individual's environment and the subsequent strength of his ego functions.

THE GOALS OF COUNSELING

In classical psychoanalytic therapy the goal of the therapists is to bring about a change in the client's personality. That is, the psychoanalyst believes that the total personality of the individual must undergo change if the individual is to be helped. The goals of ego-counseling are in a sense much more limited. The ego-counselor attempts to help the counselee with one or two particular ego defects, which are causing the counselee difficulty. As Kroeber (1964) describes the goals of counseling, the counselor does not view the counselee in terms of his defense mechanisms, but rather attempts to help the counselee divert his energy from behavior that is maladaptive to behavior that is adaptive in nature.

The ego-counselor, then, is looking for specific maladaptive ego functions within the individual and not for some unconscious evidence within the individual of a traumatic event in infancy. In short, the goals of the ego-counselor are to help the counselee see and understand his maladaptive behavior, and then help the counselee build new ego functions to deal with the particular situation in more adaptive ways. In a very real sense the chief goal is to help each individual develop what Erikson might call a sense of ego-integrity (1958).

THE COUNSELING PROCESS

Ego-counseling is designed to focus on the normal and conscious characteristics of the individual, rather than trying to uncover unconscious motivations or causes for behavior within the individual. Hence, the atmosphere of the counseling relationship is reality-oriented. The emphasis is more on the cognitive domain than on the conative. This does not mean that during the process of counseling certain material that has been repressed by the counselee will not be brought out and dealt with, nor does it mean that strong effective feelings are not expressed in ego-counseling. What it does mean is that the ego-counselor tends to be more concerned about today's behavior than past behaviors. The problem is to help the counselee with today's situation, not yesterday's.

Hartmann (1951) discussed several points that he felt were prime concerns of the ego-counselor. He emphasized the need for the ego-counselor to understand the whole behavior system of the individual, both those habitual behavior patterns that were functioning in a normal manner and those that were functioning in an abnormal pattern. That is, the counselor must strive to understand both those parts of the ego that are strong and those that are weak and unable to cope with either the innate needs of the individual or the demands of the individual's environment. The ego-counselor acknowledges that innate needs or drives may cause the individual discomfort and, hence, to behave in abnormal ways. However, the emphasis is on the situational events that threaten the individual and cause him to deal ineffectively with such events. Thus, the ego-counselor's emphasis is on the counselee's relationship with the situational events that cause him difficulty. The counselor attempts to help the counselee understand how his behavior is nonfunctional in relation to a particular situation. As was pointed out earlier in this discussion, the emphasis of the counselor is on the reality of here and now, and not on the unconscious antecedents of behavior.

Counseling then, as seen by the ego-counselors, is much less intense and of shorter duration than psychoanalysis. While both counseling and psychotherapy are concerned with the personality of the client, the counselor is not concerned with reshaping the whole personality of the individual. As Bordin points out, "personality is dealt with only as it bears on the decision or problem situation and the client is not encouraged to go much further afield" (1955, p. 336). ". . . it seems foreign to the concept of a counseling process intended to further normal [ego] development, to commit this process to extensive efforts at personality reorganization" (Hummel, 1962, p. 466).

It is the counselor's task to keep the specific goals of counseling in mind and to so direct the counseling relationship that the main emphasis is on the current problem. This ". . . . means that the counselor influences the counseling deliberations as early as his assessment of a counselee warrants, so that a gradual focus is made on a set of counselee construct with relation to some (significant) role or relationship in reality" (Hummel, 1962, p. 469). The counselor accomplishes this task by giving selective attention to the counselee and by defining the counseling relationship. The emphasis of the counseling is on rational thought processes and on the cognitive dimensions of the relationship. In essence then, it is the counselor who controls the nature of the relationship, not the client.

While the counselor needs to control the counseling relationship to achieve optimum growth for the client, it would be a mistake to think of this control in a mechanistic way. The manner in which the counselor functions in the counseling relationship will affect the manner in which the client responds. Hence, the counselor must be warm and spontaneous. The client must perceive the counselor as being someone who is not only professionally competent to help him, but also concerned with the client and willing to make some commitment to that concern. This requires that the counselor be a good and objective listener; that is, he must communicate to the counselee his acceptance of him and his willingness to help, but must do this while avoiding becoming over-involved with the counselee.

It is necessary for the counselor to maintain an objective frame of reference if he is to help the individual. Without this objectivity the counselor may become so involved with the counselee that his own need pattern comes into the picture. The counselor who responds to the counselee by suggesting some solutions to the problem that have worked for the counselor himself is involved to such an extent that it is likely he has lost his effectiveness. But as Bordin points out, some involvement on the part of the counselor is necessary. It would seem difficult to fully understand the feelings of others without relying to some extent on one's own emotional experience (Bordin, 1955). The important concern is to not let one's emotional experiences get in the way of meeting the needs of the counselee. As Hummel (1962) points out, the ego-counselor is aware of the power of the relationship, but is also aware that there is a need to go beyond the relationship. There are not only feelings, but facts, alternatives, and decisions that need to be examined and resolved.

The process of counseling, then, is a relationship in which one individual, the counselee, comes to another individual, the counselor, with a problem for which the counselee feels he needs aid. In turn, the counselor is a professionally trained individual who should be able to give this aid. The concern of counseling is not, on the whole, reorganization of the individual counselee's personality, but on specific patterns of behavior that are maladaptive for the individual. In order for the counseling to be effective, there must be some commitment on the part of both the counselee and the counselor to solving the particular concern. This is not accomplished in a sterile mechanical atmosphere, but is accomplished in an atmosphere where mutual trust, understanding, and acceptance predominate. The counselor, by the nature of his professional training, has the responsibility for controlling the counseling relationship so that the counselee can achieve optimum growth. The emphasis of the counseling process is upon first assisting the client to understand how his own behavior in relation to certain situational events has been maladaptive, and then to help the client develop new patterns of behavior that are adaptive. In short, the goal is to restore the ego functions to full strength.

Since counseling is seen as being concerned with relatively normal individuals who function somewhat adequately in most situations, but are troubled by specific concerns, the duration of counseling is seen as being relatively short, five to six sessions. "We are assuming that a relatively well-integrated person can make use of a brief counseling experience to set in motion a learning process that carries far beyond the relationship itself." (Bordin, 1955, p. 334). As counseling terminates, it is this precise feeling with which the client should be left; that is, he should be made to feel that he will now be able to deal effectively with new situations as they are presented to him. The counseling process is best terminated on a positive note, such that when new difficulties arise for the individual he will not feel the need for a counselor.

Techniques of Ego Counseling

The techniques of counseling are not a set of prescribed methods that the ego-counselor must follow rigidly. Rather, they are a set of preferred attitudes and strategies to be used flexibly by the counselor while he respects the client's right to be himself (Hummel, 1962).

The actual process of counseling begins when a counselee comes to the counselor with a difficulty for which he feels he needs assistance. In the initial stages of counseling it is the responsibility of the counselor to try to develop an understanding of the counselee, while at the same time imparting what is expected of him during the process of counseling. Thus, in ego-counseling as with other theories, the initial stages of counseling are concerned with establishing a relationship between the client and the counselor as well as laying the ground rules under which they will operate. Bordin (1955) emphasizes the need for the counselor to allow as much freedom to the client as possible in the early stages of counseling. It is through this freedom that the client will express to the counselor his concerns which, in turn, enables the counselor to define the task before them. It is important to note that in ego-counseling it is essentially the counselor who defines the task after careful attention to what the client has presented. As Bordin (1955) indicates, the inexperienced counselor often has difficulty because he is not patient enough to listen carefully and completely to the client before he defines the problem area or task.

As the professionally trained person in the relationship, the counselor has the responsibility for controlling the counseling relationship. While the counseling is designed to build the ego strength of the individual, it is the expertise of the counselor that facilitates this process. One of the critical ways in which the counselor controls the relationship is by keeping the relationship focused on the task at hand. The counselor selects the aspects of the individual's problem to work on and then keeps the relationship focused on this goal. " The counselor does this by selective responsiveness and by helping the client to establish greater intellectual control over other conflicting responses" (Bordin, 1955, p. 340).

The counselor also controls the relationship through control over the cognitive and conative dimensions of the counselee's expressions. The cognitive dimension refers to those behaviors that are generally labeled overt behaviors or expressions, while the conative dimension refers to the emotions of the individuals. The aim of the counselor is to keep a balance between the two dimensions. Counseling cannot be geared just to the expression of emotion because the reality of the problem may be lost in the expression of affect. Nor can counseling be geared just to the cognitive aspects of the problem while ignoring the client's feelings about the problem. The ego-counselor strives for a balance between the two dimensions by not letting the client communicate in only one dimension to the exclusion of the other. Hence, when a client is dealing solely with affect, the counselor may attempt to get him to deal with the cognitive aspects of the problem, or when the client is being purely intellectual, the counselor will attempt to get the counselee to deal with the emotional aspects of the problem.

The use of ambiguity by the counselor is also an effective technique designed to control the counseling relationship. Ambiguity refers to the lack of structure within a particular situation, and is needed in counseling so that a client does not feel compelled by the situation to behave or respond in prescribed ways. In general, the counselor should strive to establish a highly ambiguous situation in the early stages of counseling so that the counselee will feel free to express himself. The counselor does need to define some areas of the relationship, such as what topics are appropriate and what the limits are on the relationship between client and counselor, but the counselor should keep in mind that the more defined the relationship, the less ambiguous the situation. For example, non-directive techniques where there is little talking by the counselor increase the ambiguity of the relationship, while directive techniques where the counselor takes the lead in the interaction process decrease the amount of ambiguity.

Bordin (1955) suggests three purposes for the use of ambiguity in the counseling relationship. First, an ambiguous counseling situation provides a background against which the feelings of the client can be contrasted. Secondly, ambiguity elicits responses from the client that represent unique aspects of his personality and this, in turn, facilitates the development of transference through projection. It is this phenomenon of transference that enables the counselor to understand the reasons for the individual's behavior. In an ambiguous situation the client reveals to the counselor the patterns of behavior he uses to deal with his problems.

It is important that the amount of ambiguity offered to a particular client be appropriate to the problem. The more cognitive the problem of the individual, the less ambiguity needed. As with the cognitive-conative dimension of the counseling relationship, it is important that the counselor recognize the power of ambiguity, and that he control its use in the counseling relationship. The inexperienced counselor often will present a very ambiguous situation to an individual without realizing what he is doing and will thus encourage a very intense relationship, a relationship he may not be equipped to handle. Hence, the beginning counselor is cautioned to be very cognizant of the amount of ambiguity presented to any individual.

While the ego-analysts acknowledge that the pheonmenon of transference may occur in counseling, they do not subscribe to this phenomenon the importance given to it by Freud. In the classical sense, transference occurs when the client displaces feelings from previous situations onto the therapist. The therapist becomes a substitute figure for a person from the client's past. The ego-analysts tend to treat this in terms of counseling as a feeling developed by the counselee for the counselor. In general, they believe that the essentially normal individual can work through his problems in the counseling relationship without a reliance on transference. Hummel feels that for most counseling cases the use of transference phenomenon is not necessary. He sees it as an inappropriate technique for individuals who are relatively free of crippling neurotic defenses (1962).

The control of the dimensions of the counseling relationship that the counselor exercises facilitates the self-exploration of the client which, in turn, enables the counselor to come to a full understanding of the client. Based on this understanding, the counselor, as the acknowledged professional, makes a tentative diagnosis of the problem. While this diagnosis is tentative in nature and should not be imposed upon the client, it is the responsibility of the counselor to define the problem and share that diagnosis with the client, helping him to fully understand it. The chief technique the counselor uses to help the individual come to this understanding is interpretation. Interpretation should be used by the counselor to help the client crystallize his thoughts or feelings, to compare conflicting ideas, and to point out the defense mechanisms that are being misused. In using interpretation, the counselor is attempting to put what the client has said into a more understandable perspective such that the client may be able to see the reasons for his behavior or feelings. Even though the counselor is the acknowledged expert, he must be careful that he does not impose his interpretation or diagnosis on the client or use interpretation too early in the interview. In either case the client may resist the interpretation by establishing his defense mechanisms even more firmly. ". . . [T]he counselor introduces new meanings into their discourse as one who is trying not to convert the counselor but to join him in a mutual effort at comprehension." (Hummel, 1962, p. 475). Thus, the timing of interpretations is extremely important and the counselor must be aware of the individual's readiness to deal with it. It is only as the individual is ready to deal with the interpretation that the interpretation will have meaning for him, and thus help the counseling process.

The principal techniques with which the ego-counselor operates then are concerned with the manner in which the counseling relationship is controlled. This control is exercised chiefly through the use of the cognitive-conative dimensions, and the control of the amount of ambiguity offered to the client. Within this setting the counselor comes to some understanding of the client's difficulties from the expressions and behaviors exhibited in the counseling relationship. These behaviors and expressions are often facilitated through the use of modified or moderate transference phenomena. Once the counselor has come to an understanding of the counselee's difficulty, he attempts to bring the counselee to that understanding through the use of interpretative statements, being fully aware of the counselee's readiness to accept the interpretation.

Hummel (1962, pp. 479–480) has outlined a series of steps that a typical counselor and client might follow from an ego-counseling frame of reference. The problem of the client used in this illustration is of academic study.

1. The first step is to help the client examine his feelings about his life in school, his role in the school, his performance in school, and other school-related tasks.
2. The client is then encouraged to project himself into the future. The counselor endeavors to get the client to discuss his career and life goals. The counselor then attempts to have the client see some relationship between his present behavior and his future goals.
3. The counselor then attempts to discuss with the client those obstacles to the client's reaching his goals and how these obstacles might be removed.
4. As the discussion of obstacles is continued, the counselor, through interpretation and reflection, attempts to get the client to examine himself and his external circumstances. Further, the counselor attempts to have the client see the interrelated nature of his feelings and behaviors.
5. Finally, the counselor helps the client establish a revised set of intentions in relation to academic study, and then, if possible, get him to rehearse his new behaviors. The rehearsal involves having the client envision how he will behave in various hypothetical situations, such as how he might set up a study schedule.

In effect, the purpose of ego-counseling is not just to produce changes in specific behavior; e.g., better grades; but in ". . . the complex of meanings and organizing principles which guide the counselee in his transactions within the sector of academic study." (Hummel, 1962, p. 479).

Summary

While ego-counseling is based largely on classical psychoanalytic theory, its main emphasis is on the functioning of the ego. Ego-counselors believe that the ego functions operate to control or account for more of an individual's behavior than do the psychoanalysts. Their emphasis is on the conscious aspects of an individual and they attribute a large part of a person's behavior to conscious control. Hence, they tend to give more credit to the role the person's environment plays in his development and subsequent behavior. Further, ego-counseling is much more concerned with the relatively normal individuals and in helping these individuals develop stronger and more fully functioning egos, rather than placing emphasis on the abnormal and complete personality reorganization.

Ego-counseling is designed to help individuals develop the coping aspects of the personality. It is designed to help the individual cope with the realities of the world through the building of the ego functions. As Grossman (1964) points out, ego-counseling is concerned with getting the ego to the point where it can deal with problems in the real world, while helping the individual to remove from his behavior those defense mechanisms that hinder his interaction with the real world. In short, the goal of ego-counseling is to expand and strengthen the functioning of an individual's ego system.

ADLERIAN CONTRIBUTIONS

The inclusion of a discussion on Adlerian contributions to counseling within the framework of a psychoanalytic chapter is somewhat misleading. While Adler is most often considered one of the great Freudians, much of his theoretical position is in direct contrast to the classical psychoanalytic position. Nonetheless, it is because his name is most often associated with the neo-Freudian thinkers that the discussion is included in this chapter.

Adler was the first major individual to break away from Freud and establish his own school of thought. The name he gave to this school of thought, " Individual Psychology," was chosen to represent his conception of man as a holistic individual. He saw each individual as a consistent and unified whole, which acted in total toward a chosen life goal: a goal that each individual chooses for himself and for which each individual develops his own characteristic ways of attempting to reach that goal. Adler believed that the way to understand an individual was to determine what his goal was and what life style the individual had developed to reach that goal. This position is far different from Freud's belief that man's behavior was determined by innate drives largely out of his conscious control. The Adlerian position places much more emphasis on the importance of the individual and his interaction with his environment. Hence, Adler's emphasis was on neither the environment nor heredity as determiners of behavior; rather, it was on the interaction of the environment, heredity, and the individual as the determiner of behavior.

Adler saw the causation for behavior lying in the individual's perception of events. It was not the events themselves that determined behavior, but the way in which the objective observer perceived the event and interpreted that event to himself. An objective event in the individual's life, such as a physical deficiency, broken home, or an intolerable teacher, only acted indirectly on how an individual might respond. In such cases the actual event might affect the likelihood of home behavior developing, but by itself would not determine behavior. What is of most importance is how the individual perceives and interprets events. Adler referred to these perceptions of the individual as " fictions " and emphasized that they were not to be confused with the actual reality. Even though they are not completely accurate representations of reality, each individual behaves as though the " fictions " he creates in his mind were the actual reality.

In addition to each individual creating " fictions " of the real events, Adler believed that each individual developed for himself a life goal. This goal is developed in response to the individual's striving to overcome his own inherent weaknesses in the face of the world. The attainment of each individual's goal represents his overcoming this inherent weakness and securing ultimate happiness. Just as the individual's interpretations of events are " fictions," so the goal that one chooses is a " fiction." It is acted upon as if it will bring the individual happiness. It was Adler's belief that this " fictional goal " for each individual served as the unifying force. All individual behavior is directed toward the accomplishment of the chosen goal. Adler referred to this pattern of the individual's behavior as his " life style."

Adler also placed a great deal of emphasis on the importance of the social context of human behavior. He emphasized that all human behavior developed within a social context. The child is born into a family and its interactions first within the family and then with others establishes certain conditions upon the type of behaviors that may develop (Ansbacher, 1956). In effect, all of man's behavior is, in reality, an interaction with other beings. " For this reason, we can presume one basic desire in all human beings; the desire to belong, which Adler called 'social interest.' " (Driekurs, 1961, p. 60). Hence, whatever man does, he does in relationship to a social group. This perspective led Adler to the belief that the only way one could effectively study human behavior was to study it within the social context. It was for this reason that Adler considered his theoretical conceptions of human behavior as a social psychology (Ansbacher, 1956). In order to understand how the concepts just discussed affect the development of the individual we need to examine the sequence of events that affect personality development.

PERSONALITY DEVELOPMENT

Adler, like Freud, held the belief that most of what an individual becomes in adult life is formed during the first four or five years of the child's existence. It is during the early stages of development that the child develops habitual patterns of behavior, the life style, which are geared toward the attainment of his fictional goal—a goal that represents all that is good.

Adler believed that every individual comes into this life with a built-in feeling of inferiority. The infant as he comes into this world is in a helpless state in the face of his environment. Even if he enters as a perfectly developed and normal individual, he is not capable of coping with his world. An additional burden to the infant would exist if there were also a physical defect of some type. Adler contended that the infant soon perceives this inferiority, which results in an uncomfortable state within the individual. This development is in every sense normal, it is inevitable, and takes place in every individual to at least some degree. In fact, it is this very basic feeling of inferiority that Adler contended was the ultimate driving force of man. As the child perceives that he is inferior, either because of an organ defect or simply because of the basic nature of the infant, he begins to try and find ways to overcome his feelings. He seeks to develop means by which he can reduce the uncomfortable feelings caused by his own subjective evaluation of himself as inferior.

This feeling of inferiority within the individual has as its direct consequence the development of a striving for superiority. Adler's concept of this drive for superiority should not be confused with a drive toward social eminence or leadership. It is conceived as a much more basic drive within each individual to master his environment. This is the force that Adler contended causes man always to be moving forward and improving his situation. In Adler's words: " All our functions follow its direction. They strive for conquest, security, increase, either in the right or in the wrong direction. The impetus from minus to plus never ends. The urge from below to above never ceases" (Adler, 1930, p. 398). The focus of this drive is the fictional goal the individual has chosen for himself.

As the child searches for means of dealing with a world in which he feels inferior, he must first create in his own mind some order out of the chaos that confronts him. The child accomplishes this task by using his inherent capacity to attend to certain events in his environment and then interpret those events to himself. In effect, the child builds a world of perceptions about events. As an increasing number of these perceptions are developed, they become habitual in nature as well as interrelated. Soon the child has an organized picture of his world; a picture that may or may not be accurate. Some of these perceptions, " fictions," become concerned with future objectives, the attainment of which will allow the child to value himself as superior, thus removing the unpleasant feelings created by his feelings of inferiority.

As the child matures, he begins to focus on one particular goal. As stated earlier in this section, Adler believed that the child eventually chooses one overriding goal as the organizing element for all of the individual's behavior. The child projects this goal in front of him with the belief that its attainment will permit him to overcome all obstacles and bring him perfect security. Hence, each individual develops a goal that is uniquely his early in his life. This goal then will determine his style of behavior. His goal will determine in what things he will be interested, in what kinds of situations he will involve himself and, finally, what kinds of behaviors he is most likely to develop.

It is important at this point to note that in conjunction with the child's development of a " fictional goal " around which his behavior is organized, the child's innate social interest is also developed. Adler believed that, given favorable conditions in the child's early interactions with his family, this social interest would be encouraged. Hence, these responses are developed in an interrelationship with the child's other behaviors such that the child's striving for superiority becomes fused with his social interests. In this manner the child becomes a social being for, while he is interested in the attainment of his goal, he seeks to attain that goal in ways that will benefit both him and others. One of the best ways to overcome the uncomfortable feeling created by one's own feelings of inferiority is to believe that one is contributing to the welfare of others and is therefore valuable (Ansbacher, 1956).

Once the child has selected a goal toward which he is working and his habitual patterns of behavior designed to reach this goal have been established, he has developed what Adler referred to as a life style. The concept of life style is the most encompassing level of behavior that Adler describes. It is the individual's life style that dictates all that is considered an individual's personality: ". . . it is the whole that commands the parts." (Hall and Lindzey, 1957, p. 123). While everyone in life has the same ultimate goal of superiority, the objective that will satisfy that goal is somewhat different for everyone and the manner in which that goal is sought will also be unique. Hence every individual has a life style, but no two of these styles are exactly the same. It was in this manner that Adler accounted for the individuality of man.

Adler saw the development of an individual's life style as taking place about the time a child had reached the age of 5. From that time onward the personality of the individual remains in the same basic form. Once it is established, it dictates everything a person does from that time on (Ansbacher, 1956). Important to an understanding of this concept is the knowledge that Adler believed the individual is not fully aware of his own life style. He believed an individual could not explain fully to himself his own life style because much of that life style was formed before the child had developed the ability to symbolize events through the use of language. This explains not only why an individual does not understand all his behavior, but why the patterns of behavior remain relatively the same throughout life. If behavior cannot be verbalized, then it would be very difficult for the individual to change. As we shall see, this is one of the prime reasons why people who are experiencing difficulty need someone outside of themselves to explain their life style to them.

In summary, Adler saw personality development in terms of the child's struggle to remove himself from a position of inferiority to a place of superiority. In order to accomplish this task, the child forms " fictions," which allow him to bring some sense of order out of the chaos around him. Part of these fictions are goals toward which the individual moves in order to remove his feeling of inferiority. Gradually the individual selects one goal around which his behavior is organized and this, in combination with the individual's innate social interest, fuses together to form the individual's basic life style. It is at this point that the development of personality has taken place.

It is now appropriate to turn to a consideration of what happens within this normal progression that accounts for the abnormal behavior of some individuals.

ABNORMAL DEVELOPMENT

Adler believed that there were two basic reasons for an individual developing abnormal patterns of behavior. Abnormality, as he saw it, was first a result of an individual having greater feelings of inferiority early in his life. Secondly, the individual, in an attempt to deal with the overwhelming tension created by these feelings of inferiority, developed inappropriate patterns of behavior.

Adler proposed that an individual could develop increased feelings of inferiority by being born with a physical defect, being pampered by parents, or being subject to neglect. While Adler believed that children who were born defective in some way were likely to develop an increased feeling of inferiority, this was not an automatic development. The importance of the event in the development of the child is his reaction to the event as well as the reaction of those around him. If his reaction is positive, then development is liable to follow a normal course. If, on the other hand, he and those around him react to the defect as a serious liability, then the probability of abnormal development occurring is heightened.

Adler also stressed that a child who is pampered and constantly cared for will come to believe that he is unable to take care of himself, thereby increasing his feelings of inferiority. Similarly, the child who is neglected is not very likely to develop in a normal pattern. A child who is constantly rejected or punished is, instead, very likely to see himself as being quite inferior. While there could be other reasons for an individual's developing an over-abundance of inferiority feelings, Adler believed that these three were the basic causes of this phenomenon.

Once the individual had developed an abnormal amount of tension due to his increased feelings of inferiority, the likelihood of his subsequent behavior being abnormal was increased. One form this behavior could take was an over-striving for superiority. In an attempt to deal with his tension, the individual would establish an extremely high fictional goal for himself, and his behavior, in attempting to reach that goal, would likely be extremely rigid. Adler likened it to seeking a godlike state of perfection.

A second result of intense feelings of inferiority is related to the individual's development of his social interest. The child who is pampered, neglected, or in some way treated as different is not likely to have human encounters that are very encouraging. He begins to expect that interactions with others will not be very satisfying. This leads the child to conclude that cooperation with others in pursuit of his goals is not likely to prove a fruitful venture (Ansbacher, 1956). As a result, the child selects objectives that he believes will satisfy his own needs without any consideration of common objectives that may serve others as well. In short, rather than become socially oriented, he becomes selfish in his goals and behavior. This, in turn, affects the amount of interaction he will have with other beings. While Adler did not spend a great deal of time on this concept, he did believe that the individual who developed in abnormal ways had an activity level less than the activity level of his normal counterpart.

In Adler's view, then, abnormal behavior development was the result of the same kinds of factors that accounted for normal personality development. The differences lay with the abnormal feelings of inferiority created within the individual, and the subsequent development of inappropriate patterns of behavior in the individual in his attempt to deal with the heightened tension created by his inferiority feelings. Given this kind of development in the individual, we now need to consider the ways in which Adler felt the individual could be helped.

Goals of Counseling

The goals of counseling as seen by the Adlerians are very simply to help the individual change his concept of himself. While this may seem a rather simplistic goal, the reader must remember that Adler saw the development of abnormal behavior as being directly related to the individual's feelings of inferiority in regard to himself. The more specific goals of counseling concern taking the individual back along his developmental path in an attempt to restructure that development. The first of these specific goals is to help the individual reduce his negative evaluation of himself—his feelings of inferiority. The second goal is to help him correct his perceptions of events, and at the same time help him to develop a new set of objectives toward which he can direct his behavior. The final goal is to redevelop within the individual his inherent social interest with its accompanying social interaction. It was this last step that Adler felt was most crucial. If the goal of increasing social interest and participation was not reached, then the rest of the process was largely wasted (Ansbacher, 1956).

The Process of Counseling

Adler was one of the first to recognize the importance of the relationship between the counselor and his client. In his view, therapy was essentially a social relationship. In effect, the whole process of counseling is viewed as a process of socialization. The client's problems are largely a result of his lack of socialization. The process of counseling can thus be a powerful tool in redeveloping this process within the individual. It has this potential largely because of the social interaction between the counselor and client. This relationship is unique in that for many clients it is the first time that they are in a situation with another individual where they need not be afraid. Given a permissive and warm atmosphere by the counselor, the client will feel that he is accepted and for the first time will be able to deal openly with his feelings of inferiority.

In order to establish the appropriate relationship, the counselor must be an objective and attentive listener who can communicate to the client his liking for and concern about him. Further, he must have the ability to be patient with the client, even in the face of hostility and resistance. Adler contends that in no sense should the client ever be offended by the counselor. Thus, the counselor must have the ability to state things to the client in such a way as to have them acceptable to him. This last point is extremely important for it is the counselor, not the client, who will develop an understanding of what is causing the client difficulty. If the counselor cannot communicate this understanding to the client in ways that the latter will accept, then the client will never come to understand his own behavior. It follows that if there is no understanding on the part of the client, then there will be no change in behavior.

Adler also believed that it was important to the process of counseling that the client be treated as a responsible individual. The counselor must communicate to the client that it is his responsibility to act. As Rudolf Dreikurs (1961) points out, the counselor needs to be human in his interaction with the client. Anything that detracts from the spontaneous nature of the relationship can only be detrimental to the process of counseling.

Adler believed that, given the establishment of the proper relationship, the process of counseling would then proceed through three stages. The first stage is the period during which the counselor strives to develop an understanding of the goals and life style of the client. Once this analysis of the client is completed, the counselor strives to interpret to him his own behavior. In effect, the counselor is explaining the client to himself. Central to this process is helping the client understand the goal of his behavior and how that goal determines his disturbing attitudes, thoughts, and behavior. Once this understanding is achieved by the client, he is able to select new goals which, in turn, result in new behaviors. Finally, Adler believed in the importance of developing the social interest of the client. Adler saw the therapist as functioning similarily to the role of a mother; that is, giving the client the experience of a loving contact with another human being, and then helping him to transfer this heightened social interest to positive feelings toward others. Ultimately this would bring the client's private goals in line with goals of the larger society, and give the individual the confidence that any problem he is confronted with can be solved in cooperation with others.

Having gone through this process, Adler assumed that the behavior of the individual would be changed. This was the real test of counseling for Adler, since he did not believe that an individual could develop true understanding of himself without a subsequent change in behavior. If there was no change, then there was no self-understanding, and counseling had not been successful.

Techniques of Counseling

In the area of specific techniques in counseling Adler did the least of his writing. This may be one of the prime reasons for the relative lack of use of his therapy system despite the widespread use of many of his concepts.

From Adler's perspective, the first and most important task of therapy is for the therapist to develop an understanding of the life style of the individual. In attempting to come to an understanding of that life style it is necessary for the counselor to start with an examination of the client's present behavior. This is accomplished by asking the client questions about his current existence; that is, having him describe the events in his life and his reactions to them. At the same time, the counselor is observing the behavior of the client within the counseling situation. The permissive atmosphere of the situation is designed not only to enhance social interaction, but also to permit the client to behave in an open fashion. In this way the counselor can gain a first-hand knowledge of the client's behavior patterns. Once the present situation has been understood, the counselor then tries to develop an understanding of the entire life style of the individual. It is important to note that Dreikurs, a student of Adler, believes it is at this point that we can distinguish between counseling and psychotherapy. He believes that in the areas of vocational counseling, marriage counseling, and child guidance there is no need to go into the entire life style of the individual. Rather, these problems can be solved by an examination and understanding of the current behavior. He illustrates this point by stating that, in order to solve a problem in marriage, we do not need to explore the life style of each individual; rather, what must be done is to change the erroneous behaviors of the two partners toward each other (1961, p. 89).

Adler did identify two specific techniques to be used by the counselor during this analysis stage: empathy and intuitive guessing. The feeling of empathy is necessary for the counselor to truly understand the subjective feelings of the client. Only by trying to step into the shoes of the client is the counselor really able to understand the feelings of the client that are guiding his behavior. The intuitive guessing described by Adler can be likened to the ability of the counselor to interpret from what the client is saying the kinds of processes that are going on in his mind. This is necessary because the counselor cannot fully rely on the self-reports of the client, since the client is unable to verbalize all the reasons for his behavior (Ford and Urban, 1963).

If an understanding of the complete life style of an individual is necessary, then the counselor must engage the client in a discussion of his early recollections. Adler believed that the memory of each individual is biased and that he remembers only those events that have meaning in his current life style. Hence, if the counselor could understand the events upon which the individual had based his life style, he would be in a position to present a new understanding of these events to the client.

A second method used to understand the development of the individual's life style is for the counselor to examine the family constellation of the individual in his formative years. By understanding this constellation, the counselor can come to understand the unique interactions between individuals that may have affected his client's life style. It is this particular technique that is receiving increasing attention in the field of counseling, particularly at the elementary level. In increasing numbers, counselors are turning to an observation of the child in his home and school setting in an attempt to try and understand the causes of a particular child's difficulty.

Once the counselor has developed an understanding of the client, he needs to interpret this understanding to the client in a manner such that the client will accept this new information about himself. Unfortunately, Adler never really defined how this was to be done. The only thing that is really clear about his thinking on this topic is that the counselor needs to be flexible and use whatever methods he feels will develop new understanding in the client.

Once the client has developed this new understanding of his behavior, Adler believes that his behavior will change. Dreikurs (1961) feels that the counselor can enhance this process by providing encouragement to the client. He believes that encouragement is essential if improvement in the client is to occur. In large part, this encouragement takes the form of helping the client understand that he was the one who was causing his own difficulty and, further, he is the one in whom the responsibility lies for improving his situation. This knowledge of power over oneself tends to free the individual. He now realizes that he has the power to move himself from a minus to a plus state and counseling can terminate.

SUMMARY

Even from this brief discussion of Adlerian thinking it should be clear to the reader that his thinking has had a wide impact on the field of counseling. While his early training was with Freud, his theory of personality is perhaps the first of the phenomenological approaches. Many of the concepts he first used, such as inferiority, life style, compensation, empathy, and respect, can now be found in a variety of counseling approaches. In some ways it is unfortunate that he did not spend as much time writing about his theory of therapy as he did his theory of personality for, while his concepts are clearly understood, he left few guidelines for a counselor attempting to implement his theory. For the reader who wishes to delve further into the thinking of Adler, there are several fine books listed in the annotated bibliography at the end of this chapter.

RESEARCH

There can be little question that psychoanalytic theory and those theories, such as ego-analysis and Adlerian psychology, that are based on psychoanalytic thought have been subject to vast amounts of research. Freud, in constructing his original theory, developed exhaustive case studies of his patients. Likewise, those that have followed Freud have collected vast amounts of clinical data. Most of this research, however, has been of a case study type and has been devoted to the development of the theory itself with little research on the application of the theory to counseling. That is, much of the research has been devoted to the actual formalization of the theory of personality and its use in diagnosis. There is still very little empirical research on the application of the theory to counseling. Hence, it is difficult to substantiate whether certain counseling techniques that are proposed by theorists of this persuasion are effective or not and, beyond that, in what kinds of cases are they effective and with what kinds of clients.

As Rapaport (Knoch, 1959) indicates, the development of the field of ego-counseling may facilitate future research in this area. With their emphasis on the normal individual and the functions of the ego, the ego-analysts are giving some formal structure to the theory, which may be more amenable to empirical research. He further concludes that the present evidence is very inconclusive as only a few studies offer any evidence that is really acceptable to the field of psychology. It would seem then, that a major need for those involved with ego-counseling is to develop a systematic investigation into the effectiveness of ego-counseling techniques and assumptions about behavior. It is only as such data are accumulated that the theory can be translated into a working one. As was indicated in Chapter 1, it is the responsibility of those interested in the concepts put forth by ego-counseling to test these assumptions for themselves. A theory that is not subjected to investigation and revision based on the results of those investigations is not really a theory, but rather an accumulation of somewhat related thoughts or ideas.

It should be pointed out to the reader that most of the research done on the effectiveness of psychoanalytically oriented theories has been done with abnormal patients. That is, it has been conducted in hospital or other clinical settings and has been done with patients having severe mental disorders. It is only speculation at this point whether any of the findings using these kinds of subjects are really applicable to the field of counseling. Hence, the results of such investigations are not included here for review.

REFERENCES

Adler, A. "Individual Psychology." In Murchison, C. (Ed.) *Psychologies of 1930*. Worcester, Mass.: Clark University Press, 1930.

Adler, G. (Ed.). *Current Trends in Analytical Psychology*. London: Tavistock Publications, 1961.

Alexander, F. "Review of O. Rank and S. Ferenczi." *Entwicklungspiele der Psychoanalyse. International Journal of Psychoanalysis.* 6:484–496.

Alexander, F., and Selesnick, S. *The History of Psychotherapy*. New York: Harper and Row, 1966.

Alexander, F. *Psychoanalysis and Psychotherapy*. New York: Norton, 1956.

Ansbacher, H., and Ansbacher, Rowena. *The Individual Psychology of Alfred Adler*. New York: Basic Books, Inc., 1956.

Bordin, E. S. *Psychological Counseling*. New York: Appleton-Century Crofts, 1968.

Driekurs, Rudolf. "The Adlerian Approach to Therapy." In Stein, M. I. (Ed) *Contemporary Psychotherapies*. New York: The Free Press, 1961.

Eisenstein, S. "Otto Rank, The Myth of the Birth of the Hero." In Alexander, F.; Eisenstein, S.; and Grotjahn, M. (Eds.). *Psychoanalytic Pioneers*. New York: Basic Books, 1966.

Erikson, E. H. "Ego Development and Historical Change." *The Psychoanalytic Study of the Child*. Vol. 2. New York: International Universities Press, 1946.

Erikson, E. H. "Identity and the Life Cycle: Selected Papers." *Psychological Issues* 1:18–171.

Ferenczi, S. "Review of Technik der Psychoanalyse I Die Analytische Situation." *International Journal of Psychoanalysis* (London) 8:93–100.

Ferenczi, S. *The Selected Papers of Sandor Ferenczi*. New York: Basic Books, 1950 (4 volumes).

Ford, D. H., and Urban, H. B. *Systems of Psychotherapy: A Comparative Study*. New York: John Wiley and Sons, Inc., 1967.

Freud, S. "Psychogenic Visual Disturbance According to Psycho-Analytical Conceptions." In *Collected Papers*. Vol. 2. London: Hogarth Press, 1924, pp. 105–112 (First published in German, 1910).

Fromm, E. *Man for Himself*. New York: Rinehart, 1947.

Gaier, E. L., and Collier, M. J. "Adult Reactions to Preferred Childhood Stories." In Muensterberger, W., and Axelrod, S. (Eds.). *The Psychoanalytic Study of Society*. New York: International Universities Press, 1962.

Grossman, D. "Ego Activating Approaches to Psychotherapy." *Psychoanalytic Review* 51:65–68.

Hall, Calvin S., and Lindzey, Gardner. *Theories of Personality*. New York: John Wiley and Sons, Inc., 1957.

Hartmann, H. "Contribution to the Metapsychology of Schizophrenia." In *The Psychoanalytic Study of the Child*. Vol. 8. New York: International Universities Press, 1953.

Hartmann, H. *Essays on Ego Psychology*. New York: International Universities Press, 1964.

Hartman, H. "The Mutual Influence in the Development of Ego and Id." *Psychoanalytic Quarterly* 20:31–43.

Hummel, Raymond C. "Ego-Counseling in Guidance: Concept and Method." *Harvard Educational Review* 32:461–482.

Jones, E. *The Life and Work of Sigmund Freud*. New York: Basic Books, Volume 1, 1953; Volume 2, 1955; Volume 3, 1957.

Jung, C. G. "Answer to Job." *Psychology and Religion*. London: Routledge and Kegan Paul, 1958.

Jung, C. G. "A Psychological Approach to the Dogma of the Trinity." *Psychology and Religion*. London: Routledge and Kegan Paul, 1958.

Karpf, F. B. *The Psychology and Psychotherapy of Otto Rank*. New York: Philosophical Library, 1953.

King, Paul T., and Neal, Robert. *Ego Psychology in Counseling*. Guidance Monograph Series, Boston: Houghton-Mifflin Company, 1968.

Kroeber, Theodore C. "The Coping Functions of the Ego Mechanisms." In White, Robert W. (Ed) *The Study of Lives*. New York: Atherton Press, 1964.

Kubie, Lawrence. *The Neurotic Distortion of the Creative Process*. Kansas: University of Kansas Press, 1958.

Rank O. *The Trauma of Birth*. New York: Robert Brunner, 1957. (Originally published in London, 1929.)

Rank, O. *Truth and Reality*, translated by J. Taft. New York: Knopf, 1936.

Rapaport, D. *The Organization and Pathology of Thought*. New York: Columbia University Press, 1951.

Rapaport, D. "The Theory of Ego Autonomy: A Generalization." *Bulletin of Menninger Clinic* 22:13–35.

Sacks, H. "Review of Rank, O. Das Trauma der Geburt und seine Bedeutung fur die Psychoanalyse." Vienna: *International Psychoanalytisde Biblithek* 6:499–508.

Stafford-Clark, David. *What Freud Really Said*. New York: Shocken Books, 1966.

Taft, J. *Otto Rank*. New York: The Julian Press, 1958.

ANNOTATED BIBLIOGRAPHY

The following bibliography is presented for those readers who may wish to study in more depth either the ideas of ego-counseling or the ideas of psychoanalytic thought. It is suggested for those that are interested in ego-counseling that you will need a sound basis in psychoanalytic thought and should at least look at one of the concise texts on Freudian thought.

Ansbacher, H. L., and Ansbacher, R. R. (Eds.) *The Individual Psychology of Alfred Adler*. New York: Harper Torchbooks, 1964.

Adler's writings are organized into systematic textbook presentation dealing with the major thrusts of his ideas. Adler's original writings are used in the presentation. Well-organized book, which makes it easy to rapidly cover the major concepts of Adlerian thought.

Alder, A. *Individual Psychology*. Translated by P. Radin. Paterson, New Jersey: Littlefield, Adams and Company, 1963.

Individual Psychology, dealing with the psychical bases of homosexuality, hallucination, insomnia, prostitution, and compulsion, is Adler's first complete presentation of his theory.

Adler, A. *Problems of Neurosis*. Edited by P. Mairet. New York: Harper Torchbooks, 1964.

In the process of presenting 37 case histories, this book exemplifies some of the most salient concepts in the fully developed Adlerian system. Such concepts as lack of social feelings, useless goals to superiority, and neurotic style are discussed and illustrated. The underlying theme of this book is that neurosis develops from a lack of social interest, a lack of interest in the common welfare. Because of its clarity and examples, this book can serve as a good introduction for the beginning Adlerian student.

Adler, A. *Understanding Human Nature*. Translated by W. B. Wolfe. New York: Fawcett World Library, 1965.

In *Underling Human Nature*, Adler presents an introduction to the fundamental principles of individual psychology. Here the emphasis is on the normal rather than the maladjusted. Adler attemts to teach every human being the practical applications of these principles to everyday experiences. His book gives the reader a feeling for Adler the man and the theorist.

Adler, G. *Studies in Analytical Psychology.* London: Routledge and Kegan Paul, 1948.

This book represents a collection of lectures given by Gerhard Adler in the years from 1936 to 1945. The first essay, "A Comparative Study of Analytical Psychology," deals with the differences among Jung's *Analytical Psychology*, Freud's *Psychoanalysis*, and Adler's *Individual Psychology*. Also discussed are the pitfalls of relying upon one particular form of therapy for all individuals. The portions of the essay that outline differences among Jung, Freud, and Adler make the essay worthwhile for the reader who is not familiar with them.

The second essay, "Study of a Dream," includes the concepts of the collective unconscious and archetypes as well as the practical application of these concepts in treatment. One would do better to read Jung's own works in this case, especially his essays "On the Psychology of the Unconscious" and "The Relation Between the Ego and Unconscious."

The third and fourth essays both approach the problems of psychic growth and individual differences. A practical approach is used in "The Ego and the Cycle of Life" whereas in "Consciousness and Cure" the problems are presented from a theoretical perspective.

A fairly theoretical discussion of Jung's views on religion follows in the fifth essay. It deals with religion as a creative effort as Jung saw it, rather than as a form of sexual gratification or father image as Freud would have it.

The last essay deals with Jung's contribution to modern consciousness. Adler feels that Jung's major contribution to the world is a very optimistic philosophical outlook on man in a time when he needs it badly. The "superpersonal" images of the collective unconscious and the archetype make this possible.

Adler, K. A., and Deutsch, Danica (Eds.). *Essays in Individual Psychology: Contemporary Application of Alfred Adler's Theories.* New York: Grove Press, 1959.

Essays in Individual Psychology is a contemporary attempt to apply Adlerian theoretical principles and therapeutic practices to current research problems and case histories. Primarily emphasized are Adler's concepts of "inferiority feelings," "life style," and man's social embeddedness. This collection summarizes the latest advances in the application of Adlerian psychology in the clinic, in social and educational fields, and in the areas of child guidance and family counseling.

Alexander, F., and French, T. M. *Psychoanalytic Therapy: Principles and Application.* New York: Ronald Press, 1946.

This work, containing a collection of articles by Alexander's students and associates at the Chicago Institute for Psychoanalysis, offers a variety of suggestions for the empirical handling of Freudian doctrines in clinical situations.

Ansbacher, H. L., and Rowena, R. (Eds.). *The Individual Psychology of Alfred Adler.* New York: Basic Books, 1956; Harper Torchbooks, 1964.

The Individual Psychology of Alfred Adler is an organized and systematic presentation of Adler's individual psychology. It begins with his early philosophy and concepts, exemplifies how he moves away from a biological, objective, orientation toward a holistic, subjective orientation, and demonstrates how Adler arrived at his mature theory of striving for superiority to overcome the three major problems of life. Also presented are Adler's views of maladjustment, therapeutic treatment, crime disorders, and communal problems. This book gives the reader a clear, comprehensive understanding of individual psychology.

Bassin, F. V. "Consciousness and the Unconscious." In Cole, M., and Maltzman, I., Eds. *A Handbook of Contemporary Soviet Psychology*. New York, London: Basic Books, Inc., 1969.

This study is of interest because of the official rejection of Freud after 1925 with the advent of Stalin to power. The parallel with Nazi Germany's rejection of the psychoanalytic school as "A Jewish Science" is a fairly well-known one. While the writer stresses continued opposition to Freudian ideas, he repeatedly cites Pavlov for his recognition of the existence of non-cognized form of psychic activity.

Brenner, Charles. *An Elementary Textbook of Psychoanalysis*. New York: International Universities Press, Inc., 1955.

The basic principles of psychoanalysis are defined in a clear, understandable fashion. Brenner has the material well organized and cites the manner in which Freud's theories have changed over the years.

Brill, Dr. A. A. (Ed.). *The Basic Writings of Sigmund Freud*. New York: Modern Library, 1938.

This book is a translation of six of Freud's works. In the first book, *Psychopathology of Everyday Life*, Freud writes of those common faulty actions of everyday life; mistakes in writing, slips of the tongue, forgetting names, etc. He shows that these are not accidental and how analysis brings out the disturbing influences behind such slips.

In the second book, *The Interpretation of Dreams*, Freud writes of the dream as a normal function of the mind and explains how it represents the hidden fulfillment of an unconscious wish.

In the third book, *Three Contributions to the Theory of Sex*, Freud describes sexual aberrations, infantile sexuality, and the transformation of puberty.

Book Four, *Wit and Its Relation to the Unconscious*, discusses those unconscious underlying thoughts, which are brought to the consciousness in the disguise of wit.

Book Five, *Totem and Taboo*, refers to the restrictions that primitive races impose on themselves and how people now create such taboos for themselves.

In the last book, *The History of the Psychoanalytic Movement*, Freud relates the history as he sees it. He states that his theory is his creation and therefore "nobody knows better than I what psychoanalysis is, wherein it differs from other methods of investigating the psychic life, what its name should cover."

Cox, D. *Jung and Saint Paul*. New York: Longmans, Green and Co., 1959.

Jung and Saint Paul compares Christianity and analytical psychology as stated by Jung. The book, as Cox presents it, is a formidable one involving interpretation and translation of Christian and Jungian terms into a "neutral" language so that the comparisons can be made. His findings that Jung and Christianity, although not exactly alike, are very similar in their teachings, ideals, conceptions of man, etc., are hardly as important as the actual comparisons themselves and the discussion of the various concepts involved.

Crichton-Miller, H. *Psycho-Analysis and Its Derivatives.* London: Oxford University Press, 1945.

Crichton-Miller presents a brief summary of the nature of psychoanalysis, criticisms of it, and points of similarity and contrast between psychoanalysis and other theories of Jung, Adler, and Prinzhorn.

Erikson, E. H. *Childhood and Society.* New York: W. W. Norton and Company, 1963.

Erik Erikson, a psychoanalyst, writes about the social significance of childhood. Roughly, he divides this book into the three aspects of man—the biological, the social, and the psychological. In the first part, he discusses the biological basis of psychoanalytic theory, Freud's schedule of libido development. In Part Two, he considers a social problem—how to educate the American Indian children today in light of their tribal past. Part Three considers the laws of the ego as revealed in ego pathology. Here Erikson considers the eight stages of man, for which he is famous. In the final part, he considers how the changing conditions of the United States, Germany, and Russia affect the child's entrance into the adult world.

Fenichel, O. *The Psychoanalytic Theory of Neurosis.* New York: W. W. Norton and Company, 1945.

This is an invaluable text and handbook encompassing all psychoanalytic theories in 1945. In order to clarify techniques for treatment, it details: (1) mental (and personality) development; (2) the neurotic conflict with its defense mechanisms and symptomatology; (3) specialized data relative to special neurosis (4) character disorder problems and theory; (5) clinical, therapeutic, and prophylaxis areas.

Ford, D. H., and Urban, H. B. *Systems of Psychotherapy: A Comparative Study.* New York: John Wiley and Sons, Inc., 1965.

This is a good overall basic reference that goes beyond Hall and Lindzey's introduction to psychoanalysis. This volume contains chapters on the systems of Adler, Horney, Rank, and Sullivan, as well as the ego-analysts.

Freud, S. *The Ego and the Id.* New York: Norton and Company, 1960.

Written in 1923, *The Ego and the Id* offers a description of Freud's structural model of the mind and how it works. In addition to a discussion of consciousness and the unconscious, the ego, id, superego, instincts, and the dependent relationships of the ego are considered. This book is an excellent introduction and foundation for readings in Freudian theory.

Freud, S. *Group Psychology and the Analysis of the Ego.* New York: Bantam Books, Inc., 1965.

Written late in the twenties, this work offers a description of Freud's conceptualization of the psychodynamics of the individual in society. The concepts of identification, internalization, and the superego are of prime concern in this work. In addition, it is concerned with hypnosis and the "herd instinct." It is in this volume that Freud gives some importance to the cultural and social points of view in relation to man's development.

Freud, S. *An Outline of Psychoanalysis.* New York: W. W. Norton and Company, Inc., 1949.

In *An Outline of Psychoanalysis* the Freudian doctrine is brought together in a concise and positive form. The observational and experiential nature of psycho-analytic theory is stressed. Whether or not one accepts Freudian theory, this work is extremely useful not only for understanding Freud, the so-called "orthodoxist," and the "reformed," but for understanding the "deviants" and neo-Freudians.

Freud, S. *The Question of Lay Analysis—An Introduction to Psychoanalysis.* New York: W. W. Norton and Company, Inc., 1950.

Besides being a summary of Freud's personality theory, the book deals with the techniques of analysis and the analytic situation.

Freud, S. *Therapy and Technique.* New York: Collier Books, 1963.

Therapy and Technique is a collection of essays written between 1888 and 1937. The essays range from early case histories and a discussion of hypnotism and suggestion to recommendations in the technique of psychoanalysis, dynamics of the cure, and sections on the practice and theory of dream interpretation. This book is especially interesting because the span of time over which the essays were written permits one to observe the development and refinement of ideas that took place in Freud's thinking.

Fromm, E. *The Art of Loving.* New York: Harper and Roe, 1963.

Fromm is a social psychologist. He is interested in the well being of society. In this volume, he shows his deep concern for people and the concern that people should feel for each other. He divides this small book into major parts—the theory and the practice of love. In the theory section, Fromm considers the love between man and his fellow man, the love between a mother and a child, brotherly love, motherly love, erotic love, self love, and the love of God. In the practice of love, Fromm requires of his reader discipline, concentration, patience, and supreme concern. According to Fromm, these qualities must be a part of one's life structure if one really wishes to practice the art of loving.

Hall, C. S. *A Primer of Freudian Psychology.* New York: The New American Library.

Most of the material contained in this small volume also appears in Hall and Lindzey's *Theories of Personality.* The "Primer" does have an excellent beginning chapter on the scientific theories and discoveries that influenced Freud.

Hall, C. S., and Lindzey, C. *Theories of Personality.* New York: John Wiley, 1957.

Hall and Lindzey devote three chapters of this book (viz. 2, 3, and 4) to the psychoanalytic school. One chapter is devoted to Freud, another to Jung, and a third to Adler, Fromm, Horney, and Sullivan. The authors for the most part divide each chapter into six parts: an introductory section, the structure of personality, its dynamics, its development, characteristic research and research methods, and current status and evaluation. From this breakdown, one gets a good idea of the personality theory of each school. Freud is strong on the libidinal theory, which is rejected by Jung and Adler. Jung claims that man's behavior is conditioned not only by individual and racial history but also by his aims and aspirations. Adler with the neo-Freudians, on the other hand, stresses the social aspect of personality.

Jung, C. G. *Flying Saucers.* New York: New American Library, 1969.

This fascinating essay is one of Jung's very latest works. It is an excellent application of his analytical psychology. The essay is especially appreciated if the reader possesses a substantial knowledge of Jung's theories.

Jung, C. G. *Modern Man in Search of a Soul.* New York: Harcourt, Brace, and World, Inc., 1933.

Modern Man in Seach of a Soul is a group of essays ranging in topics from analysis to the spiritual problems of man. The core of many of Jung's theories are presented herein; i.e., a psychological theory of types, the stages of life, and basic postulates of analytic psychology. In addition, there is a discussion of contrasts between Jung and Freud and of the aims and problems of modern psychotherapy.

Jung, C. G. *Psyche and Symbol.* Garden City, New York: Doubleday and Company, 1958.

Psyche and Symbol is a volume of selected essays specifically chosen because of their preoccupation with Jung's universal archetypes of the collective unconscious. Especially worthwhile is the section on the symbolism of the self, which includes description of the ego, the shadow, the syzygy, the self and Christ as a symbol of the self. In addition, there are sections on the phenomenology of the Spirit in fairy tales, the Child Archetype, I Ching, Nature and the Psyche, and a psychological commentary on the Tibetan Book of the Dead.

Jung, C. G. *Two Essays on Analytical Psychology.* Cleveland: World, 1953.

This volume contains "On the Psychology of the Unconscious" and the "Relations Between the Ego and the Unconscious." Both essays are in a sense "primers" in analytical psychology and, for the most part, relatively easy to read.

Two essays deal with Jungian methods and principles as well as theoretical concepts including archetypes, collective and personal unconscious, persona, anima-animus, attitude types, and the relationships between them.

The volume, in addition to the two essays, contains Jung's prefaces to the first, second, third, and fifth editions as well as the original drafts of the two essays in separate appendices. The original drafts contain the first tentative formulations of Jung's concept of archetypes and the collective unconscious as well as his germinating theory of types. His theory was formulated, at least in part, as an attempt to explain the conflicts within the psychoanalytic school from which he had recently seceded. Historically, then, the drafts are of interest in that they mark the end of Jung's association with Freud. The prefaces to the various editions are also worth reading because they explain, in brief, how each edition differed from the preceding ones and thereby span 30 years of change of thought and consequent theory maturation.

Jung, C. G. *The Undiscovered Self.* New York: New American Library, 1957.

The position of man in today's scientific and mass society is explored in this work. The possibility of the individual being overwhelmed and suffering a loss of meaning is discussed. As a way out of this dilemma, Jung focuses upon religion ("reciprocal relationship between man and an extramundane authority . . .") and the individual's understanding of himself in terms of self-knowledge and self-awareness.

Munroe, R. L. *Schools of Psychoanalytic Thought: An Exposition, Critique, and Attempt at Integration.* New York: Dryden Press, 1955.

Ruth Monroe is a psychologist writing about psychoanalytic schools of thought and describes her book as a "lengthy, semi-technical account of the ideas" of the leaders of these groups. This fairly well describes her very readable volume.

The author begins with an overview. Here she considers an approach to psychoanalytic thought and some concepts of the various schools. The next three sections consider the three major groups of psychoanalytic thought. Freud and the "Freudians" are treated in the first part; Adler and the "neo-Freudians" in the second part; and Jung and Rank in the third part. Miss Munroe concludes Part I with an epilogue.

The chapters in Parts 2 and 3 are entitled: "The Terms of the Organism" (the biological inheritance or human nature), "The Terms of the Milieu" (the influence of the environment), "The Genetic Process" (the child as father to the man), "The Dynamics of the Functioning Personality" (Why does Johnny act that way?), and "Pathology and Treatment." Interspersed throughout are the author's critical comments.

This volume is a fairly complete introduction to the psychoanalytic approach.

Rank, O., and Sacks, H. "Psychoanalysis as a Science and as an Art." *American Image 1964* 21:8–133.

The role of psychoanalysis as therapy for individual mental treatment, for social-pedagogical aims, as a science, and as an art is discussed. The particular significance of applicability of psychoanalysis for the humanities is developed with exploration into the concepts of the unconscious and its forms of expression.

Rank, O. *Psychology and the Soul.* New York: A. S. Barnes and Company, Inc., 1950.

Rank recognizes the philosophical nature of this work but sees philosophy as the true heir of investigation of the spiritual aspects of man. Rank surveys the religious, sexual, and psychological stages of spiritual history as well as dreams, symbolism, and its relation to will.

Rank, O. *Will Therapy and Truth and Reality.* New York: Knopf, 1950.

Essentially Rank saw the goal of therapy as the release of creative courage founded upon faith in the self. This volume spells out the basic assumptions for treatment by the Rankian method.

Riviere, Joan (Ed.). *A General Introduction to Psycho-Analysis.* New York: Liveright Publishing Corporation, 1935.

This book consists of three separate courses of lectures delivered by Freud at the University of Vienna in 1915–17. The first two courses (15 lectures) assume no knowledge of the subject and so are quite elementary in style—almost conversational. They cover such subjects as errors, dreams, wish fulfillment, and others, in an interesting way. The third course (13 lectures) is more technical and includes the concepts of resistance, repression, and sexual life.

Rosen, J. *Direct Analysis.* New York: Grune and Stratton, 1953.

Dr. Rosen's book reflects the optimism of his successes in the initiation of his particular therapy with psychotic patients at Temple University Hospital, Philadelphia. His work briefly describes his alterations of the classical technique of Freudian psychoanalysis. He designed this specialized approach for work with "transference" neuroses, hysteria and compulsive obsession in order to apply it to the "narcissistic" neuroses, often called psychoses (or insanity in legal terms). Instead of waiting for patients to produce "free associations" of thought and feeling to indicate the directions of their diseases, Dr. Rosen confronts them with the results of his diagnosis, informing them plainly about their psychoses. For treatment, he engages himself in the patient's fantasies, enacting roles of individuals who were crucially important in the patient's infancy, and interpreting the fantasies with bold openness. The shock effects of the physician's daring, along with manifest identification and comprehension in patient's derangements, often roused some communication with the patient.

Strachey, James (Ed.). *An Outline of Psychoanalysis.* New York: W. W. Norton and Company, Inc., 1949.

This translation of Freud's final book, in which he attempted to state the doctrines of psychoanalysis as clearly and concisely as possible, is an elementary summary for the beginning student.

Strachey, James (Ed.). *Studies on Hysteria,* 1893–1895. New York: Basic Books, Inc., 1957.

Studies on Hysteria is a translation of Joseph Breuer's and Sigmund Freud's studies. The mechanism of hysteria is discussed in detail. Five complete case histories are followed by Breuer's theoretical discussion and Freud's psychotherapy of hysteria.

Waelder, Robert. *Basic Theory of Psychoanalysis.* New York: International Universities Press, 1960.

This book deals with basic theory and questions psychoanalytic interpretations in an attempt to combat misunderstandings.

3

Self-Theory Contributions to Counseling

Many of the basic concepts that underlie current concepts of self-theory have been expressed in the literature of psychology for many years; however, it is in the last quarter-century that self-theory has received most of its attention. As is the case with psychoanalytic theory, there are many conceptions of self-theory. Indeed there are far too many interpretations of self-theory to describe in this text. If time and space permitted, we could deal with conceptions of self as defined by Snygg and Combs, Sarbin, Mead, and Koffka just to mention a few. However, none of the aforementioned theorists have had the impact on self-theory and, more importantly, the relationship of self-theory to counseling than has the theorist upon which this chapter is based, Carl Rogers. At this point in time, Rogers' conception is the most fully developed and certainly the most researched position on self-theory.

As was the case with Freud, the ideas of Carl Rogers have had a profound impact on the field of counseling and, at the same time, have been highly controversial. Ever since the publishing of his first book in 1942, *Counseling and Psychotherapy*, Rogers has been willing and eager to have his ideas put to the test through evaluative research. Indeed, to this day he maintains that his theoretical formulations are in no way finalized. If the reader will recall, in our discussion of theory in Chapter 1 we pointed out that one of the attributes of a good theory is that it be in a continual state of development through the employment of research and other evaluative techniques. It is evident that Rogers has been serious in his statements about an evolving theory. As one examines his original theoretical statements as they appeared in the 1942 book and then compares them with his text, *Client-Centered Therapy*, published in 1951, and again with his 1959 book, *A Theory of Therapy, Personality, and Interpersonal Relationships, as Developed in the Client-Centered Framework*, one can see a number of highly significant changes in his position. His recent articles continue to indicate the evolving nature of his theoretical position. In his own words, theory is "a fallible, changing attempt to construct a network of gossamer threads which will contain the solid facts . . . a stimulus to further creative thinking" (1959, p. 191).

Perhaps it is Rogers' willingness to express his theoretical position and his desire for it to be questioned and tested that account for the impact of his self-theory, called client-centered theory, upon the field of counseling. As was the case with Freud's development of psychoanalytic theory, Rogers developed this client-centered theory from his work as a therapist.

BACKGROUND

Through his own work as a therapist Rogers was able to bring together elements of his own experience plus the influence of other theorists into a theory of personality and therapy. Early in his own life he was subjected to the Thorndiken influence at Columbia, and his first practical experience as a therapist was at the Institute for Child Guidance, which was dominated by Freudian thought. While on the staff of the Child Guidance Center in Rochester, Rogers began to be influenced to some degree by the thinking of Otto Rank. In 1940, Rogers moved from a clinical setting to a position on the faculty of The Ohio State University. It was here that he began to crystallize his own experiences of working with people into a theory of therapy. While much of his theory is a synthesis of theorists such as Lecky, Snygg and Combs, Rank, Sullivan, and others, the major theoretical hypothesis came from his own experiences. In 1955, he wrote about the influence of his experiences as a therapist upon his thinking. "To me they seem to be the major stimulus to my psychological thinking. From these hours and from my relationships with these people I have drawn most of whatever insight I possess into the meaning of therapy, the dynamics of interpersonal relationships, and the structure and functioning of personality" (Rogers 1955, p. 5). Hence, it was basically due to what he found in working with people that he began to think in new directions. His first theoretical formulations concerned the process of therapy. It was only later in his own development that he began to broaden his theory of therapy into a more comprehensive theory of personality.

THEORY OF PERSONALITY

While Rogers believes that his theory of therapy is stronger than the more general theory of personality because of its experiential base, it suits our purposes better if we begin with his notions about personality, its development, and the nature of normal and abnormal behavior.

NATURE OF MAN

Rogers rejects the Freudian concept of man as being basically an irrational, unsocialized, and self-destructive being that has little control over itself. Instead he sees man as being basically good. In the Rogerian view, man is rational, socialized, and to a large extent determines his own destiny. This . . . "means that the individual has the capacity to guide, regulate, and control himself, providing only that certain definable conditions exist. Only in the absence of these conditions, and not in any basic sense, is it necessary to provide external control and regulation of the individual" (Rogers, 1959, p. 221). Thus, the individual, given a reasonable situation in which to grow and mature, will develop his full potential, and this development will take place along constructive lines. Man, then, is basically good and under the proper conditions for growth will be a forward-moving, positive, and constructive individual; one who will be relatively free from internal anxiety, and one who will operate in a satisfactory fashion in society.

STRUCTURE OF PERSONALITY

Rogers builds his theory of personality around three essential ingredients, which he calls the organism, the phenomenal field, and the self. The term *organism* refers to the total individual. "The organism is at all times a total organized system in which alterations of any part may produce changes in any other part" (Rogers, 1951, p. 487). The organism then is all that a person is, his thoughts, behaviors, and physical being. The *phenomenal field* refers to all that a person experiences. "Every individual exists in a continually changing world of experience of which he is the center" (Rogers, 1951, p. 483). The *self* as referred to by Rogers is a differentiated portion of the phenomenal field. It is composed of a series of perceptions and values about the "I" and "me."

In this basic structure Rogers believes that the organism acts in a holisitc fashion to the phenomenal field. That is, at any point in time the individual acts as an organized entity in his attempts to satisfy its needs. Secondly, the organism has as its one basic motive the need to become actualized, . . . "the urge to expand, extend, develop, mature" (1961, p. 351). Stated simply, this is a desire by the organism to develop fully and to be free of external controls. Finally, the organism acts in a manner that allows some experiences to become symbolized in the consciousness while denying or ignoring other experiences. It shall be seen that what the organism tends to be aware of and to symbolize are products of learning, the more adequate this awareness, the more likely an individual will experience normal development.

The phenomenal field as described by Rogers refers to the ever-changing world of experience, and experience includes not only those experiences external to the individual but also those events that are internal. Some of these experiences are consciously perceived, but some are not. It is also important to note that what is perceived by the individual in his phenomenal field is what is important, not the actual reality. It is what the individual perceived to be occurring that is his reality.

The most important of Rogers' principles of personality is his conception of the "self." In Rogers' conception of the structure of personality, the self is in the center of the structure, the focal point around which the personality evolves. The self develops out of the organism's interaction with the environment. As it develops, it tends to integrate as well as distort some of the values of other people. The self integrates those values consistent with the self and distorts other values in order to maintain consistency. Through this process the self is striving to maintain the consistency of behavior of the organism and its own consistency. Experiences that are not consistent with the self are perceived as a threat to the self. Central to the idea of self is that the self is always in process, it grows and changes as a result of its continuing interaction with the phenomenal field.

In studying Rogers' conception of the structure of personality, one should keep in mind that central to his theory is the belief that the personality is always in a state of process; that is, the three components of personality continue to interact and produce changes in the individual. Further, he attributes all of man's behavior to only one motive, self-actualization. This motive provides man with a goal toward which he is constantly striving. His behavior is goal-directed, directed toward the control of the environment and the individual's place in that environment. Moreover, behavior is assumed to be positive and forward moving. It is innately good and need not be subject to control under normal circumstances. The individual need not be subjected to control from external forces because each individual is capable of "a balanced, realistic, self-enhancing, other-enhancing behavior" (Rogers, 1961, p. 105).

In examining Rogers' position on the structure of personality, we need to keep in mind his conception of reality. His position toward reality states that what is perceived by the individual is reality. Hence, it makes little difference what actually happens in an event; what is important is the individual's perception of what happened. In this view the person responds to his perception of the event, not the actual event. An individual chooses his responses to an event based on his perceptions of that event. Hence, man is not a reactive being, but responds to situational events by an active thought process. He is not passive in the situation, but an active agent.

In Rogers' view, then, personality is a product of a continuing interaction between the organism, the phenomenal field, and the self. Personality is not static, but is in a continual state of change. Human behavior acts in a unitary and positive fashion toward the goal of self-actualization. Finally, man is basically good and, given normal conditions for development, will be responsible for his own actions. He is not a reactive being but one who takes an active role in his own behavior based on his perceptions of his experiences.

Having examined the basic structure of personality as set forth in Rogers' conception of self-theory, we now turn to a discussion of how this structure develops in individuals. We will first examine the course of normal personality development, and then move to a consideration of ways in which this normal development is impaired.

PERSONALITY DEVELOPMENT

In Rogers' view each individual comes into this world with an inherent tendency toward actualization. This inherent tendency is the motivational system for the infant, and it is the same motive that moves all of us. Thus, from the outset the infant's behavior is goal-directed, directed toward the need to satisfy the organism in interaction with reality. Reality for the infant is what he experiences; that is, the infant's perception of his experiences is his reality. As Rogers points out, the infant exists in an environment that is of his own creation and can really be understood only from the infant's inter-

nal frame of reference (Rogers, 1959). If the infant is placed in a new situation and perceives that situation as being frightening, it makes no difference if the "reality" of the situation is not a threat to him. What is important is his perception of that situation; that is the real world to him. Certainly, if he is continually put in this situation and his experiences lead him
to believe that he should not be frightened, then his perception of the reality of the situation will change; however, it is the perceived reality that
affects behavior regardless of whether that perception is in fact an accurate
one. As the individual interacts with his perceived reality, he interacts as
a unit. He begins to evaluate his experiences as to whether they do or do
not meet his need for self-actualization. Those experiences that the infant
perceives as not meeting his needs are given a negative value, while those
that are perceived as fulfilling his need are given a positive value. Rogers
refers to this process as an organismic valuing process (Rogers, 1959).
Through this valuing process, the individual begins to pay attention to those
experiences that are evaluated positively, and to avoid those experiences
that are valued negatively.

Out of the organism's interaction with the perceived reality, the self of
the individual begins to develop. The individual's experiences begin to be
differentiated and symbolized in awareness as self-experience. As the individual interacts with his environment, most importantly those significant
others in his environment, this awareness of self-experiences develops into
a concept of self, which is a differentiated part of the phenomenal field. Up
to this point in the development of the personality the infant has been concerned only about satisfying his own need for actualization. As an awareness of self develops, he learns that certain behaviors cause people to respond to him in warm and loving ways, which the infant finds innately satisfying. Likewise, he learns that certain behaviors are responded to with anger and rejection, which are not satisfying to the infant. Hence, the individual begins to respond with behaviors that will elicit the satisfying responses of others and to avoid those behaviors that do not elicit responses
satisfying to the infant.

Hence, we can say that the individual has acquired a need for positive
regard. The individual learns from others what behaviors are to be valued
positively. This leads him to adopt a set of self-evaluative thoughts based on
the behaviors that are valued by others. Through this process he develops a
need for positive self-regard. He begins to judge his own behavior as good
or bad because of what others value, regardless of whether the behavior is
satisfying to him or not. Given this development, the individual now has two
processes by which he evaluates his own behavior: his own innate organismic valuing process and the values of others he adopts. Often the evalua-

tion of others becomes so important to the individual that his behavior is dominated not by what will be innately satisfying to him, but what will cause others to respond to him in favorable or positive ways. If this process is carried far enough, the individual begins to like or dislike himself based on the evaluations of others. In this case his need for self-regard causes him to introject into the self system the values of others. He is now in a situation where he cannot value himself in a positive light unless he behaves in terms of these introjected values, regardless of whether the behavior is innately satisfying or not. At this point Rogers states that the person has developed conditions of worth. The individual gives positive value to some experiences that are not innately satisfying, and he gives negative value to some experiences that are innately satisfying (Rogers, 1959).

It is quite possible that the above sequence need not take place. Earlier in this chapter we referred to the proper conditions for normal development of the personality, and it is the need for positive self-regard that plays a large part in establishing these conditions. Given constant positive evaluation by the significant others in the individual's environment, the individual will develop a healthy personality. In this kind of situation the individual constantly experiences positive evaluation from others, which is satisfying to him even though some of his behaviors may not be accepted. Thus, if a child always feels loved by others even though they do not accept some of his behavior, then no conditions of worth will develop. In this situation the child is experiencing unconditioned positive regard, which leads him to experience only unconditional self-regard. It is these conditions that lead to the development of a healthy personality for, if no conditions of worth are developed, the individual's organismic valuing process and his needs for self-regard and positive regard are congruent. Hence, an individual will evaluate his behavior based on whether he believes it will lead to a positive or negative effect. Rogers believes that those behaviors that will bring positive effects to the individual will not only be personally satisfying but, because of the nature of man, will be basically accepted and positively valued by the society. As a result of the sequence just described, the individual will be a well-adjusted socialized individual (Rogers, 1959).

In Rogers view, then, an individual who is given the proper conditions for growth, which we have just discussed, will develop into what he terms a fully functioning individual. Under these conditions the individual will be open to all his experiences and will have no need to apply defensive mechanisms. He will be aware of all his experiences and will be able to symbolize them accurately. His organismic valuing process will determine his behavior, and he will be in a continual state of change as he has new experiences. He will be able to deal in creative and adaptive ways to new situations be-

cause he will have no need to distort or deny to awareness any of his experiences. He will be a socially effective individual who "will live with others in the maximum possible harmony, because of the rewarding character
of reciprocal positive regard" (Rogers, 1951, p. 234). It is important to
note that Rogers does not use the term, *well-adjusted*, to describe this individual; rather, he chooses the term *fully functioning person* because he
believes that the latter term implies a continuing process whereas the former implies a static state. In his view, then, there is no static state of adjustment, rather, there is a continuing process of development toward self-
actualization. "The fully functioning person would be a person-in-process,
a person continually changing. Thus, his specific behaviors cannot in any
way be described in advance. The only statement which can be made is that
the behaviors would be adequately adaptive to each new situation, and that
the person would be continually in a process of further self-actualization"
(Rogers, 1959, p. 235).

Given then that all men come into this world with the potential for good,
and with the one basic motive of actualizing the organism, how does the
individual develop psychological maladjustments; that is, how is he prevented from becoming the fully functioning individual? It is to this important question that we must now direct our attention.

THE DEVELOPMENT OF MALADAPTIVE BEHAVIOR

Recall that in the normal course of an individual's development there develops a need for self-regard. This need leads the individual to perceive his
experience in a selective fashion in terms of the conditions of worth he has
introjected into his own self. Those conditions of worth are developed because of others' reactions to the individual. They are not necessarily congruent with nor based on his own innate valuing system, but on the values
of others. Consequently, the individual perceives and symbolizes in awareness only those experiences that are in agreement with his conditions of
worth. Those experiences that are not are perceived in distorted fashion or
are denied to awareness. These distorted perceptions of experience cause
the individual to move away from an integrated state. As experiences in the
organism are not recognized as self-experiences (integrated), they are not
brought into the structure of the self in accurate form. Hence, from the
time that the individual first develops conditions of worth and perceives his
experiences based on these conditions of worth, the possibility for a state
of incongruence between the self and the organism's experience may exist.

It is this incongruity between the organism's experiences and the self that lead the individual to the state of vulnerability and psychological maladjustment. The individual can no longer act as a unified whole because his self-perceptions conflict with some of his experiences. Sometimes his behavior is controlled by his organismic valuing process, but at other times it is controlled by the introjected conditions of worth. In essence, we have a situation where the house is divided against itself.

In Rogers' view this situation is the basic estrangement of man. "He has not been true to himself, to his own natural organismic valuing of experience, but for the sake of preserving the positive regard of others has now come to falsify some of the values he experiences and to perceive them only in terms based upon their value to others" (Rogers, 1959, p. 226). This is a tragic development in the individual that takes place early in infancy where the individual has learned certain values that cause him to be untrue to himself. The reader has only to consider his own behavior in relation to his children or to remember his own childhood to see how this learning takes place. A child does many things that are innately satisfying to himself but that cause others to become angry or reject him. The child may be noisy when his parents want him quiet, he may fight when he should not fight, he may play with things he should not touch, he may show too much interest in sexual activities, and we could go on and on. The point is that when the child behaves in these ways, he does not receive positive regard, but instead receives anger, rejection or, in short, a negative feedback. This loss of positive regard is very important to the child, so he begins to develop the conditions of worth that lead to the incongruity between self and experiences. Hence, the conditions are present for the development of vulnerability and psychological maladjustment.

As a result of the development of incongruity between self and experiences, the individual develops incongruities in his behavior. Some of his behaviors will be consistent with his self-concept, and will act to maintain and enhance the self-concept (the process of self-actualization). Other behaviors will be based on the conditions of worth and will not enhance or maintain the self-concept, but will maintain and enhance those aspects of experience that are not a portion of the self-structure. In order to maintain itself, the self will distort these experiences or deny them as part of his self-experiences. The behavior of the individual in this state may take the form of having sexual relations at one point in time because it is innately satisfying, while at other times he avoids sexual relations because of others' values that it is bad. This pattern of behavior is not only consistent, it most probably will cause the individual to experience anxiety.

If the behavior of the individual is not distorted or denied, but instead is accurately symbolized in the person's awareness, the self-concept will be exposed to its inconsistency and thus arouse feelings of anxiety. Rogers suggests "the conditions of worth would be violated, and the need for self-regard would be frustrated." (Rogers, 1959, p. 226.) "Experiences which seem to the behaver to be threatening to his existing concepts of self are likely to be rejected with great vigor." (Combs and Snygg, 1959, p. 113). If the individual feels threatened, then he has no choice but to defend himself. Combs and Snygg, Hilgard, as well as Rogers have suggested that the common defense mechanisms as outlined in psychoanalytic theory are means by which the individual may deal with this threat. The process of defense keeps those experiences that are inconsistent with the self-concept from being accurately symbolized in the awareness of the individual.

The process of the defense mechanisms acts to keep the perceptions of the individual experiences consistent with the individual's self-structure. This is accomplished through selective perception or distortion of the actual experience, or through the denial to awareness of the experience. The individual who projects his feelings on to others as if they were not his own is utilizing the defensive process. The individual who uses rationalization to justify what he has done is also using a process of defense. In both cases the individual is trying to disavow his own behavior so that he can protect the consistency of his own self-concept. As Hilgard states, "The need for self-deception arises because of a more fundamental need to maintain or restore self-esteem" (1949, p. 376). The difficulty in using the defensive mechanisms is that the behavior that causes the anxiety or threat to the self does not change. Hence, the conditions that cause the individual to deny or distort his experiences does not change; the individual's behavior is not flexible or adaptive. As a consequence, the behaviors of the individual become increasingly rigid, as his perceptions of experiences are continually distorted. The individual is prevented from fully functioning because his experiences are not brought into accurate awareness and are not assimilated into the structure of the self.

To some degree or another most of us employ some defenses to protect our self-image. The question then is when do these defenses cause the individual enough difficulty so that his functioning is impaired? If an individual has a high degree of inconsistency between his concept of self and his experiences, and he is suddenly confronted with this inconsistency by some experience he cannot deny or distort, then the organisms' process of defense will be unable to cope with the situation. This situation causes anxiety in the individual, the extent of which will depend on the degree to which the self is threatened.

The defense mechanisms have not been successful and the experience or behavior can no longer be denied to awareness or distorted in awareness. The consistency of the self is disrupted and a state of disorganization will depend on the severity of the threat to the self. In such a state the individual will behave at times in ways that are consistent with experiences that have previously been distorted or denied to awareness, and at other times will behave in ways that are consistent with his self-concept. He may at times behave in ways that are openly hostile to other people, while at other times he may behave in a manner that is quite socially acceptable. In short, the behavior of an individual in a state of disorganization is unpredictable to either the individual or those around him.

In Rogers' view, then, what are the characteristics of the individual who is experiencing personal difficulty or maladaptive behavior? He is generally in a constant state of anxiety or tension. His behavior tends to be rigid because of his inaccurate perceptions of his experiences. He is not able to be flexible or adapt new behaviors to meet new situations; that is, he cannot assimilate new experiences into the self-structure. Hence, he tends to avoid new situations and to misjudge many of his current situations. Further, he is unaware of much of his behavior because he tends to deny it to awareness or distort the experience to fit his self-concept. His behavior is unpredictable and often irrational, and he often has the feeling that his behavior is out of his control. In short, he is an individual who cannot satisfy his need for self-actualization because he does not have adequate confidence in his own ability to control his behavior.

What are the ways then through which the self-theorists would attempt to help such individuals return to a position where they could move toward self-actualization? Before we consider the means whereby this process takes place, we need to examine the objectives of self-theory, or client-centered counseling.

THE GOALS OF COUNSELING

One of the most important aspects of client-centered counseling is the question of who sets the goals of counseling. In the client-centered, or self-theory view, it is extremely important for the counselor to allow the client to set the goals. It must be remembered that in the client-centered viewpoint the individual has, as an innate motivating force, the need for self-actualization. Hence, each individual, given the proper circumstances, can develop and regulate his own behavior, and this behavior will be positive and socially acceptable. Thus, if the counselor were to set the goals for the client, he would be interfering with the basic nature of man. In Rogers' view, the counselor is unable to help an individual learn to rely upon himself if he, the counselor, sets goals. In essence then, the goal of the client-centered counselor is to establish the proper conditions whereby the normal developmental pattern of the individual can be brought back into play.

In a more specific sense, however, the goal of the client-centered counselor is to help the individual become more mature and to reinstitute the process toward self-actualization by removing the obstacles to this process. The objective is to free the individual of those learned behaviors that are faulty and that hinder his innate tendency toward self-actualization. The desire is to help the individual move forward in a positive and productive manner by helping the individual redevelop his own resources and potential (Boy and Pine, 1963, p. 43). Hence, the goals for all clients are the same: to remove those obstacles in the individual that hinder a true perception of his experiences so that he may gain new insight into his experiences and self-structure. In Rogers' view, the goal of counseling is simply to release an already existing force in a potentially adequate individual.

Before we leave the discussion of the goals of client-centered counseling, it should be pointed out that in the client-centered view the complete goals of counseling have not been accomplished when the person leaves counseling. Rather, at the termination of the counseling process, only the pattern for future change has been established. That is, the obstacles to growth have been removed and new ways of perceiving experiences have been established so that the individual can proceed along the road toward self-actualization. This fits with Rogers' belief that there is no such thing as the static state of well-adjusted, rather, a process toward becoming a fully functioning individual.

THE COUNSELING PROCESS

The client-centered approach to counseling has been described as an *if-then* approach to counseling. It is stated that if certain conditions exist, then a process will take place that has certain definable characteristics. If this process occurs, then the counselor can expect certain changes to occur in the client. The basic hypothesis of client-centered counseling, then, is that, given the establishment of the proper conditions for growth, the client will be enabled to gain self insight and then take positive steps to solve his difficulties. The central concept of client-centered counseling is a belief in the importance of certain conditions in the process of counseling. It is to these necessary conditions that we now need to turn our attention.

Conditions of the Counseling Process

In understanding the client-centered approach to counseling, it is important to remember that in this approach the conditions that are set forth as necessary for counseling are also assumed to be sufficient for counseling. That is, if the conditions exist or are provided, then change will take place in the client. The following conditions are those Rogers believes are both necessary and sufficient for counseling.

The first essential condition in the process of counseling is that two people be in contact. In his earlier expositions of his counseling theory, Rogers used the word *relationship*, but it is now replaced with the word *contact*. This construct refers to the need for the counselor and the client to be in at least a minimal state of psychological contact. In Rogers' terms, it is the least experience between two people that could be referred to as a relationship.

The second essential condition is that the client be in at least a minimum state of anxiety, vulnerability or incongruence. Earlier in this chapter, in the section on the development of personality, we discussed the fact that anxiety or vulnerability occurred when an individual was experiencing incongruity between his self-concept and his behavior. The more anxious the individual is about this incongruity the more likely that successful counseling will take place. In essence, the individual has to be concerned enough to want to make some changes in himself.

The third condition that is essential to the process of counseling is that the counselor must be congruent to the relationship. That is, the counselor must basically be an integrated or whole person, one whose conception of self allows him to be aware of all his behaviors and to experience them in accurate awareness. Another word often used in place of congruent is *genuine*. What is implied here is that the more closely the counselor approaches the state of a fully functioning individual the more effective a counselor he will be. This state of congruity in the counselor allows him to be aware of and honest with himself about the kinds of feelings the client is eliciting in him, so that these feelings do not interfere with the process of counseling.

The fourth necessary and sufficient condition that must be present is that the counselor experience unconditioned positive regard toward the client. This condition is of central importance to the client-centered counselor. To have unconditioned positive regard for an individual means that you respect the person, regardless of the differential values that you might place on his various behaviors. To maintain unconditioned positive regard for a person, the counselor must be non-evaluative. He does not judge one behavior as being positive and another negative; rather he accepts the individual for what he is regardless of his behaviors. It is much like the feeling a parent has toward a child, where the child is valued and loved for himself even though the parent may not place equal value on all his behaviors. When this condition is provided to the client, he comes to believe that he is a person of worth, irrespective of his behavior.

The fifth essential condition is that the counselor experiences empathic understanding of the client's internal frame of reference. In Rogers' view, no one can ever fully understand the internal frame of reference of an individual except the individual himself. But the term *empathic understanding* means that the counselor is able to understand the internal frame of reference of the client to the greatest degree of accuracy possible for another person. It is an attempt to try and understand the client as if the counselor were the client. The counselor can never be the individual but must try to understand him as if he were the individual.

The final necessary and sufficient condition is that the client perceives, at least to some degree, the counselor's unconditioned positive regard for him as well as the counselor's empathic understanding. The important point here is that it is not sufficient for the counselor to possess empathic understanding of and unconditioned positive regard for the client, but that these conditions must be communicated to the client and he, in turn, must perceive that those conditions are present.

In the client-centered view, the conditions just discussed are the necessary and sufficient conditions for counseling. As stated previously, it is an *if-then* position. *If* these conditions are provided to the client by the counselor, *then* the process of counseling will take place and, if the process of counseling takes place, certain definable outcomes will occur. These outcomes center around the return of the individual to a state where he is once more on the road to self-actualization. Rogers (1959) feels that the greatest flaw in his statement of necessary and sufficient conditions is that they are stated as if they were an all or none phenomenon. Yet, all of the conditions, except possibly the first one, exist on some kind of continuum. Recent research, which will be dealt with in more detail later, appears to indicate that, indeed, these conditions do exist on a continuum. Not only is it important that the conditions exist, but the degree of their existence may be of more importance.

Given the six conditions just presented, what kind of process can a counselor using this theoretical position expect to take place? What can he expect to happen in the process of counseling? What changes will occur in the transactions between client and counselor, and what changes can we expect in the client?

Given the proper conditions, it is expected that the client will increasingly feel free to express his feelings. In the counseling situation, the client finds himself in a threat-free, non-possessive, accepting atmosphere in which he feels that he is valued for his own sake; hence, he comes to realize that he will be valued by the counselor regardless of the kinds of thoughts he expresses. There is no threat to his receiving positive feedback from his statements since he is receiving an unconditional positive regard from the counselor. In essence, it makes no difference if he expresses hatred of his brother because he will not receive negative feedback from the counselor for expressing this feeling. As the client increasingly feels comfortable in the counseling situation, more and more of his statements will take on the character of self-reference. In the initial stages of counseling many of his feeling statements will refer to nonself matters, which are safer to discuss; however, as the process of counseling continues, he will increasingly deal with "I" or "me" statements. For example, the client may change from discussing how difficult it is for brothers to get along to how difficult he finds it to get along with his brother.

As the number of self-reference statements increases, he begins to see his experiences and feelings in a more realistic light. He is more able to accurately symbolize his experiences in his consciousness. He now finds himself in a situation where he can examine his feelings and experiences in an objective manner without a threat to the self. He can examine the incongruity between certain of his experiences and his concept of self because, in the counseling situation, there is no threat in doing so. In a situation outside of counseling he may not be able to express his feelings of hatred for his brother because of the threat to the self that would be incurred by such a statement. In the atmosphere of the counseling situation, however, he can express that feeling without the self being threatened by another's reactions.

In the counseling situation the counselee is now able to express his true feelings and to examine in an objective manner those experiences that have in the past been denied or distorted because of the threat to the self. As he examines these experiences in an objective manner, his concept of self becomes reorganized and complemented by the assimilation of these new experiences. As the reorganization of the self-concept continues, the individual's experiences and self-structure become increasingly congruent. This lessening of incongruity between self and experiences means that there are fewer situations that are a threat to the self and this, in turn, leads to less defensive behavior on the part of the client. He no longer has to protect the self by denying or distorting experiences because more of his experiences are congruent with his conception of self. The client increasingly is able to feel an unconditional positive self-regard, and he redevelops the ability to react to his experiences based on his own organismic valuing process, rather than on the introjected conditions of worth. In short, he becomes his own man once again. He is not only able to deal with situations that have caused him difficulty in the past, but he is open to new situations. His behavior is flexible and adaptive. He is once more in the process of becoming a fully functioning individual.

Those who follow the client-centered approach or, as some now call it, the relationship theory approach, make no attempt at explaining the reasons for the above process. As Rogers (1959) points out, no one really knows why when a piece of steel is rubbed by a magnet, that the piece of steel will point north if it is allowed to rotate freely. Likewise, it really is not important to their way of thinking why the individual goes through the previously discussed process in counseling. What is important is that, given the proper conditions, this process will occur in the individual and will lead to certain outcomes; namely, the individual will be able to perceive his experiences accurately, evaluate those experiences based on his own organismic valuing process, and then act accordingly.

IMPLEMENTING THE PROCESS OF COUNSELING

In Rogers' first exposition of his theory in 1942 he placed a great deal of importance on specific techniques that had grown out of his own experience as a practicing therapist. In his book he advanced concrete procedures that a therapist or a counselor should use, and these were accompanied by partial transcripts of actual therapy situations. By 1951, Rogers had rejected this approach and in his second book emphasized that two different therapists could use the same technique but get different results. The emphasis had shifted to the importance of the therapist or counselor in the relationship. Hence, he now talks less about technique and more about the attitudes of the counselor. Given the proper attitude, the counselor in the client-centered framework has a great deal of freedom as to what he actually does in the counseling interview. Put simply, the counselor's role is to create the proper conditions to make it possible for the counseling process to take place which, in turn, will result in changes in the client.

Of prime importance in implementing the process of relationship or client-centered counseling is the counselor's attitude toward the worth and integrity of the individual. Rogers believes that a counselor can be client-centered only to the extent that he has respect for the worth of the individual (Rogers, 1959). To this end the counselor attempts to implement the process of counseling by being as perceptive and sensitive as possible to the client and his experiences. In essence, the counselor must perceive the internal frame of reference of the individual as accurately and completely as possible, and then feed his perceptions back to the client. In one sense the client-centered counselor becomes an alter ego for the client, a self out of the self. This allows the individual to see and examine his own attitudes, feelings, and perceptions as worn by another. He therefore can view them without the complications of emotion and in a more objective manner. The assumption is that the client, having perceived these elements more closely in a non-threatening way and in a non-judgmental atmosphere, will come to accept these elements into the structure of the self.

Of major importance in the establishment of the counseling process in the client-centered view is the nature of the relationship. This is a relationship that is established because the client has come to the counselor seeking help. Hence, the responsibility for the relationship is the client's, not the counselor's. In defining the nature of the relationship to the client, the counselor must make it clear that he is not an answer man; rather, it is the client himself who has the answers. The counselor is there to assist the individual in finding his own solutions to his difficulty. The major responsibility for the success of the counseling will rest with the client. Perhaps the most unique aspect of self-theory or client-centered counseling is this emphasis placed on client responsibility.

The other limit the counselor should place on the relationship concerns time. This refers to the need for the counselor to specify the length of each session. In addition, he may also desire to set some limit on the number of sessions. There are two primary reasons for establishing these time limits for counseling. The first is the obvious reality of limited amount of time a counselor has available, but perhaps more important is the belief that, given certain time limits, the client may sense a need to make the sessions as productive as possible. While setting this limit to the relationship, it must be made clear that what occurs within these time limits is still the basic responsibility of the client.

The emphasis in the counseling relationship is on the individual and not on a particular concern or problem. This is in line with the self-theory belief in the wholistic nature of behavior; that is, one aspect of behavior is related to the whole system of behavior. Hence, it is the entire system that requires attention, not a particular aspect of the system. Within this context, it is expected that the counseling relationship will help the individual develop better ways of dealing with life in general and that the individual will become a more mature, more socialized, and more self-enhancing individual. This is not to say that specific problems or concerns of the client will not be solved, but that they will be solved as a by-product of the individual's growth toward self-actualization. All of this implies that no specific goals are established for the counseling; rather, the goal is simply to provide the necessary conditions to bring about meaningful change in the client.

The self-theory position also puts a great deal of emphasis on the here and now of the individual's existence, both inside and outside the counseling relationship. A knowledge of the nature and background of the client's difficulties is believed to be unnecessary in self-theory. What is important is not what has happened in the individual's past that may have led to his present difficulties; rather, what is important is the manner in which he is now operating. If we go back to the illustration of the client feeling hatred for his brother, the client-centered position would be that it makes no difference that this hatred developed because the brother came along and displaced some of the parent's affection. What is important is the individual's present feelings toward his brother and how this affects his whole pattern of behavior. Thus, one of the counselor's roles is to help the client focus on his present feelings by expressing them verbally in the counseling relationship.

The emphasis on the here and now is reflected in the self-theory position on the place of diagnosis in counseling. The self-theorists argue that there is no place for diagnosis in counseling. It is considered undesirable because of the connotation that a few have the power to decide what is right for the many. Further, it violates the major assumption that each individual is a self-determining being, responsible for his own actions. Secondly, only the client can accurately see his internal frame of reference, thus it is dangerous for the counselor to attempt a diagnosis no matter how accurate he feels his perceptions of the client's internal frame of reference may be. Finally, diagnosis implies a denial of the basic uniqueness of each individual. To diagnose is to place people in categories, and the client-centered counselor wishes to avoid this trap. Rather than diagnose the client's difficulty, the counselor should respond to the individual as a unique person with a potential for diagnosing his own difficulty and then remedying the situation.

As well as an emphasis on the present situation and the lack of a need for diagnosis, the client-centered approach emphasizes the need for an emphasis on the emotional elements in the relationship rather than on the intellectual. Pure knowledge or intellectualization does not help the client because the impact of the knowledge is blocked from awareness by the emotional satisfactions the individual achieves through his present behavior. Put another way, the individual may know intellectually what the real situation is but, because of his emotional feelings, this knowledge does not help him change his behavior.

Earlier in this chapter we discussed the point that it was the individual's perceptions of his various situations, the emotion, not the so-called reality of the situation, that was his reality. So regardless of what the real situation is, it is the individual's feelings about the situation that are important, and these are what must concern the counselor. Thus, in client-centered counseling the counselor attempts to help the client focus on feelings about himself, other people, and the events that take place in his world. For example, when a client is expressing disappointment in himself, it is the counselor's role to point this feeling out to the client. He reflects to the individual as accurately as possible the feelings that the client is expressing at that point in time. It is then hoped that the client will be better able to view these feelings objectively.

The emphasis on the emotional aspects of the counseling process is coupled with the client-centered view of the role of information in counseling. In general, the client-centered approach does not believe that the counselor should bring information into the counseling process. This approach does not deny the importance of information, rather it proposes that it should be the client who brings information into the counseling process; information that has been gathered outside of counseling, perhaps under the counselor's direction. Thus, the actual counseling experience is devoted to helping the individual sift through the information, with the emphasis again being placed on the client's feelings toward that information. As with the other intellectual elements in the process of counseling, it is the counselor's responsibility to help the client focus on his feelings about information. It is the feeling about the information, not the information per se, that is important.

This view on the use of information in the process of counseling also holds true for a specific kind of information—testing. In current client-centered thinking it would seem that the use of tests in counseling would not be completely excluded, but that their use may be somewhat limited. As with other types of information, what is held as important is how the client feels about the test and its information. In speaking about the use of tests in counseling, Rogers (1946, p. 142) has stated that "The client, may, in exploring his situation, reach the point where, facing his situation squarely and realistically, he wishes to compare his aptitudes and abilities with those of others for a specific purpose. When tests come as a real desire from the client, they may enter into the situation." Even in this situation it may be more important to discuss why the client wishes to take a particular test. If, for example, a client were to ask, "Do you have a test that will tell me what occupation I should enter?" the counselor, instead of listing all the tests that might do the requested job, should first focus on why the client feels he needs a test to make this decision for him.

It should be clear to the reader that the relationship, client-centered, or self-theory approach to counseling does not place a great deal of emphasis on counseling techniques. The emphasis is almost exclusively on the importance of the relationship. The emphasis is not on technique but on the ability of the counselor to establish a relationship in which the six necessary conditions, which were outlined earlier in this chapter, are present. To the degree that these conditions are present and perceived as being present by the client, the counseling process will be effective.

The key element in establishing these conditions is the counselor and his relationship with the client. The counselor must be a patient and expert listener, one who fully accepts each individual by offering to that individual an atmosphere of unconditional positive regard and empathic understanding. His attempt is to help the client develop insight into his difficulty by encouraging free expression from the client and then reflecting these feelings to the client. In a very real sense, the counselor becomes an alter-ego for the client. In this process it is not a specific problem, nor information, nor other intellectual elements that are discussed; rather, the focus is on the individual in his current state and on his current feelings.

SUMMARY

If this process is followed, then the necessary and sufficient conditions for counseling will be established. Having established these conditions, the client will be able to go through the process of articulating his feelings, developing insight and self-understanding, and finally developing re-oriented goals and new modes of behavior. While counseling may end at this stage, it is not the end of the process. The client has simply been returned to a state where he is able, on his own, to continue the life-long process toward self-actualization. He is an individual who once again is in control of his behavior. His conditions of worth, which were the introjected values of others, have disappeared and his organismic valuing process has taken its proper place as the evaluator of experiences and controller of behavior.

RESEARCH

One of the outstanding contributions that has been made to the field of counseling by those of the self-theory orientation has been the willingness to submit their methods of counseling to the test of research. From the beginning, client-centered or relationship counselors, led by Rogers, have made it clear that their theory should be submitted to research and then reformulated on the basis of that research. As was pointed out earlier in this chapter, Rogers' own theory has undergone several changes since he first wrote about his approach in 1942. While initial research on the theory consisted mainly of analysis of tapes from counseling sessions, the various approaches used in researching the theory includes a wide range of techniques. The one major criticism of much of this research has been that most of it is based on client self-reports. This approach, however, fits with the basic assumption of the theory that only the client can really tell whether the counseling has been beneficial or not.

There does appear to be extensive evidence from the research that the necessary and sufficient conditions hypothesized by those of the client-centered orientation are sufficient in some cases. An early study by Seeman (1954) found that therapeutic success was related both to the degree that the counselor felt a liking for the client and the degree to which the client felt that he was liked by the counselor. More recent research by Truax (1961), Carkhuff (1967), and Carkhuff and Berenson (1967) indicate that, indeed, in many cases these conditions are sufficient to bring about change in the client. Truax and Carkhuff (1967) conclude that an individual who can communicate warmth, genuineness, and accurate empathy is more effective in helping other people. It appears then that at least to some degree these conditions can be measured in the counseling interview and that the conditions do have a beneficial effect for the client.

Studies on the actual process of counseling include some early research by Rogers and Dymond (1954), Hogan (1948), and Raskin (1949). These studies indicated that as counseling progressed there was a decrease in the amount of defensiveness of the client, there was an increased congruence between the self and experience, and a trend toward the person seeing himself as the locus of evaluation was observed. Later studies by Rogers (1967), Truax and Carkhuff (1967), and Carkhuff and Berenson (1967) demonstrate that, given the necessary and sufficient conditions, a client will move into self-exploration, which will lead to positive changes in the individual. As with the research on the effects of the conditions, the research on the changes an individual goes through during the counseling process appears to be confirmed.

The research on the outcomes of counseling is perhaps both the most interesting and the most important. That is, given the conditions and the process of counseling, what kinds of outcomes can be expected? An overview of the research in this area seems to be the segment of the theory that is least confirmed. Studies by Cowen and Combs (1950) and Grummon and John (1954) tend to support the fact that individuals who have gone through client-centered counseling do have better overall adjustments. A study similar to these, conducted by Carr (1949), did not find any evidence of better adjustment following counseling. As was pointed out earlier, much of this research is of the self-report type and thus is extremely difficult to evaluate. There are now appearing in the research literature more and more studies that tend to lend support to the effectiveness of counseling, given that the necessary conditions hypothesized by the client-centered theorists are present.

Truax (1963) found that schizophrenic clients who had therapists offering high levels of the necessary conditions did show improvement after counseling. He also discovered that those clients who had therapists offering low levels of these conditions tended to show negative personality changes. Truax and Carkhuff (1965) also reported that changes in the level of the conditions offered affected the amount of self-exploratory behavior on the part of the client. A study by Holder, Carkhuff, and Berenson (1967) found that the depth of self-exploration of a low-functioning client was related to the amount of the necessary conditions offered by the counselor. A study of Truax, Wargo, and Sibler (1966), found that when high levels of the necessary conditions were provided, counseling could be effective with the culturally disadvantaged. This research would seem to indicate that not only are the conditions necessary, but the levels of the conditions offered affects the outcomes of counseling in either a positive or negative direction. Coupled with this research on how the level of the necessary conditions affected counseling outcomes was the development of scales to measure four of the necessary conditions. Carkhuff and Truax (1967) developed such scales to measure the level of empathy, unconditional positive regard, self-congruence, and concreteness.

An interesting and controversial development in the research generated by the client-centered approach in the mid-1960's was the research on the effectiveness of "lay" counselors. Carkhuff and Truax (1965) provided a brief training period for five lay hospital personnel in the facilitative conditions, who then ran group counseling with hospital patients. Their findings led them to conclude that the lay therapists were successful in bringing about improvement in the clients. Subsequent investigations by Berenson, Carkhuff, and Myrus (1966), and Pierce, Carkhuff, and Berenson (1967) have further established the viability of training lay persons to function at minimally facilitative levels, permitting them to initiate some behavior change in clients. Studies in this area have used screened college graduates as well as volunteers from lay personnel in schools, hospitals, and communities. Further, there is some research evidence from Kratochvil, Carkhuff, and Friel (1968) that lay persons will function at higher facilitative levels than do professional counselors, and that their clients will consequently function at higher levels.

If the research developments continue along this line, it would appear that some revision in counselor preparation programs is warranted. Until this research has had further elaboration, however, it should be viewed with some caution. Nevertheless, this research does add support to the belief in the importance of the necessary conditions hypothesized by the client-centered theorists.

Most of the research findings discussed in this section of the chapter are based in large part on the verbal reports of clients and, hence, must be viewed with some caution. Regardless of this shortcoming, the amount of research generated by the client-centered position is indeed awesome. Only a small representative portion of the research conducted has been presented here. Not only is the sheer amount of research voluminous, but the results of that research deserve serious consideration by prospective and practicing counselors. Certainly it would seem that there can be little question of the importance of the conditions called necessary and sufficient by the client-centered theorists. The question not yet answered is whether these conditions are sufficient in all cases and are the conditions found in all good counseling, regardless of the theory used by the counselor.

Readers interested in exploring further the research in the client-centered position should refer to the following annotated bibliography. Particular attention should be paid to the works of Truax, Carkhuff, and Berenson.

REFERENCES

Berenson, B. G.; Carkhuff, R. R.; and Myrus, Pamela. "The Interpersonal Functioning and Training of College Students." *Journal of Counseling Psychology* 13:441–446.

Boy, Angelo V., and Pine, Gerald J. *Client-Centered Counseling in the Secondary School.* Boston: Houghton-Mifflin Company, 1963.

Carkhuff, R. R. *The Counselor's Contribution to Facilitative Processes.* Urbana, Illinois: Parkinson, 1967.

Carkhuff, Robert R., and Berenson, Bernard G. *Beyond Counseling and Therapy.* New York: Holt, Rinehart, and Winston, Inc., 1967.

Carkhuff, R. R., and Truax, C. B. "Training in Counseling and Psychotherapy: An Evaluation of an Integrated Didactic and Experiential Approach." *Journal of Consulting Psychology* 29:333–336.

Carkhuff, R. R., and Truax, C. B. "Lay Mental Health Counseling: The Effects of Lay Group Counseling." *Journal of Consulting Psychology* 29:426–431.

Carr, A. C. "An Evaluation of Nine Nondirective Psychotherapy Cases by Means of the Rorschach." *Journal of Consulting Psychology* 13:196–205.

Combs, A. W., and Snygg, D. *Individual Behavior: A Perceptual Approach to Behavior.* (Rev. ed.). New York: Harper and Row, 1959.

Cowen, E. L., and Combs, A. W. "Follow-up Study of 32 Cases Treated by Nondirective Psychotherapy." *Journal of Abnormal Social Psychology* 45:232–258.

Grummon, D. L., and John, Eve S. "Changes over Client-Centered Therapy Evaluated on Psychoanalytically Based Thematic Apperception Test Scales." In C. R. Rogers and R. F. Dymond (Eds.). *Psychotherapy and Personality Change; Co-ordinated Studies in the Client-Centered Approach.* Chicago: University of Chicago Press, 1954.

Hall, Calvin S., and Lindzey, Gardner. *Theories of Personality.* New York: John Wiley and Sons, Inc., 1957.

Hilgard, E. R. "Human Motives and the Concept of Self." *American Psychologist* 4:374–382.

Hogan, R. "The Development of a Measure of Client Defensiveness in the Counseling Relationship." *Unpublished Dissertation.* University of Chicago, 1948.

Holder, Todd; Carkhuff, R. R.; and Berenson, B. G. "The Differential Effects of the Manipulation of Therapeutic Conditions upon High and Low Functioning Clients." *Journal of Counseling Psychology* 14:63–66.

Martin, J. C., and Carkhuff, R. R. "The Effects upon Trainee Personality and Interpersonal Functioning in Counseling Training." *Journal of Clinical Psychology.* In press, 1967.

Pierce, R.; Carkhuff, R. R.; and Berenson, B. G. "The Effects of Differential Levels of Therapist-Offered Conditions upon Lay Mental Health Counselors in Training." *Journal of Clinical Psychology* 23:212–215.

Raskin, N. J. "An Analysis of Six Parallel Studies of the Therapeutic Process." *Journal of Consulting Psychology* 13:206–220.

Rogers, C. R. (Ed.), with the collaboration of Gendlin, F. T.; Kiesler, D. L.; and Truax, C. B. *The Therapeutic Relationship and Its Impact. A Study of Psychotherapy with Schizophrenics.* Madison: University of Wisconsin Press, 1967.

Rogers, C. R. "Psychometric Tests and Client-Centered Counseling." *Educational Psychological Measurement* 6:139–144.

Rogers, C. R. "A Theory of Therapy, Personality, and Interpersonal Relationships as Developed in the Client-Centered Framework." In S. Koch (Ed.). *Psychology—A Study of a Science: Volume III. Formulations of the Person and the Social Context.* New York: McGraw-Hill, 1959.

Rogers, C. R. "A Theory of Therapy, Personality, and Interpersonal Relationships, as Developed in the Client-Centered Framework. *Unpublished Manuscript,* 1955.

Rogers, C. R. *Client-Centered Therapy; Its Current Practice, Implications, and Theory.* Boston: Houghton-Mifflin, 1951.

Rogers, C. R. *On Becoming a Person. A Therapist's View of Psychotherapy.* Boston: Houghton-Mifflin, 1961.

Rogers, C. R., and Dymond, R. F. (Eds.). *Psychotherapy and Personality Change; Coordinated Studies in the Client-Centered Approach.* Chicago: University of Chicago Press, 1954.

Seeman, J. "Counselor Judgments of Therapeutic Process and Outcome." In C. R. Rogers and R. F. Dymond (Eds.). *Psychotherapy and Personality Change.* Chicago: University of Chicago Press, 1954.

Truax, C. B. "The Process of Group Psychotherapy." *Psychological Monographs,* 1961, 75 (7, Whole No. 511).

Truax, C. B. "Effective Ingredients in Psychotherapy: An Approach to Unravelling the Patient—Therapist Interaction." *Journal of Counseling Psychology* 10:256–263.

Truax, C. B. "Clinical Implementation of Therapeutic Conditions." In C. R. Rogers. *Therapeutic and Research Progress in a Program of Psychotherapy Research with Hospitalized Schizophrenics.* Symposium presented at the meeting of the American Psychological Association, New York, September, 1961.

Truax, C. B., and Carkhuff, R. R. *Toward Effective Counseling and Psychotherapy: Training and Practices.* Chicago, Aldin, 1967.

Truax, C. B., and Carkhuff, R. R. "Personality Change in Hospitalized Mental Patients during Group Psychotherapy as a Function of the Use of Alternate Sessions and Vicarious Therapy Pretraining." *Journal of Clinical Psychology* 21:327–329.

Truax, C. B.; Wargo, D. G.; and Silber, I. D. "Effects of High Accuracy Empathy and Nonpossessive Warmth during Group Psychotherapy with Female Institutionalized Delinquents." *Journal of Abnormal Psychology* 71,267–274.

ANNOTATED BIBLIOGRAPHY

Carkhuff, Robert R., and Berenson, Bernard G. *Beyond Counseling and Theory.* New York: Holt, Rinehart & Winston, Inc., 1967.

Must reading for counselors regardless of their own theoretical beliefs. Excellent discussion of the facilitative conditions for counseling.

"Client-Centered Therapy." *The Counseling Psychologist* I, Number 2, *Summer 1969.*

This particular edition of *The Counseling Psychologist* is devoted to client-centered or relationship therapy, with the major contribution by C. H. Patterson.

Rogers, C. R. *Client-Centered Therapy. Its Current Practice, Implications and Theory*. Boston: Houghton-Mifflin, 1951.

> This book is the result of the University of Chicago Counseling Center staff's presentation of client-centered therapy and its application to play therapy, group therapy, student-centered teaching, and the training of counselors and therapists.

Rogers, C. R. *Counseling and Psychotherapy*. Boston: Houghton-Mifflin, 1942.

> Non-directive counseling, a new pathway in psychotherapy, is presented in comparison with the older methods of counseling. Noted by the author are differences in goals, characteristic steps in the therapeutic process, and problems faced by the counselor. A major portion of the volume defines and illustrates the development of insight in the counseling relationship.

Rogers, C. R. *On Becoming a Person. A Therapist's View of Psychotherapy*. Boston: Houghton-Mifflin, 1961.

> This book, which contains addresses made by Carl Rogers throughout the country, presents the characteristics of his helping relationship as well as the importance of developing the fully functioning person.

Rogers, C. R. "A Theory of Therapy, Personality, and Interpersonal Relationships as Developed in the Client-Centered Framework." In S. Koch (Ed.). *Psychology—A Study of a Science: Volume III. Formulations of the Person and the Social Context*. New York: McGraw-Hill, 1959.

> This systematic statement of Rogers' developing theory for the American Psychological Association in connection with its study of status and development of psychology in the United States analyzes the general structure, presents the theory in detail, and reviews the program of research.

Rogers, C. R. (Ed.). With the collaboration of Gendlin, F. T.; Kiesler, D. L.; and Truax, C. B. *The Therapeutic Relationship and Its Impact. A Study of Psychotherapy with Schizophrenics*. Madison: University of Wisconsin Press, 1967.

> This is a comprehensive analysis of the research study done at the University of Wisconsin with hospitalized schizophrenics and normal individuals to test whether or not the process movement is positively related to the presence of relationship elements. It was found that the attitudinal qualities of the person-to-person relationship are effective with schizophrenics. The outcome of this particular research program gave Rogers the empirical backing he needed for his theory to be completely accepted by many of today's leading clinicians.

Thompson, J. M. "Relationship between Carl Rogers' Helping Relationship Concept and Teacher Behavior; Client-Centered Therapy." *California Journal of Educational Research*. 20:151–161.

4

Learning Theory Contributions to Counseling

Counseling is an activity that is designed to bring about behavioral changes in people. It is undertaken with the assumption that the counselor is going to help the counselee change some behavior such that, following counseling, the counselee will behave in new and more adaptive ways. Many counseling theorists would say that what the counselor is attempting to do is to help the counselee learn new patterns of behavior. Further, they would say that if we can make that assumption, then counseling itself should be an application of theories of learning. It is from this base that the various behavioral learning theory approaches to counseling have grown.

The behavioral approach to counseling makes the basic assumption that client problems are problems in learning. Further, counselors should view their task as attempting to help those who come to them learn new behaviors leading to a solution to the client's problem. In effect, the counselor is a special kind of learning specialist (Krumboltz, 1966). This approach to counseling is not a congolomeration or a bag of tricks that is applied mechanically to counselees, but is a system of counseling based on laboratory investigations of the effects of conditioning on behavior (Michael and Myerson, 1962).

Basic to the learning theory approach is the assumption that "Inherited genetic and constitutional determiners are not under the control of, or subject to, direct experimentation by behavioral scientists." (Michael and

Meyerson, 1962, p. 383). Hence, what counselors must be concerned about are observable patterns of behaviors, for that is the only thing that we can meaningfully control. The behavioral counselor is concerned with the interaction of the individual and his environment, and the ways in which this environment may be modified to bring about changes in the individual.

While there has long been a great deal of concern about the relationship between counseling and learning theory, it has received the greatest attention only in the last few years. The early attempts to apply learning theory principles to counseling centered largely on an attempt to put the already existing theories of counseling and psychotherapy into a learning theory framework. The work of such theorists as Dollard and Miller (1950) and the Pepinskys (1954) are examples of this kind of attempt. More recently, the work of such theorists as Salter, Wolpe, and Krumboltz has concentrated on building theoretical approaches to counseling without attempting to tie them to past theories of counseling and psychotherapy. While the work of such people as Dollard and Miller was extremely important to the field of behavioral counseling, it is with the more recent theoretical developments that this chapter will be mainly concerned. Readers who are concerned with examining the field of behavioral counseling in depth should examine the works of such theorists as Dollard and Miller (1950) and the Pepinskys (1954).

THEORY OF PERSONALITY

The basic assumption of the learning theory approach to personality is that man's behavior is learned. The behavior he learns is the result of his interaction with the environment. Man does not come into this world as innately bad or good; rather, he comes into this world neutral like the Lochian idea of a *tabula rosa* (Hosford, 1969). That is, man enters this world with the potential for either good or evil; he has no inherent drives in one direction or the other. He is neutral, and the manner in which he develops his personality depends upon his interaction with the environment. Hence, from the learning theory framework man should be viewed as a reactive being. He reacts to stimuli as they are presented to him in his environment. As he reacts, his patterns of behavior and ultimately his personality are formed.

Most learning theorists would concede that some behavior may be a result of an individual's innate characteristics and the interaction of these characteristics with the environment. However, since innate characteristics cannot be controlled or defined by man, our attention should be focused on those things we can control or explain, which is the observable interaction between the individual and his environment.

Within the framework of learning theory, man's behavior is determined by the goals he sets for himself and, sometimes, by those imposed by society. His behavior is always directed to these goals. "An individual responds with those behaviors that he has learned will lead to the greatest satisfaction in a given situation." (Rotter, 1964, p. 57). His motives for behaving are developed through experience, and gradually the individual develops a set of differentiated motives or needs.

This process can be illustrated by examining the interaction between a mother and a child. The initial stages of the infant's interaction with his mother result in satisfaction through feeding. This satisfaction gradually becomes generalized to the extent that the infant receives pleasure simply by being in the presence of his mother. That is, he learns to want attention from his mother, a goal or motive that is separate from the first goal of reducing his feelings of hunger. Through their continuing interaction the child learns that some of his behaviors result in pleasurable attention from his mother and other behaviors do not. In order to receive this pleasurable attention, the child will strive to do those things that will please his mother and focus her attention on him. Finally, this process may generalize to the extent that the child behaves in certain ways even when the mother is not present because he has learned that she would approve of these behaviors, and this in itself is satisfying to the individual. Thus, motives, drives, or needs are developed not through instincts or other innate characteristics but through the individual's experience, his interaction with the environment.

From the preceding illustration it can be seen that, as the individual continues to interact with his environment, there develops a network of motives or needs that acts to guide his behavior. These needs or motives will vary from being very specific, as a need for a mother's love, to very general, as the need for good interpersonal relationships. The more specific the need, the more possible it is to predict the pattern of behavior in a given situation (Rotter, 1964).

Rotter (1964) has outlined three rather broad characteristics of these learned needs: need potential, freedom of movement, and need value. Need potential refers to a set of behaviors that are directed toward a particular need, such as receiving attention from others, and the probability of their occurrence in a given situation. Freedom of movement refers to the belief of the individual that certain patterns of behaviors will lead to certain satisfactions or rewards. The individual learns that crying when he is young will bring him attention from others, but this same behavior as a teenager will likely bring him not attention but rejection. Finally, each need of the individual has some value. That is, in any given situation one need or goal may have more value than some other goal in the same situation. A student may have a need to please his teacher, but he may also have a need to be seen in a favorable light by his peers. The relative value he attaches to these two needs in a given situation will in part determine what patterns of behavior he chooses to use.

It can be seen from this example that a type of need hierarchy forms. Each individual is born with an innate hierarchy of needs, such as food and water. However, most of these needs are formed through learning. This concept of placing needs in a hierarchy serves as a tool to explain the fact that in any given situation an individual may have the potential for several responses, and each of these responses has a probability for occurrence that can be ranked. If we go back to the example of the students in the classroom, we can illustrate this principle. One student may value pleasing the teacher more and his response is governed by that need. To another student in the room the need to please his peers may have more value and he will respond accordingly. Yet another student may value neither one of these needs and behave quite differently from the other two.

From the learning theory framework, then, man's personality is determined largely by his interaction with the environment. That is, if we can understand the psychological situation of the individual, we can understand the structure of his personality and predict his behavior. The individual learns through experience that certain situations will present certain satisfactions or dissatisfactions to him. Through this experience the individual develops different patterns of needs, which lead to different patterns of behavior. Further, individual differences develop because individuals perceive a specific situation differently. The child who has received love from his mother will react to her presence in certain predictable ways, and this pattern of behavior will be different from the individual who has been rejected by his mother. In essence, each individual has learned through experience what a given situation means to him, and he reacts to the situation on that basis.

The basis for the structure of an individual's personality then is his learned patterns of behaviors. Obviously, much of this learning takes place early in the individual's development. Hence, not unlike other theoretical approaches to personality, the learning theory approach recognizes the importance of early childhood experiences in the development of personality. Unlike other approaches, however, the learning theory approach to personality does not attribute much of personality to innate characteristics of the individual, but rather ascribes the needs of the individual to those experiences that he has learned will bring him satisfaction.

PERSONALITY DEVELOPMENT AND
PRINCIPLES OF LEARNING

Given the learning theory position that an individual's personality is the result of his interaction with his environment and can be attributed largely to learning rather than innate characteristics, how does this learning actually take place? What are the factors that produce the learning of behavior? For our purposes we can examine two related, but different ways in which the organism learns new behaviors: classical conditioning and operant conditioning. It is upon one of these two models that most learning theories of personality and counseling are based.

CLASSICAL CONDITIONING

The man usually given credit for the beginning of the classical conditioning theory is Pavlov. His work in conditioning led to the establishment of the basic principles of classical conditioning. Pavlov demonstrated that dogs could be conditioned to salivate when they heard a bell, if that bell had been paired several times with the presentation of food to the dogs. In this case the food was an unconditional stimulus and the bell was the conditional stimulus. In effect, the dogs learned to respond to the bell in the same manner as they had previously responded to the food. Pavlov also found that behavior could be extinguished if a particular response was not given any reinforcement.

Classical conditioning makes use of the fact that some events in an individual's environment are related to some human neuromuscular and glandular responses (Michael & Meyerson, 1962). The taste of a lemon, for example, causes salivation in most of us. The lemon is a stimulus that causes an automatic reaction in the organism, which is a response. Many such stimulus-response connections are present at birth, and most of them are concerned with maintaining the existence of the organism.

A different stimulus that has not been a part of an innate stimulus-response relationship can become a conditioned stimulus, which creates a response by being paired with an original unconditioned stimulus. In turn, the response to the conditioned stimulus is called a conditioned response. This then is the chain of learning from a classical conditioning framework. As mentioned earlier, this new relationship will not remain as part of the organism's behavior if the conditioned stimulus is presented often enough without the presentation of the unconditioned stimulus. In the case of the dogs, if the bell was presented frequently without any accompanying presentation of food, the conditional stimulus (bell) would lose its power to evoke a response. This is the process of extinction.

While classical conditioning may explain the manner in which some behavior is learned, many writers in the learning theory camp feel that much of an individual's behavior cannot be explained by the classical model. To explain how most of an individual's behavior is learned, these theorists turn to the assumptions of operant conditioning.

Operant Conditioning

The basic principles of operant conditioning have been outlined by B. F. Skinner (1938). Skinner's contention was that most of human behavior occurs at random, and the critical question is what are the environmental consequences of the behavior. This type of behavior " operates " on the environment, which is different from behavior that responds to prior stimuli (Michael & Meyerson, 1962). Basic to operant conditioning is a law of learning postulated by Skinner (1938), which states that if a certain behavior is followed by an event in the environment that brings satisfaction to the individual, then the probability of that behavior occurring in the future is increased. This is very similar to E. L. Thorndike's "Law of Effect," which stated that an act may be altered in its strength by its consequences.

To illustrate this principle, we can consider the child who sucks his thumb. At some point in time the infant randomly stuck his thumb in his mouth and the sensations generated were pleasurable, hence rewarding. Because the behavior was rewarding, the probability of that behavior reoccurring is increased. In short, the behavior of thumb-sucking has been learned. Thus, learning through operant conditioning is the opposite of learning through classical conditioning. The former occurs because of what happens after a particular behavior while the latter is concerned with the stimulus in the environment that causes the organism to respond. In operant conditioning the organism first must behave in a certain manner. This behavior is then shaped by the consequences of the events in the environment that follow it.

It is perhaps appropriate at this point to examine in more detail some basic principles of learning that derive from both the classical and operant conditioning models.

REINFORCEMENT

In general there are two rather broad categories of reinforcement, which are termed positive or negative. A reinforcement that has a positive valence is often referred to as a reward, and it generally brings some form of pleasure or satisfaction to the organism. Some of these positive reinforcers or rewards are vital to the maintenance of the organism, e.g., food and water. Other events in the environment, such as money, praise, or love, may become positive reinforcers because the individual has learned to value them. More often than not the individual has learned to value them because of the approval or disapproval of others, by praise or blame, by promises or threats. Such reinforcers can be termed conditioned or secondary reinforcers. Many of them become generalized conditioned reinforcers; e.g., money becomes a positive reinforcer because the individual has learned that money in and of itself will bring many kinds of satisfactions.

At the opposite end of the continuum are the negative reinforcers or, as they are sometimes called, aversive stimuli. This class of reinforcers is negative because they bring pain or unpleasantness to the individual. While some of these reinforcers actually physically bring pain to the individual, others, such as social rejection, become negative through learning. As with the positive reward of money, social rejection can be termed a conditioned reinforcement or generalized conditioned reinforcement. That is, the force of social rejection as a reinforcement will cause the individual to respond in certain ways in many different situations.

It is important to note that in either the case of positive or negative reinforcement the reinforcement may take place without the individual being consciously aware of it. While there are many times that the individual is aware that he has been rewarded, there are other cases where he will not be aware. However, it makes little difference in the operant model whether he is consciously aware of the reinforcement or not.

In both models of conditioning the phenomenon of extinction is extremely important. Behavior is said to occur for as long as that behavior receives some reinforcement. If, however, the behavior ceases to be reinforced either positively or negatively, the behavior will cease. If this phenomenon of extinction did not occur, a response, once learned, would persist indefinitely. The stronger the response the longer it will take to be extinguished, but it will disappear in the absence of reinforcement.

An extremely important principle of learning is the idea of generalization. Generalization refers to the assumption that not only does a reinforcement accompanying a particular stimulus increase the probability of that stimulus to elicit a particular response but also that the effect spreads to other similar stimuli. Hence, the stimulus that is similar to the one accompanying the reinforcement will also elicit the particular response. Thorndike referred to this law of learning as " response by analogy." That is, to any new situation in the environment an individual will respond as he would to a similar situation. The infant who receives satisfaction from being held by his mother and responds accordingly may generalize this satisfaction to the stimulus of being held by his father and will respond in the same manner. This process of generalization is extremely important because no two stimuli or stimulus situations are exactly the same. However, the more closely the new stimulus resembles the original, the more probable will be the original response. If individuals did not have this ability to generalize from one stimulus to a similar stimulus, there would be no learning.

As the previous example demonstrates, the ability to generalize from one situation to the next is so often taken for granted that we pay very little attention to it. The young child who calls everything that is big and has four legs a horse is generalizing from one stimulus to another. Granted that the response produced is not accurate, it still demonstrates the principle of generalization and, at the same time, leads us to a consideration of how these generalizations do become accurate.

Discrimination

In conjunction with the concept of generalization we must consider the manner in which the individual learns to tell the difference between two stimuli: the process of discrimination. It is apparent that an individual cannot go through life responding in the same fashion to related but different stimuli. The child cannot go through life referring to all large four-legged animals as horses. He must learn the difference between horses and cows and, indeed, between the different kinds of horses. In short, he must learn to discriminate between stimulus situations. The law of discrimination states that the relationship between stimuli and responses that has been generated through the process of generalization may be separately broken down. This occurs through a process of combining reinforcement with extinction. In this process the correct response to a stimulus is given reinforcement while the incorrect response to a similar stimulus is not given reinforcement. In the case of the child calling all large four-legged animals horses, we would reinforce his verbal response to the correct stimulus, a horse, but we would not reinforce his responding to a cow as a horse. Eventually, the child would make the correct response only in the presence of the correct stimulus. If we are concerned with further discrimination between horse and colt, or between various kinds of horses, we could follow a similar pattern of reinforcement and discrimination. The level of discrimination we will need depends in large part on how important the stimulus situation is to us. The ability to discriminate between good and bad art is important to some, but relatively unimportant to others. It is quite obvious that each individual is forced to make many thousands of discriminations in his everyday life, hence the extreme importance to our learning process.

SCHEDULES OF REINFORCEMENT

Before moving to a discussion of how the various responses of an individual are molded into complex behavior patterns, we need to return to the concept of reinforcement once again to consider the importance of the rate and timing of reinforcement.

Skinner and his followers have concentrated much of their research on this very topic. The term *schedule of reinforcement* refers to the particular pattern of reinforcement applied to a particular response. The simplest schedule of reinforcement is that of continuous reinforcement, which simply means that after every response of a given nature a reward or reinforcement is applied. While this is the simplest form, it is also the least effective. If the reward is continuously given, the effects of the reward are lessened. If a parent gives her child a cookie to keep the child quiet, and continues to do this, the cookie soon loses its effect.

Much more effective than continuous reinforcement is some schedule of reinforcement on an intermittent basis. Such schedules can be divided into two rather large categories: fixed ratio reinforcement and interval reinforcement. If the frequency of the reinforcement depends on the rate of responses, we have ratio reinforcement; that is, after so many correct responses a reward is applied. An interval schedule of reinforcement is based simply on the passage of a given amount of time. On this schedule it does not make any difference how many responses are made; the reward is delivered only after the proper amount of time has passed. In most cases individuals who have been exposed to either of the intermittent schedules will retain the learned responses longer than if they had been on a continuous schedule; the response is more difficult to extinguish. Hence, when trying to instill a particular response in an individual, it is far more effective to use one of the intermittent schedules of reinforcement. In either case a response learned through this application of reward will last longer without an additional reward. The child who is rewarded for his good behavior on an intermittent basis will maintain that behavior over longer periods of time without an additional reward.

Shaping

The question that remains to be answered is, " How do all these responses that are learned come together to form complex behaviors? " Skinner has referred to this process as shaping. The complex behavior is shaped through a number of successive approximations, during each of which certain behavior is reinforced and other behavior is not. Through this process the behavior gradually comes closer and closer to the desired pattern. Hill (1963) gives an illustration of how shaping might be used in training a rat, and that illustration will serve here to illustrate the basic process of shaping. The problem is to train a rat to press a level, pick up a marble and carry it across the cage and deposit it into a hole, then receive his reward of food. Quite obviously this is not a pattern of behavior that we could normally expect of a rat but, through the process of shaping, the rat can be trained to perform this task.

In order to train the rat, we would first deprive him of food until such time as we were sure he was quite hungry. The rat would first be trained to eat from an apparatus into which food was placed. While he was eating at the apparatus, a small sound would be produced intermittently. Soon the rat would be trained to go to the apparatus when he heard the sound. The next part of the shaping process would be to require the rat to touch a lever after he hears the sound, but before the food is delivered. The next step is to add the requirement of touching the marble, than taking it across the cage, and finally putting it in the proper hole. Throughout this process the rat has been rewarded after coming closer to the desired response.

As with this illustration, human behavior is formed through the process of shaping. The child learning to ride a bike goes through this very same process. As he learns each small behavior or response required to ride a bike, he receives the reward of self-satisfaction, or praise from his father. Soon he has put together all the necessary responses into the rather complex behavior of riding a bike, perhaps to the extent that he can ride it with no hands. The point is that complex patterns of behavior are formed through a process of shaping. As with the learning of simple responses, these shapings take place every day in our lives; some we may be consciously aware of, others may take place outside our conscious thought.

Mediating Responses

If the principles of learning just outlined apply to man as well as to other animals, the question then is how is man different, or is he different, from other animals. Man is unlike other animals for he has the capacity to develop mediating responses that allow him to respond to his environment in new ways by permitting him to plan and evaluate his responses to that environment. These mediating responses, referred to by Dollard and Miller (1950) as "higher mental processes," consist largely of the use of language and symbolism. Because man has the capacity to use symbols and language, he can label stimuli and can mediate their effects. That is, because of language he can go through a reasoning process when he is confronted with a particular stimulus and delay any immediate response to the stimuli. A man who sees a symbolization of food, despite the drive that it calls forth in him, is able to delay the response to that stimulus until it is time to eat. He is mediating his response to a given stimulus, and much of human behavior is so governed. In fact, most of human behavior goes through a process of mediation, and it is this process of mediation that makes man not only different from other animals but exceedingly more complex.

Imitative Learning

It has been apparent to most learning theorists that some of an individual's behavior is learned through a process that does not involve the direct receiving of a reward. Such learning is said to take place through the process of imitation or vicarious learning. This very simply is the process whereby an observer learns a particular response by observing some other person (the model) in his environment perform the response. Miller and Dollard (1941) referred to this process as "matched dependent behavior." They felt that the individual learned the response only if he matched the behavior of the model. Mower (1960) felt that the response of the model could be learned by the observer simply by rewarding the model, not the observer. In this process, it is assumed that the reward given the model is a vicarious reward for the observer. Recent work by Bandura (1962, 1965a) suggests that imitative learning can take place without either the model or the observer being rewarded. His contention is that imitative learning can take place simply through one individual observing another individual respond. He does point out, however, that while the pattern of behavior may be learned simply through observation, it may take actual reinforcement in order for the observer to perform the behavior. In a sense, the behavior may lie dormant until it is called forth through reinforcement.

It is apparent how important this notion of imitative learning is to the learning theory position. We all have observed children who model their behavior after someone they admire. The boy who holds a bat just like his favorite ballplayer, or the girl who wants to talk like her favorite star, are exhibiting learning through modeling. Recent research in this area indicates that this is an extremely important way in which individuals learn, and it goes hand in hand with the other laws of learning.

SUMMARY

This section has attempted to present an overview of the basic principles of learning. In no way do we claim that it is an exhaustive treatment of the field of learning. Indeed, many thousands of words have been written on the principles of learning, and in our limited space we could not hope to give the reader a full background in the field. Our attempt rather has been to provide the reader with the basic notions of learning theory.

If we now retrace our steps to the beginning of this chapter, the statement that man's behavior or personality is determined largely by his interaction with his environment may have more meaning. As man interacts with his environment, he is subject to the laws of learning that have just been presented, thus his personality is formed through this process of learning. As the individual is subjected to reinforcements from his environment, some behaviors are strengthened or learned while others are weakened or extinguished. In addition, the individual may also learn some patterns of behavior through the imitation of others. If the individual observes some other individual successfully completing some behavior he would like to accomplish, he may imitate the behavior of the second individual. This learning in turn leads to generalizations and discriminations by the individual and the gradual shaping of simple responses into complex behaviors. Further, as the individual develops, there develops in him, largely through the use of language, the ability to make mediating responses. These mediating responses allow him to plan and formulate his response to various stimuli, or to withhold an immediate response to a particular stimulus. This then is the process of personality development, and the form of the personality in large part depends on the environment in which the individual develops.

ABNORMAL PERSONALITY DEVELOPMENT

As we have seen, the main emphasis in a learning theory approach to personality development and counseling is on the importance of the individual's environmental situation. It is largely through the interaction of the individual with the environment that personality is learned. In the same manner as what are considered normal patterns of behavior are learned, so also are abnormal or maladaptive patterns of behavior learned. " Man's personality consists of both his positive and his negative habits. Those habits which are inappropriate (i.e. deviant) are learned in much the same way as appropriate behaviors" (Hosford, p. 2, 1969). That is, the inappropriate behavior has been learned because it has been rewarded at various points in time. The child who is a constant behavior problem in class may behave in that manner because he has learned that it is the only way he can receive attention. When the teacher shouts at him, he is receiving satisfaction or a reward for the behavior. Even though we may consider this behavior inappropriate, it has brought him a reward that he values: attention. Likewise the child who is withdrawn, one who might be termed a social isolate, has learned to behave in that manner. By being a social isolate, she may be avoiding a situation, or people with whom she is uncomfortable. Her reward is that she does not have to participate in a situation that causes fear in her, a fear that has also been learned because of past experience.

The point of these illustrations is that learning theory is concerned with observable behavior and does not try to take into account any inner reason for an individual's maladaptive behavior. In the case of both the attention-seeking child and the social isolate we have examples of individuals who have simply learned bad habits. The bad habits just as the good habits are formed through the learning process outlined earlier.

From a learning theory framework then, an individual's behavior or personality is determined in large part by the kinds of reinforcements he has received in his interaction with various environmental situations. Maladaptive behavior is different from normal behavior, not in the manner in which it was learned, but only to the degree that the behavior is typical or maladaptive to the observers (Hosford, 1969). In other words, we could describe maladaptive behavior as behavior that is not satisfying either to the individual or to those near him. In very large part, it is the culture with which the individual exists that determines what is good or bad behavior. We are all aware that behavior may be perfectly acceptable in one culture while in another culture it would be completely unacceptable. For example, in some parts of the world it is completely acceptable behavior to have more than one wife, but in many other countries it is so unacceptable that one can go to jail for such behavior.

In summary, learning theory is concerned with observable patterns of behavior, not the internal state of the individual. The learning theorists hold that one can explain maladaptive behavior just as we can explain normal patterns of behavior. All behavior is formed through a learning process; it makes no difference whether the behavior is adaptive or maladaptive. The individual has adopted that pattern of behavior because it has brought him some reinforcement, some satisfaction.

GOALS OF COUNSELING

Before we can examine the manner in which the learning theory position is translated into counseling practice, we should examine the goals of that counseling. That is, what is hoped to be accomplished through the process of counseling?

Rotter has stated his goals of counseling as " helping the patient to lead a more constructive life, to contribute to society, to maximize his potential for achievement, to maximize his feelings of affection or contribution to others." (Rotter, 1962, mimeo). In short, his goal is to help the individual reach a state of happiness and pleasure. On the surface this definition is not very different from the definitions that have been given as goals of counseling for the self-theory or the psychoanalytic position. There is, however, an important difference in the goals. While the learning theorists would not argue that these goals are the ultimate goals of counseling, they would say that they are too global to work with in counseling. Their position is that we need more immediate goals that can be dealt with by the counselor and the counselee.

Krumboltz (1966) states that the goal of counseling must be stated in specific terms. We must talk about particular behaviors that are in need of being changed. People come to counseling because they have particular problems that they are unable to resolve by themselves, and they believe that the counselor will be able to help them with this concern. The goal of counseling must be to help each of these individuals resolve the problem that they bring to the counseling situation. Not very often will a client come to a counselor saying "I need a better self concept"; rather they are more inclined to say "I feel inadequate when with a group of people." Granted that the problem of feeling inadequate with a group of people may be indicative of what we term a poor self-concept, the behavioral counselor would choose to deal with the specific concern, not the global feeling. It may well be that other aspects of the self-concept also need some work, but the behavioral position is that the counselor needs to work on one specific concern at a time. It is only in this manner that appropriate behavior changes can be brought about.

The goals of counseling then must be stated in specific terms and, because they need to be stated in such a manner, the specific goal of counseling may be different for each individual. Granted that the ultimate goal of counseling will be close to Rotter's definition, it is with the more specific goals that counselors should first be concerned.

From this frame of reference it is necessary that both the client and the counselor decide on the goals of counseling. The counselor should respond to the goal that the counselee brings to the counseling situation rather than have some preconceived idea about the ultimate goal of counseling for all individuals. There may be times when the goal that the client has in mind is out of the realm of the counselor, because of interests, competency, or ethical considerations of the counselor. In these cases the counselor must tell the client that this goal is inappropriate and uncomfortable for him, the counselor. In essence then, the counselor and the client must work together in setting the goal for counseling. They must both agree that this is a goal that they want to achieve, and that through counseling there is a possibility of achieving the goal.

The critical element of this position regarding the setting of the goal for counseling is that the method by which the counselor will operate is not rigid. Rather he responds, within limits, to the goal that the counselee presents, and it is the accomplishment of that goal that is of utmost importance. As we shall see, the methods the counselor utilizes to help each client may be quite different, depending on the counselee and the problem that he brings to the counseling situation.

THE PROCESS OF COUNSELING

The counseling process as viewed from a learning theory position is simply a learning situation. Both the counselee and the counselor should recognize the situation as such, and the counselor should view himself as an aid in this learning process (Krumboltz, 1966). Any changes that come about as a result of the counseling process are a direct result of the same laws of learning that apply outside of the counseling situation. Hence, the process of counseling is concerned with the application of these same laws of learning.

The question that immediately arises in many individuals' minds at this point is, "Isn't this a very mechanistic view of counseling, and is the counselor nothing more than a practitioner with a bag of tricks?" The answer, of course, is no. Wolpe (1958) emphasizes the need for the therapist to be accepting, to try to understand the client and what he is communicating, and to be non-judgmental. " All that the patient says is accepted without question or criticism. He is given the feeling that the therapist is on his side" (Wolpe, p. 106, 1958). Krumboltz, likewise, believes that it is essential for the counselor to be understanding and to communicate this understanding to the client. He must be warm and empathic, and hold each individual in high regard. If these conditions are not present, it is impossible for the counselor to determine what is the client's difficulty and to gain the necessary cooperation of the client (Krumboltz, 1966). If a good working relationship is not established between the counselor and the client, then no counseling will take place. The Pepinskys (1954) and Dollard and Miller (1950) state similar positions on the need for the counselor to be a person and to establish a warm, permissive atmosphere for the client.

It is in this kind of atmosphere that the client is given the freedom to express his concerns. He finds that his statements are not received with a judgmental or shocked attitude, but are accepted. He discovers that the counselor is someone who will listen to his concerns and, perhaps for the first time in his life, the client feels that he has found someone with whom he can really talk (Miller and Dollard, 1950). When this kind of atmosphere is established, the problem of the client can be clarified and his feelings about that problem can be understood by the counselor. It is only after this stage of the process of counseling has been completed that the two participants in the relationship can begin to work on resolving the difficulty. Unless the problem is brought into a sharply defined focus, resulting in a clear understanding of the problem by both the counselor and the client, counseling will not progress.

Central to the process of counseling, then, is the defining of the client's particular concern. From a learning theory framework it is not enough to define a client's difficulty as having a poor self-concept. The problem must be stated in workable terms in the counseling situation. In essence this means that the concern or difficulty must be stated in terms of overt behavior. Instead of defining a problem as a poor self-concept, the behavioral counselor attempts to have the client define the concern in specific terms, such as "I am unable to relate to individuals of the opposite sex", or "I stutter in front of a group of people." These are examples of specific behaviors and can be dealt with through counseling. This is not to say that behavioral counselors are not concerned with an individual having a good self-concept, or self-actualization. The contention is only that these global concepts must be translated into specific behaviors that are desired. It is only when the appropriate behaviors have been so defined that the counselor and the client can work toward the achievement of those behaviors. The successful achievement may indeed lead the client to have a better self-concept, which is of course desirable, but is not a workable original goal.

In conjunction with the clarification of the client's concern into specific behaviors is the notion that only one specific desired behavior should be concentrated upon at a time. From the learning theory perspective it is not an advantage to try to deal with or modify the whole structure of personality at any one time. As Bijou (1966) indicates, such global attempts are doomed to failure because there is just too much behavior to be dealt with at any one point in time. It is far better to work on one concern and, once that one has been resolved, to move on to another concern, if one exists. In this manner both the counselor and the client have a clear notion as to their goal and when it is accomplished. Therefore, the counseling situation is structured to work on only one particular concern at a time.

THE COUNSELOR

It is implied in the foregoing discussion that the counselor is an active participant in the counseling process. He helps the client define the specific concern that has brought him to the counseling situation, but it is the counselor who decides whether the kind of help that he can offer will help the client. Further, from a learning theory framework the counselor has the responsibility to decide on the particular course of the counseling. He decides what particular techniques he will utilize in the counseling situation. Once the concern has been defined and agreed upon by both the client and the counselor, it is the counselor who controls the process of counseling and accepts the responsibility for its outcome. As Krumboltz (1966) states, once the counselor has agreed to work with the counselee, the responsibility for the outcome of counseling is largely his. It is the counselor's responsibility to launch his counselee on a course of action that will eventually help that counselee reach a resolution of his difficulty. In order to accomplish this end, the counselor must control the counseling process. This is not an arbitrary manipulative control that goes against the client's wishes, rather it is a control specifically designed to meet the goals of the client.

In summary, the process of counseling as viewed from the learning theory framework is first a learning situation in which the same laws of learning that apply outside of counseling apply within. In order to utilize these laws of learning, the counselor must first establish an atmosphere in which there is mutual trust between the counselor and counselee. Secondly, the counselor and the counselee must come to some understanding about the concerns that brought the individual to counseling, and this must be stated in specific behavioral terms. That is, the client and the counselor must establish what are the desired ends of counseling. If at this point the counselor feels that he can help the client, the process of counseling continues largely under the control of the counselor. In the exercise of this control the counselor may use whatever ethical techniques he feels will lead the client to the desired behavior. Some of these techniques will be applied in the counseling situation itself, but the counselor may also involve himself in the individual's environment outside the counseling office. Thus, the counseling process is often more than just the face-to-face meeting of the client and the counselor. It often involves others in the client's life.

TECHNIQUES OF COUNSELING

While most of the approaches to learning theory counseling would be in general agreement about the process of counseling, albeit with different emphasis, the contrasts are somewhat greater when considering techniques of counseling. There are those that basically follow the classical conditioning model, while others operate from an operant conditioning model. Hence, in this section we will attempt to present the basic techniques in each of these camps. By doing this, we do not mean to imply that there is no overlap between the various branches of learning theory; however in the interest of clarity the techniques will be largely divided into the classical and operant models.

CLASSICAL MODEL

The man most closely identified with the classical model of conditioning in counseling is Joseph Wolpe. His theory of reciprocal inhibition is receiving increasing attention in the field. According to Wolpe (1958) the fundamental aim of counseling must be to remove the feelings of anxiety that are brought about by stimuli that are objectively harmless. The effectiveness of counseling is based on breaking down this learned response to the stimuli so that a more appropriate response may occur.

In order to accomplish the goals of counseling, the client usually has from one to a dozen interviews. During this time the counselor strives to establish the kind of relationship we discussed earlier on the process of counseling. It is important that the client should feel that the counselor likes him and is not judging him, while the client gives the counselor all the information possible about his childhood, family, school experience, vocational plans, and anything else that may relate to who he is at the present. This information is helpful to the counselor as he attempts to understand the client in his present state; however, it is not essential that a great deal of the past be brought into the counseling situation. What is important is an understanding of the manner in which the client behaves at the present time.

After the initial interviews are over, the client may take some inventories designed to give information about the kinds of activities that elicit inappropriate individual responses. This information is used in conjunction with information gained from the counselor's discussions with the client. The information is combined in order to establish a hierarchy of conditions that cause anxiety in the individual and to which the individual responds in an inappropriate manner. The following illustration may be helpful in understanding the forming of such a hierarchy. An individual may present himself to the counselor by stating that he is fearful or anxious when others are observing him. The counselor then attempts to establish the hierarchy by ascertaining what kinds of people observing him cause him the most anxiety. The counselor may find that the counselee is quite comfortable at home being observed by family, a little less comfortable when in the company of friends, a little more uncomfortable when in the company of strangers, and quite uncomfortable when alone with another strange individual. While this is a rough illustration, it serves to illustrate the increasing evidence of anxiety in different situations. It is upon this hierarchy that the crux of the counseling rests. The actual techniques used are termed assertive responses, sexual responses, and relaxation responses.

Assertive Responses

" In general, assertive responses are used for anxieties evoked in the course of direct interpersonal dealings" (Wolpe, 1958, p. 113). These responses are very similar to what Salter refers to as excitatory responses. The assertive response simply involves trying to get the client to express his feelings during interactions with others. An individual who is hurt by something someone else has done to him is encouraged to tell the person his feelings. In effect, the client is told that there is no reason not to express these feelings, and his anxiety over expressing them is groundless. The counselor attempts first to get the client to be assertive in the counseling interview; that is, to state his feelings to the counselor. Once this is accomplished, the client is instructed to attempt the same kinds of responses outside of counseling. The principle of conditioning involved here is that, in expressing assertive responses to the counselor, the client finds that there is no punishment or anxiety accompanying the response. Hence, the expression of the assertive response is teamed with a relaxed situation rather than an anxiety-producing situation. The counselor needs to use as much pressure as he feels necessary in order to get the client to perform the assertive behavior outside of the counseling situation. In some cases the counselor will be unable to motivate the client to do this and may have to resort to role playing in the interview (Wolpe, 1958).

Sexual Responses

While most counselors would not have a need for using this technique, it is included here as an example of another technique from the classical model. These responses are used when the client has anxiety connected with sexual situations. In short, all this response involves is instructing the client to participate in sexual activities only when there is no anxiety accompanying the situation. As with the assertive technique, the critical issue is to motivate the client to follow the instructions of the counselor. In this way only pleasurable feelings are generated by sexual situations, because sexual situations that cause anxiety are avoided. Gradually, it is felt that these pleasurable feelings will expand to cover other sexual situations.

Relaxation Responses

Relaxation responses are appropriate for any kind of anxiety, but are most appropriate when the stimulus causing the anxiety is an inanimate object. The technique was originally developed by Jacobson. The technique involves instructing the client in relaxation of the muscles. Clients are instructed that relaxing is a way of combating anxiety. While relaxation of the muscles is a technique in and of itself, it is most often used by Wolpe in conjunction with systematic desensitization.

Systematic Desensitization

The technique of systematic desensitization uses the hierarchy of anxiety-producing situations that evolved from the initial interviews as well as the techniques of relaxation. Once the hierarchy has been established, and the client is trained in muscle relaxation, the treatment can begin. The client is asked to imagine the least anxiety-producing situation in the hierarchy while he is in this relaxed anxiety, then the next situation on the hierarchy is imagined. This pattern is followed until the client can imagine the most fear-producing situation in his hierarchy without the feeling of anxiety. In essence, the client is being conditioned to a new response to the formerly fear-producing stimulus situations. Instead of an anxiety response, he is being conditioned to a relaxed response, and the two are incompatible. Hence, the anxiety response disappears.

While each of the techniques just outlined is somewhat different, they have in common the idea of changing an old inappropriate response to a stimulus to a response that is more appropriate. The aim of the counselor using these techniques is to break down the learned response to a particular stimulus in order that a more appropriate response may occur. This is accomplished following the classical conditioning model of teaming stimuli with more appropriate or desired responses.

Behavior Modification in the Classroom

A final technique deserving of consideration is that of behavior modification in the classroom. While it is usually considered as belonging with the classical model, this technique is an example of combining specific techniques from both the operant and classical models.

Often the best method to change the behavior of an individual involves bringing about changes in his environment that will remove the old behavior and replace it with a more desirable one. To illustrate this technique, we can examine what might be done in trying to change the behavior of an aggressive child in the classroom. In such a case the first step to be taken would be the establishment of the child's baseline behavior. This involves a simple tabulation of the number of times the child behaves in an aggressive manner in the classroom. This data is used to determine whether the technique is having any impact on the child's behavior. The second step is to remove the child from the classroom and into a room where he is isolated every time he exhibits some aggressive behavior. The length of this time-out period will vary with each individual and with the child's age. The use of the time-out procedure is combined with the use of positive reinforcement. The positive reinforcement is used whenever the child is engaging in normal social interactions. The reward takes two forms. One form of reward is the social reinforcement of the teacher's attention and praise. The second form is the use of tokens. When the child engages in normal social interaction, he receives a token. These tokens may be used by the child for later rewards such as food or a certain amount of free time. In this illustration the child receives positive reinforcement in the forms of praise and tokens when the desired behavior is exhibited and receives an aversive stimulus when the undesirable behavior is exhibited. One behavior is reinforced and one is extinguished.

While the list of techniques presented here does not exhaust the range of those used by therapists following the classical model, they are the ones most frequently used. For a more detailed account of these techniques, the reader is referred to the writings of Joseph Wolpe, Andrew Salter, and Albert Bandura.

OPERANT MODEL

As was true in the case of those counselors who generally follow the classical model of counseling, those who basically follow the operant model place an important emphasis on the establishment of the relationship between the counselor and the client. As Krumboltz (1967) points out, " The client is likely not to describe the totality of his problems unless he thinks his listener will understand things from his point of view"; and "the counselor's ability to communicate his understanding of the client's problem to him establishes the counselor as an important person in the client's life and therefore one able to be an influential model and effective reinforcing agent" (p. 244). Hence, the first goal of the behavioral counselor is to establish a relationship with the client in which the client feels free to express himself to the counselor, whom the client views as an individual really interested in attempting to help him with his difficulty.

Once this relationship has been established the actual techniques used by the counselor will vary depending upon the client and the nature of his concern. The techniques used most often in the counseling relationship itself will include operant conditioning, imitative learning, and cognitive learning. However, it is important to note that the behavioral counselor may rely on more than the face-to-face meetings with the client. Because of his belief in the importance of the environment in establishing and maintaining inappropriate behaviors on the part of clients, the behavioral counselor will often attempt to make changes in the environment of the individual. Thus, in some cases he becomes a behavioral engineer, actually manipulating the individual's environment in order to provide an environment that will aid the process of behavioral change. While some may object to this manipulation, the behaviorists are quick to point out that the manipulation used is done so as to enhance the probability that the client will accomplish his desired behavior. The counselor does not set the goal; the client sets the goal.

Operant Conditioning

Obviously, the most frequently used technique of those following the operant model is that of operant conditioning. This technique involves the modifying of behavior through the use of reinforcement. Earlier in this chapter the principles of reinforcement were outlined so there is no need to repeat them in detail here. The important point to remember is that in operant conditioning the response must first occur, then the reinforcement is applied. It is this reinforcement that shapes the behavior in the desired direction. Thus, in the counseling situation, the emphasis is first on the client behavior patterns that are in need of change. Once these have been established by both the client and the counselor, the counselor can begin reinforcing those statements made by the client that indicate some direction toward the desired behavior. The actual reinforcement used to encourage further responses in the desired direction may consist of the counselor giving particular attention to a statement or by inattention to certain statements. He may express verbal approval of certain statements and disapproval of others by not responding or responding negatively. In short, the form of the reinforcement may be verbal or non-verbal, positive or negative, and through this reinforcement certain responses are reinforced and certain responses are extinguished.

Hosford (1969) has outlined four crucial considerations in the use of operant conditioning in counseling. First, the counselor must be sure that the reinforcement he is using is strong enough to motivate the counselee to perform the desired behavior. In essence, the same kind of reinforcement will not work as well for all clients, and the counselor needs to find the reinforcement that has the greatest potential for increasing the desired behavior. Secondly, the counselor must use the reinforcement in a systematic manner. As Krumboltz (1966, p. 15) states ". . . the question is not whether the counselor should or should not use reinforcement—the question is how the counselor can time his use of reinforcement in the best interests of his client." In the initial stages of counseling it is important that each response indicating movement in the desired direction be reinforced. As counseling progresses, however, the reinforcement should be applied on a systematic but intermittent basis. As we discussed earlier, the intermittent schedule of reinforcement tends to have the most long-lasting effect on behavior. The third necessary element is the contingency between the demonstration of the desired response and the application of the reward. For best effectiveness the reinforcement must follow closely the demonstrated desired response. Closely related to this continguency is the fourth crucial element, which is that the desired response must be first elicited by the counselor. This often involves the use of cue statements by the counselor. A cue statement is one designed so that the client can hardly avoid responding in the desired direction. What, in effect, the counselor is doing is giving a verbal prompting to the client. This prompting or giving of cue statements may be particularly important in the early stages of counseling but, as the effects of reinforcement begin to act, there should be less need for these kinds of statements.

The technique of operant conditioning in counseling, then, involves the gradual shaping of the client's behavior toward the desired behavior through the use of positive and negative reinforcement. This reinforcement can be of a verbal or non-verbal form. It must be strong enough to motivate the client and be applied consistently in close proximity to the desired response.

Imitative Learning

A second technique that is receiving increasing attention from the behavioral counselors is the use of imitative learning. The application of imitative learning to the field of counseling involves the presentation of a model or models to the counselee which demonstrates the desired behavioral outcome and with which the counselee can easily identify. As was discussed earlier, imitative or vicarious learning is one of the principal means by which people learn new behaviors. In the counseling situation the counselee may be so ignorant of ways to modify his behavior or to develop new behaviors that reinforcement techniques may be inappropriate in the early stages. Instead, it may be more appropriate to present some type of model to the individual which represents the desired behavior. The client, in observing the behavior of the model, may learn the new behavior simply through observation. Whether the counselee learns the new behavior or not will depend to some extent on the degree to which he identifies with the model.

Kagen (1963) states that models can be effective agents for behavior change because they are identified by individuals as examples of their ideal selves. The model represents some desirable goal that the individual would like to command. " The most salient of these include: (a) power over the environment . . . ; (b) competence and instrumental skills; (c) autonomy of action; and (d) the receipt of love, affection, and acceptance from others" (Kagen, 1963, p. 82). The model that is presented to the counselee may show more control over his own destiny than the counselee has; he may have greater ability in dealing with certain situations; he may be more readily accepted by other individuals; and, because of these strengths, he may be able to be more independent in his behavior. The effectiveness of the technique of presenting a model or models to clients depends upon how closely the client can identify with the behavior of the model—for the closer the identification, the more imitative learning that will take place.

There are three basic types of models that have been used in counseling: filmed, taped, and live. In all three cases the model is presented to the clients as an example of the desired behavior. Once the models have been presented, the counselor may use cue statements to lead the clients to a discussion of the model's behavior. The counselor can then employ verbal reinforcement techniques to further shape the behavior of the clients in the desired direction. Seldom in counseling is the principle of imitative learning used by itself. More often, it is used in conjunction with the principles of operant conditioning.

Cognitive Learning

A third technique that may be used by some counselors following a behavioral model is that of cognitive learning. In some respects cognitive learning is very similar to the assertive technique discussed earlier in this chapter. There may be occasions when the client knows the behavior that he wishes to engage in, but is unaware of how to accomplish the behavior. In such cases it may be appropriate for the counselor to instruct him as to what to do. In essence, what is involved in this technique is a contract between the client and the counselor. Having agreed upon the desired behavior, the client agrees to try what the counselor suggests for a certain period of time. While this may seem like an over-simplified technique for a counselor to use, and in fact may not be considered by some as counseling, it may be an effective technique in some cases. Obviously, as with other techniques, it should not be used in a mechanical manner but should be used as just one technique in the process of counseling.

As was indicated in the section on modeling techniques, the behavioral counselor will usually use the techniques that have been outlined in combinations. With some clients the counselor may employ all the techniques discussed at various times during counseling, or he may use particular combinations of techniques. We also do not wish to imply that the techniques discussed here are the only ones used in behavioral counseling. What we are saying is that these are the basic techniques around which behavioral counseling revolves. Certainly, each of the many theorists and practitioners within the field of behavioral counseling has variations of these techniques as well as other techniques that they use. Nonetheless, the behavioral counselor finds his rationale for counseling in the laws of learning that have been discussed in this chapter. Though each will have his own emphasis, it is the basic laws of learning which are essential.

RESEARCH

Research has shown that the verbal behavior of a person can be influenced in an orderly, predictable, and lawful fashion by what another person says and does (Thoresen, 1967). Krasner (1958) reviewed 39 studies of verbal reinforcement, the majority of which showed that when subjects were reinforced for some class of behavior, the behavior increased. Several research studies indicate the nature of the results from these early investigations. Verplanck (1955) found that the number of opinion and attitude statements made by subjects could be increased through verbal reinforcement. Greenspoon (1955), using verbal reinforcement, increased client responses of plural nouns; Buss and Durkee (1958) increased the number of verbal responses of effect made by subjects; Adams and Hoffman (1960) increased the number of subject self-references; and Matarazzo (1963) even increased the length of time the interviewee spoke. Thus, there appears to be ample evidence that verbal reinforcment can increase the number and kind of verbal responses made by subjects.

A further question to be answered was whether verbal reinforcement made by counselors could help a counselee learn new patterns of behaviors and attitudes. One such investigation was carried out by Krumboltz and Ryan (1964). They investigated the effects of verbal reinforcement counseling on the decision-making of 60 male college students enrolled in a first-year psychology course. One 20-minute counseling session was held with each subject during which decision and deliberation responses made by the counselees were reinforced by the counselor. It was found that, after counseling, the number of decision and deliberation responses made by the counselees increased and the frequency of decision responses generalized to situations outside of the counseling office. They also found that some counselors were more effective than others in using reinforcement techniques. Other investigations have shown that reinforcement techniques have been effective in modifying hyperactive and aggressive behavior (Vance, 1969); in developing appropriate classroom behavior (Castle, 1969); and in improving academic performance (Scoresby, 1969).

MODELING

In early investigations of the effects of modeling on children, Bandura and Huston (1961) found that children did imitate the aggressive behavior of a model while in the presence of that model. Bandura, Ross, and Ross

(1961) noted that children who observed an aggressive model took on the behavior of that model and generalized this behavior to new situations.

Bandura, Ross and Ross (1963) investigated the effects of three types of models on 96 nursery-school children. The children were divided into three experimental groups and one control group. The children in the first experimental group were exposed to a real-life aggressive model, the second experimental group was presented a filmed aggressive model, and the third experimental group was presented a cartoon film showing aggressive behavior. The results of this study indicated that the aggressive behavior of the children in all three experimental groups rose significantly above that of the children in the control group. All three types of models were equally successful in increasing the aggressive behavior of the children. They also found that the effectiveness of the model was somewhat a function of the sex of the model, the sex of the child, and the reality cues of the model.

In a later study, Bandura, Ross, and Ross (1963b), using essentially the same methodology as in their previous study, with 80 nursery-school children again found support for the effectiveness of models in transmitting desired kinds of behaviors. They also noted that the degree of success of the model's behavior had an effect upon the rate of the childrens' learning. That is, the more positive reinforcement the model received for certain behavior, the more likely this behavior would be picked up by the children.

The above studies indicate that learning takes place not only through direct reinforcement of responses, but also through vicarious reinforcement or imitative learning. Several investigations have shown that imitative learning or vicarious reinforcement is also effective in counseling. Much of this research has been carried out in combination with verbal reinforcement research.

Verbal and Model Reinforcement

Krumboltz and Thoresen (1964, 1967) studied the effects of both verbal-reinforcement and model-reinforcement counseling on students' information-seeking behavior. A total of 192 eleventh-grade students were assigned to either individual or group counseling. In the verbal-reinforcement groups the students were given positive verbal reinforcement when they made statements indicating information-seeking behavior. In the model-reinforcement groups a tape-recorded interview with a model was presented to the group. During the tape, the model was given positive reinforcement when he made statements concerning information-seeking behavior. This was followed by discussion during which the counselor reinforced those statements made by the counselees indicating information-seeking behavior. The results showed that model-reinforcement counseling and verbal-reinforcement counseling both produced significant results. The subjects not only increased their number of information-seeking responses, but they also increased their information-seeking behavior outside of the counseling situation. The model-reinforcement counseling was most effective with the male students, while the verbal-reinforcement counseling was most effective with the fe-males. The data also indicated that different counselors had varying degrees of success with the two methods, but that there was no overall difference between individual and group counseling.

In an investigation that used the same methods and types of subjects as mentioned in the previous study, Krumboltz and Schroeder (1965) found that verbal-reinforcement and model-reinforcement counseling increases the amount of career planning done by high school students. Further, they agreed with previous studies (Krumboltz and Ryan, 1964; Krumboltz and Thoresen, 1964) that the increase in the desired behavior generalized to situations outside of the counseling office.

In most of the research on models in counseling found in the literature, the models are of either a taped or a film variety. Recently there have been some studies on the effectiveness of peer models who actually take part in the counseling sessions. Hansen, Niland, and Zani (1969) investigated the effects of live peer models on elementary school children of low sociometric status. The models were peers selected by the students as "stars" of the school, and they actually participated in the group sessions. The stars were not informed that they were acting as models during the group sessions. The results indicated that there was significant improvement in social ac-ceptance for the low sociometric group following counseling. The effective-ness of using both verbal-reinforcement counseling and model-reinforce-ment counseling, using live peer models in reducing alienation among high school students, was demonstrated by Warner and Hansen (1970) and Warner (1971). In a similar investigation conducted by Warner, Niland, and Maynard (1970), model-reinforcement counseling was found to be ef-fective in helping elementary school children set realistic achievement goals.

DESENSITIZATION

The research literature also lends considerable support to the technique of desensitization. Wolpe (1961) reported that his technique of desensitization was effective in helping 35 out of 39 randomly elected clients. The proce-dure has also been found to be effective with test anxiety (Weinstein,

1969) ; school phobia (Garvey and Hegrenes, 1966) ; and sexual devia-
tions (Lazarus, 1963). In a review of 50 case articles and 20 empirical investigations, Paul (1968) concludes that there is overwhelming evidence to
support the use of desensitization with a wide variety of client problems.

COGNITIVE LEARNING

The literature contains few studies that deal exclusively with cognitive learning. Kensey (1957), (1969) does report the technique as being effective in
helping students who are chronic classroom behavior problems. Shier
(1969) also found positive results with classroom behavior problems.

SUMMARY

From the studies cited in this section, it would appear that counseling based
on learning theory does hold promise. Certainly it would seem that those
who adhere to this position are quite willing to submit their approach to
the rigors of empirical investigation. Readers who desire a more thorough
review of the research in this area should refer to the texts of Krumboltz
and Thoresen (1969), and Bandura (1969).

REFERENCES

Adams, J. S., and Hoffman, B. "The Frequency of Self-Reference Statements as a Function of Generalized Reinforcement." *Journal of Abnormal and Social Psychology* 60:384–389.

Baer, D. M. "The Effect of Withdrawal of Positive Reinforcement on an
Extinguishing Response in Young Children." *Child Development*
32:67–74.

Bandura, A. "Behavioral Modifications through Modeling Procedures." In
Krasner, L., and Ullmann, L. (Eds.). *Research in Behavior Modification.*
New York: Holt, Rinehart and Winston, 1965.

Bandura, A. *Principles of Behavior Modification.* New York: Holt, Rinehart
and Winston, 1969.

Bandura, A. "Social Learning through Imitation." In Marshal Jones (Ed.).
Nebraska Symposium on Motivation, 1962. Lincoln: University of Nebraska Press, 1962.

Bandura, A., and Huston, A. C. "Identification as a Process of Incidental
Learning." *Journal of Abnormal and Social Psychology* 63:311–318.

Bandura, A., and McDonald, F. J. "The Influence of Social Reinforcement and the Behavior of Models in Shaping Children's Moral Judgments." *Journal of Abnormal and Social Psychology* 67:274–281.

Bandura, A.; Ross, D.; and Ross, S. A. "A Comparative Test of the Status Envy, Social Power, and Secondary Reinforcement Theories of Identificatory Learning." *Journal of Abnormal and Social Psychology* 67:527–534.

Bandura, A.; Ross, D.; and Ross, S. A. "Imitation of Film-Mediated Aggressive Models." *Journal of Abnormal and Social Psychology* 66:3–11.

Bandura, A.; Ross, D.; and Ross, S. A. "Transmission of Aggression through Imitation of Aggressive Models." *Journal of Abnormal and Social Psychology*, 63:575–582.

Bandura, A., and Walters, R. H. "Aggression." In *Child Psychology: The Sixty-Second Yearbook of the National Society for the Study of Education*, Part I. Chicago: The National Society for the Study of Education, 1963.

Bijou, S. W. "Implications of Behavioral Science for Counseling and Guidance." In Krumboltz, J. D. (Ed.). *Revolution in Counseling: Implication of Behavioral Science*. Boston: Houghton-Mifflin, 1966.

Buss, A. H., and Durkee, A. "Conditioning of Hostile Verbalizations in a Structure Resembling a Clinical Interview." *Journal of Consulting Psychology* 6:415–418.

Caslle, Wanda K. "Assuming Responsibility for Appropriate Classroom Behavior." In Krumboltz, J. D., and Thoresen, C. E. (Eds.). *Behavioral Counseling: Cases and Techniques*. Holt, Rinehart and Winston, 1969.

Dollard, J., and Miller, N. E. *Personality and Psychotherapy*. New York: McGraw-Hill, 1950.

Dulany, D. E. "Hypothesis and Habits in Verbal Operant Conditioning." *Journal of Abnormal and Social Psychology* 63:251–263.

Gahoon, D. D. "A Comparison of the Effectiveness of Verbal Reinforcement Applied in Group and Individual Interviews." *Journal of Counseling Psychology* 12: 121–126.

Garvey, W. P., and Hegrenes, J. R. "Desensitization Techniques in the Treatment of School Phobia." *American Journal of Orthopsychiatry* 147–152.

Greenspoon, J. S. "The Reinforcement Effect of Two Spoken Sounds on the Frequency of Two Responses." *American Journal of Psychology* 68:409–416.

Hansen, J. C.; Niland, T.; and Zani, L. P. "Model Reinforcement in Group Counseling with Elementary School Children." *Personnel and Guidance Journal*, April 1969.

Hosford, Ray E. "Behavioral Counseling—A Contemporary Overview." *The Counseling Psychologist* 1:1–33.

Kagen, J. "The Choice of Models: Conflict and Continuity in Human Behavior." In Lloyd-Jones, Esther, and Weatervalt, Esther M. (Eds.). *Behavioral Science and Guidance: Proposals and Perspectives.* New York: Columbia University, 1963, 63–85.

Kanfer, F. H., and Marston, A. R. "Conditioning of Self-Reinforcement Responses: An Analogue to Self-Confidence Training." *Psychological Reports* 13:63–70.

Keirsey, D. W. "Systematic Exclusion: Eliminating Chronic Classroom Disruptions." In Krumboltz, J. D., and Thoresen, C. E. (Eds.). *Behavioral Counseling: Cases and Techniques.* New York: Holt, Rinehart and Winston, 1969.

Kramer, Howard C. "Effects of Conditioning Several Responses in a Group Setting." *Journal of Counseling Psychology* 15, 1:58–62.

Krasner, L. "Studies of the Conditioning of Verbal Behavior." *Psychology Bulletin* 55:148–170.

Krumboltz, J. D. "Changing the Behavior of Behavior Changers." *Counselor Education and Supervision* 46:6, 222–229.

Krumboltz, J. D. (Ed.). *Revolution in Counseling.* Boston: Houghton-Mifflin, 1966 (b).

Krumboltz, John D. "Behavioral Goals for Counseling." *Journal of Counseling Psychology* (a) 13, 2:153–159.

Krumboltz, J. D. "Counseling for Behavior Change." Paper presented at the American Personnel and Guidance Association Convention, Boston, Massachusetts, April, 1963 (mimeo).

Krumboltz, John D. "Parable of the Good Counselor." *Personnel and Guidance Journal* 43:118–124.

Krumboltz, John D., and Emery, John P. "Standardized vs. Individualized Hierarchies in Desensitization to Reduce Test Anxiety." *Journal of Counseling Psychology* 14:204–209.

Krumboltz, J. D., and Schroeder, W. W. "Promoting Career Exploration through Reinforcement." *Personal and Guidance Journal* 44:19–26.

Krumboltz, J. D., and Thoresen, C. E. *Behavioral Counseling: Cases and Techniques.* New York: Holt, Rinehart and Winston, 1969.

Krumboltz, J. D., and Thoresen, C. E. "The Effect of Behavioral Counseling in Group and Individual Settings on Information-Seeking Behavior. *Journal of Counseling Psychology* 11:324–333.

Krumboltz, John D., and Thoresen, Carl E. "Relationship of Counselor Reinforcement of Selected Responses to External Behavior." *Journal of Counseling Psychology* 14:140–144.

Krumboltz, John D., and Varenhorst, Barbara. "Molders of Pupil Attitudes." *Personnel and Guidance Journal* 44:443–446.

Krumboltz, J. D.; Varenhorst, B.; and Thoresen, C. E. "Non-Verbal Factors in the Effectiveness of Models in Counseling." *Journal of Counseling Psychology* 14:412–418.

Lazarus, A. A. "The Treatment of Chronic Frigidity by Systematic Desensitization." *Journal of Nervous and Mental Disease* 136:272–278.

Lomont, James, and Edwards, James. "The Role of Relaxation in Systematic Desensitization." *Behavior Research and Therapy* 5:11–25.

Lovaas, O.; Freitas, Lorraine; Nelson, Karen; and Whalen, Carol. "The Establishment of Imitation and Its Use for the Development of Complex Behavior in Schizophrenic Children." *Behavior Research and Therapy* 5:171–181.

Marston, A. R. "Response Strength and Self-Reinforcement." *Journal of Experimental Psychology* 68:537–540.

Matarazzo, J. D.; Waitman, M.; Saslow, G.; and Weins, A. N. "Interviewer Influences on Durations of Interviewee Speech." *Journal of Verbal Learning and Verbal Behavior* 1:451–458.

Michael, J., and Meyerson, L. "A Behavioral Approach to Counseling and Guidance. *Harvard Educational Review* 32:382–402.

Migler, B., and Wolpe, J. "Automated Self-Desensitization: A Case Report." *Behavior Research and Therapy* 5(2):133–135.

Miller, N. E., and Dollard, J. *Social Learning and Imitation.* New Haven: Yale University Press, 1941.

Mowrer, O. H. *Learning Theory and the Symbolic Processes.* New York: John Wiley and Sons, 1960.

Mowrer, O. H. "Some Philosophical Problems in Psychological Counseling." *Journal of Counseling Psychology* 4:103–111.

Neuringer, Charles; Myers, Roger A.; and Nordmark, Torberg, Jr. "The Transfer of a Verbally Conditioned Response Class." *Journal of Counseling Psychology* 13:208–213.

Paul, G. L., and Shannon, D. T. "Treatment of Anxiety through Systematic Desensitization in Therapy Groups." *Journal of Abnormal Psychology* 73:119–130.

Pepinsky, H. B., and Pepinsky, Pauline, N. *Counseling: Theory and Practice.* New York: Ronald Press, 1954.

Poser, Ernest. "Training Behavior Therapists." *Behavior Research and Therapy* 5:37–41.

Rotter, J. B. *Clinical Psychology.* Englewood Cliffs, New Jersey: Prentice-Hall, 1964.

Rotter, J. B. "Some Implications of a Social Learning Theory for the Practice of Psychotherapy." Mimeographed paper, 1962.

Ryan, T. A., and Krumboltz, J. D. "Effect of Planned Reinforcement Counseling on Client Decision-Making Behavior." *Journal of Counseling Psychology* 11:315–323.

Scoresby, A. Lynn. "Improving Academic Performance." In Krumboltz, J. D., and Thoresen, C. E. (Eds.). *Behavioral Counseling: Cases and Techniques.* Holt, Rinehart and Winston, 1969, pp. 64–69.

Shier, David A. "Applying Systematic Exclusion to a Case of Bizarre Behavior." In Krumboltz, J. D., and Thoresen, C. E. (Eds.). *Behavioral Counseling: Cases and Techniques.* Holt, Rinehart and Winston, 1969, pp. 114–125.

Singer, R. D. "Verbal Conditioning and Generalization of Pro-Democratic Responses." *Journal of Abnormal Sociology* 63:43–46.

Skinner, B. F. *The Behavior of Organisms.* New York: Appleton-Century-Crofts, 1938.

Thompson, Andrew. "Conditioning of Work Oriented and Work Aversive Statements of Neuropsychiatric Patients." *Journal of Counseling Psychology* 12:115–120.

Thoresen, C. E. "Using Appropriate Models." *American Psychologist* 21:688.

Thoresen, Carl E., and Krumboltz, John D. "Similarity of Social Models and Clients in Behavioral Counseling." *Journal of Counseling Psychology,* 15, 5:393–401.

Thoresen, C. E.; Krumboltz, J. D.; and Varenhorst, B. "Sex of Counselors and Models: Effect of Client Career Exploration." *Journal of Counseling Psychology* 14:503–508.

Thoresen, C. E., and Stewart, N. S. "Counseling in Groups: Using Group Social Models." Paper presented at the American Educational Research Association Convention, February, 1967.

Thoresen, C. E. *An Experimental Comparison of Counseling Techniques for Producing Information-Seeking Behavior.* Unpublished dissertation. Stanford University, 1964.

Vance, Barbara J. "Modifying Hyperactive and Aggressive Behavior." In Krumboltz, J. D., and Thoresen, C. E. (Eds.). *Behavioral Counseling: Cases and Techniques.* Holt, Rinehart and Winston, Inc., 1969, pp. 30–33.

Verplanck, W. S. "The Control of the Content of Conversation: Reinforcement of Statements of Opinion." *Journal of Abnormal Social Psychology* 51:668–676.

Warner, R. W.; Niland, T. N.; and Maynard, P. E. "Model Reinforcement Group Counseling with Elementary School Children." *Elementary School Guidance and Counseling,* 1970.

Warner, Richard W., Jr., and Hansen, James C. "Alienated Youth: The Counselor's Task." *Personnel and Guidance Journal* 48:443–448.

Warner, R. W, Jr. "Alienated Students: Six Months after Receiving Behavioral Group Counseling." *Journal of Counseling Psychology,* Summer, 1971 (In press).

Warner, R. W., Jr, and Hansen, J. C. "Verbal-Reinforcement and Model-Reinforcement Group Counseling with Alienated Students." *Journal of Counseling Psychology* 17:168–172.

Weinstein, F. "Reducing Test Anxiety." In Krumboltz, J. D., and Thoresen, C. E. (Eds.). *Behavioral Counseling: Cases and Techniques.* New York: Holt, Rinehart and Winston, 1969.

Weiss, R. L.; Krasner, L.; and Ullman, L. P. "Responsibility to Verbal Conditioning as a Function of Emotional Atmosphere and Patterning of Reinforcement." *Psychological Report* 6:415–426.

Whittemore, Robert, Jr., and Heimann, Robert. "Modification of Originality Responses." *Journal of Counseling Psychology* 13:213–218.

Wolpe, J. *Psychotherapy by Reciprocal Inhibition.* Stanford: Stanford University Press, 1958.

Wolpe, J. "The Systematic Desensitization Treatment of Neuroses." *Journal of Nervous and Mental Disease* 132:189–203.

Wolpe, J. "The Formation of Negative Habits: A Neurophysiological View." *Psychological Review* 59:290–299.

Wolpe, J. "An Interpretation of the Effects of Combinations of Stimuli Patterns Based on Current Neurophysiology." *Psychological Review* 56:277–283.

Wolpe, J. "Isolation of a Conditioning Procedure as the Crucial Psychotherapeutic Factor: A Case Study. *Journal of Nervous and Mental Diseases* 134(4):316–329.

Wolpe, J. "Learning Theory and 'Abnormal Fixations.' " *Psychological Review* 60:111–116.

Wolpe, J. "Learning Versus Lesions as the Basis of Neurotic Behavior." *American Journal of Psychiatry* 112:923–927.

Wolpe, J. "The Prognosis in Unpsychoanalyzed Recovery from Neurosis." *American Journal of Psychiatry* 118:35–39.

Wolpe, J. "Quantitative Relationships in the Systematic Desensitization of Phobias." *American Journal of Psychiatry* 119(11):1062–1068.

ANNOTATED BIBLIOGRAPHY

Bandura, Albert. *Principles of Behavior Modification.* New York: Holt, Rinehart and Winston, Inc., 1969.

This book is an excellent treatment of the whole field of behavioral counseling. Students interested in a current and in-depth treatment of the area would be hard pressed to find a better source.

"Behavioral Counseling." *The Counseling Psychologist* 1:N4, 1969.

This entire volume of *The Counseling Psychologist* is devoted to behavioral counseling. An excellent and current overview of the field.

Ford, D. H., and Urban, H. B. *Systems of Psychotherapy: A Comparative Study.* New York: John Wiley and Sons, Inc., 1967. Section II of the systems. Chapter 8, "The Reciprocal Inhibition Psychotherapy of Joseph Wolpe," pp. 273–304.

Probably the most thorough and comprehensive presentation of Wolpe's approach, this chapter deals in detail with many of the lesser emphasized aspects as well as the major tenets. Aside from the original sources, this summary is probably the best reference for anyone seeking to learn the theory and therapy of Wolpe since the content draws heavily from many of his research findings and journal articles.

Goodstein, Leonard. "Behavior Theoretical Views of Counseling." In Bufford Stefflre (Ed.). *Theories of Counseling.* New York: McGraw-Hill, 1965, pp. 140–192.

Goodstein provides an overview of current theory, role of fear and anxiety, unconscious processes, methods used to reduce fear and anxiety in counseling, and the counselor as a variable in the process. He uses case illustrations to provide insight into theory.

Holland, J. G., and Skinner, B. F. *The Analysis of Behavior.* New York: McGraw-Hill, Inc., 1961.

Holland and Skinner have applied the principles of reinforcement to the writing of this book on conditioning and behavior. They have programmed the book into various sections; the reader must respond to every sentence before continuing. The workbook contains such topics as the beginnings of conditioning in psychology, the terminology employed, various principles of shaping, and schedules of reinforcement.

Jung, John. *Verbal Learning.* New York: Holt, Rinehart and Winston, Inc., 1968.

Many of the behaviorists' concepts, especially those of Krasner on verbal conditioning, relate directly to concepts included in this book. Jung discusses such topics as experimental approaches to learning, cognitive factors in the learner, transfer of training, long- and short-term memory, and associated learning.

Krumboltz, John D. "Behavioral Counseling: Rationale and Research." *Personnel and Guidance Journal* 44:383–387.

> According to Krumboltz, the rationale for counseling is that people have problems that they cannot solve by themselves. The client requests the ends and the counselor, in turn, supplies the means. By using behavioral techniques, the counselor can improve testing, information seeking, and general behavior.

Krumboltz, John D. "Behavioral Goals for Counseling." *Journal of Counseling Psychology* 13:153–159.

> Krumboltz discusses criteria for three types of behavioral goals: (1) altering maladaptive behavior, (2) learning the decision-making process, (3) preventing problems. The consequence of stating behavioral goals argues against the practice of stating broad categorical goals such as self-acceptance, which cannot be operationally measured.

Patterson, C. H. *Theories of Counseling and Psychotherapy.* New York: Harper and Row, 1966. Part II, "Learning Theory Approaches to Counseling," Chapter 7, "Psychotherapy by Reciprocal Inhibition: Wolpe," pp. 154–179.

> For an introduction into the basic philosophy and concepts, therapy process, and techniques of Wolpe's theory, this chapter provides a good review. The two interviews presented exemplify the implementation of several of his techniques. The summary and evaluation section highlights the strengths and weaknesses of Wolpe's approach.

Truax, Charles. "Some Implications of Behavior Therapy for Psychotherapy." *Journal of Counseling Psychology* 13:160–169.

> Truax attempts to examine a total spectrum of behavior therapy, culling out those elements most effective or useful for all psychotherapists. He concludes that therapists high in empathy, warmth, and genuineness will be more effective. They are potent positive reinforcers and will elicit higher positive affect from the client. Persons low in the same qualities will be aversion-negative reinforcers and will elicit negative affect from the client.

Ullman, L., and Krasner, L. (Eds.). *Research in Behavior Modification.* New York: Holt, Rinehart and Winston, Inc., 1965.

> Ullman and Krasner present studies of the latest research done in the area of behavior modification. Especially useful is Chapter 9 entitled "Verbal Conditioning." In this chapter Krasner presents research studies dealing with verbal learning experiments in the laboratory as well as isolated variables in the counseling setting. Krasner describes the procedures used to control variables in the therapeutic setting in order to isolate specific verbal conditioning effects.

Ulrich, Roger; Stacnik, Thomas; and Mabry, John. *Control of Human Behavior.* Glenview, Illinois: Scott, Foresman and Company, 1966.

> This book contains a collection of research studies in the area of behavior modification as well as discussion of the moral implications involved. In addition to the beginnings of behavioral work, the studies cover work in hospital and clinical settings with psychotics, behavior modification in educational settings, advertising, and viewer responses to television programs.

Wolpe, J. "Behavior Therapy in Complex Neurotic States." *British Journal of Psychiatry* 110 (464) :28–34.

Wolpe contends that the techniques are applicable for both "simple" and "complex" neuroses.

Wolpe, J. "Experimental Neuroses as Learned Behavior. *British Journal of Psychology* 43:243–268.

Wolpe's findings, through study of cats receiving shock during feeding, provide support for his contention that behavioral changes characteristic of experimental neuroses are learned responses.

Wolpe, J. "Need-reduction, Drive-reduction and Reinforcement: A Neurophysiological View." *Psychological Review* 57:19–2.

Wolpe's earlier exposure to Hull and a medical background are exemplified in this article, which contends that learning is not mere reduction of primary needs but reduction of central neural excitation or drive; learning is always preceded by drive-reduction.

Wolpe, J. "The Neurophysiology of Learning and Delayed Reward Learning." *Psychological Review* 59:192–199.

Through his neurophysiological theory of reinforcement, Wolpe argues against secondary reinforcement as a learning process and/or explanation of delayed reward learning.

Wolpe, J. "Phobia Reactions and Behavior Therapy." *Conditioned Reflex* 2(2) :162. (*Psychological Abstracts*, 1963, 2672)

The view that fear response habits associated with complex stimuli may be treated just like the classical phobias is presented in this journal article by Wolpe.

Wolpe, J. "Primary Stimulus Generalization: A Neurophysiological View." *Psychological Review* 59:8–10.

Borrowing heavily from the research of Hull, Pavlov and Hovland, Wolpe contends primary stimulus generalization is attributable to similar stimuli exciting various afferent neurons.

Wolpe, J. "Psychotherapy Based on the Principle of Reciprocal Inhibition." Chapter 13, p. 353–382. In Burton, A. (Ed.). *Case Studies in Counseling and Psychotherapy*. Englewood Cliffs, New Jersey: Prentice-Hall, Inc., 1959.

This chapter provides a capsule summary of the rationale of Wolpe's approach, experimental background, procedure in therapy with the various responses inhibiting the neurotic reaction cited, and the detailed amount of a case. The addendum that follows this paper is very helpful and answers ten questions frequently posed to Wolpe.

Wolpe, J. *Psychotherapy by Reciprocal Inhibition*. Stanford, California: Stanford University Press, 1958.

This is the original, primary, and most relevant reference for understanding Wolpe's psychotherapy. The first part of the book deals with his contention that neuroses are learned and with his neurophysiological view of learning. The second part focuses upon the use of reciprocal inhibition procedures in psychotherapy.

Wolpe, J. "Psychotherapy: The Nonscientific Heritage and the New Science. *Behavior Research and Therapy* 1(1):23–28.

This paper lauds the "scientific orientation" of conditioning therapy methods and disfavors the "speculation premises" of psychoanalysis.

Wolpe, J. "Reciprocal Inhibition as the Main Basis of Psychotherapeutic Effects." *Archives of Neurology and Psychology* 72:205–226. In Greenwald, H. (Ed.). *Active Psychotherapy.* New York: Atherton Press, 1967.

One of the most often quoted and earliest attempts to develop his viewpoint, this article presents some of Wolpe's original research findings. Seven of his deconditioning techniques for neurotic habits are cited through nine illustrative cases.

Wolpe, J. "Theory Construction for Blodgett's Latent Learning." *Psychological Review* 60:340–344.

In this article, Wolpe explains latent learning according to his view of the learning process: "Amount of synapse formation varies with amount of reinforcement-sensitivity upon which the drive-reduction acts."

Wolpe, J., and Lazarus, A. A. *Behavior Therapy Techniques: A Guide to the Treatment of Neuroses.* First Edition, New York: Pergamon Press, 1966.

In this book, many of the techniques utilized in behavior therapy are presented along with case examples. The emphasis is on methodology and treatment. Techniques involved in assertive training, systematic desensitization, sexual responses, thought stopping, group desensitization, and aversive conditioning are discussed by the authors.

Wolpe, J.; Salter, A.; and Reynn, L. J. (Eds.). *The Conditioning Therapies: The Challenge in Psychotherapy.* New York: Holt, Rinehart and Winston, Inc., 1964.

As a result of a "Behavior Therapy Conference," which included leading proponents of the behavioral therapy viewpoint, 11 separate papers are presented dealing with current experimental studies and problems in the field. The group of papers is one of the most current and enlightening collections available in book form.

Wolpe, J., and Rachman, S. "Psychoanalytic 'Evidence': A Critique Based on Freud's Case of Little Hans." *Journal of Nervous and Mental Diseases* 131:135–148.

This article vehemently opposes Freud's analytic case presentation of Little Hans.

5

Toward a Theory of Counseling: Where Are We Now?

The three preceding chapters have been devoted to examining three basic theoretical approaches to counseling. While acknowledging that there are many variations within these three rather broad categories, it is our contention that the approaches discussed form the basis from which many individual theories of counseling have been developed. It is this very diversity that causes many in the field a great deal of concern about the future of counseling. Some writers feel that the profession of counseling is doomed because of the many differences within our own ranks, while others view the situation as a healthy climate in which new ideas and assumptions can be tested. As is usual in this type of situation, the better answer lies somewhere between these two extremes; for despite the many different theoretical approaches to counseling, there are many similarities. The purpose of this chapter is to examine the areas of agreement and disagreement between the three most divergent views of counseling presented in the preceding chapters; ego-counseling, self-theory, and learning theory. In order to facilitate this comparison, the chapter will be divided into the same format that was followed in the preceding three chapters. Within each section we will examine the similarities and differences among the three approaches.

139

NATURE OF MAN

One of the most difficult questions that must be addressed by every approach to counseling concerns the nature of man. One must decide what is man's place in this world before one can hope to be able to help him. Yet, man is the most complex organism known. Hence, the question about his nature is not an easy one to answer and this very difficulty is reflected in the diversity of answers to the question.

In the ego-counseling view man is a reactive being. He reacts to his own innate drives and needs. Those drives and needs are developed and profoundly influenced by his early childhood experiences and frustrations. In this view, man's nature is largely determined during the first five years of his existence. During these five years the child has many emotional experiences related to his sexual growth, and these experiences form the basis for his later behavior. Man's behavior is not under his own control, but is under the control of unconscious determiners. These determiners of behavior are largely concerned with gratifying the basic biological needs. In short, all of man's behavior is determined, and if we knew enough about the unconscious part of the mind, we could predict all of his behavior.

The learning theorists take a similar approach to the ego-counseling theorists in relation to the nature of man. They also view man as a reactive being. In the learning-theory view, man does not react to his own innate drives, rather he reacts to the world around him. In this view, man is a biological being who reacts to the stimuli in his environment. As with the ego-analysts the learning theorists believe that man's behavior is determined, but it is determined by the environment in which he exists. Hence, man does not control his own destiny but is controlled by forces outside of himself. Man's adult behavior is a direct result of his early childhood environment, for in this environment he learns patterns of behavior in reaction to the environment. These learned patterns determine his later reactions to the stimuli in his adult environment.

Contrasting with the positions of the ego-counselors and the learning theorists is the position taken by the self-theorists. In their view, man is a being in the process of becoming, a being that is basically good and with the potential for controlling his own behavior. In this view, man's behavior is not determined by forces outside of his own control but is controlled by the individual through a conscious and thoughtful process. In effect, man is not an irrational, controlled individual, but a rational being who, to a large extent, determines his own destiny.

It should be noted that while the self-theorists maintain that their position toward man is non-deterministic, there is an element of determinism inherent in their theory. If man has a natural, innate characteristic of moving toward self-actualization, his behavior is then determined by this goal. Further, the self-theorists, following the lead of Snygg and Combs, believe that the phenomenal field of the individual largely determines the individual's behavior. Both of these beliefs are somewhat deterministic in nature. However, the self-theorists' answer to these deterministic tendencies in their theory would revolve around the individual's interaction with these concepts. While they agree that self-actualization is a general goal that everyone moves toward, the general goal does not determine specific behavior because self-actualization is different for every individual. Likewise, they would contend that it is the individual's perception of the phenomenal field that determines behavior, not the field itself. Nonetheless, as the reader goes through the rest of this chapter, he should be aware that there is more determinism in the self-theory position than the self-theorists might care to admit.

At this point it would seem that the three approaches to counseling have little in common relating to their conception of the nature of man. Certainly, the learning-theory approach and the ego-counseling approach are somewhat similar in that they both view man's behavior as being determined and outside of his own control; while the self-theorists, despite what has been previously pointed out, maintain that man is free. There is, however, an implied commonality about the nature of man among all three approaches. This commonality is implied by the fact that there exist these three approaches to counseling. The notion of counseling is to help people bring about changes in their behavior. Hence, all three approaches acknowledge that man's behavior has the capacity to change. Related to this common assumption is the common belief that certain events in an individual's life can cause him difficulty, and these difficulties are serious enough to need some kind of change. So, while at first examination it would seem that the three approaches have little in common, they do share the belief that an individual is sometimes in situations that cause him to need help, and that help can be offered to the individual with the expectation that a change in the situation will occur.

DEVELOPMENT OF PERSONALITY

The ego-counseling approach to the development of personality is based largely on the work of Freud. In this view, man's personality is seen as an outgrowth of the constant struggle within the individual between the id, ego, and superego. Man is thus seen as always being in a state of conflict. It is a dynamic conception of personality. The unconscious feelings of the individual are constantly striving to reach consciousness, and the individual expends energy to keep these thoughts in the unconscious. Therefore, man is in a constant state of internal conflict of which he is unaware.

While not all who call themselves ego-counselors agree, many of the ego-counseling theorists see the personality of the individual as being composed of the id, ego, and superego. The id represents that part of the individual that strives to bring satisfaction to the organism. The superego represents that which is ideal within the individual. It is really composed of those things the individual believes he could not do and those things that the individual would like to be. In the ego-counseling view, the ego, or the executor, is the most important part of the personality. It is the ego that mediates between the drives of the id and the outside world. It is the interaction of these three component parts of the personality (id, ego, superego) that determines the personality of the individual.

The development of the personality occurs as the individual moves through a natural growth pattern and learns to overcome the tension and anxiety resulting from his conflicts, frustrations, and threats. Through this process the individual develops mechanisms designed to rechannel the original impulses from the id into more accessible and acceptable sources or objects. This development occurs in an orderly fashion and is related to the body areas from which the individual derives pleasure. Unlike the Freudian position, the ego-analysts believe that man also reacts to and is affected by situational events. Hence, they place importance on the healthy development of the ego and its functions. It is the ego that must learn to mediate between the internal needs and the situational events. The manner in which the ego learns to cope with both the internal and external demands is of central importance to the individual's personality.

As in the Freudian position, the ego-analysts place a great deal of importance on the early childhood. It is during this period that the ego learns how to mediate between the different demands. Most of this learning takes place through interaction with the significant others in the child's environment. The manner in which the ego learns to deal with the various demands in childhood largely determines how the ego will operate in adult life. From this position man then has the potential for learning how to deal with life in a defensive fashion, as in the classical Freudian view, or for learning how to deal with life in a positive coping manner.

In short, the ego-analysts tend to see man's personality development in a more positive light than do the classical Freudians. The personality is made up of many patterns of behavior, which are interrelated. Some of these patterns are developed in response to inante drives. However, as the individual matures, more and more behavior patterns are developed because of conscious thought by the ego as it reacts to various environmental situations. The important point is that, regardless of the generating point of the pattern of behavior, that pattern generates in reaction to something.

As was the case with the various conceptions of the nature of man, the learning-theory approach to personality development is somewhat similar to the ego-analytic position; that is, personality is formed in reaction to something. In the case of the learning theories, personality is formed as man reacts to the stimuli he finds in his environment. From this perspective all behavior, hence personality, is learned. Like the other approaches to counseling, learning theory recognizes the importance of early childhood experiences in the development of personality. As the child is exposed to various environmental reinforcements, some behaviors are strengthened or learned while others are weakened or extinguished. In effect, it is the laws of learning that determine how the personality develops. The learning may take place through direct reinforcement or by vicarious reinforcement or imitation. Nevertheless, this learning leads to the formation of generalizations and discriminations by the individual and the gradual shaping of simple responses into complex behavior. Through the use of language, the individual develops the ability to make mediating responses that allow him to plan his responses to various stimuli or to withhold an immediate response to a particular stimulus.

In essence, then, the personality of the individual is largely determined by the environment in which the individual develops. In the ego-analytic view, personality was formed in a reaction to both innate and external demands, while in the learning-theory view, personality also develops in reaction, but it is reaction only to the stimuli found in the environment. The individual learns through experience that certain situations will present certain satisfactions to him while others will not. Thus, the individual develops different patterns of needs, which lead to different patterns of behavior.

As do the ego-analytic and learning-theory approaches, the self-theory approach places a great deal of importance on the environment of the individual in the development of personality. Unlike the other two approaches, however, the self-theory approach views man not as a reactor to this environment, but as a being that takes an active role in his own behavior based upon his perceptions of the environment. The individual is seen in a wholistic fashion. He is basically good and, given the proper conditions for development, he will be responsible for his own actions. Personality development is seen as always being in an emerging process. It is a product of a continuing interaction between the individual and his perceived environment, and is always moving toward the ultimate goal of self-actualization.

As the individual interacts with his perceived reality, a conception of self begins to develop. As this self-concept develops, and as the individual becomes aware of others' reactions and begins to respond to those behaviors that will gain satisfying responses from the significant others, the individual will develop a healthy personality. In this state the individual is able to evaluate each of his experiences in an honest fashion and behave accordingly. Thus, the individual's behavior is not predetermined, but is based on an active conscious evaluation of present experiences. From this perspective, behavior and personality are in a continuing process of change, a change toward self-actualization.

As one examines these three conceptions of the nature of personality and its development, it is clear that they agree on the importance of early childhood experiences. All three emphasize the impact of these experiences on the adult personality. While the ego-analytic and learning-theory position both believe that man is a reactor, they differ somewhat on what he reacts to. In the ego-analytic view, man reacts both to his innate drives and to his environment while, in the learning-theory view, man basically reacts to the stimuli in the environment. In either case, man is not believed to have a great deal of conscious control over his own behavior.

At the other extreme is the self-theory position, which attributes all of man's behavior to his own thoughtful control. Man is viewed as being able to evaluate his own experiences and then act accordingly. In the self-theory view, we find the rather optimistic notion that man acts on his environment and is in control of his own personality development. In the other two approaches we find a rather pessimistic view that man reacts to stimuli, innate or external, and his personality development is largely outside of his own conscious control. Regardless of this central difference, it is clear that all three approaches agree on the importance of the environment in the shaping of personality. The differences among the three approaches center on how they view the interaction between the individual and the environment.

MALADJUSTMENT DEVELOPMENT

All three approaches to counseling acknowledge that during early childhood the individual can have experiences that lead to maladjustment or maladaptive behavior later in life. The ego-analysts view this type of behavior as generating from a breakdown in the functioning of the ego; that is, in some manner the ego functions were not able to cope with certain situations in a meaningful and positive fashion and so suppressed the experiences into the unconscious. They may arise later and cause the individual difficulty because he never learned to deal with them in the first place. Somewhat similarly, the self-theorists see the maladaptive behavior as resulting from uncomfortable situations, the memory of which is pushed into the unconscious. In their view, the individual either distorts the original experience or denies its existence because it does not fit with his introjected conditions of worth. Hence, both of these approaches to counseling view the maladaptive behavior as stemming from experiences that have been denied awareness which, in turn, prohibit the individual from learning how to cope with them in a positive fashion. From this perspective, then, the maladaptive behavior is only a symptom of some underlying cause.

Quite different from this approach is the learning-theory position, which concerns itself almost exclusively with the maladaptive behavior. From this perspective maladaptive behavior is acquired in the same manner as is normal behavior. The inappropriate behavior is learned because it has been rewarded at various points in time. The learning theorist is not concerned with underlying causes, but is concerned only about the maladaptive behavior. It differs from normal behavior not in the manner in which it has been developed but only to the degree that it is atypical or maladaptive to the observer. Hence, behavior is not caused by hidden motives or drives, but occurs because it brings some satisfaction to the individual. As we shall see, differences in opinion as to the nature of maladaptive behavior will be reflected in the various approaches to the counseling process.

THE COUNSELING RELATIONSHIP

Basic to an understanding of the counseling relationship is an understanding of the goals of counseling. In the cases of both the ego-analysts and the self-theorists these goals tend to be stated in global fashion and deal with the underlying causes of the maladaptive behavior. On the other hand, the learning theorists maintain that the goals of counseling must be stated in very specific terms and must be stated in terms of removing a particular maladaptive behavior. The first two approaches tend to view the goals of counseling as being the same for everyone, while the latter approach requires that different goals be established for each individual.

Somewhat unlike the traditional Freudian approach to counseling, the ego-analytic counseling relationship is reality oriented. The ego-counselor is concerned with understanding the whole network of the individual's behavior, but he is more concerned about present behavior as opposed to past behavior. He is concerned primarily with helping the individual to understand why some of his ego functions are not operating and then helping him to restore those ego functions to full operating capacity. The chief goal then is to re-establish the ego as the executor of the personality; to, in effect, rebuild the ego in the areas where it was in need of repair. From this perspective it is the counselor who controls the relationship and defines the areas in which the ego is in need of strengthening. In effect, the counselor diagnoses the difficulty and then prescribes the appropriate treatment.

The basic goal of the self-theorist is to establish the proper conditions for growth in the counseling relationship. Given this situation, the counselee will be able to gain insight into himself and will then be able to take positive steps toward the solution of his difficulties. The emphasis here is on helping the client gain insight into his difficulties, assuming that this insight will lead to changes in his behavior. The goal of counseling is global and is the same for everyone; establish the conditions for counseling. This is quite different from dealing with specific ego-function breakdowns, or specific maladaptive behaviors.

The learning theorist views the counseling relationship as differing little from other learning environments. The goal of counseling is to help the individual learn more adaptive behavior. The concern is not with the underlying causes of the behavior, but only with the specific, observable behavior that is causing the individual difficulty. Of the three approaches, this is by far the most action-oriented approach, the former two being concerned more about gaining insight into the causes of behavior. The learning theorists believe that both the counselor and counselee must define what are to be the goals of counseling for this particular client. Once these goals have been established, it is the counselor who dictates the appropriate treatment.

It is certainly obvious at this point the one thing that all three approaches have in common in relation to the goals of counseling is that counseling is designed to facilitate changes in behavior. The self-theorist sees this goal from a wholistic approach, the ego-analyst sees it in terms of particular ego functions, and the learning theorist sees it in terms of specific behaviors. The goals move from very global to very specific. The question then must be, "How do these different goals affect the way in which the counseling relationship is handled?" As one might suspect, there are striking differences, but there are also striking similarities.

The most striking similarity among the three approaches to the counseling relationship is the shared feeling about the necessity for a good relationship. All three stress the need for the counselee to feel accepted and understood in the relationship. The counselee must feel that the counselor is concerned and is able to help him. Also involved is what is usually referred to as therapist genuineness or honesty with the client. In effect, the counselor must come across to the client as a real person, one who is deserving of his trust.

A second common element to all three approaches is the notion that the counseling process will lead to some change on the part of the client, and that this change can be aided through the use of the counseling interview. It is true that some of the learning theorists stress the need for manipulation of the client's outside environment, but they also place a great deal of importance on the counseling interview. In terms of the amount of change expected through the use of counseling, there are differences in degree, but not in expectation. Some theorists are expectant of a complete change in personality while others expect changes only in particular areas. We should hasten to add that most theorists take the latter position.

It would seem then that most approaches agree on the need of an appropriate counseling relationship. This relationship is built on the assumptions that counseling can lead to behavioral change, that this change is facilitated through the interview process, that the relationship must be based on mutual trust and understanding between the counselor and the client, and that both members of the relationship must have confidence in the ability of that relationship to bring about changes in the client.

Central to the differences among the three approaches is the role of the counselor in the counseling process. Both the ego-analytic and learning-theory positions hold that the counselor is some kind of expert to whom the client has come with a problem that he cannot resolve by himself. This assumption leads both schools to the belief that the counselor must take a somewhat active role in the counseling relationship. The ego-analysts see the counselor as controlling the relationship, balancing it between the affective and cognitive domains. Further, they see the counselor as being responsible for making a diagnosis of the problem and then presenting to the client what he must do to resolve his situation. Likewise, the learning theorist sees the counselor as prescribing the method of treatment once a diagnosis of the difficulty has been determined. We should point out that this is not done in a cold mechanistic fashion, because both approaches emphasize the need for the client to feel confidence in and respect by the counselor. Further, they both agree that the client must agree with the diagnosis before any particular treatment will be effective. Nevertheless, both approaches tend to see the counselor as the controlling agent of the relationship. Their model of the relationship is quite similar to the medical model.

A quite different view of the relationship is held by the self-theorists. They argue that because of man's inherent growth tendency, the client has the capacity and motivation to solve his own problem if provided with a nonthreatening atmosphere. Thus, the self-theorists have strongly emphasized that the counselor's presence or behavior in the counseling relationship does not directly influence the client's behavior. In their view, then, there is no need for diagnosis on the part of the counselor and, in fact, it is held that diagnosis is detrimental to the process of counseling. In their view, diagnosis places the locus of evaluation on the counselor when it should be on the client. Further, it creates dependency needs in the client when he should be helped to develop his own self-strength. The self-theorists believe that if the counselor controls the relationship and sets the goals for the client, he is interfering with the basic nature of man. From this perspective, then, the counselor's role is to simply provide the conditions so that the client may reinstitute his self-actualizing tendency. The counselor is active only to the extent that he controls the conditions, not what the client does.

The three approaches also hold different views in relation to the cognitive vs. affective dimension. The more cognitive or rational position is held by the learning theorists. They emphasize the need to pay attention to the particular behavior in question. They are concerned with the observable behavior of the client that is in need of change, not with the affective or conative emotions that may or may not be causing the behavior. In their view, these cannot be dealt with because they cannot be seen, but the behavior can be seen and therefore be dealt with. In effect, one can characterize the counseling relationship from this perspective as being one that emphasizes a rational learning experience.

We can place the ego-analysts in the center of this affective-cognitive dimension. The counselor, through the use of selective attention to the counselee, attempts to keep a balance between the cognitive and affective dimensions of the relationship. In the ego-analysts' view, both dimensions are important to the process of counseling, as the client first needs to gain insight into himself. Find the underlying emotion that is causing the difficulty; then, through a rational thought process, the client plans with the counselor means by which he may correct his weak ego functions.

The self-theorists place the greatest emphasis on the affective dimensions of the counseling relationship. In their view the counseling relationship is designed to elicit from the client those feelings about himself which, to that point in time, he had denied to his awareness. It is assumed that once these feelings have been expressed in the threat-free atmosphere of the counseling relationship, the client will gain self-insight and this insight will lead to behavioral change. The emphasis here is almost exclusively on the affective expressions of the client, for it is those expressions that are most important, not the real world.

It is obvious at this point that the counseling relationship is viewed quite differently by the ego-analysts, the learning theorists, and the self-theorists. We can move from the very cognitive, action-oriented learning theory approach, through the somewhat balanced ego-analytic approach, to the affective, insight-oriented self-theorists. The self-theorists believe that insight, by itself, will lead the client to change, while the ego-analysts contend that the counselor must in effect prescribe the necessary changes for the client. On the other hand, the learning-theory approach is exclusively action oriented. To the learning theorists the symptom is not an indication of some hidden difficulty, but is the problem that needs to be handled. It is also clear that, as one moves from an insight-oriented approach to an action approach, the degree to which the counselor assumes responsibility for the outcome of counseling is affected. The counselor is not only more active in the actual counseling relationship, but he may also take an active role in the outside life of the client.

Having examined these differences and similarities in the views of the counseling relationship, we need to examine how these differences are translated into the actual techniques used in counseling.

TECHNIQUES OF COUNSELING

An examination of the techniques stressed by the three approaches indicates that the learning theorists tend to place the most emphasis on the actual techniques of counseling. The self-theory position places almost no emphasis on techniques, unless we consider the ability of the counselor to establish minimal psychological contact with the individual while conveying his genuineness, his unconditioned positive regard for the client, and his emphatic understanding of the client. No other techniques are needed.

The ego-analytic position places its emphasis on the ability of the counselor to control the dimensions of the relationship. This is largely accomplished by controlling the amount of ambiguity offered to the client, and through the use of partial interpretations. In this manner the counselor provides the structure necessary for the client to express his feelings and then be led to an understanding of his difficulty through the partial interpretations of the counselor. In effect, the counselor, having made his diagnosis, leads the client down the road to self-awareness through the use of interpretation.

The techniques of counseling as proposed by the various branches within the learning-theory position follow the laws of learning. The learning theorists' view of counseling as simply a type of learning experience leads them to a reliance on the same laws of learning that apply in everyday life. Hence, they place a great deal of reliance on the laws of reinforcement, shaping, imitative learning, and cognitive learning. It is the counselor who decides which principles of learning will be most effective with a particular client and then applies those laws to the counseling process. In the learning-theory approach it is the technique that is important, in the ego-analytic position it is the control of the relationship that is important, and in the self-theory position it is the relationship itself that is of crucial importance.

While each of the approaches to counseling has different views of the techniques required, they do have in common one essential technique. All three require that some form of verbalization take place between the client and the counselor. If this kind of exchange does not take place, then the process of counseling does not take place. One of the constant criticisms of counseling is that it is basically designed, regardless of the theory being used, for those who can verbalize. In point of fact this criticism may be valid and more attention should be paid to how counselors can operate with those potential clients whose possession of verbal skills is somewhat limited.

This examination of the similarities and differences among the ego-analytic, learning-theory, and self-theory positions has shown that there are a great many similarities as well as differences. The differences appear to generate from different conceptions of man and how the events around him influence his life. In some cases these differences are the result of different perceptions about similar events, and in some cases they are generated from a simple difference in semantics. While these differences may, in some cases, be extremely important, they are often blown out of proportion. That is, often they are not so great or, indeed, so important that some type of rapprochement between the various approaches to counseling cannot be made. To that end, it may be appropriate to examine some research that has studied and compared different theoretical approaches to counseling.

RESEARCH

As has been demonstrated, there are differences between various theoretical approaches to counseling. Some of these differences have been demonstrated in the research literature. Sundland and Barker (1962), using a Therapist Orientation Scale, studied 139 psychotherapists. The questionnaire contained some 16 subscales and in nine of the scales there were significant differences between the therapists classified as Freudians, Sullivanians, and

Rogerians. It should be pointed out that, in the development of the Therapist Orientation Scale, items upon which therapists agreed were discarded. Further, when these same therapists were grouped by level of experience, differences were found on only one scale.

Wallach and Strupp (1964) examined the differences between four different classifications of therapists: Freudians, General Psychoanalytic, Sullivanian, and Client-Centered. Using a scale of Usual Therapeutic Practices, they found that the four groups could be differentiated on the amount of personal distance maintained in the counseling relationship.

McNair and Lorr (1964), using a scale based on the Therapist Orientation Scale, studied 265 therapists. As with the previous studies cited, they found differences between the therapists on three separate dimensions.

While these studies indicate that there are differences in counseling practice, one must remember that these researchers were looking for differences. Perhaps an even more important question concerns the outcome of counseling. Did it make any difference in the outcome when different approaches were used? To a large extent this question has not yet been answered by the research. Hence, we really do not know whether the differences that were found have any significant meaning.

Just as there is evidence of differences between various theories, there is a growing body of evidence that there are many similarities. Fiedler's classic studies (1950a, 1950b, 1951) demonstrated that there is little difference between various approaches to counseling. Much of the evidence on this side of the ledger demonstrated some rapprochement between the self-theory and the behavioral or learning-theory positions. Sapolsky (1960) found that the effectiveness of reinforcement techniques was related to the success of the relationship. Ullman and Krasner (1965) also emphasize the importance of the relationship regardless of the theoretical approach of the counselor.

In one of the most recent investigations of how theory affects proactive children, Truax (1966) analyzed a single, long-term successful case handled by Carl Rogers. Truax concluded that the data from this case indicated Rogers was quite successful in using the techniques of reinforcement. This investigation is important because it is an indication that perhaps the positions of the self-theorists and the learning theorists are really not far apart, at least in actual practice.

In a further study, Truax (1968) found that when three of the necessary conditions for counseling promulgated by the self-theorists, accurate empathy, non-possessive warmth, and genuineness, were used as reinforcers, clients increased the amount of self-exploration. As does the previous study, this investigation indicates that the actual practice of counseling may have elements of both learning theory and self-theory.

In an investigation by Anderson, Douds, and Carkhuff (1967), there was a further indication that while theories may be different, practices at the very least are overlapping. In examining 40 counseling interviews, they found that those counselors who were operating at a high level of functioning, offering high levels of the necessary conditions for counseling, were more effective in the use of confrontations with their clients. The technique of confrontation is one that is more typically associated with the action approaches to counseling; i.e., learning theory or ego counseling; yet it was found to be an effective technique when used from a self-theory orientation.

Just as we saw that some research evidence supports the notion of differences between theories, it is also possible to find research supporting the similarities between the various theoretical approaches. As before, we still have very few answers as to whether any of these differences or similarities do make a real difference in the outcome of counseling.

SUMMARY

At this point one may wonder whether there is any possibility that the day will come when there is a theory of counseling. While it is still far too early to answer this question, we may speculate that there is some hope. Rogers (1961), in writing about the many differences within counseling, stated that the differences "seem irreconcilable because we have not yet developed the larger frame of reference . . ." In a similar vein, Allport (1961) wrote, "The trouble with our current theories of learning is not so much that they are wrong, but that they are partial." In effect, both of these men are saying that we need to further develop the theories that we now have and, as this development occurs, we may see a rapprochement between the various theories. Certainly there is already some indication that there is basic agreement on some crucial issues.

There is little question that most approaches to counseling recognize the importance of the client-counselor relationship. While some argue that it is sufficient by itself, all agree that it is necessary. It is also clear that all approaches to counseling recognize that difficulties do arise in a person's life, and these difficulties can be overcome through the process of counseling. With these basic agreements, perhaps the differences that exist are not insurmountable.

It is perhaps appropriate here to restate what was said in the first chapter of this book. A theory is only a set of assumptions in the process of testing. It is not something that is final and stagnant, but should always be changing.

As stated in Chapter 1, it is most important for each counselor to strive to develop a theory for himself; a theory that is based on certain assumptions, but that is also open to revision. The logical place to begin this process is by studying the present theories in the field and the research related to them. Once this has been accomplished, the counselor is ready to try these theories in his own practice and research, and also to develop his own theory out of his experiences. Crucial to this process is the development by the counselor of an understanding of himself. He must know himself as a person if he ever hopes to successfully develop his own mode of counseling. Having discussed the various theoretical contributions to the field of counseling, then, it is now appropriate to turn to an examination of the importance of understanding the counselor as a person.

REFERENCES

Allport, A. W. "Psychological Models for Guidance." *Harvard Educational Review* 32:373–381.

Anderson, Susan; Douds, John; and Carkhuff, Robert B. "The Effects of Confrontation by High and Low Functioning Therapists." *Unpublished Research*, University of Massachusetts, 1967.

Fiedler, F. "The Concept of an Ideal Therapeutic Relationship." *Journal of Consulting Psychology* 14:235–245.

Fiedler, F. "A Comparison of Therapeutic Relationships in Psychoanalytic, Non-Directive and Adlerian Therapy." *Journal of Consulting Psychology* 14:436–445.

Fiedler, F. "Factor Analysis of Psychoanalytic, Non-Directive, and Adlerian Therapeutic Relationships." *Journal of Consulting Psychology* 15:32–38.

McNair, D. M., and Lorr, M. "An Analysis of Professed Psychotherapeutic Techniques." *Journal of Consulting Psychology* 28:265–271.

Rogers, C. R. "Divergent Trends." In R. May (Ed.). *Existential Psychology.* New York, Random House, 1961.

Sapolsky, A. "Effect of Interpersonal Relationships on Conditioning." *Journal of Abnormal and Social Psychology* 60:241–246.

Sundland, D. M., and Barker, E. N. "The Orientation of Psychotherapists." *Journal of Consulting Psychology* 26:201–212.

Truax, C. B. "Reinforcement and Non-Reinforcement in Rogerian Psychotherapy." *Journal of Abnormal Psychology* 71:1–9.

Truax, C. B. "Therapist Interpersonal Reinforcement of Client Self-Exploration and Therapeutic Outcome in Group Psychotherapy." *Journal of Counseling Psychology* 15:225–231.

Ullman, L. P., and L. Krasner. *Case Studies in Behavior Modification.* New York: Holt, Rinehart and Winston, 1964.

Wallach, M. S., and Strupp, H. H. "Dimensions of Psychotherapists' Activities." *Journal of Consulting Psychology* 28:120–125.

6

The Counselor
as a Person

It would be naive to presume that the counselor as a person would not be an integral part of the counseling process. Surely, personalities have an effect in any interpersonal relationship; teacher-student, doctor-patient, salesman-customer, as well as counselor-client. The outcome of a relationship may depend more upon the personalities involved than on the technical competence. Wouldn't you rather buy a car from a "nice guy" than from one you dislike even though he is a skilled salesman? Doesn't a student respond more favorably to a teacher whose personality is agreeable to him? A few years ago a student counselor drew an example of personality interaction from literature. Would the crew of the Pequod have been destroyed except for the demonic, warped personality of Captain Ahab? He certainly was a competent seaman, well versed in technical knowledge, but his personality was so twisted, yet powerful, that he overcame the members of his crew and led them to destruction. Although the counselor's personality will not have such drastic effects, it may influence the outcome of the counseling process.

ROLE OF THE COUNSELOR AS A PERSON

There was a time when the counselor as a person was to be withheld from the therapeutic relationship. Early forms of psychoanalytic and client-centered theories emphasized the role of specific conditions of therapy and specific actions of the counselor as a therapeutic agent. In fact, the early technical specifications of a blank screen argued for minimizing the counselor as a real person. The client-centered approach began by emphasizing the freedom that characterized the counselor's relationship and permissiveness with the client. Departures from this approach were seen as personal intrusions into the counseling. Most learning-theory or behavioral approaches to counseling did not focus on the counselor as a person but on the techniques he used. However, recent literature has stressed a personal relationship, which calls attention to the counselor as much as, or more than, his technical skills. When talking about the personality of the counselor, do we go beyond specifying how counselors must act to be effective in a change process? Are these actions a reflection of some enduring characteristics of the counselor that does not depend upon his education? If such is the case, to what extent do we remove from counseling the prominence of theory and concepts regarding the process of action?

If the counselor's personality is of paramount importance, we should explore the following pertinent questions. Is there a relationship between counselor personality and choice of theoretical orientation? Are there some personality characteristics or patterns that are therapeutic and can be differentiated from technical skill? Do some personality characteristics influence counselor effectiveness? Do client personality differences influence counselor behavior?

THEORETICAL ORIENTATION AND THE COUNSELOR AS A PERSON

One must question whether the choice of a particular theoretical orientation is conditioned by factors in the personality makeup of the counselor. Theory is an inescapable part of the counselor's professional behavior. Classification and determination about what is germane are integral parts of the counseling process. Theory may be explicit in detail or implicit in formulations based upon experiences that are important factors in the selection of an explicit theory. This is evidenced by the wide variety of theoretical applications that cannot be explained by internal consistency and comprehensibility. "It seems essential to recognize that a theory is a tool of discovery, chosen partially because of the utility it has had and our discovery of ourselves and the ordering of events and experiences of which our own lives are made" (Shoben, 1962). The contributions of theory to counseling are making articulate a set of ideas that the counselor can discover or are providing a structure to create necessary order out of the confusion of the counseling process. In general, systematic ideas may be regarded to a significant degree as a part of the counselor as a person. It is essential for the counselor to have a thorough knowledge of himself and his theoretical frame of reference (Shoben, 1962). Shoben believes that the counselor's adaptation to any particular theory is a reflection of his own personality traits.

Strupp (1962) has made the most extensive study of the reactions of counselors representing different orientations, professional training, and level of experience. However, his studies do not include personality characteristics of the counselor. There is good reason to believe that the theoretical orientation does influence how a counselor thinks about counseling, and also how he views his clients. In an early study comparing client-centered and psychoanalytic counselors, Strupp (1958) found client-centered counselors more optimistic, more reluctant to attach diagnostic labels, more likely to give differentiated descriptions of defense mechanisms, and more able to state specific counseling goals. In comparing their reactions in a simulated counseling situation, he found that client-centered counselors use reflection as a primary response mode, while psychoanalytically oriented counselors generally answered direct questions, used exploratory questions, and responded in a mode involving greater interest and initiative.

There have been few studies bearing directly on whether there are personality correlates of a preference in response and no research directly on the question of the relationship between theoretical orientation and personality. Bohn (1965) studied the relationship between dominance as a personality characteristic and directedness as a characteristic of counseling behavior and obtained negative results. Cannon (1964), using the Omnibus Personality Inventory, found that the higher the regression-suppression score and the lower the schizoid functioning score, the greater likelihood that the counselor would express positive effect toward the client.

The Fiedler (1950) investigations found that better-trained counselors of varying theoretical orientations agreed more with each other in their concept of the ideal therapeutic relationship than they agreed with less well-trained counselors within their own orientation. He also found that the therapeutic relationship provided by experts of one orientation resembled more closely the relationship offered by experts of other orientations than it resembled the relationships created by neophytes in the same orientation. However, Sundland and Barker (1962) made an analysis of the relationship between experience and therapy attitude and found, contrary to Fiedler, that experienced therapists are more similar to inexperienced therapists of their own orientation than they are to other experienced therapists.

Anthony (1967) continued earlier studies by Fiedler (1950) and by Sundland and Barker (1962). The two former studies used different counselor subjects at the experienced and inexperienced levels. This study made a longitudinal analysis of the shifts in the therapeutic approach as the therapist became more experienced and asked, does experience bring therapists of originally dissimilar orientation more closely together in their goals? Their results showed that all original groups became more interpretative and thought more about how their clients were relating to them. They became more personal with clients and viewed therapy as less of a conceptual and more of a non-conceptual process. They assigned more importance to the client's understanding of himself and, in general, formulated the most specific goals for therapy. They also reported that the unconscious processes uniformly became a subject of less importance and, for all, despite four years increase in experience, they reported a feeling of increased insecurity in the psychotherapeutic setting. One can conclude that experience does bring therapists of an originally dissimilar orientation more closely together.

On the basis of his study, Wrenn (1960) postulated that theoretical orientation in the counselor is of little influence in determining the manner in which experienced counselors respond, even though special counseling situations were used that should have maximized the effect of theory differences. Glasgow and Bergman (1962) wondered whether clinically trained raters might view as more warm and accepting those responses that seemed better in the light of their own theoretical orientation to therapy. The findings were negative and indicated that good agreement could be obtained in ratings on the warm-accepting–cold-rejecting dimension and that there was no appreciable influence due to the theoretical orientation of the raters.

Williamson (1962) has described the counselor as a technique, indicating that the counselor's philosophy of human development should show through his behavior and that his efforts at relating effectively with the client must come from his acceptance of himself as he is. The person is a technique not only in what he does or says but in how he conducts himself in the manner of his unverbalized communication. Even the counselor's style of living is an important and effective technique of counseling, since desirable characteristics of the counselor as a human being exist that may be closely related with the effectiveness of counseling.

Lister talks about the counselor's personal theory. He maintains that the beginning counselor has already spent a number of years formulating, testing and modifying hypotheses about himself and others. He believes that the counselor thereby has his own personal theory and suggests that this personal theory refers to the hypothesis he has come to view as a reliable guide to personally effective and satisfying human relations. "Although many such hypotheses are largely implicit and articulate, they nevertheless constitute patterns for counseling behavior even before the students are introduced to formal courses in counseling or personality theory" (Lister, 1964).

The formal theory chosen by a counselor is probably related to his own personal theory. As Shoben (1962) has suggested, to the extent that one's choice of theory depends on something other than the internal consistency of a system of ideas, its comprehensiveness, or the degree to which it is clearly buttressed by evidence that meets the criteria of scientific validity, it seems at least possible that mere personal and temperamental factors may be determinative. The choice of a theory may be "partially a function of the extent to which such ideas validate one's inarticulate and implicit impressions of how behavioral events can be ordered and understood" (Shoben, 1962).

Such unions of personal and textbook theories would provide an explanation for those who feel comfortable using the client-centered, learning-theory, or any other systematic counseling approach. The ease with which this occurs would seem to depend upon the access of the formal theory that articulates one's personal theory and the freedom to adapt and implement that theory. A counselor may begin by leaning more heavily on the formal theory to understand and explain the client's behavior as well as his own counseling behavior—particularly since he has to describe this to his supervisor. As he becomes more experienced, he may rely less on the explicit theory and more on his personal theory, using the theoretical terms only to explain feelings that he has and to communicate with other persons.

PERSONALITY OF THE COUNSELOR

In examining the literature in this area, one may divide it into the hypothetical personality, which has evolved a great deal of speculation, and the research contributions regarding the personality of the counselor. In the area of hypothetical personality, many authors have listed the counselor traits they think are necessary for effective counseling. Most of these authors want the counselor to be a psychologically healthy person and tend to reflect a general idealized personality.

The Hypothetical Personality

Several years ago the APA Committee on Training in Clinical Psychology (1947) compiled the following list of traits for a counselor.

1. Superior intellectual ability and judgment
2. Originality, resourcefulness and versatility
3. Fresh and insatiable curiosity; self-learner
4. Interest in persons as individuals rather than as material for manipulation—a regard for the integrity of other persons
5. Insight into own personality characteristics; sense of humor
6. Sensitivity to the complexities of motivation
7. Tolerance
8. Ability to adapt "therapeutic" attitude; ability to establish warm and effective relationships with others
9. Industry; methodological work habits; ability to tolerate pressure
10. Acceptance of responsibility
11. Tact and cooperativeness
12. Integrity, self-control, and stability
13. Discriminating sense of ethical values
14. Breadth of cultural background—"educated man"
15. Deep interest in psychology, especially in its clinical aspect

Another early description of the characteristics of counselors is found in the National Vocational Guidance Association publication on Counselor Preparation (1949). That statement proposed that general characteristics of counselors include a deep interest in people, and patience with them, sensitivity to the attitudes and the actions of others, emotional stability and objectivity, a capacity for being trusted by others, and respect for facts. More recently, the Association for Counselor Education and Supervision (1964) indicated that the counselor should have six basic qualities: (1) belief in each individual, (2) commitment to individual human values, (3) alertness to the world, (4) open-mindedness, (5) understanding of self, and (6) professional commitment.

Appell (1963) believes the most significant resource a counselor brings to the relationship is himself and the most important variable is that the counselor understands himself. He needs to experience himself as a person of worth and individuality before he can afford such privileges to a client. Arbuckle (1954) feels that the self shows in counseling and the counselor cannot be effective if he plays a role. He must have an understanding of the extent to which his technique is an expression of himself. If the technique is impaired by his personality, his counseling will be ineffective. Dreyfus (1967) suggests that it is not a counselor's training and what he does as a counselor, but rather his ability to be human that is of prime importance. There has been a stress on the need for a genuine interpersonal encounter and a de-emphasis on the importance of a particular school or theory of therapy. Dreyfus believes that looking at various therapeutic orientations has failed to demonstrate the efficacy of any one of them and explains that a single variable—humanness—seems to underlie all therapeutic approaches and may account for the positive result obtained by all approaches.

Williamson (1962) describes some desirable characteristics of the counselor using himself as a technique. The counselor should have optimism about the outcome of the human experience and confidence that his service will enhance the likelihood of the client's attaining fullness of humanity. He must accept himself as he is, must be his best as a result of his effort to actualize his potentialities. His manner should be one of warm, friendly equality in the interview, demonstrating belief in the dignity and worth of the individual. He must have unquestionable personal integrity of which the client is aware. His style of relating must demonstrate expertise in helping and showing a penetrating understanding of individuals. He should be broadly informed. His behavior should show commitment to educating youth toward full actualization of potentialities. He must exemplify and promote objectivity in his work and must be perceived as advocating and practicing persistent striving for personal excellence in all dimensions of development. He should have a broad scope of relevant knowledge, dialectic agility in the use of knowledge, and sensitivity to persons. His private and personal life should exemplify "academic virtues," diligence, moral honesty, and commitment to academic freedom.

Parker (1966) asserts that the counselor should have a sensitivity to others, the ability to analyze objectively another person's strengths and weaknesses, awareness of the nature and extent of individual differences, and the ability to identify learning difficulties. According to Mowrer (1951), personal maturity is the most important criterion for a counselor to possess. He admits there is no valid way to measure it. Hobbs (1958) picks as his ideal a "compleat" counselor. This person is without question technically competent but is also aware of the world, its social and political issues, and can be creative in an unlimiting, unlimited world view.

Fullmer and Bernard (1964) review Maslow's hierarchy of needs and believe self-actualization is the most difficult to obtain yet the most important attribute of the ideal counselor. Tyler (1969) recognizes intellectual competence and general emotional stability as necessary for counseling. In addition, she adds the basic attitudes of accepting and understanding people as necessary characteristics. She also points to the personal traits that are detrimental in counseling as being rigidity, hostility, indifference, and obtuseness.

Several years ago, Farson (1954) stated that the "counselor is a woman." This is based on the thesis that the work of the counselor calls for behavior that is more closely in tune with social expectations for women than for men. The feminine role is generally perceived as tender, gentle, loving, dependent, receptive, passive, more concerned with interpersonal relations than with things, while the masculine role is seen as clever, tough, strong, courageous, independent, and more concerned with things than with people.

The work of the counselor generally requires him to comfort and to work with any and all of the client's feelings. This capacity to deal with the affective and interpersonal behaviors is generally perceived to be more feminine than masculine. Carkhuff and Berenson (1969) suggest that a counselor is both a man and a woman. They believe that the counselor is not only gentle, tender, loving, and passive-receptive, but also active and assertive and able to confront and interpret immediacy when it is appropriate. They believe that the functional definitions of masculinity and femininity suggest the counselor would initiate communication and be action oriented as well as responsive and facilitative, Carkhuff and Berenson state that counselors who offer the highest level of facilitative conditions also offer the highest level of action-oriented dimensions.

In 1968, McClain attempted to investigate the question, is the counselor a woman? He used the 16 Personality Factor Questionnaire as the research instrument. He concluded that the overall picture of men counselors in the study indicated they possess feminine qualities necessary for the counseling role as well as most of the personal strengths to be hoped for. The timidity and dependency that was suggested by certain test scores could interfere with optimum effectiveness as counselors. The women counselors in the study had the essential feminine qualities requisite to the helping role. It appeared that both men and women possess in acceptable degrees the fundamental femininity and requisite ego strength that have been deemed appropriate for a successful counselor.

Siegel (1959) discussed the role of the counselor's religious values in counseling, stating that, to the extent that either the counselor or client allows his own values to impede the true evaluation of the client's problems and his feelings about them, to this extent the values interfere with the goals of the helping relationship. He also felt that the real requisite of the therapist is to be aware of what his values are with regard to religion and to be sensitive enough so that whatever communication of these values occurs from himself to the client does not interfere with the exploration of the client's feelings and attitudes toward this value area. Again Siegel expressed that the counselor needs to be secure enough about his own religious values so that he allows the client to question those very same values without selecting a goal for the client.

Bugental (1964) described the subjective influences and patterns in the psychotherapist he thought to be influential in determining the success of therapy. He listed inappropriate gratification for the therapist as well as appropriate gratification. The inappropriate gratifications were the seeking for one-way intimacy, the imaging of omnipotence, the attempt to master contingency, the protected and disguised giving of tenderness, and displaced rebelliousness. The appropriate gratifications for the therapist were listed as participation, personal growth, the emerging in psychological processes, and the contribution to patient growth. Furthermore, Bugental defined maturity in the therapist as expressed through humility, selective participation, genuine encounter, and the acceptance of the guilt of being a therapist. Fisher (1967) suggested that a crisis hits the experienced therapist as he progresses away from the academic atmosphere of his training into his own private and largely unchallenged work. This crisis comes with a lessening of external restraints formerly caused by coursework and degree requirements, the erosion of his goals with clients, the profession's diverse indoctrination method, inadequacy of his own conceptual skills, the changing attitudes of society toward therapy, the customs and politics within the profession, and discontent in his own private life.

CONCLUSION

What type of personality should the counselor possess in order to produce the most effective counseling relationship? We could list adjectives to show the characteristics necessary for successful counseling such as sympathetic understanding, common sense, good judgment, emotional stability, fairness, sincerity, good character, approachability, flexibility, adaptability, intelligence, leadership, friendliness, sense of humor, tact, tolerance, integrity, vitality, sensitivity, and so forth. The list could go on and on. With such a list of traits, one would expect the counselor to walk on water! It is impossible to expect anyone to possess all of these admirable traits. So where do we draw the limit? Are there certain criteria or should one possess five or ten of certain traits to become a successful counselor? Possibly the research on counselor characteristics is more explicit.

RESEARCH ON COUNSELOR PERSONALITY

Research has been conducted on the types of people who enter the counseling field and the reasons for their vocational decisions. Some studies have used instruments to measure the personal needs of counselors and several have compared counselors and administrators. Research has also been conducted on the effect of counselor education in changing the counselor's attitudes and responses.

Since the growth of personality is developmental, perhaps it is worthwhile to examine the childhoods of those who enter the profession. The Michigan group has been pursuing a line of theory and research regarding personality factors and vocational choice that may have applications to counseling. Their position is that part of the intrinsic attractiveness of an occupation includes the ways it affords for seeking gratification and reducing anxieties. Grater, Kell, and Morse (1961) contend that those who go into a social service such as counseling must have a need for nurturing in order to be successful and to find job satisfaction. This need to take care of and be close to other people develops in childhood. When a child learns that he can obtain positive emotional response from his parents by his nurturant behavior, he can reduce the anxiety-producing threat of desertion by establishing conditions in which he is needed and helpful. He learns to postpone gratification of his need for affection until his parents can respond to him; this brings loneliness and limited dependence to the child's life. In his adult life he is reticent about expressing personal needs and reluctant or unable to make demands on other people. This is ideal for the counseling relationship in that the counselor nurtures the client and does not expect anything from the client but his acceptance of the nurturance. His past pattern of adjustment has been continued and is successful in adult life. Hence, job satisfaction results from administering to the needs of others.

Galinsky (1962) found predicted differences between the reports of childhood experiences by graduate students in physics and clinical psychology. He found that, as children, the psychologists had more opportunity to be curious about interpersonal relationships, behavior of people was discussed often in the home, emotional expression was characteristic in the family, and frank discussion of people behavior was characteristic of family conversation.

Schutz and Mazer (1964) studied graduate students who were enrolled in guidance and counseling programs to identify their motives for determining vocational choice. They report that motives could be arranged in three general categories; adient, abient, and global appeal. Ten factors were adient, reflecting a positive purposeful aspect of counseling; the search for personal status and prestige, means of directing others, means of helping others, opportunities to do research, ladder to further success, possibility of listening to others and learning about one's self, a way of extending one's personal influence, a means of obtaining personal acceptance and support, opportunity to be creative, and ways of maintaining school relationships.

Five variables were abient, reflecting avoidance of adversative elements in counseling; personal threat, the business world, physical labor, competition, and health threat. Global appeal factors focused on socially acceptable stereotyped reasons for entering the profession. The extent to which any single individual uses all dimensions was not answered by the study. The multiplicity of factors shows great heterogeneity in the sources of vocational interest.

Throughout the literature related to professional education, there are numerous studies attempting to differentiate the personality characteristics of school counselors from school administrators. Polmantier (1966) reported that literature dealing with the personality of the counselor shows different needs for principals and counselors. He suggests that nurturance and affiliation are significant aspects of personality in counselors. Other traits assigned to the counselor include the ability to perceive self and others realistically, empathy, emotional stability and expression of self.

Significant differences between the psychological needs of counselors have also been found by Kemp (1962). Principals were described as having greater need for achievement, deference, order, and aggression, while counselors scored higher on personality scales of intraceptions, exhibitionism, and affiliation. Chenault and Seegars (1962) investigated the personality factors of principals and counselors while using an intrapersonal diagnostic technique. Both groups perceived administrators as being more competitive and aggressive, but less kind and tolerant than counselors. Stefflre and Leafgren (1962) report a study on the vocational values of counselors and administrators. The counselors were significantly higher on measures of altruism and self-realization, whereas the administrators obtained high scores on measures of control and financial reward. However, when values were ranked according to means, the two groups showed commonalities.

Donnan and Harlan (1968) used the 16-factor questionnaire to study the personality of counselors and administrators. Five factors were found to significantly differentiate between the two groups. On the emotional versus emotionally stable factor, counselors' scores indicated higher ego strength while administrators' scores showed them to be more affected by feelings. On the expedient versus conscientious factor, administrators' scores indicated stronger superego strength while counselors' scores tended to be in the expedient direction. On the tough-minded versus tender-minded variable, counselors' scores reflected a sensitive characteristic as opposed to the realistic scores of the administrators. Administrators' scores on the trusting versus suspicious factor were higher than those of the counselors, reflecting a more suspicious nature for them versus the counselors' more trusting attitude. The counselors' scores were in the forthright direction while administrators were in the shrewd direction on the forthright versus shrewdness factor. However, these studies show only that counselors are different from administrators, not that the characteristics affect their counseling.

COUNSELOR EDUCATION

One aspect of the personality-technical skills issue is the effect the educational process has on the counselor as a person. Does the knowledge gained from class make him a competent counselor? Does the educational program affect him personally as well as teaching him skills? Joslin (1965) examined the relationship between knowledge and counseling competence. The conclusion of the study was that "the low correlations between knowledge and counseling competence certainly provide evidence for doubting the effectiveness of counselor education programs composed entirely of didactic courses." From those findings there is little reason to believe that students who achieve high levels of knowledge will automatically become highly competent counselors.

Patterson (1967) reported on the effect of counselor education on the personality of the counselor. He administered the California Personality Inventory, the Barron Ego Strength Scale, the F Scale, and a counseling attitude scale to an NDEA Institute, a regular counseling group, and a non-counseling group of students. There were some differences between the counselor and non-counselor students at the beginning of the year. The counselors scored higher on well-being, psychological-mindedness, ego strength, and counseling attitude but were lower on the F Scale. At the end of the year, the counseling students were higher on self-acceptance, psychological-mindedness, ego strength and counsel attitude. The total counselor group increased in ego strength, counseling attitude and decreased on the F Scale. The non-counseling students also increased on the counseling attitude and decreased on the F Scale; however, the counselors remained higher.

Munger and Johnson (1960) reported that counselors in training changed in terms of their responses on the Porter Test of Counselors' Attitudes. Over the institute training period there was a continuing increase in understanding those attitudes the counselor would respond to a client and a corresponding decrease in the value setting and probing attitudes in the counselors' responses. However, a follow-up study reported by Munger, Myers and Brown (1963) found that in a three-month follow-up on attitudes, the changes had all but disappeared. In a 27-month follow-up after the end of the institute, the Porter was administered again with indications that there were further losses in terms of the understanding attitudes expressed by the counselor responses. On the basis of these data, there is reason to suspect that the attitude changes that occurred in an eight-week beginning institute were discouragingly transitory. In the same article, the same effects were investigated with a semester-long institute. It was found that there were more understanding responses and fewer probing responses in a three-month follow-up; however, this group was really indistinguishable from the back-sliding attitudes of the short-term institute. Also, trainees who were later employed as counselors maintained their understanding attitude more persistently than those who were not employed as counselors.

Conclusion

These research studies add little to the hypothetical list of characteristics. We have learned that people desiring to become counselors have needs to fulfill and that counselors have some different needs from administrators. The most significant finding is that the educational program does not seem to have a lasting effect on the counselor. Hence, one would assume that selecting persons who have the personal characteristics and potential would be important. What characteristics are related to affecting counselor behavior?

EFFECTIVENESS AND COUNSELOR CHARACTERISTICS

Shertzer and Stone (1968) reviewed the literature on the characteristics that distinguish effective from ineffective counselors. They concluded that these characteristics may be separated in terms of three dimensions: experience, type of relationship established, and non-intellective factors.

Experience

Campbell (1962) studied whether inexperienced counselors used the same interview subrole behaviors as did experienced counselors and investigated the influence of the counselor's personality and background on his subrole pattern. The findings for the former were positive; in the latter case they discovered that the counselor's background had more influence on his subrole behavior than did his present personality traits. Grigg (1961) studied clients' ratings of those who had earned a doctorate degree (A), experienced trainees (B), and inexperienced trainees (C). He found differences among groups A, B, and C as follows: (1) A and B tend to wait and allow the client to initiate discussion while C is more active and chatty. (2) There were no significant differences on the use of questions although twice as many counselors from all three groups were seen as not using questions frequently. (3) Both B and C utilized interpretations more than A. (4) C gave advice and made suggestions more than A or B. (5) A and B allowed the client to control the hour more than C and yet (6) the client's feelings about improvement were independent of the experience level of the counselor.

Bohn (1965) examined the relationship of counselor dominance, experience, and the type of client with the amount of counselor directiveness. He concluded that experienced counselors were significantly less directive than less experienced counselors and that dependent clients elicited the most directive behavior from counselors. Mills and Abeles (1965) studied the counselors' need for affiliation and nurturance as related to their liking for clients in the counseling process. They found that a significant relationship between the need for nurturance and liking existed only for practicum students. It was not significant for interns or a senior staff of experienced counselors. They interpreted their results as meaning that as experience increases, the beginning counselor foregoes his need for nurturance, especially during internship, but that the need appears again in future experience.

PERSONAL VARIABLES

Demos and Zuwaylif (1966) reported that effective counselors possessed more nurturance and affiliation while less effective counselors were higher in autonomy, abasement, and aggression. Combs and Soper (1963) found that there were clear distinctions between good and poor counselors, as rated by faculty members, on the basis of aspects of their perceptual organization; that is, the ways of perceiving one's self, others, and the task of counseling. Allen (1967) tried to anticipate the effectiveness of counselor trainees by means of the higher-order personality variable of psychological openness. His results suggest that the effective counselor is a person who is on relatively good terms with his own emotional experience and that the ineffective counselor is one who is relatively uneasy in regard to the character of his own inner life. The criterion for this study was supervisor rating. None of the estimates of academic aptitude, the Graduate Record Examination, Miller Analogies Test, the number of psychology courses, or the admission ratings predicted the subjects standing on the criterion at a level beyond chance likelihood.

Milliken and Patterson (1967) investigated the relationship of dogmatism and prejudice to counseling effectiveness. They asked a coached client and a supervisor to assess the effectiveness of counselors on a 16-item counselor effectiveness scale. The counselors also completed the Dogardum Ethnic Distance Scale and the Rokeach Dogmatism Scale. The counselors who were rated as "good" were lower on all of the scales of the EDS and RDS. However, only the supervisors' global rating significantly differentiated the "good" and "bad" counselors, who were differentiated by their prejudice and dogmatism. Kemp (1962) investigated the influence of dogmatism on the training of counselors. His study indicated that open-minded or low-dogmatic counselors were more understanding and supportive on a beginning written test and in an actual counseling situation. On the other hand, closed-minded or high-dogmatic counselors made more permissive responses on the beginning written tests and showed more understanding and support. In the actual counseling situation, however, where there was no chance to reflect as on the first written test, they responded in accordance with their customary dogmatism.

Brams (1961) discovered that effective communication in counseling interviews is positively related to the trainee's tolerance for ambiguity as measured by the Berkeley Public Opinion Questionnaire. Other relationships measured were inconclusive. Gruberg (1969) investigated the tolerance of ambiguity as it related to the orientation of the counselor's verbal behavior. He found that high-tolerance counselors used counseling leads of clarification, acceptance, and silence in their responses significantly more often than did low-tolerance counselors. The low-tolerance counselors used leads of advising, diagnosis, direct questions, and evaluation significantly more often than did the high-tolerance counselors. The responses of counselors with average tolerance of ambiguity included leads with approximately the same frequency as did those of high-tolerance counselors. Analysis of data for the talk ratio indicates a significant difference between the high- and low-tolerance counselors, with the latter speaking more often during the interview. Counselors having a high tolerance of ambiguity were rated by counselor educators as being more effective in their skills of responding to clients' statements than were counselors having a low tolerance of ambiguity.

Bandura (1956) investigated the relationship between counselor anxiety and effectiveness. He hypothesized that competent counselors are less anxious than those judged to be less competent and possess greater insight into the nature of their own anxieties than do less competent counselors. A total of 42 counselors from four clinical settings participated in the study. Each counselor rated himself and all other subjects as to degree of anxiety with respect to dependency, hostility, and sex. The average rating assigned to each counselor constituted the anxiety measure. The inside measure was defined in terms of the relative discrepancy between the counselor's self rating and the average group rating for him. Supervisor ratings were used as a criterion measure of counseling competence. The findings indicate that anxious counselors were rated less competent than those low in anxiety but neither the counselor's degree of insight into the nature of his anxiety nor counselors' self ratings of anxiety were significantly related to supervisors' ratings of competency. Bandura concluded that the presence of anxiety, whether it is recognized or not, affects a counselor's ability to perform successful counseling.

Johnson *et al* (1967) conducted a study of counselors' characteristics by exploring the relationship between certain counselor characteristics and some criterion measure of effectiveness. They used a multiple regression analysis to find the relationship between five predictor measures of counselor characteristics and five criterion measures of counselor success or effectiveness. From this analysis, the authors concluded that effective male counselor trainees were characterized as confident, friendly, affable, accepting, and liking. They were generally satisfied with themselves and their surroundings. The effective female candidates were described as more outgoing and efficient, giving an appearance of confidence. They appeared to be assertive and person-oriented. Effective male and female counselors tended to be more like each other than like members of the less effective group of their own sex.

Kazienko and Neidt (1962) investigated the personality characteristics of male counselor trainees from 25 summer NDEA counseling and guidance institutes. Each trainee had been identified by the staff as being in the top or bottom 25 percent of their institutes. The trainees described themselves in terms of self-concept, motivating forces, values, and feelings about others. They were compared on those variables. In comparing self-concepts, the good counselors perceived themselves as serious, earnest, patient, soft-spoken, aware of personal self-centeredness, being more domestic than social, and not mechanically inclined. The poor counselors did not describe themselves as serious or patient, but tended toward loudness of voice, were not aware of any personal self-centeredness, and saw themselves as normally domestic and social, as well as mechanically inclined. In their description of motivation, the good counselors were concerned about possessing a measure of. security but tended to reject the need for wealth, while the poor counselors were neither motivated nor unmotivated by prospects of security or riches. The good counselors did not value cunningness and shrewdness but did hold a value that people should have the right to be different and did not value severity or strictness. The poor counselors emphasized conformity and tended toward strict adherence to rules. The good counselors viewed people as possessing an adequate measure of intellectual ability while the poor counselors gave others no particular credit for intellectual talent.

Stefflre, King, and Leafgren (1962) used Q-sort judgment by peers as a criterion for designating nine most effective and nine least effective counselor trainees. They reported significant differences between the effective and ineffective counselor samples on four dimensions. The effective group earned higher scores on academic aptitude and performance. They also had higher scores on the Strong Vocational Interest Blank Social Welfare Scales and significantly higher deference and order scores on the Edward Preference Scale than did the ineffective group. Significant differences in the group's discrepancy score of the Bill's Index of Adjustment and Values and Discrepancy suggest that, in terms of self-concept, the effective counselors underestimated themselves and the ineffective counselors overestimated themselves. Gade (1967) also used a sociometric index in relation to counselor-predicted effectiveness. He concluded that from a self-contained counselor education program there was a positive relationship between the rankings of counselor effectiveness and one's sociometric status.

RELATIONSHIP

Wallach and Strupp (1960) concluded that the personality of the counselor is an integral part of his clinical judgments and counseling practice. They found that a warmer therapist attitude was associated with more favorable perceptions of the client, including clinical judgments, prognostic estimates, and treatment plans. They also found that a more highly motivated client engendered a warmer attitude in the therapist.

There is a growing body of research that indicates effective counseling is related to the type of relationship provided by the counselor. In the much quoted Fiedler studies (1950), common characteristics in the relationships were achieved by the expert clients regardless of their orientation. The experts were reportedly better able to communicate with and understand their clients, maintain an appropriate emotional distance, divest themselves of status concerns, and show positive regard for their clients. Rogers (1962) reported on a series of investigations with the major finding that clients in relationships marked by high levels of counselor congruence, empathy, and positive regard show constructive personality change and development. Extensive research has been reported by Carkhuff and Berenson

(1967) and Truax and Carkhuff (1967) supporting the quality of these facilitative conditions as the most important variable in counseling success. Additional research suggests that low levels of these facilitative conditions contribute to client deterioration.

CONCLUSION

Studies of the relationship between counselor effectiveness and personal characteristics indicate that effective counselors may be distinguished from less effective counselors in terms of having more experience, higher affiliation and nurturance needs, more openness and less dogmatism, and greater tolerance of ambiguity. It also appears that peers can agree on who is the most effective and that these judgments are similar to supervisor ratings. The largest amount of data and most consistent findings show the more effective counselor as being able to provide a meaningful relationship with the client. Is the counselor's ability to be congruent and to communicate positive regard and empathy a personality characteristic, or is it learned in a training program? Possibly both. The counselor must have a life style that permits him to behave in a facilitating manner, and it may be possible for the training program to assist in this process.

Just what does effective counseling mean? Most of these studies used supervisor or peer ratings, with very few client ratings included. The first two are external judgments in which the counselor behaved as they liked. The research in this area does not examine client behavior change nor does it follow up to note other effects of counseling. Actually, the research in this area does not yield conclusive evidence that certain characteristics of the counselor are related to his effectiveness. One might wonder if the interaction of the client and counselor personalities is a meaningful area to pursue.

THE RELATIONSHIP OF CLIENT CHARACTERISTICS AND COUNSELING

Counseling involves both a counselor and a client, thus the characteristics of both persons may have an effect on the process and outcome. Various client characteristics have been examined as well as the similarity of the two persons. A review of some literature will yield the tone of this area.

Goldstein (1960) investigated the effect of client expectation about psychotherapy as a factor in the improvement. He concluded that the amount of attention and contact, such as the form of intake, periodic interviewing, and testing, gives a client the expectation or sort of placebo effect that does lead to their improvement. He found that with 15 no-therapy control clients his idea that spontaneous recovery is not really spontaneous but is a function of such identifiable factors was supported. Actually, improvement is in part due to a favorable expectation of improvement from counseling. It may well be, then, that part of the success would depend upon the personality and expectations of the client.

A similar factor is the faith that the counselor has in his ability to influence change, and the faith the client has in the counselor. Frank (1961) presents a case for the client's faith in the treatment as a therapeutic agent. If faith is a therapeutic agent, it is probable that the counselor's faith influences the faith that the client feels. Kirtner and Cartwright (1963) found that the length-by-outcome of counseling was related to the personality structure of the clients at the beginning of therapy. The "short-success" group was generally at a higher level of personality integration, the participants more open in their impulse life, less confused about their sex role than were those of other groups. The "short-failure" group was generally in a low level of personality integration and expressed an extreme underlying sense of incapacity to deal with life situations.

Apparently, the counselor's behavior in the interview is related to client perception and liking of the counselor. Tomczyk (1968) found that when clients with a positive attitude toward their counselors were compared with clients having a negative attitude toward their counselors, the clients with a positive attitude perceived their counselors as being less verbally active while discussing affective problems, but more verbally active when discussing cognitive problems. These counselors were generally more verbally active over a wide range of verbal roles and provided a stronger working relationship with the client. The counselors expressed fewer non-accepting remarks but provided more approval and reassurance to the client. They discussed the counseling process with the client and provided more information while discussing affective problems and also gave more help with study methods.

What role does the counselor's like or dislike of the client play in his effectiveness within the relationship? There have been a few studies predicated on the assumption that a counselor will be more successful if he likes the client. McNair, Lorr, and Callahan (1963) failed to find any differences in liking for clients in counselors who eventually withdrew from therapy prematurely as compared to those who stayed. Stoler (1963) found that likable clients are more successful in therapy but that research designs must provide a discrimination as to whether it is the counselor's liking or the student's likability that is the important factor. If the counselor's liking for the client proves to be related to therapeutic success, then the next step calls for action in two directions. One is to ascertain in what way liking influences the change process; that is, it may increase the counselor's empathic understanding and act as an immediate gratification that cements the relationship. The other direction is to study what personality factors may influence a general tendency to like clients or particular kinds of clients. Abeles (1964), using the Rorschach, found a negative relationship between liking the client and the counselor's readiness to project hostility and anxiety and to receive form accurately. In another study with Mills (1965), Abeles attempted to relate need for affiliation and nurturance with liking, obtaining only partial results since the counselors in training demonstrate the relationship but experienced counselors do not.

Munson (1960) reviewed the literature on counselors' motivation, which supported her conclusion that nurturance and inquisitiveness are two important needs served by counseling and that the choice of doing counseling is, in part, an attempt to gratify these needs. She went on to assume that conflicts in achieving either or both of these gratifications would provide a source of difficulty for the counselor when he encountered a client whose own behavior or personality blocked one or the other of these satisfactions. She conducted an evaluation of this assumption by having two counselors who worked with clients in conflict with these needs and one counselor who worked with clients having no conflict with respect to either need. She found that counselors in conflict were less likely to respond in a manner that facilitated client expression if the client was highly resistant. However, a non-conflicted counselor's responses were unaffected. The conflicted counselor's expression of satisfaction, judgment of the client's suitability for counseling, and enjoyment of the counseling relationship were similarly influenced. Most of the effect seemed attributable to clients expressing opposition to help, and it seemed to make no difference whether the counselor was under- or over-sensitive to his conflict.

In a study of therapy with schizophrenic patients, Betz and Whitehorn (1962) found that certain Strong Vocational Interest scores could differentiate successful from unsuccessful counselors and thus derived a scale for obtaining this differentiation. However, McNair, Callahan, and Lorr (1962) found a reverse relationship of the Betz scale with success and treatment of neurotic clients. In other words, where Betz and Whitehorn found that A therapists were more successful than B therapists with schizophrenics, Mc-Nair *et al* found that B counselors were more successful than A counselors with neurotics. An interaction is suggested between the client and counselor types in determining outcome. Carson, Harden, and Shows (1964) investigated the nature of these interacting factors and suggested that the A-type counselor responded more actively and more freely to persons either distrustful and expectant of harm and hostility or ready to be self-indulgent, while B-type counselors responded similarly to persons who were trusting, acceptant of help, and self-critical.

SIMILARITY OF COUNSELOR AND CLIENT CHARACTERISTICS

Mendelsohn and Geller (1963) matched counselors and clients for similarity on judgment-perception, thinking-feeling, sensation-intuition, and extroversion-introversion. They found that the greater the counselor-client difference score for each dimension, the fewer the number of sessions. In a replication of the study, Mendelsohn (1966) reported that although client personality variables affect the decision to seek counseling, the counselor-client matching is more important in determining its outcome. Lesser (1961) investigated the relationship of counseling progress to similarity, felt or perceived similarity, and empathic understanding. He concluded that the counselor's accurate perception of similarity facilitated communication both in word and feeling. The counselor is able to overcome the negative aspect of similarity in the counseling process when he correctly perceives the similarity. Baer (1967) concluded that the dissimilarity of counselor-client personality was much more often associated with high ratings of counselor success. The clients and counselors under study agreed that counseling was successful when the counselors were unlike the clients on the variables of original thinking, vigor and responsibility. Baer's findings suggest *not* matching counselor and client.

Several studies have indicated a curvilinear relationship between the similarity of personality variables and success in counseling. A study by Mendelsohn and Geller (1965) paired counselor and client in terms of high, middle, and low similarity and as same or opposite sex. With the criterion variables of evaluation, comfort-rapport, and judged competence, the effects of similarity on outcome did vary according to the different criteria. Evaluation was curvilinear in relation to similarity, with the middle similarity producing the highest scores. The comfort-rapport scores were related to high similarity for freshmen but to middle similarity for the non-freshmen. The effects of similarity were more pronounced in opposite than in same sex matching. High ratings of judged competence were associated more with extroversion-introversion and thinking-feeling dimensions of the client personality rather than with counselor-client similarity.

Carson and Heine (1962) also found a curvilinear relationship between counselor-client similarity and counseling success. They concluded that either extreme similarity or dissimilarity impedes counseling. Gerler (1958) also found support for the curvilinear relationship between client-counselor similarity in personality traits and favorable outcome. Tuma and Gustad (1958) report that closer similarity between counselor and client measures of dominance, social presence, and social participation was possibly related to the client's self-learning in counseling. Cook (1966) compared high, medium and low counselors and clients on similarity and values, suggesting a curvilinear relationship with a medium similarity group showing a more positive change in meaning than the high or low group

Some investigation has been made of the complementary aspects of personality and counseling outcome. Complementary characteristics are those that mutually make up what is lacking in the other person. The most extensive study was conducted by Snyder (1961) and extended over four years in which he was a therapist with 20 clients. After each interview the counselor and the client completed an Affect Scale. Snyder classified and analyzed his data on three variables of affect, control, and disclosure. Through the course of therapy the clients were categorized into "better" and "poorer" groups. The therapeutic relationship and interaction appeared to be better when the client and counselor complemented each other on three characteristics.

CONCLUSION

This review of the literature suggests that the personality of the client will affect the counseling situation. Success is partially dependent on liking the counselor and expecting success. Also it apparently helps to have the counselor like the client. If the client meets some of the counselor's needs he is probably more apt to like him and the two will work toward success. Other studies show that different counselor behaviors are more effective with certain types of clients. This raises a question regarding the effect of similarity of personalities on counseling. Most studies suggest a curvilinear relationship so that personalities too similar or too different interfere with counseling. All of this leads to a conclusion that the two personalities need to be compatible if they are going to work together and be successful. However, we do not have a formula for matching counselors with clients.

A conclusion for the whole chapter can best be stated by noting the importance of the person-technician balance. A counselor uses two balanced components—personal relationship skills and technical skills. He must make a conscious effort to examine his personal growth as well as his methods.

Brammer and Shostrom (1968) show an interest in the person-technician balance by listing five local points as a base for their book. (1) The counselor is engaged in helping others but is also a human being with personal weaknesses and problems of his own. He has the capacity to grow and learn from his clients, but he must then take the responsibility for his own constant personal growth through counseling for himself, group experience, or some other self-renewal experience. (2) The counselor is an expert in helping others but has no mystical or technical solutions. His technical training can be helpful but only through his continuous attempt to increase his own self-understanding and awareness can he believe in what he is attempting to do with clients. Counseling is only partially a technique, the rest being subtle human relationship effectiveness. (3) Both the client and the counselor are unique individuals. (4) Therefore, counseling must be viewed as a workshop for the growth of both individuals. (5) The central emphasis for the counselor must be the development of a core of valid techniques along with the flexibility for adding new ideas and disgarding old approaches. Counseling techniques should be developed for the client and, most of all, be consistent with the counselor. Counseling should not be guided primarily by one theory of thought but viewed rather as a dynamic interplay of a unique relationship between two distinctive individuals.

REFERENCES

Allen, T. W. "Effectiveness of Counselor Trainees as a Function of Psychological Openness." *Journal of Counseling Psychology* 14 (1):35–40.

American Psychological Association Committee on Training in Clinical Psychology. "Recommended Graduate Training Program in Clinical Psychology." *American Psychologist* 2:539–558.

Anthony, N. "A Longitudinal Analysis of the Effect of Experiences on the Therapeutic Approach." *Journal of Clinical Psychology* 23 (4):512–516.

Appell, M. L. "Self-Understanding for the Guidance Counselor." *Personnel and Guidance Journal* 42:143–145.

Arbuckle, D. "The Self Shows in Counseling." *Personnel and Guidance Journal* 33:159–161.

Association for Counselor Education and Supervision. "The Counselor: Professional Preparation and Role." *Personnel and Guidance Journal* 42:536–541.

Bandura, A. "Psychotherapists' Anxiety Level, Self Insight, and Psychotherapeutic Competence." *Journal of Abnormal and Social Psychology* 52:333–337.

Baer, C. E. "Relationship of Counselor Personality and Counselor-Client Personality Similarity to Selected Counseling Success Criteria." *Journal of Counseling Psychology* 14 (5):419–425.

Bohn, M. ., Jr. "Counselor Behavior as a Function of Counselor Dominance, Counselor Experience and Client Type." *Journal of Counseling Psychology* 12 (4):346–352.

Brammer, L. M., and Shostrom, E. L. *Therapeutic Psychology*. Englewood Cliffs: Prentice-Hall, Inc., 1968.

Brams, J. M. "Counselor Characteristics and Effective Communication in Counseling." *Journal of Counseling Psychology* 8:25–30.

Bugental, J. F. T. "The Person Who Is the Psychotherapist." *Journal of Consulting Psychology* 28 (3):272–277.

Campbell, R. E. "Counselor Personality and Background and His Interview Subrole Behavior." *Journal of Counseling Psychology* 9 (4):329–334.

Cannon, H. J. "Personality Variables and Counselor-Client Affect." *Journal of Counseling Psychology* 11 (1):35–46.

Carkhuff, R., and Berenson, B. *Beyond Counseling and Therapy*. New York: Holt, Rinehart and Winston, Inc., 1967.

Carkhuff, R., and Berenson, B. "The Counselor Is a Man and a Woman." *Personnel and Guidance Journal* 48:24–28.

Carson, R.; Harden, Judith; and Shows, W. "A–B Distinction and Behavior and Quasi-Therapeutic Situations." *Journal of Consulting Psychology* 28:426–433.

Carson, R. C., and Heine, R. W. "Similarity and Success in Therapeutic Dyads." *Journal of Consulting Psychology* 26 (1):38–43.

Chenault, Joan, and Seegars, J. "The Interpersonal Diagnosis of Principals and Counselors." *Personnel and Guidance Journal* 41:118–122.

Combs, A. W., and Soper, D. W. "The Perceptual Organization of Effective Counselors." *Journal of Counseling Psychology* 10 (3):222–226.

Demos, G., and Zuwaylif, F. "Characteristics of Effective Counselors." *Counselor Education and Supervision* 5:163–165.

Donnan, H. H., and Harlan, A. "Personality of Counselors and Administrators." *Personnel and Guidance Journal* 47 (3):228–232.

Dreyfus, E. A. "Humanness a Therapeutic Variable." *Personnel and Guidance Journal* 45 (6):573–578.

Farson, R. "The Counselor Is a Woman." *Journal of Counseling Psychology* 1:221–223.

Fiedler, F. "A Comparison of Therapeutic Relationships in Psychoanalytical, Nondirective, and Adlerian Therapy." *Journal of Counseling Psychology* 14:436–445.

Fisher, K. A. "Crisis in the Therapist." *Psychoanalytic Review* 54 (1):81–98.

Foulds, M. L. "Self-Actualization and the Communication of Facilitative Conditions during Counseling." *Journal of Counseling Psychology* 16 (2):132–136.

Frank, J. *Persuading and Healing: A Comparative Study of Psychotherapy.* Baltimore: Johns Hopkins, 1961.

Fullmer, D., and Bernard, H. *Counseling: Content and Process.* Chicago: Science Research Associates, Inc., 1964.

Gade, A. M. "The Relationship of Sociometric Indices and Counselor Candidate Effectiveness." *Counselor Education and Supervision* 6 (2):121–124.

Galinsky, M. "Personality Development and Vocational Choice of Clinical Psychologists and Physicists." *Journal of Counseling Psychology* 9:299–305.

Gerler, W. "Outcome of Psychotherapy as a Function of Client-Counselor Similarity." *Dissertation Abstracts*, 1958, 18, #1864.

Goldstein, A. "Patient's Expectancies and Non-Specific Therapy as a Basis for (Un)Spontaneous Remission." *Journal of Clinical Psychology* 16:399–403.

Grater, H.; Kell, B.; and Morse, Josephine. "The Social Service Interest: Roadblock and Road to Creativity." *Journal of Counseling Psychology* 5:267–275.

Grigg, A. E. "Client Response to Counselors at Different Levels of Experience." *Journal of Counseling Psychology* 8:217–223.

Gruberg, R. "A Significant Counselor Personality Characteristic: Tolerance of Ambiguity." *Counselor Education and Supervision* 8 (2):119–124.

Hobbs, N. "The Compleat Counselor." *Personnel and Guidance Journal* 36:594–602.

Johnson, D.; Shertzer, B.; Lindon, J. E.; and Stone, S. C. "The Relationship of Counselor Candidate Characteristics and Counseling Effectiveness." *Counselor Education and Supervision* 6 (4):297–304.

Joslin, L. C., Jr. "Knowledge and Counseling Competence." *Personnel and Guidance Journal* 43 (8):790–795.

Kacienko, L., and Neidt, C. "Self Descriptions of Good and Poor Counselor Trainees." *Counselor Education and Supervision* 1:106–123.

Kemp, C. "Counseling Responses and Need Structures of High School Principals and of Counselors." *Journal of Counseling Psychology* 9:326–328.

Kemp, C. G. "Influence of Dogmatism on the Training of Counselors." *Journal of Counseling Psychology* 9 (2):155–157.

Kirtner, W., and Cartwright, D. "Success and Failure in Client-Centered

Therapy as a Function of Client Personality Variables." *Journal of Consulting Psychology* 22:259–264.

Lesser, W. "The Relationship between Counseling Progress and Empathic Understanding." *Journal of Counseling Psychology* 8:330–336.

Lister, J. "The Counselor's Personal Theory." *Counselor Education and Supervision* 3:207–213.

McClain, E. W. "Is the Counselor a Woman?" *Personnel and Guidance Journal* 46 (5):444–455.

McNair, D.; Lorr, M.; and Callahan, D. "Patient and Therapist Influences on Quitting Psychotherapy." *Journal of Consulting Psychology* 27:10–17.

McNair, D. M.; Callahan, D. M.; and Lorr, M. "Therapist 'type' and Patient Response to Psychotherapy." *Journal of Consulting Psychology* 26 (5):425–429.

Mendelsohn, G. "Effects of Client Personality and Client-Counselor Similarity on the Duration of Counseling: A Replication and Extension." *Journal of Counseling Psychology* 13:228–234.

Mendelsohn, G. A., and Geller, M. H. "Effects of Counselor-Client Similarity on the Outcome of Counseling." *Journal of Counseling Psychology* 10 (1):71–77.

Mendelsohn, G. A., and Geller, M. H. "Structure of Client Attitudes toward Counseling and their Relation to Client-Counselor Similarity." *Journal of Consulting Psychology* 29:63–72.

Milliken, R. L., and Patterson, J. J. "Relationship of Dogmatism and Prejudices to Counseling Effectiveness." *Counselor Education and Supervision* 6 (2):125–129.

Mills, D., and Abeles, N. "Counselor Needs for Affiliation and Nurturance as Related to Liking for Clients and Counseling Process." *Journal of Counseling Psychology* 12:353–358.

Mowrer, O. H. "Training in Psychotherapy." *Journal of Consulting Psychology* 15:274–277.

Munger, P., and Johnson, C. "Changes in Attitudes Associated with an NDEA Counseling and Guidance Institute." *Personnel and Guidance Journal* 38:751–753.

Munger, P.; Myers, R.; and Brown, D. "Guidance Institutes and the Persistence of Attitudes: A Progress Report." *Personnel and Guidance Journal* 41:415–419.

Munson, Joan. "Patterns of Client Resistiveness and Counselor Response." *Ph.D. Thesis,* University of Michigan, 1960.

National Vocational Guidance Association. *Counselor Preparation.* Washington: The Association, 1949.

Parker, C. "The Place of Counseling in the Preparation of Student Personnel Workers." *Personnel and Guidance Journal* 45:259–260.

Patterson, C. "Effects of Counselor Education on Personality." *Journal of Counseling Psychology* 14:444–448.

Rogers, C. "The Interpersonal Relationship: The Core of Guidance." *Harvard Educational Review* 32:416–429.

Schutz, R. E., and Mazer, G. E. "A Factor Analysis of the Occupational Choice Motives of Counselors." *Journal of Counseling Psychology* 11 (3):267–271.

Siegal, S. J. "The Role of the Counselor's Religious Values in Counseling." *Journal of Counseling Psychology* 6:270–274.

Shoben, E. J., Jr. "The Counselor's Theory as a Personality Trait." *Personnel and Guidance Journal* 40 (7):617–621.

Snyder, W. *The Psychotherapy Relationship.* New York: The Macmillan Company, 1961.

Stefflre, B.; King, P.; and Leafgren, F. "Characteristics of Counselors Judged Effective by Their Peers." *Journal of Counseling Psychology* 9 (4):335–340.

Stoler, N. "Client Likability: A Variable in the Study of Psychotherapy." *Journal of Consulting Psychology* 27 (2):175–178.

Strupp, H. "The Performance of Psychoanalyitc and Client-Centered Therapists in the Initial Interview." *Journal of Consulting Psychology* 22:265–274.

Strupp, H. "The Therapist's Contribution to the Patient's Treatment Career." In Strupp, H., and Luborsky, L. (Eds.). *Research in Psychotherapy.* Washington, D. C.: American Psychological Association, 1962.

Sundland, D. M., and Barker, E. N. "The Orientations of Psychotherapists." *Journal of Consulting Psychology* 26 (3):201–212.

Tomczyk, J. R. "Determinants and Effects of Counselor's Verbal Role." *Personnel and Guidance Journal* 46 (7):694–701.

Truax, C., and Carkhuff, R. *Toward Effective Counseling and Psychotherapy.* New York: Holt, Rinehart and Winston, Inc., 1967.

Tuma, A., and Gustad, J. "The Effects of Client and Counselor Personality Characteristics on Client Learning in Counseling." *Journal of Counseling Psychology* 4:136–141.

Tyler, Leona. *The Work of the Counselor.* New York: Appleton-Century-Crofts, Inc., 1969.

Wallach, M., and Strupp, H. "Psychotherapists, Clinical Judgments and Attitudes toward Patients." *Journal of Consulting Psychology* 24:316–323.

Waskow, J., and Bergman, P. "Does Theoretical Orientation Influence Ratings of 'warmth-acceptance'?" *Journal of Consulting Psychology* 26 (5) :484.

Whitehorn, J., and Betz, B. "A Study of Psychotherapeutic Relationships between Physician and Schizophrenic Patients." *American Journal of Psychiatry* 111:321–331.

Whiteley, J. M., *et al* "Selection and Evaluation of Counselor Effectiveness." *Journal of Counseling Psychology* 14 (3) :226–234.

Williamson, E. G. "The Counselor as Technique." *Personnel and Guidance Journal* 41:108–111.

Wrenn, R. L. "Counselor Orientation: Theoretical or Situational?" *Journal of Counseling Pychology* 7:40–45.

PART TWO

COUNSELING
PROCESS

7

Initiating
Counseling

"The initial interview is the hardest part of our task—the part that demands from us the most intensive concentration. Each person constitutes for us a new adventure in understanding. Each is destined to broaden our own lives in directions as yet uncharted. Each initial interview renews our appreciation of the challenge and the fascination of the counseling task" (Tyler, 1969).

The principal task in the first interview is to establish a good relationship so the client feels comfortable enough to present and work on his problem. There are many factors that might affect the kind of relationship that is established. Prior to the client seeing the counselor, there may be factors that influence the ease with which rapport is established. In a school or college situation, the counselor and counseling center may have a reputation that either facilitates or hinders the beginning of counseling. The degree of anxiety the client is experiencing when he comes to the counselor's office will also affect the ease in establishing rapport. The client is aware of a problem and wants to talk with the counselor. Even when the client is a self-referral, he may be struggling with whether or not he wants to confide in the counselor. The immediate impressions the client receives from the counselor also will affect his early attitudes.

The counselor in particular must be sensitive to the client's feelings, attitudes and expectations as he enters counseling. This chapter explores client expectations and preferences and how they are involved in the initial interview. In addition, we will explore the goals, phases, and certain counselor behaviors in the interview.

CLIENT EXPECTATIONS OF COUNSELING

Each person approaching a new experience has a conceptualization of the events before him and certain perceptions of his role as well as the role of others in this situation. The individual's conceptualization of the coming event is a definite factor in determining his behavior in his new environment. Role theorists have emphasized the importance of expectations in determining people's behavior in their roles. The two people approaching counseling have apprehensions and anticipations about the forthcoming relationship. The counselor and the client will bring certain expectations of counseling to the counseling interview which may affect their behavior.

The counselor should be aware of his expectations and attempt to operate from his own frame of reference yet be aware of the client's frame of reference. He must have a construct of himself and the client. It is feasible that an awareness of the client's expectations will help the counselor form a construct of the client to meet him at the level of his expectations.

What Do Clients Exect?

What do clients expect of counseling? How do they expect the counselor to behave and what techniques do they expect him to use? Do clients have a preference for certain topics of discussion in the interview? These are the questions that have stimulated researchers to study the preferences and expectations of clients.

Secondary School

Two studies have focused on junior-high-school-aged students. Poppen and Peters (1965) investigated the expectations of students prior to seeing counselors in an NDEA Institute. They report that the students expected more advice and direction than was offered by the counselors. It appears that the counselors were more interested in establishing a relationship during the first interview than focusing on specific topics. One unique aspect of this study was the comparison of expectations of students who had previously seen a counselor with non-counseled students. The conclusion was that few differences in expectations existed despite whether or not they had seen a counselor. All of the students generally expected a school counselor to be a friendly, competent person who knows the answers, but did not expect him to support or agree with their views when there was disagreement with teachers or parents.

Perrone, Weiking, and Nagel (1965) used case descriptions to gain students', parents', and teachers' views on counseling. Parents were in favor of more intensive counseling than either students or teachers. Students who indicated they had more problems recommended more counseling for the "homely" student type, while the student checking fewer problems recommended more counseling for the "queer" student type.

In a study conducted at the high school level with nine schools in New York, Grant (1954) reported that students perceived counselors as being able to help in the vocational and educational planning areas. The counselor was not ". . . seen by students as being an effective or at least an acceptable source of help in the broad area of personal emotional problems."

Heilfron (1960) used case descriptions to elicit high school students' concepts of who needed counseling. The students indicated that counseling was not necessary for bright students or those performing effectively in school but should be used with students displaying problems. This is contrary to the concept of "counseling for all," which educators have espoused for schools.

College

Several studies have investigated college students' expectations. Form (1953) developed a scale of attitudes toward counseling consisting of 22 items to be classified as "strongly agree" or "strongly disagree." Using this counseling attitude scale, he conducted a study at Michigan State to get the student's perception of the Counseling Center in four areas. It was found that students feel more free to take problems to the Counseling Center in this order: Educational, Vocational, Social, and Personal. He found that students generally have favorable attitudes toward counseling and that the more contacts they had with counselors, the more favorable the attitude.

In a study of expectancies of clients at Michigan, Bordin (1955) found the tendency for clients to anticipate either a personal relationship between client and counselor or an impersonal process devoted primarily to receiving information and advice.

Severinsen (1966) investigated client satisfaction as related to expectations of counseling and what clients perceived the counselor did in an educational counseling interview. Client dissatisfaction was related to the dissimilarity of expected counselor empathy and perceived counselor empathy, irrespective of the direction of the dissimilarity. This suggests that satisfaction at the end of the first interview seems to be a function of how closely the counselor approximates the client's expectation.

A study of how various campus groups viewed counseling was conducted by Warman (1960). A total of 250 college students responded to a 100-item questionnaire. The students rated vocational choice as the most appropriate topic for the counseling center, followed by college routine problems, with adjustment to self and others listed as least appropriate. Wilcove and Sharp (1971) extended this approach to have students, their parents, faculty and counselors give their perceptions of the counseling center. Significant differences were found among the various groups. The counselors thought adjustment problems were more appropriate than did any of the other groups. Parents rated all the problem areas as more appropriate to discuss with the counselor than did the students. The students ranked college routine, vocational choice, and adjustment problems as the order of appropriateness. The authors of both studies note that their student publics have differing expectations from the counselors regarding appropriate concerns to bring to the counseling center. The counselors may need to re-educate the student population or at least recognize that students may have different expectations. The counselors could re-evaluate their own expectations in light of student concerns.

Isard and Sherwood (1964) investigated the effect of client expectations of an interview focused on presentation and interpretation of test data. They found that what the client expected of the counselor was related to the degree of satisfaction with counseling. Whether the counselor introduced the test data or the client asked about it did not matter. The dissatisfied clients had expected the counselor to point out the best area for them to study, to tell them what the tests proved, or they expected nothing would come of it and nothing did. However, Grosz (1968) reported that college students' positive and negative expectations of counseling had no effect on the quality of the relationship established with a counselor. The counselors' ratings also indicated no differences between relationships with students having positive and negative expectations.

Clinical Setting

There has been some study of the client expectation of counseling and the improvement that takes place. There have been conflicting findings, with some research suggesting a positive, linear relationship and others reporting an absence of correlation between them. Goldman and Shipman (1961) speculated that the relationship might be curvilinear. Their findings indicate a significant curvilinear relationship between the degree of client anticipation of symptom reduction and the reduction they perceive occurring during their initial interview. A moderate client expectation of gain is associated with the greatest satisfaction. They suggest that moderate expectation may be the most accurate expectancy on an objectivity-subjectivity dimension. Clients with very high or low expectations may be evidencing behaviors that contribute to their problems.

In another clinical study, client expectations were obtained before experiencing either a structured or unstructured initial interview (Clemes and D'Andrea, 1965). Clients experiencing interviews compatible with their expectations rated their anxiety significantly lower than clients having interviews incompatible with their expectations. Also, the therapists rated those interviews that were incompatible with the clients' expectations as the most difficult. Too great a discrepancy could lead to premature termination. It is suggested that the counselor strive for an optimal level of discrepancy conducive to behavior change; i.e., enough compatibility for the client to remain but sufficient discrepancy so he has to deal with the difference. Findings from other studies have indicated that incompatibility of expectations is associated with increased strain during therapy and early termination (Linnard and Bernstein, 1960; Overall and Aronson, 1963).

CLIENT PREFERENCES

Pohlman (1964) comments that in business the customer is always right but in counseling the client's preferences for the counselor are often treated as irrelevant. Several earlier studies show that clients' attitudes toward and satisfactions with counseling suggest that clients prefer counselors who are not nondirective. Even though there may be an immediate, but temporary, favor of the client-centered approach, Forgy and Black (1954) found in follow-up that the clients experienced more satisfaction with the more active method. Grigg and Goodstein (1957) found that "Those clients who see their counselor as taking an active role, making suggestions, and helping with specific plans, are more likely to report a favorable outcome for their counseling experience than those clients who see their counselor as a passive listener." A study of Sonne and Goldstein (1957) suggests that a moderately directive interview may give the client an impression of greater effectiveness and of accomplishing more than does a client-centered interview.

Biddle (1958) found that the counselor's nonconformity to the norms the client perceived for him led to less progress in all phases of the interview than did conformity. Grater (1964) hypothesized that clients who prefer affective counselor characteristics would be more likely to focus on a discussion of personal-social problems in the first interview than clients preferring more cognitive characteristics. To test this hypothesis, college students completed a short Cognitive-Affective Inventory prior to seeing a counselor. A comparison was then made of the focus of their interview. The hypothesis was supported, lending support to Bordin's idea that the characteristics a client considers important in the counselor are indicative of the type of problem he will discuss.

Pohlman (1961) studied changes in client preferences during counseling. College students rated their liking of counselor activities before experiencing counseling with a counselor in an on-campus practicum. After eight sessions they repeated the rating. Significant changes in preference took place as a result of counseling. However, the clients' preference did not come into line with the counselors' behaviors, so there were still differences at the conclusion between client preference and counselor behaviors. Some of the items that the clients wanted more often than the counselor did that were significantly larger than members who wanted it less include:

1. Tell me what he thinks I should do
2. Understand what I am saying
3. Give me information
4. Give an opinion of his own, different from one I expressed
5. Take a personal interest in my problems
6. Refer to his own experience, life, problems
7. Express confidence in me
8. Let me know what he thinks is morally right or wrong for me to do
9. Let me know what we are trying to do
10. Understand my true feeling
11. Seem sure of himself

The items that were wanted significantly less include:

1. Repeat what I have just said, in the same or other words
2. Have me do the talking
3. Have me introduce new topics, instead of introducing them himself
4. Answer questions by asking other questions of me, such as "What do you think?"

There was no preference as to topic of discussion among vocation, study habits, use of time, religion or moral questions, or purposes and goals of living. The clients preferred that the counselor do the decision-making and advice-giving and use techniques in keeping with this emphasis.

Koile and Bird (1956) investigated the preferences of freshmen who would seek help. Males preferred a male counselor on far more problems than a woman counselor and women students preferred a woman counselor. There were a greater proportion of women willing to consult a male counselor than men consulting a woman counselor. The men expressed a preference more frequently than did the women.

Similar findings were reported by Fuller (1964) using clients and nonclients. The male students preferred a male counselor. Female clients with a personal problem preferred male counselors more frequently than female students who were not really entering counseling. Of those students who experienced counseling, those preferring a female counselor previously were more likely to change preference after counseling than those who had preferred male counselors.

What Causes Client Expectations?

Types of Problems. The purposes of coming for counseling apparently affect the client's expectations of the counselor. Bordin (1955) reported that the client who seeks information tends not to place so much importance on the personal characteristics of the counselor. Characteristics such as "fatherly, someone you can lean on" were detrimental to counseling. The clients expecting to talk about personal problems and themselves were more inclined to see the personal characteristics of the counselor as an important part of the process. They were not just seeking information but going to talk about themselves—and you do not talk about yourself to just anybody.

The client expects the counselor to act differently if he has a different problem. The client who comes seeking information expects the counselor to participate more in the process. In other words, he expects the counselor to tell him the answer, help him find it, or give him information to read. This is the type of client that becomes angry or does not return if the counselor assumes a role that is too passive. Most clients with personal problems recognize they need to talk more and the counselor will participate less.

What about the client who presents a facade? Robinson (1950) has pointed out that there is more counselor change-in-role, moving from an information-type interview to personal problem-type interview with the same person, than in the role he plays with different clients. If the client begins with a vocational information problem, the counselor focuses on it; should the client then introduce other personal concerns, the counselor's behavior can be adjusted.

Social Influence

Patterson (1958) suggests that the expectations and preferences of clients in counseling are biases, that they are socially and culturally determined.

The child develops an attitude toward specialists in our society. The doctor, the lawyer, and the teacher do things for us and to us, or tell us what to do. The relationship is one of dependency and reliance on authority. These attitudes transfer to others who are identified as authority figures; i.e., to counselors. Through experience with other authorities, the counselor-client relationship is the signal for the assumption of a dependent pattern. The client expects to be informed, to be questioned, to speak only in response to the counselor, to be dependent upon the lead of the counselor, who takes the responsibility for the relationship.

McGowan and Schmidt (1962) comment that many counselors add to their difficulty in this area without even being aware of it. Counselors frequently complain to their supervisor that "the client just wouldn't talk, and I had to start off by asking questions." If the interview has been observed, if the supervisor has had a chance to evaluate the counselor's non-verbal behavior for cues as to his ease in the initial part of the interview, and if a clear recording of the interview is available, the answer to the counselor's problems is usually evident. The counselor has simply never given the client an opportunity to talk, nor has he created an atmosphere in which the client felt free to talk. Often the counselor feels uneasy during the first short silence and so asks questions or structures the interview in some subtle way. This meets the general social expectation of the client and he learns during this initial stage that he can sit back and wait for the counselor to ask questions. Actually the counselor has stimulated the client behavior he complains about. Counselors need to be conscious of these cues and look for them when listening to recordings of their own interviews.

Referral

Before the interview begins, the client may have formed an attitude or expectancy because of the person who referred him to the counselor. The client who is a self-referral on the recommendation of a friend expects to be treated as the friend was. Such clients are usually quite positive. However, if he was referred by the principal or a teacher, the client will expect an authority quite similar to the one who sent him. This is generally a wary, defensive, and noncommunicative client. Another type of client expectation is caused if he is referred for a mental health examination. Such a client may be very apprehensive and fearful.

Attitude Toward People

The sex of the counselor may affect the expectation of the client. A child develops some general conceptions of what men and women are like. Some of the clients' feelings about the sex as a whole may affect the counseling relationship. A young boy may be quite bashful talking to a young woman counselor (or a young girl talking to a young male counselor). The client may perceive an older woman as a mother figure or a man as a father figure, and assume the usual role. If the client has had a bad previous experience with someone like the mother figure, he may transfer these feelings to the counselor and expect the same behavior again.

There is a question as to the value of having a counselor and client of opposite sex. It may be beneficial, as many persons find it easier to talk to counselors of the opposite sex. Counseling is a learning process, a situation in which emotional attitudes are modified; thus it might be better for a boy to find out that all women are not like his mother or teachers.

Previous Counseling Experience

The client's previous experience may help or hinder the relationship. Previous unpleasant experiences of a client may cause the counselor to start an interview with two strikes against him. Likewise, lack of clear-cut understanding on the part of the client of the nature of counseling is a widespread source of improper expectations of counseling. It is important that the client know the limitations and possibilities of counseling as well as such bits of information as the length of interviews, probable length of the process, or how he makes an appointment.

What Is the Counselor's Role?

Even though there seems to be some agreement regarding client expectations, clients obviously approach a counseling situation with individual expectations. The question at the beginning of this chapter was, what are the client expectations of counseling? An even more pressing question seems to be, what do you do when you find the answer? Do you meet the client's expectation? Do you change his expectations to meet yours? There seems to be support for both sides of this issue.

Bordin (1955) suggests one adaptation to client expectations is in the definition of the counseling task. Although psychologically oriented counselors do not use the psychoanalytic concept of free association, they do tend toward only slightly more structured definition of the task. The counselor can offer a definition of counseling after the initial period, during which the client has explained why he came to the counselor. The client who comes to the counselor without any admissions of inability to deal with his problems and with no expectations of becoming personal or giving up responsibility for himself is not prepared to accept a free-association task definition.

The counselor then will try to convey the idea that the client must be concerned with and communicate about his feelings as they bear upon the problem. Counseling is not concerned solely with the rational manipulation of factors in his situation. The counselor must convey the definition of the task in verbal terms and non-verbal cues. It is important for the counselor to structure the situation and lay out the rules of the game, thereby taking the mystery out of the situation.

Patterson (1968) feels that counseling is a learning process, which is an opportunity for the client to learn to be independent and to accept responsibility for himself. If these are goals of counseling, then it appears appropriate to begin the learning in the counseling process itself. Patterson believes that clients can and do learn this during counseling when given the opportunity to do so. Counselors need not accede to the preferences and expectations of the client but can teach the client to enter a relationship and assume the appropriate responsibility.

Shaw (1955) states the rather unusual approach of up-ending the client's expectancies. The up-ending of expectancies is conceived as a kind of catalytic function whereby the counselor fosters the adopting of latent construction already entertained to a limited degree by the individual. This is sort of an "ice breaking" technique. The counselor's action can be understood as a matter of up-ending expectancies in hoped-for directions. Rather than presenting himself as the highly poised professional the client might have expected, he reveals himself as no less human than the client. This may increase readiness on the part of clients to expose themselves to a person of this kind and risk further re-orientation. The up-ending of expectancies in hoped-for directions can be analyzed as a matter of upsetting a particular expectancy while, at the same time, fostering a larger perspective. A client's expectancy of defeat, for example, met with, "Well, you can't win them all, anyway," might do as much to up-end the expectancy of defeat as a discussion of probabilities of winning versus not winning or of the dynamics of defeatism. These ideas would force the client to change his expectancies to meet the methods of the counselor.

How easy is it to change the client's expectations?

Pohlman (1961) found that significant changes took place during the period of counseling in client preferences about counselor behaviors. But counseling did not change client preferences to the point where they came into line with counselor behavior. There were still many significant post-counseling differences between client statements of what they would like counselors to do and what the counselor did.

In the Poppen and Peters study (1965), little difference existed between the expectancies of those who had previously seen a counselor and those who had not. In fact, the nine most frequent expectancies were the same, with only slight variation in order. This would indicate that even when a client has seen a counselor, his expectations are not always changed.

Conclusion

Rogers stated that one of the necessities of the helping relationship is that the client and counselor be in psychological contact. Often we see a client who has certain expectations of counseling and a counselor who has different expectations or goals. These two may be talking in the same room, but they are not in psychological contact. Many clients want information while counselors want psychological problems. If there is to be a meaningful experience, they must get together. If we believe the unique goals of the counselor in the mental health field are his preventive and positive contributions, then it is important for the counselor to accept clients and to work with them when they have not yet reached a stage where they are aware of and willing to admit emotional problems. He must be willing and able to talk with clients about those problems at the client's present level of thinking.

This is a point that many counselors have difficulty grasping. Often their early studies have so overemphasized the technique that they enter into a counseling relationship with an idea about how they want to respond, but with limited knowledge of what this will involve in terms of their giving of themselves personally in order to meet the true needs of the client, and not just his initial expectations. If counselors are themselves confused about the true nature and controlled involvement of the relationship, and the client is even more naive, how can we reasonably expect growth to occur? The counselor must be aware of himself as a person, his ideas and techniques of counseling. It may be that a planned and gradual introduction into the personal involvement required for the counseling relationship, as well as an increased need for self-awareness on the part of the counselor, is necessary before he can meet the personal needs of the client. Then he can appropriately structure the counseling interview for the client.

THE INITIAL INTERVIEW

Having explored some of the factors that are present before the interview, attention is now focused on initiating counseling. The counselor needs to be aware of the goals to be accomplished in this interview. By accomplishing the primary goals, the counselor has set the counseling relationship in motion. In meeting these goals, the counselor will carry out certain roles and the interview will frequently flow through a three-phase pattern.

GOALS

Tyler (1969) has suggested that there are three goals to be accomplished during the initial interview. The most important of these is to lay the foundation for the counseling relationship. This relationship is characterized as one of warmth and acceptance in which the counselor communicates that he understands or is attempting to understand the client, in which the counselor responds as a genuine human being rather than playing the role of a counselor. (The characteristics of a facilitative relationship are covered in more detail in Chapter 8.) Tyler suggests that the process of finding out what the client wants, what he prides himself on, and what he is concerned about is likely to produce a warm feeling as a by-product.

A second goal of the initial interview is to begin opening all the psychological realities in the client's situation. Tyler emphasizes the opening-up characteristic as a difference between counseling and usual conversation. When a friend expresses anxiety or doubt, one's impulse is frequently to reassure the person. In counseling, however, we help the client to explore more deeply the feelings he is trying to express or look at the area more closely. The degree of client exploration in the initial interview will depend upon various circumstances. At this point the counselor will follow the client's train of thought and feelings but will not probe deliberately for hidden meanings.

Within this major goal, Wolberg (1954) lists several other goals that are established. The counselor will get pertinent information from the client to help establish the tentative dynamics and make a tentative diagnosis. This exploration will permit the counselor to tentatively assess the strengths and weaknesses of the client.

The third goal of the initial interview is to structure the situation for the client. Each counselor will probably have some type of structuring orientation in which he gives the client some idea of what the counseling is like, what is expected of him, what he can expect from the counselor, and how to make plans for further work. The purpose of this structure is to eliminate as many misconceptions as possible and to give him some idea of what he can expect when they begin the next interview. The counselor should give the client only as much as he can use at this time rather than laying out a full description and lecture of the process of counseling.

Counselor Behavior

Preparation for Counseling

The degree of preparation for the first interview will depend upon the counselor's concept of his function as a counselor, the amount of time available and, of course, whether the client appears suddenly and unannounced. Many counselors prefer to have a cumulative folder with a great deal of information about the client prior to seeing him. Other counselors feel that they do not want previous information about the client and would prefer to start with his initial presentation. They assume that reading information about the client may bias them in their attitudes toward the client. Other counselors assume that they can quickly learn information that may otherwise take a long time for the client to contribute (Arbuckle, 1965).

History Taking

Among the researchers, some believe the counselor may need a formal case history in some clinical situations, while others challenge the value of history taking with the client. Those in favor insist that great gaps in information are present when reliance is placed solely on the spontaneous unfolding of the history and that only a careful inquiry into various aspects of the person's life will reveal a complete picture of what has happened to the client. Without an adequate history, it may take months before the client gets around to talking about an aspect of his problem that may give the client an entirely different perspective of the client in his situation.

On the other hand, there are many reasons why counselors hesitate to take complete case histories. Exhaustive histories are not necessary from a diagnostic point of view and are not believed to be of therapeutic value. The therapeutic value of counseling is not composed of collecting information but of helping the client to develop insight into himself and a new outlook leading to a change in behavior (Wolberg, 1954). It may also be argued that asking the client to give a schematic account of himself may increase his resistance in concealing some significant facts about himself. A client may also assume that, once he has made the report of his history, he can sit back and expect the counselor to solve his problems. In a setting where a case history is required, many counselors have the client fill out a questionnaire form or have another person do the history taking.

Counselor Role

Buchheimer and Balogh (1961) describe the counselor as a collaborator as he works with the client in the process of self-exploration, problem-solving, and gaining new perceptions into the person's life situation. This counseling process is both intimate and objective. It is intimate in that the two people become close to each other and the client has freedom to express his feelings. It is objective in the sense that the counselor will help examine and clarify his feelings and attitudes. For many clients this will be a new kind of experience and a different type of relationship with another person. It is hoped that the client will not feel the need to maintain a facade as he does in most social relationships. Experiencing a facilitative relationship will lead him out into the open to explore himself in this objective partnership. This position of a collaborator is complex in that the counselor is not a peer and, although he does not want to be perceived as a superior, this is difficult to communicate to the client.

It is important for the counselor to be sensitive to what is happening in the interview. He must be aware of several factors that are influencing the situation and make responses that seem most likely to bring about progress. During the first interview the counselor will want to determine the type of problem the client presents. From his research on the types of counselor behaviors that occur in interviews, Robinson (1960) suggests that a simple decision as to whether it is a skill or adjustment problem will affect the counselor's behavior. Experienced counselors tend to change their behavior in dealing with these types of problems.

The counselor will also concern himself with the motivation exhibited by the client. An anxious client who feels a need for counseling will be more highly motivated than a client who is referred or called in to see the counselor. A motivated client will usually keep the interview on the topic even when the counselor misses a point, while a less motivated client will be much more resistant to talking about himself or the situation. Working with the "unmotivated" client is one of the major difficulties for a counselor. The counselor's major goal in the interview is to overcome the client's resistance and low motivation by providing a relationship that will make him feel secure enough to bring out his problems. When the client realizes that the counseling situation offers no threat to his control of his own development and that counseling is a source of help but not domination, he may be motivated to express himself.

The counselor will also want to assess the client's stage of insight. If the client has been active in thinking through his problem, his behavior and that of the counselor will be different from the case of a client who is merely flabbergasted by his problem. Robinson (1950) emphasizes that the counselor's communication should be effective in keeping the client motivated, helping him gain insight into his problems, and making him willing to accept that which is discovered and needed.

Usually a counseling interview will be more effective if the client seeks help on his own rather than being referred. Once the client appears, the counselor must provide an atmosphere that makes it easier for the client to discuss his problems. Successful interviews are structured so that the client remains motivated throughout the necessary number of interviews; that is, until he can gain insight and develop internalized methods to solve his problems and change his behaviors.

The goal of moving toward self-insight suggests several necessary characteristics for counseling. The client must be provided with an optimum relationship for thinking through his problem. Under these conditions, or through the contribution of the counselor's ideas, the client can frequently gain new insights into his own efforts. Once the client has new understandings of his feelings and attitudes in a situation, he can slowly try out new behaviors in an effort to cope more effectively with himself and his social situation.

A client's personal problem is often vaguely and poorly verbalized; thus the first step in solving the problem is to be able to see it clearly. The counselor must help the client overcome feelings of distaste and embarrassment in facing his problems, especially before another person.

Robinson (1955) states that research studies have shown four dimensions of counselor behavior to be useful in the interview: an acceptance attitude, responding to the core of what the client says, division of responsibility, and degree of lead.

The counselor should frame his remarks so that the acceptance attitude is evident. As the chart in Chapter 9 (page 232) indicates, counselors vary in their ideas, from considering this the most important part of their relationship to merely calling it interested friendliness.

In dealing with the core of the client's remarks, the counselor must be sensitive to the real problems brought out by the client. He must avoid responding to irrelevant cues and be careful not to diagnose the problem according to his thinking rather than the client's. He may respond to the core of the theme behind the content of what the client is communicating.

Division of responsibility in the counseling interview is determined to a great extent by the problem to be solved. Usually, at the beginning of the interview, the client has a responsibility for stating the problem. His responsibility continues as he explores a personal problem, while the counselor assumes a listening role. However, he follows closely the client's remarks so that he can help the interview along as necessary. When the client has a skill problem or needs information, the counselor will necessarily assume more responsibility for the interview once the problem has been stated. The division of responsibility tends to be different not only with different types of problems but also in handling a given problem from moment to moment. As long as the client is progressing, he is allowed to carry primary responsibility but, as he runs into momentary difficulties, the counselor may enter. Therefore, the primary responsibility shifts back and forth in a collaborative relationship in which neither person has the impression that he alone has responsibility for the relationship.

The amount of lead that a counselor will assume in his remarks depends upon the client's needs and interests. The situation is described as a ladder in which the counselor's remarks should be at the very next rung above the client's thinkings so as to stimulate his development. However, this next level should be close enough to be easily understood and accepted by the client without arousing resistance (Robinson, 1955). A description of various leads is presented in the section on communication techniques.

Action Orientation

Most of the studies indicate that lower-class clients are less likely to seek counseling and, when referred, many are likely to drop out of counseling in a very short period of time. There appear to be a lower rate of success and a higher rate of dropout; therefore, there is a need to do something in the initial interview to motivate the client. Baum and Felzer (1964) believe that early, flexible, and meaningful activity in the initial interview is essential to the establishment of the therapeutic relationship. Such activity should be geared to discussing the expectations of the client, as well as his understanding of counseling and how it works.

As a result of the studies that describe the inaccessibility of the lower social class client, many authors have recommended changes in counseling technique. The concept is appropriate for all clients. It is believed that it is a wasteful procedure to include lower-class clients in the process of teaching insight counseling. It is up to the counselor to assess the client's motivation, as well as work with it and try to develop it in the initial session. It is the counselor's responsibility, not the client's. The clients are frequently vague about counseling and have no clear concept about the possibility of help for their problems. They see little relationship between talking and the resolution of their conflicts or eliminating the problems. They are fearful about counseling and tend to look for direction from an authority figure. To combat these tendencies, it is suggested that there be more re-education and preparatory work on the part of the counselor, particularly in the initial interview, to stimulate the client.

Baum and Felzer (1964) point out that there is difficulty in establishing a common area of understanding. Counselors should resist trying to make a client out of someone who is not interested in becoming one. There is a strong tendency to let the interviews carry themselves, which may work out with better motivated and more sophisticated clients. The counselor may not be able to sell insight to all clients. Baum and Felzer believe that there needs to be early and meaningful activity in the relationship. By "activity" they mean a flexible and spontaneous initiative applied to the particular needs of each client in order to bring about an optimum bridge of communication. This may mean active listening and observing or it may mean explanation and education as to what counseling is about. At other times the counselor may be active in describing the resistances the client has to counseling. The client must be encouraged to air his expectations, what he hopes to get, the concept of his problem, and the concept of counseling. It is important for the counselor to communicate the idea of what might be going on in a straightforward language.

PHASES IN THE INTERVIEW

Buchheimer and Balogh (1961) divide the initial interview into three phases: statement of the problem, exploration, and the closing and planning for the future. This theoretical framework of the initial interview represents a purposive and goal-directed approach to the interview. It is only a guide and the counselor should not attempt to force the interview into any particular pattern. A progression through the initial interview would be from the counselor-client agreement on the problem on which they are going to work, to their exploration of this problem, to the client incentive to become involved in a counseling relationship, to the resolution of the problem through self-understanding, to action that is based on that understanding.

Statement of the Problem

The client is a person in quest. He may be only dimly aware of the nature of his quest or the path he might take. He may not be able to see any way to solve his problem. His quest may stem from dissatisfaction with himself or from others who may have indicated their dissatisfaction with him. He may be dissatisfied with others. His concern may be related to personal development and typical tasks related to his development. It could be an educational-vocational type of concern, or it may be more closely involved with personal and social concerns. The problem the client is able to state at the beginning of counseling is only what he is able to acknowledge at the time and may not represent his major concerns. It is important for the counselor to permit the client the freedom of self-expression and freedom to describe himself in terms of his environment, problems, and goals. The counselor must be careful, however, not to assume that there is always some underlying problem lurking beneath the surface that he must ferret out (Buchheimer and Balogh, 1961).

During the first part of the interview, the client will be given an opportunity to express his problem and his interest. The client may describe himself and his view of life. If this information is sufficient for the counselor, then no further information need be gathered. However, if the counselor is concerned with doing a great deal beforehand, it is important for him to obtain the background information in a systematic and discriminating way. The counselor may go about getting information with a structured intake interview in which he elicits significant background information. This background information should be tailored to the specific client and should deal with his self-perceptions, personal constructs, and perception of his environment.

As the client begins to state his problems, he will present his perception of himself in a particular situation. There may be some hesitancy on his part because he cannot accurately verbalize his feelings. He may describe one or more symptoms at this point, and some of these may not be related to the main problem disturbing him. The counselor's use of general leads or reflections concerning the symptomatology should allow the client to give a more complete picture of his main concern and the history of his problem. The client will talk spontaneously and should not be interrupted. When there is a pause, the counselor may encourage him to continue by showing interest through careful attention and non-verbal communication.

The client who is particularly anxious may deluge the counselor with a wave of unimportant details designed to keep the counselor off balance and allow the client to minimize his anxiety by controlling the content of the interview. In this case, the counselor may need to subtly focus the client's attention on the main aspects of his problem.

The counselor tries to indicate both verbally and non-verbally that he is interested in what the client has to say. This is the first active helpful thing the counselor can do for the client. Clients frequently apologize for coming in with their problems. They may say that others have more serious problems and theirs are really not very important. The counselor, however, assures the client that he is interested in hearing more about what the client has to say and communicates that he considers him worth the time. It is not unusual for the clients to be excessive in formality, restrained in behavior, using formal speech patterns and, in most ways, attributing to the counselor the status of authority (Holland, 1965). The verbal assurances and non-verbal expressions of interest the counselor makes contribute to the client's feelings of being of some significance or importance.

The counselor is predominantly receptive in the initial interview. The client may suggest he does not know what to say; the counselor indicates confidence in the client's judgment by suggesting that he tell him whatever he feels is important at the time. The counselor will use the communication techniques of reflection and clarification to direct the client's content and feelings to gain a better understanding of what the client is experiencing.

As soon as the counselor comes into contact with the client, he begins his observation and initial assessment. This is done by observing as much as possible about the client in an unobtrusive manner. The observation should include the overall impression of dress, the individual's carriage, walk, facial expression, and any special mannerisms he may present. Observation of the client will continue throughout the entire interview. This initial assessment is tentative and any conclusions are subject to later verification (Wolberg, 1954).

When opening the interview, the counselor sets the stage for the rest of the counseling session. It is important, therefore, that he exhibit a warm and interested manner. What happens in the opening moments of the interview can either facilitate or hinder communication in the rest of the sessions.

The principal objective of the initial interview is the establishment of a working relationship. Without such a relationship there is no counseling progress, since the relationship is so important to the success of counseling. All tasks must be subordinate to this objective and its achievement. If the counselor plunges into the exploration of provocative conflicts prematurely, the counseling process will be hampered. The client will not endure the anxiety nor cope with the resistance that occurs even in the early parts of the interview. The attitudes of respect, trust, and confidence in the counselor must be established.

The client must be motivated to work with the counselor. If the client has been referred and really has a low level of motivation, the counselor will have to concentrate his efforts in creating in the client the proper incentives for counseling. No matter how tempted he is to work on the dynamics of the client, he will have to inhibit this until the client is more strongly motivated.

It is necessary to clarify the goal and purpose of the interview so the client will be aware of his situation and his relationship to the counselor. When one attempts to establish goals, he may discover that the client's expectations of therapy are far beyond what could be reached. Some discussion of this problem, with explorations of possibilities, should take place at some point during the interview. It may have to wait, however, until further information is gathered.

The counselor may also have the task of clarifying and removing misconceptions about counseling. Movies and periodicals have often depicted the counselor as a "kook" and the client may therefore be somewhat apprehensive. Many others coming for counseling have been filled with fear that the counselor can read minds and may be frightened that the counselor can see right through them. Countless other misconceptions may burden the counseling effort and interfere with a proper counseling relationship.

Wolberg (1954) discussed some of the frequent resistances that occur in the early phases of counseling. The client may boycott any attempt to convince him that he can be helped. He has invested certain needs in his inappropriate behavior and continues to act on them. The client may refuse to accept the counselor's ideas of counseling because *he* has ideas of what should happen and under what conditions he will cooperate.

Probably the greatest interferences at this point are the client's habitual interpersonal activities. The client has a style of life and, even though parts of it are causing him difficulty, he will not want to give it up. Dealing with resistances to a harmonious relationship constitutes the primary pursuit of the opening phases of counseling.

To illustrate the phases in the initial stages, an interview with a senior high school boy is presented. Parts of later interviews with Tom will be used in the chapter to continue illustrating the relationship.

C   Good morning, Tom.

S   Good morning.

C   I noticed that you made an appointment for this morning. Anything in particular that you'd like to talk about?

S   Well I'm not really sure you know what, what it is, what's been happening. I've just been—I suppose some of the teachers have told you—I've been having some trouble—and my work isn't good—I've been in trouble in some of the classes. I don't really know, you know, what's, what's wrong for that matter. They told me I'd better come and see you—I'm not sure exactly what it is.

C   You sound a little bit confused—uh—maybe about what's going on inside of you and what's therefore led to the kind of behavior you're having—that other people are saying—

S (interrupting) Yeah—I don't—in other words I seem to be having a problem—but I'm not sure why—I just don't know what's
happened Ah-h-h school, everything seems different just over the
—probably nothing I can put my finger on, you know what I
mean—but school just doesn't interest me that much any more
and I find it kind of boring—I just can't put myself into it.

C It sounds like everything has just sort of lost meaning for you.

S That meaning's a good—a good word, yeah, because it doesn't
make sense, I guess meaning and sense are the same thing. In
other words I'd—why should I be doing this, eh, where is it getting me, what for? I don't particularly like school, I always did
well, although in the last year you know I haven't done well.
Um-m-m, it's not any one thing I can put my finger on, it seems
the classes kind of bore me.

C Gosh, you almost sound hopeless, not just about—not just about
classes or grades but—gosh I hear a hopelessness of saying what's
the sense of doing anything, there's just no hope for—

S (interrupting) Yeah, where does it get you—what—or not only
what—eh—where do you want to go—where am I heading um-m
if I could see where school was going to get me or why I am here
or if I just enjoyed doing it but I don't, ah, you know, I don't see
any—let's say that I do stay in school and graduate and go to college, you know I won't be doing it because I want to do it or because I see that it's going to get me some place—I don't see any
place that I really want to get to, I don't see where I'm going to
fit in maybe.

C If you feel this hopeless—that—that doing anything in school or
making any sort of plans is so hopeless, I'm wondering if you feel
the same way about talking with me.

S Well, I don't think I would have come, you know, if I—wasn't
forced to come but I don't think I would have, um, I don't think
you can answer, you know, you can't tell me what to do. But I'm
willing.

C So you feel enough hope, enough, maybe confidence in yourself
or strength in yourself that you're looking for meaning for something to make sense out of life.

S Well you kind—

C Maybe we're able to grapple with some of this here and, and
maybe out of our discussions we can give you some ideas to make
some steps toward—

S I'd like to feel that way, but, you know, I have a kinda hard
time—

C   I'm sure—but we can work together toward clarifying your feel-
    ings. Then maybe you can consider plans about the present as
    well as the future. Does that make sense to you?

S   Yes, I guess so—ok.

Exploration

The client will explore himself when he feels the climate is safe enough.
Some clients describe things immediately, others wait until they feel more
comfortable. Even when the client explores his problem and cries during
the interview, it may be that he is not dealing with the depth of his feelings
or his problem but is still focusing at a fairly cognitive level and talking
about his feelings (Buchheimer and Balogh, 1961). The concept of rapport deals with the comfortableness of the relationship and mutual confidence between the client and the counselor. Many people talk about rapport
being established before counseling can begin; therefore, counselors frequently invent devices designed to establish rapport. Actually, rapport
evolves from the relationship between the two people and is not something
that can be established. Many counselors begin interviews by talking about
the weather or some other small talk in an effort to put the client at ease.
If the client has come to the counselor on his own, he has something he
wants to say and five minutes of small talk may only get in the way. If
the counselor has initiated the interview, the client is wondering why he
was called and again has a certain level of anxiety.

The counselor will generally gain pertinent information from the client
by listening to his spontaneous account and then focusing on selective information that will continue to move the client toward his self-exploration.
The counselor will assess the existing dynamics of the client; however, this
assessment will need constant revision as new data emerges through the
course of counseling. The formulation of existing dynamics will vary according to the counselor's theoretical bases, his skill, training, and experience. No matter how skilled and trained the counselor may be, it is
frequently not possible to gain an understanding of the dynamics of the
client in the initial interview. Many of his patterns are not identifiable to
the counselor and many clients are incapable of verbalizing sufficiently to
give the counselor an idea about their dynamics. As a rule, several interviews will be required before the dynamics begin to unfold (Wolberg,
1954). Clients who are able to talk more freely about themselves and their
feelings will be more capable of revealing sufficient clues about their problems to enable the counselor to make some tentative assumptions about the
dynamics. The key word must be *tentative*.

As the client describes himself and his situation, the counselor should note the client's strengths and weaknesses. It will be important to note the areas of living in which the client is succeeding. There will be times when the counselor will want to know where the client is strong and the areas from which he draws strengths. It is important for the counselor to look for the positive aspects of the client's life as well as his weaknesses. All too frequently, counselors write up interviews describing only the defense mechanisms and weaknesses that a client uses, avoiding the positive parts of the person's life.

C   Why don't you tell me sort of what you feel behind this hopelessness, what leads to this overall hopeless feeling.

S   I can't say exactly what it is—it's just there all the time. You know I used to think that I wanted to be, you know, a success, I wanted to go to college and graduate and be a success and everything just seemed to fit together and I didn't really question things but, ah, as I look around now I don't, I can't, see anything that I want to be, or to do. I don't see, ah, anything very attractive—I don't see where I fit in, I feel that there isn't anything really worth doing and then I don't do anything and then that just makes me feel worse, um, I think maybe—

C   You sound, ah, really awfully lonely you know—sort of isolated, you keep saying that you don't belong—fit in—

S   Yeah—

C   There is a desperate feeling of not belonging, of not doing anything and when you don't do anything, you sort of get in trouble.

S   Well that's exactly—where do you belong? How do you find where, who you—that's—gets to who you are—where—who—how do you know who you are and where you fit in and lonely, I don't know, I mean, I have friends and, and you know I have a good girl friend and everything but it, ah, it isn't enough, ah, you know, we do the same things and go to the same places and lately I've been drinking a lot you know and, but it's nowhere, it's just not anywhere, and it's not their fault, and,

C   In playing the game, you know, studying and making those kinds of plans that you used to have are also nowhere—you don't see any sense in going through that routine again.

S   What for, I can't, I just can't do it, as I sit down to do it I can't understand why I'm doing it and you know and then I just give up, so, I guess it brings you to come around to wondering just exactly where you can find where you're going to fit in or who you are or that sort of thing and I don't know, you know, I don't know what to do—I don't know where to go—I guess I know that no one can tell me—yet—and I see everyone else, not *every*one but most people just don't seem that concerned about it, they seem to know what they're doing and why they're doing it but it doesn't make—it—doesn't, I don't know, I just don't—

C   Pretty damn confusing isn't it?

S   I don't see what, yeah—how do ya—how do ya go about figuring something like that?

C   It sounds like you've gone along for a number of years with plans and ideas of who you were and where you thought you were going and all of a sudden the bottom fell out of that and it's not who you really are or think you want to be anyway.

S   Yeah. I guess that's—I wasn't really—that wasn't really me all that time you know—I was what my parents wanted me to be and what the teacher—everything that was expected to—you know, to what you were supposed to do—that was—it was ok—I didn't worry about it but you know- -I guess as you get really to know and you see your parents for what they really are and they're humans with their faults and they've worked hard all their lives and in any sense I guess they're successful, but they're not—that doesn't make them happy and their lives aren't—they're not really happy and they don't—I don't know, they're successful but they're not really happy and ah I find that—that's—that I was doing sort of doing the same thing—sometimes I get—you know— have you ever just felt scared that nothing makes sense and you're just all alone?

C   Yeah, it must be kind of desperate when you feel that way. I think maybe what I want to say to you is that—that—you're not alone in the sense that I'll spend enough time to try and help you in thinking through some of these because it appears you're looking for—for—you—that when you say the things you used to feel and think weren't you—also saying now you don't know who you are because you haven't—you haven't worked through shedding off your parents' ideas and values. Probably, you're in the process of shedding those but you haven't developed the new you yet and maybe that's what you have to search for now. saying "Gee, what are my values going to be, what is going to bring happiness to me and that some of the things that my folks have set up apparently aren't going to make me happy."

S   Man, that's it—but—what—

Closing and Planning

Near the end of the initial interview, the counselor will want to make the practical arrangements for future counseling. At this point the counselor and client should establish some tentative goals to work toward in the counseling relationship.

The counselor will also tentatively select a method with which he is going to work with the client. If the client is primarily interested in vocational or educational decision-making problems, the counselor may make arrangements for testing, some provision for occupational information, and later interviews for working through this information and decision-making.

The counselor will probably structure the interview according to his own personal mannerisms. Structuring may be done by explaining to the client the task that lies ahead and delimiting the problem area. The counselor may define both his and the client's responsibilities.

Even though the counselor will describe the situation and give some guidelines as to behavior, the content of the interview will be the client's prerogative. Each interview will be structured mutually. The type of relationship that develops between the counselor and the client must be unique.

At the end of the first interview, the client has concern for closure. Holland (1965) suggests this has several aspects. First, the client has risked himself in initiating counseling and, if he is interested in pursuing this relationship, he wants to know if the counselor is going to work with him. Secondly, he is concerned whether he has done the right thing in seeking counseling with this person. Third, he wants to know whether the counselor thinks his problems can be successfully handled.

It is very important that the closing of the interview be warm and friendly and communicate a willingness to work with a client. The counselor's manner, speech, facial expression, and tone of voice should express that there is a real satisfaction in seeing the client again.

C   You have to start saying, "What are my goals? Who am I in establishing my own identity," you know.

S   Yeah.

C   It's going to take some time for us to—ah—sort of wrestle through and find out who you are out of this.

S   You—you mean, you think then that—I—you know—you think talking about being—that—that could help?

C   Well, I think this is the place we have to start, that—as you grapple with this—ah—I can help you clarify some of the things that you're—that you're feeling, some of the inconsistencies you feel, and some of the behaviors you have—look at some of the things you fall into.

S   (Mumble)

C   Apparently you're going to have—you're in the process of developing a new identity from what you were before.

S   Umm—can I do that?

C   Well, it's a—it's a—not a simple thing obviously. I think it's a willingness of the two of us to—to work at it. If you think you want to do that why don't we set up a couple of—of interviews a week maybe and spend some time working on it.

S   Ok—well—I'm sure they'll let me out of class.

C   Let me set up a—a—an hour tomorrow—you've got a study hall tomorrow—let me set it up tomorrow—we'll start then, ok?

S   Ok.

C   Very good.

REFERENCES

Arbuckle, D. *Counseling Philosophy, Theory, and Practice.* Boston: Allyn & Bacon, Inc., 1965.

Baum, O. E., and Felzer, S. B. "Activity in Initial Interviews with Lower-class Patients." *Archives of General Psychiatry* 10 (4):345–353.

Biddle, B. J. "An Application of Social Expectation Theory to the Initial Interview." *Dissertation Abstracts* 19:186.

Bordin, E. "The Implications of Client Expectations for the Counseling Process." *Journal of Counseling Psychology* 2:17–21.

Buchheimer, A., and Balogh, Sara. *The Counseling Relationship.* Chicago: Science Research Associates, Inc., 1961.

Clemes, S., and D'Andrea, V. "Patient's Anxiety as a Function of Expectation and Degree of Initial Interview Ambiguity." *Journal of Consulting Psychology* 29:397–404.

Forgy, E., and Black, J. "A Follow-up After Three Years of Clients Counseled by Two Methods." *Journal of Counseling Psychology* 1:1–8.

Form, A. "Measurement of Student Attitudes Toward Counseling Service." *Personnel and Guidance Journal* 33:84–87.

Fuller, Frances F. "Preferences for Male and Female Counselors." *Personnel and Guidance Journal* 42:463–467.

Goldstein, A., and Shipman, W. "Patient Expectancies, Symptom Reduction and Aspects of the Initial Psychotherapeutic Interview." *Journal of Clinical Psychology* 17:129–133.

Grant, C. "How Students Perceive the Counselor's Role." *Personnel and Guidance Journal* 32:386–388.

Grater, H. A. "Client Preferences for Affective or Cognitive Counselor Characteristics and First Interview Behavior." *Journal of Counseling Psychology* 11:248–250.

Grigg, A., and Goodstein, L. "The Use of Clients as Judges of the Counselor's Performance." *Journal of Counseling Psychology* 4:31–36.

Grosz, R. "Effect of Client Expectations on the Counseling Relationship." *Personnel and Guidance Journal* 46:797–800.

Heilfron, Marilyn. "The Function of Counseling as Perceived by High School Students." *Personnel and Guidance Journal* 31:133–136.

Holland, G. *Fundamentals of Psychotherapy*. New York: Holt, Rinehart and Winston, 1965.

Isard, Eleanore S., and Sherwood, Emily J. "Counselor Behavior and Counselor Expectations as Related to Satisfactions with Counseling Interview." *Personnel and Guidance Journal* 42:920–921.

Koile, E. A., and Bird, Dorothy. "Preferences for Counselor Help on Freshman Problems." *Journal of Counseling Psychology* 3:97–106.

McGowan, J., and Schmidt, L. *Counseling: Reading in Theory and Practice*. New York: Holt, Rinehart and Winston, Inc., 1962.

Patterson, C. "Client Expectations and Social Conditioning." *Personnel and Guidance Journal* 37:136–138.

Perrone, P.; Weiking, Mary; and Nagel, E. "The Counseling Function as Seen by Students, Parents, and Teachers." *Journal of Counseling Psychology* 12:148–152.

Pohlman, E. "Changes in Client Preferences During Counseling." *Personnel and Guidance Journal* 40:340–343.

Pohlman, E. "Should Clients Tell Counselors What to Do?" *Personnel and Guidance Journal* 5:456–458.

Poppen, W., and Peters, H. "Expectations of Junior High School Pupils for Counseling." *Journal of Educational Research* 58:358–361.

Robinson, F. P. "The Dynamics of Communication in Counseling." *Journal of Counseling Psychology* 2:163–169.

Robinson, F. P. *Principles and Procedures in Student Counseling*. New York: Harper and Brothers, 1950.

Severinsen, K. N. "Client Expectations and Perception of the Counselor's Roles and Their Relationship to Client Satisfaction." *Journal of Counseling Psychology* 13:109–112.

Shaw, F. "Mutuality and Up-ending Expectancies in Counseling." *Journal of Counseling Psychology* 2:241–247.

Sonne, T., and Goldman, L. "Preferences of Authoritarian and Equalitarian Personalities for Client-centered and Eclectic Counseling." *Journal of Counseling Psychology* 4:129–135.

Tyler, Leona. *The Work of the Counselor*. New York: Appleton-Century-Crofts, 1969.

Warman, R. "Differential Perceptions of Counseling Role." *Journal of Counseling Psychology* 7:269–274.

Wilcove, L., and Sharp, W. H. "Differential Perceptions of a College Counseling Center." *Journal of Counseling Psychology* 18:60–63.

Wolberg, L. *The Technique of Psychotherapy.* New York: Grune and Stratton, 1954.

8

Diagnosis
in Counseling

The concept of diagnosis originated in the area of medicine, where it is defined as the distinguishing of an illness or disease and its differentiation from other diseases. Diagnosis is based on the attempt to classify illness or disease into discrete, mutually exclusive categories, each of which is characterized by a common origin or cause, a common course, and a common prognosis or outcome (Patterson, 1959). The concept of diagnosis was carried over into counseling through the influences of psychiatry, a branch of medicine that deals with social and emotional problems. However, the concept of classifying disease and treatment does not seem to apply when counseling with normal individuals. This has caused some controversy over the function of diagnosis in counseling. The advocates of diagnosis suggest that it plays a central role in counseling while opponents claim that problems are not sufficiently discrete nor techniques specific enough to be effective. The use of diagnosis for classification has been used, but the concept of diagnosis as "understanding the client" has gained popularity. We will explore some of the major concepts as well as some ideas regarding the process of diagnosis.

PURPOSE OF DIAGNOSIS

The purpose of diagnosis in counseling is to identify the client's life style of functioning or, more specifically, the disruptions of the life style. By

213

identifying the problem area, the counselor and client can establish the goals of the counseling process. Diagnosis can be viewed as serving different functions in the counseling process. It can be used to categorize the problem of the client and therefore label the problem area. This is a carry-over of the medical model, in which the first step is to diagnose the problem in order to prescribe the appropriate treatment.

Because most of the labels in counseling are not sufficiently discrete to suggest differential treatment, a diagnosis that gives a comprehensive picture is frequently used. The drawing together of all the information about a client and his situation as a basis for his decision is an important part of educational and vocational counseling. Another concept of diagnosis is the use of a working hypothesis to understand the client. The counselor develops a model of the client or an individual theory, which changes as the counselor learns more about him. This moment-to-moment understanding is particularly important for both personal and social problems.

In some clinical settings, a counselor may hold a diagnostic interview in which he evaluates the present psychological status of the client and the causal factors of behavior. This leads to suggesting treatment and a prognosis of future adjustment. Such an interview is used for evaluation; the counseling process begins later and frequently with a different counselor. However, in most settings the diagnosis and counseling are interwoven as the counselor begins the process with the initial interview and continues working with the client. With this concept, diagnosis is not a judgment at a point in time but an intricate part of the ongoing process of counseling.

Proponents of diagnostic evaluation base their support of it on the assumption that diagnosis brings clarity and order into a very complex field. They contend that diagnosis enables the counselor to fit many diverse items of information into some understandable pattern, which then allows the counselor to make a prediction about the client's behavior. This procedure subsequently gives the counselor a firm basis on which to construct his plans for handling the case.

A second factor in support of diagnostic evaluation is the assumption that it will aid in the selection of clients for treatment or continuation of treatment. The counselor must decide whether he or his agency can provide the appropriate kinds of treatment to help the client. It is a generally accepted fact that counselors are not equipped to work with severely disturbed clients suffering from psychotic manifestations such as delusions and hallucinations, or clients requiring hospitalization. These cases, it is felt, should be referred to a psychiatrist.

A third reason for using diagnosis in counseling is to aid the counselor in determining what the client seems to need most. Is the client lacking information, or insight? Is he in need of clarification or support? Is he in need of a combination of these? Is the reason the client stated for seeking counseling the real problem, or is it a facade? These are questions the diagnostician feels must be answered before the appropriate treatment can begin (Weiner, 1959).

DIFFERENTIAL TECHNIQUES

Underlying diagnosis is the assumption that different problems lead to differential treatment. For example, Callis (1960) theorized that new experience, perception, and generalization develop a behavior repertoire while inadequacies in behavior repertoire are due to lack of experience, distortion in perception, and errors in generalizations. To deal with these problems, there are two basic approaches to counseling. He suggests that lack of experience is most effectively dealt with by the method of counselor discovery and interpretation to the client. Distortion in perception is most effectively handled by the client's self-discovery.

Although much of counseling is remedial, it may also include developing the potential of the client. The counselor can be effective in bringing about positive aspects of development in the client's life. Developmental goals can be reached without seeking causes and remedial counseling. The counselor and client must state these goals carefully so learning efforts can be efficiently directed. This defining of the areas of positive development is one aspect of the diagnostic process.

Robinson (1963) describes a two-level division of goals. The two rows are used to contrast the remedial and developing strengths goals. The columns are Robinson's diagnostic problems. It is suggested that the counselor's techniques with a client's remedial problem would be different from those employed in developing his strengths. Obviously, these are gross areas of diagnosis and very general approaches to the counseling process.

Due to the lack of specificity in diagnosis and treatment, many counselors have not seen diagnosis as an essential part of counseling. Diagnosis was considered one of the most important skills of a counselor until the rise of the nondirective movement. Since that time, the proponents of the use of diagnosis in the counseling situation have done much research and writing in an attempt to demonstrate the positive contribution of counselor diagnosis. Two major conceptions of diagnosis involve it as either a process of classification or a process of understanding.

	Personal Adjustment	Relating To Others	Knowledge	Maturity	Skills
Remedial	Motivational conflicts Poor self-insight Neurotic tendencies	Conflict with authority figures, peers, spouse, children Loss of loved ones	Lack information about environment	Dependence	Reading disability Speech disability
Developing Strengths	Personality integration Self-insight and acceptance Educational and vocational planning Philosophy of life	Cooperation Loving	Competence	Independence Civic and family responsibility Breadth of interests	Dev. higher-level skill SQ3R study method Use of semantics Use of resources Discussion Cl. use of Co: Discussing plans As a resource

FIGURE 8-1. A CLASSIFICATION OF CLIENT NEEDS THAT AFFECT COUNSELING METHOD. F. P. Robinson, "Modern approaches to counseling diagnosis," *Journal of Counseling Psychology*, 1963, 10, 325–333. By permission.

DIAGNOSIS AS CLASSIFICATION

Many proponents of diagnosis hypothesize that it is possible to classify psychological problems and that the categories will point to differentiation in treatment. This hypothesis has led to many attempts to develop a series of diagnostic constructs to be used by the counselors in their work. The acceptability of these constructs is based upon four desired characteristics: (1) the system must result in a reliable classification of the subjects among its categories; (2) the categories must be mutually exclusive—each class should be identified by constant, discrete symptom clusters; (3) there must be greater variance among the constructs than within each category; (4) each construct should form the basis for the choice of treatment (Bordin, 1946). Over the years several category systems have been proposed.

In 1937, Williamson and Darley identified the diagnosis categories they felt would encompass all problems dealt with by the counselor. They were: vocational, educational, personal-social-emotional, financial, health, family.

Bordin (1946) expressed dissatisfaction with the Williamson-Darley diagnostic constructs because he saw them as sociologically oriented and as excluding psychological dynamics, describing the difficulty but ignoring the source. He suggested that these categories overlapped and did not lead to differential treatment. He stated that his system of classification is a "psychological description which starts at the individual describing the organization of his behavioral characteristics and predicting what his reactions will be to his social environment." Below is a summary of Bordin's set of diagnostic concepts with the common cause and treatment suggested.

Dependence

The client has not learned to take the responsibility for solving his own problems. The counselor aids the client in gaining insight into his feelings of adequacy to cope with everyday problems and to obtain experiences that will make him independent.

Lack of Information

Past experiences of the client have not provided him with the knowledge necessary to cope with the situation. The counselor must give the client the needed information or direct him to the appropriate source.

Self-Conflict

Two or more conflicting feelings are motivating the client. The counselor helps the client to recognize and accept the conflicting feelings so that he may resolve the conflict.

Choice Anxiety

The client is unable to face and accept an inevitable unpleasant situation. The counselor helps the client realize and accept his problem and subsequently make a decision.

No Problem

The client is in need of support in following through on a decision he has already made, or is checking to determine whether he is on the right track. The counselor should lend the client his support.

In evaluation of Bordin's constructs, Robinson (1963) writes that the categories do not give diagnostic indication of what might be the specific cause of the frustration and, therefore, there is little indication of the treatment to be used.

The next attempt to define and to differentiate empirically among the causal categories of client problems was made by Pepinsky (1948). Pepinsky based his diagnostic categories on Bordin's set of constructs but extended Bordin's construct of "Self-Conflict" to include three subcategories: cultural self-conflict, interpersonal self-conflict, and intrapersonal self-conflicts. He replaced Bordin's category, "No Problem," which did not explain the reason why the client sought counseling, with "Lack of Assurance." He also added a sixth category, "Lack of Skill."

Pepinsky evaluated his system constructs by studying intercounselor agreement in applying the constructs to 115 cases. Each counselor based his diagnosis on an analysis of the individual's record blanks, test scores, and other available reports. There were three important findings: (1) The constructs of "interpersonal self-conflict," "intrapersonal self-conflicts," "lack of assurance," "lack of information," and "lack of skill," which were used with consistency by the counselor-judges, were relatively mutually exclusive and seemed to identify important "cause of" factors. (2) Counselor-judges were not able clearly to distinguish between the categories, "cultural self-conflict" and "dependence." (3) "Choice anxiety" was not studied systematically because problems of this type were rarely observed in the cases used.

In Byrne's (1958) scheme the construct "Self-Conflict" and its subcategories were replaced by the categories, "Lack of Insight," and "Lack of Information." The category, "Dependence," was replaced by "Immaturity," the reason being that Byrne believed dependency to be only one expression of immaturity. "Choice Anxiety" was dropped because anxiety is a symptom, not a cause. The category "Lack of Assurance" was maintained. The construct "Lack of Skill" was altered to "Lack of Problem-Solving Skill." Byrne added a new category, "Domination by Authority, Persons or Situations." This last construct includes the client who is unable to make a choice or to plan for the future because of pressures from his environment for him to do something other than what he wills to do.

Robinson (1963) edited the Bordin, Pepinsky, Byrne and Callis systems of classification and proposed the following categories: (1) personal maladjustment; (2) conflict with significant others; (3) discussing plans; (4) lack of information about environment; (5) immaturity; and (6) skill deficiency.

A departure in diagnostic divisions was described by Callis (1965), with a two-dimension diagnostic classification plan. Along one dimension are three of the Williamson-Darley categories: 1) vocational (VOC), 2) emotional (EM), and 3) educational (ED); this dimension is labeled "problem-goal." Along what is labeled the "cause" dimension are these five dimensions: 1) lack of information or understanding of self (LIS), 2) lack of information or understanding of the environment (LIE), 3) motivational conflict within self (CS), 4) conflict with significant others (CO), and 5) lack of skill (LS) (for example, poor reading skills or poor study habits). This cause dimension attempts to focus on whatever is lacking in the client's personal resources that causes his inability to solve his problem.

This two-way system of classification makes 15 diagnostic hypotheses possible. The counselor places a client into one category from each dimension and can record his diagnostic hypothesis by using the symbols from each dimension. The problem-goal dimension is written first, with the cause dimension second. Callis' system of classification has been successfully used in record keeping.

CONCLUSION

Although many systems of diagnosis have been formulated, revised, or modified, there still is no one system that has met all four of the desired characteristics mentioned earlier. Diagnosis by classification has received considerable criticism. The major failure of the classification system has been in attempting to relate classification to differential counseling procedures. Menninger (1958) remarks, "I am somewhat ashamed to admit that it has taken me a quarter of a century to realize that this formula (treating the patient according to his diagnosis) rarely works out this way in actual experience." It would seem to be clear that a classification bearing no relationship to counseling procedures would be of little value in counseling. It has been assumed that there should be different counseling methods associated with the various categories into which client problems are classified. The attempt to look at the diagnostic categories with this in mind has led to the persistence of such attempts at classification.

The difficulty of classifying client problems can be seen by reviewing the initial interview with Tom (Chapter 7). He was having an educational problem in terms of course work and considering whether or not to attend college. The college or work decision would involve somewhat of a vocational decision problem. It was clear that Tom had a conflict within himself that he really could not describe clearly as well as the possibility of conflict with his parents. As the counselor, would you categorize Tom's problem in each area or possibly seek the one major cause? How might your counseling differ with his various problems? Do these classifications help you understand Tom?

Over the years, the antagonists of diagnosis, frequently client-centered theorists (Rogers, 1951), have not stressed structure of any sort, including diagnosis or assessment. They consider diagnosis as palliative and superficial and, at times, restricting and negative to the counseling relationship.

The most basic reason for rejecting reliance on diagnosis was the theoretical position that the client is the only one who can fully understand the dynamics of his own behavior. Change in behavior comes only through a change in perception of the "self." Rogers (1951) claimed that the client will deal with or explore problems ". . . as soon as he is able to bear the pain, and that he will experience a change in perception as rapidly as that experience can be tolerated by the self." Diagnosis places the laws of evaluation in the hands of an "expert," which may foster feelings of dependency and interfere with the emphatic relationship. Patterson (1959) also suggested that diagnosis was not necessary because all maladjustment is similar in origin and the technique of counseling was not dependent upon the nature or content of the conflict.

DIAGNOSIS AS UNDERSTANDING

The impact of the client-centered theory challenged the concept of diagnosis, particularly in terms of classification. However, dignaosis may be viewed in counseling as a process of understanding. Diagnosis is fitted into Rogers' frame of reference in a way far different from the use of diagnostic category systems. Rogers accepted the use of diagnosis in the following sense:

> In a very meaningful and accurate sense, therapy "is" diagnosis, and diagnosis is a process which goes on in the experience of the client, rather than in the intellect of the clinician (Rogers, 1951, p. 223).

We suggest that it is a process that goes on in the experience of the counselor as well as the client. Diagnosis as understanding involves working hypotheses, changing with and being revised by any new cognitive and affective factors brought into the interview by the client or, possibly, from outside-the-client sources.

How does the counselor establish the working hypothesis? In a statement de-emphasizing the use of categories, Bordin (1955) called for understanding the client and suggested "it seems more fruitful to rely on a well-differentiated theory of personality as a basis for trying to understand a particular person." This concept of diagnosis makes the counselor's understanding of the client dependent upon his adoption of a philosophy of man, personality-theory, and counseling theory.

The concept of the counselor as an hypothesis maker and model builder has been supported by many. Pepinsky and Pepinsky (1954) proposed that the counselor be a model-builder by forming a "micro-theory" of the client's behavior. They believe the counselor must distinguish between observation and inference, state testable hypotheses, test them, and reconstruct the "micro-theory" in light of new information. It is clear that the counselor's responses in the interview will result from his conception or understanding of the client.

Meehl (1954) also considered the counselor a model-builder. He described the process as the counselor bringing events and circumstances together at the moment into a "conception of this person." Wrenn (1951) discussed it as "process diagnosis" while Super (1957) talked about the counselor's "picture of the client."

It is apparent that these early writers captured the idea of diagnosis as understanding. The counselor maintains continuing understanding by formulating a personal theory for the client. That personal theory is generally based on some larger theory of personality development, maladjustment, and counseling theory.

Once again let us review the initial interview with Tom. Using the theory of development you prefer, can you begin to formulate a micro-theory or model of him? It is a short interview and we can only begin to establish some working hypothesis. With this concept of diagnosis there is no need to make a judgment—just to understand the client. Further information is provided in Chapter 10, "Continuing the Relationship," which can extend our understanding of Tom.

How successful are counselors in this process of formulating a personal theory for their clients? Several studies examine this question. McArthur (1954) had counselors predict behavior over a ten-year period. All of these counselors tended to use a variety of data and formulated hypotheses from several theories, regardless of their theoretical orientation. They were operating from some conception of the person. Two early studies point out the problem in the process. Koester (1954) recorded counselors' thought processes and found they did interpret data, synthesize the data, make hypotheses, and evaluate their hypotheses. However, he reported a reluctance to accept negative information that would refute the hypothesis. A similar finding by Parker (1957) suggested that although counselors did make a conceptual model of the client, they did not increase the richness of the model from interview to interview. Gauron and Dickinson (1966) reported that clinicians were influenced by their initial impressions. They compared the initial and final diagnosis and found that the clinician ended up with his initial impression as a final diagnosis in 18 of 36 cases. It appears that counselors are hypothesis makers in building a model of the client, but once this is done, prove to hold the model firm. This sounds more like a judgment than a changing fluid process.

A related area to the counselor hypothesis-making is the clinical vs. statistical prediction controversy. The controversy deals with the effectiveness of a counselor's clinical prediction compared with using data in a formula to make a statistical prediction. Meehl (1954) reviewed 19 studies that predicted success of some kind of training, education, or recovery from psychoses. He reported that ten studies found no difference in the effectiveness and nine found the statistical method was more effective. For years this information was used to suggest that, when possible, the counselor should use a statistical formula for prediction. In educational and vocational counseling this is frequently possible.

More recent studies on counselor prediction of student grades in college have been conducted by Watley. In one study (1966) he investigated the predictive validity among individual counselors and attempted to identify factors that differentiated between the "most" and "least" accurate predictors. He found that increased amounts of data did not affect the predictive accuracy of the counselors as a group. Predictive ability was highly individual. Although no counselor was able to predict better than the statistical predictions, some consistently equaled it. The counselors who were the best predictors obtained significantly higher Miller's Analogies Test mean scores and had higher mean P+ scores on the Minnesota Multiphasic Personality Inventory. These scores suggest the better predictors were more able to understand abstract concepts and were more compulsive with stronger needs to develop knowledge of the constructs with which they work.

A second study by Watley (1966b) investigated the counselors' confidence in the accuracy of their predictions. These findings suggest that counselors who lacked confidence in their predictions were more often correct than counselors expressing the most confidence in their judgments. Educational and vocational counseling relies heavily on the accuracy of counselor predictions. The results of these studies indicate that counselors arrive at conclusions that are inaccurate and that, unless they recognize how inaccurate their predictions are, they may be detrimental to a client.

DIAGNOSTIC PROCESS

To effectively use diagnosis as understanding, the counselor remains open to himself and to new information that is presented. The process of diagnosis is complex and involves the counselor's understanding of as many facets of the client as possible.

Robinson (1963) proposes that at least four aspects of client analysis are needed in formulating a diagnosis for a basis in selecting appropriate counseling methods. The first aspect is the traditional concept of looking for the cause of difficulty so the content of treatment can be determined. An intensive case study is necessary to understand the complex pattern of causal factors as well as the client's previous dynamics of adjusting to his situation. Much of this will be gathered in the counseling interview; however, testing may contribute valuable information.

Psychological tests present problems to be solved by the client under specified interactional conditions. In the comparison with usual interview procedures, most psychological tests provide a greater standardization of the stimulus conditions. Test results should represent objective material. The subjective element enters into the interpretation of the factual results. In other words, psychological tests are an objective aid to observation in the diagnostic process.

All too frequently, the testing is completed in a separate interview and the results of the tests are communicated to the counselor for implementation of his diagnosis. However, there is much to be gained if the person making the diagnosis also administers a test during the interview. In addition to the specific answers given in the test, it can provide a behavioral sample of the patient's reaction to a problem situation in a relatively stressful interpersonal situation. Therefore, the use of tests in the interview can be considered a miniature life experience, yielding information about the patient's interpersonal behavior and variations in his behavior as a function of the stimulus conditions (Kanfer and Saslow, 1965).

The client's modes of achieving adjustment essentially reflect reliance on particular defense mechanisms and selective responses to stimulation associated with those defenses. Responses to various test items are verbalized end-products in thought process initiated by the items. A test response, then, is more than just a score, although scores may be helpful in making comparisons with other persons or with the same patient after therapy. A test response, because it represents the person's characteristic style of thinking, allows inferences concerning his predominant behavior pattern. Hence, the person administering the test may learn more from the client than just his score on the test.

The client must be made to think in a variety of problem situations so the counselor can distinguish the pervasive aspects of his adjustment efforts. It is important that the counselor learn about the client's past adjustment efforts (as well as his application of assets and liabilities) to new problems. Usually there is considerable continuity between past and present adjustment behavior, but it is possible to have a discrepancy. From the test responses, the counselor can form a picture of the characteristic efforts at adjustment. It is imperative that the counselor check the implications of any one response or pattern against the implications of all other responses or patterns. When sufficient patterns are found that have one or two major implications in common, an interpretation is possible. The counselor seeks as few general conclusions as possible to embrace all the significant patterns.

An interpretation is a prediction that certain behavior or thinking will be found by direct observation to characterize the individual. The interpretation refers to thinking or behavior that can be immediately apprehended and does not commit the counselor to any diagnosis. The counselor gathers his test data, case experience, and observations into a set of diagnostic hypotheses about the patient.

The second focus of client analysis goes beyond looking for areas of remediation and looks for the positive. It emphasizes describing the goals involved in building the strengths of a client, thus giving direction to counseling. The diagnosis is focused on identifying those positive areas of the client's life he would like to strengthen.

A third focus of the process involves the counselor's discovering the manner in which the client responds to stimuli so he can select appropriate counseling methods. He looks for the adjustment techniques of the client so these can be reinforced. The counselor studies how the client responds to certain situations and why, which permits him to develop a model of the client. This is helpful in understanding the client and determining what will be effective with him.

The fourth aspect involves the moment-by-moment responding of the counselor to aid the client in learning more appropriate behaviors. With the conceptualization of the client—the problem area, the client's dynamics of adjustment, and the counseling goals—the counselor selects the bases for learning that best suit the purpose being worked on at the time.

Thought Process.

In the counseling interview the counselor's thought processes can involve various diagnostic styles. Gauron and Dickinson (1966) investigated diagnostic decision-making in psychiatric interviews and then described six approaches. Their illustrations seem appropriate to the processes that might be found in counseling. In the "Intuitive-Adversary" approach the counselor commits himself to a diagnosis on an intuitive basis early in the interview and then challenges the information to disprove this diagnosis. The user of this approach is dependent on his intuition and is open to pitfalls of attitudinal set, bias, or distortion.

Another approach is termed "Overinclusive-Indecisive" because a counselor starts to go in one direction, then drifts in a different direction when information suggesting another potential direction is presented. The final result is a decision maker in conflict with no apparent confidence in his ability to form conclusions. Diagnosis is reached in an impulsive manner and is probably an arbitrary decision.

The "Textbook" approach is used by a counselor who follows a rigid format. He asks for information as it appears in written records and case history write-ups. There is no concept as to which information is most valuable nor do bits of information with potential diagnostic clues cause him to deviate from his predetermined course. The "Bibliography" approach is closely related except it is not so structured. Information is not requested in any predetermined order but on the apparent basis of whim. A user of the Bibliography approach is compulsive in his need to obtain all the information but impulsive in his manner of getting it. Both of these approaches follow a textbook idea of information to gather.

Two other approaches offer more meaningful processes. In a "Diagnosis-By-Exclusion" approach, the counselor would list several broad diagnostic possibilities. He proceeds to gather information, excluding diagnostic possibilities until he ends up with the most meaningful one. It is inductive in nature since he is inferring conclusions on the basis of information and functions as a data gatherer and excluder. This approach might be an effective process if one needs to diagnose for classification.

In the "Flexible-Adaptable" approach, the counselor has no preconceived ideas about the order in which information is requested but goes where the information leads him. The counselor uses a feedback arrangement in that the data he receives modifies his thinking. His current thinking, derived from the impact of all the combined information, determines what he responds to next with the client.

If we consider diagnosis an ongoing process to understand the client—where he is at the moment as well as where he has been—the last approach would be most helpful. It seems that a more unstructured method in gathering information would permit the client more freedom to explore himself and his environmental situation. This will yield more meaningful information and help the client gain self-insight. The thought process of the counselor could be examined on a dimension labeled inductive-logical and intuitive-alogical. It seems that inductive thinking would be more productive. The logic might follow the inductive thinking process rather than a prescribed set of questions.

Diagnosis, used in the sense of a working hypothesis, seems valuable. The following excerpts from Kell and Mueller (1966) express how the best use can be made of diagnosis:

> Diagnosis . . . is an interpersonal process in which the sole purpose of the diagnosis is to understand the relationship well enough to be able to help the client to change . . . The initial diagnosis is only one of the means that the counselor has of setting the counseling relationship in motion. As the counsel process continues to progress appropriately, the process of diagnosis becomes a more intimate, idiosyncratic one . . . Whether the counselor's diagnosis changes will be a function of whether the relationship becomes closer, because only in an intimate relationship is it safe for the client to talk about the meaning that his behavior has for him . . . As the relationship grows stronger, the diagnosis necessarily becomes more specific to this person, and the counselor leaves the generic ideas farther and farther behind him as he and the client delve more deeply into the meanings of his experiences (pp. 16–17).

SUMMARY

This chapter has examined the major conceptions of diagnosis and presented some ideas on the process. There has been a controversy regarding the place of diagnosis in counseling. Proponents of diagnosis advocate that it plays a central role in counseling while opponents maintain that it involves external judgments, which interfere with understanding the client.

Several classification systems have been proposed to identify client problems with the intention of differential treatment. Actually, a classification system would be helpful in research and record keeping but generally not helpful in the counseling process. The idea of establishing working hypotheses to build a model or micro-theory of the client seems more appropriate to maintain a deeper understanding of the client.

REFERENCES

Bordin, E. S. "Diagnosis in Counseling and Psychotherapy." *Educational and Psychological Measurement* 6:35–56.

Bordin, E. S. *Psychological Counseling*. New York: Appleton-Century-Crofts, 1955.

Byrne, R. H. "Proposed Revisions of the Bordin-Pepinsky Diagnostic Constructs." *Journal of Counseling Psychology* 5:184–188.

Callis, R. "Diagnostic Classification as a Research Tool." *Journal of Counseling Psychology* 12:238–243.

Callis, R. "Toward an Integrated Theory of Counseling." *Journal of College Student Personnel* 1:2–9.

Gauron, E., and Dickinson, J. "Diagnostic Decision Making in Psychiatry." *Archives of General Psychiatry* 14:233–237.

Kanfer, F., and Saslow, G. "Behavioral Analysis: An Alternative to Diagnostic Classification." *Archives of General Psychiatry* 12:529–538.

Kell, B. L., and Mueller, W. J. *Impact and Change: A Study of Counseling Relationships*. New York: Appleton-Century-Crofts, 1966.

Koester, G. A. "A Study of the Diagnostic Process." *Educational and Psychological Measurement* 14:473–486.

McArthur, C. "Analyzing the Clinical Process." *Journal of Counseling Psychology* 1:203–207.

Meehl, P. E. *Clinical Versus Statistical Prediction*. Minneapolis: University of Minnesota Press, 1954.

Menninger, K.; Ellenberger, H.; Pruyser, P.; and Mayman, M. "The Unitary Concept of Mental Illness." *Bulletin of the Menninger Clinic* 22:4–12.

Parker, C. A. "A Study of Clinical Diagnosis and Prediction by Means of Verbal Report." Doctor's thesis, University of Minnesota, 1957.

Patterson, C. H. *Counseling and Psychotherapy: Theory and Practice*. New York: Harper and Row, 1959.

Pepinsky, H. B. "The Selection and Use of Diagnostic Categories in Clinical Counseling." *Applied Psychological Monographs* No. 15 .

Pepinsky, H. B., and Pepinsky, Pauline. *Counseling: Theory and Practice*. New York: The Ronald Press Company, 1954.

Robinson, F. P. "Modern Approaches to Counseling Diagnosis." *Journal of Counseling Psychology* 10:325–333.

Rogers, C. R. *Client-Centered Therapy*. Boston: Houghton Mifflin Company, 1951.

Super, D. E. "The Preliminary Appraisal in Vocational Counseling." *Personnel and Guidance Journal* 36:154–161.

Watley, D. "Counselor Confidence in Accuracy of Predictions." *Journal of Counseling Psychology* 13:62–67(b).

Watley, D. "Counselor Variability in Making Accurate Predictions." *Journal of Counseling Psychology* 13:53–62(a).

Weiner, I. B. "The Role of Diagnosis in a University Counseling Center." *Journal of Counseling Psychology* 6:110–115.

Williamson, E. G., and Darley, J. G. *Student Personnel Work*. New York: McGraw-Hill, 1937.

Wrenn, C. G. *Student Personnel Work in College*. New York: The Ronald Press Company, 1951.

9

Counseling
as a Relationship

Many writers in the field of counseling view the relationship as the most important aspect. In recent years, techniques have been superseded in theory by the feeling tones that lie behind them. Technique has become less stringent in order to allow expression of an important dynamic—the counselor's attitudes. These attitudes are very influential factors in producing the kind of relationship that leads or does not lead to client improvement. The factors that foster development and maintenance of an effective relationship are of primary importance. What are those factors or dimensions of the counseling relationship that make it effective? One area is the facilitative conditions the counselor communicates to the client. These seem to serve as a base for the development of a relationship. In addition, there are several dimensions that exist in the interaction between counselor and client that are influential in the effectiveness of counseling.

THE FACILITATIVE CONDITIONS

Rogers (1957) stated what he called the necessary and sufficient conditions for therapeutic personality change. These are the specific counselor attitudes that Rogers believed to be essential for the development of a counseling relationship. They are a comprehensive and systematic conception of the change-producing ingredients of the counseling process. First of all, he points out that significant change does not occur except in a relationship. He means that two people must be in psychological contact: the awareness of both the client and the counselor of each other's presence. The other necessary and sufficient conditions postulated by Rogers include the counselor's positive regard for the client, experiencing unconditional positive regard, empathic understanding, and being congruent in their relationship.

The counselor must be congruent or integrated in the relationship. He must be exactly what he is—not a facade, a role, or a pretense. He not only means what he says but his feelings also match what he is expressing. Being congruent or genuine involves a willingness to be and to express the words, behavior, feelings, and attitudes that exist within the counselor. It is only in this way that the relationship can have reality.

The second facilitative condition in a relationship is the counselor's experiencing an empathic understanding of the client's world and being able to communicate some of this understanding to the client. The counselor senses the client's private world as if it were his own, but without losing the "as if" quality. The counselor is sensing the feelings and personal meanings that the client is experiencing. When he can perceive these from "inside" as they seem to the client, and when he can successfully communicate some of this understanding to the client, then this condition is fulfilled.

The third condition for growth and change is the counselor's experiencing a warm, positive, accepting attitude toward the client. Although Rogers listed this third, it probably is the first thing the counselor is able to communicate to the client. It means that he likes the client as a person and cares for him in a nonpossessive way as a person with potentiality. This condition means that the counselor respects the other person as a separate individual and is usually termed "positive regard."

The last condition for personal change in the relationship is called unconditionality of regard. It is hypothesized that the relationship will be more effective as the positive regard is more unconditional; that is, the counselor does not accept certain feelings in the client and disapprove of others. There is an ongoing positive feeling without reservation or evaluations. The counselor's acceptance of the client is unconditional in the sense that it is nonjudgmental. There are no conditions or strings attached. It means an acceptance of and a regard for the person's attitudes at the moment, no matter how negative or positive they may be. This acceptance of the client's fluctuating feelings makes it a relationship of warmth and safety. This means that the client does not have to hide parts of himself, behave in certain ways, or play certain games for the counselor to pay attention to him, or to care for him as a person.

Rogers has contributed the most focus on these variables and their importance in the relationship. He has called specific attention to them and has based his whole counseling approach on these conditions. In fact, the concept of the necessary and sufficient conditions for change seems almost synonymous with client-centered counseling. Actually, most approaches to the counseling relationship include similar variables. Table 9-1 presents a comparison of these conditions across several theoretical approaches.

PSYCHOANALYTIC THEORISTS

The psychoanalytic writers do not name attitudes that are necessary for successful counseling. However, Adler, Horney, and Alexander, as examples of psychoanalytical orientations, seem to stress two similar variables in their writings. They say that understanding and friendly interest in the client are necessary for successful counseling to take place.

Horney (1942) writes that, by his friendly interest, the analyst gives the client a good deal of what may be called general human help. That is similar to what one friend might give to another: emotional support, encouragement, interest in his happiness. This may be the client's first experience of human understanding, the first time another person has bothered to see that he is not simply spiteful, suspicious, or demanding but, with a clear recognition of such traits, still likes and respects him as a striving and struggling human being. Alfred Adler, the first of Freud's pupils to break away, in his writing about the type of therapy called "individual psychology," gives the two main attitudes of the counselor as understanding and a friendly way. Sullivan (1954) used the word "awareness" instead of understanding and the word "respect" instead of friendly interest. He believed that respect for the other person and awareness of the other person's feeling were elements of the expertness in interpersonal relations that any client would look for in an interviewer. Sullivan is probably most noted for his concept of the participant observer. He believed the counselor could not stand off to one side and apply his sense organs without becoming personally implicated in the operation.

This concept of being personally implicated appears to be quite similar to Rogers' idea of being congruent in the relationship. Although Alexander (1963) does not talk about a condition equivalent to congruence, he does present some similar ideas. He maintains that the counselor's objective, emotionally nonparticipating attitude is artificial insomuch as it does not exist between human beings in actual life. He believes the client reacts to the counselor as a concrete person and not only as a representative of transferred feelings. He also believes that the counselor's reactions exceed what

TABLE 9-1

Rogers	Adler	Horney	Sullivan	Alexander
1. Congruence	. . .	. . .	Personally Implicated	. . .
2. Empathy	Understanding	Understanding	Awareness	Understanding
3. Positive Regard	Friendly Way	Friendly Interest	Respect	Friendly Interest
4. Unconditional Regard	. . .	. . .	. . .	. . .
5. . . .	Intuitive Guessing	. . .	. . .	. . .

Dollard and Miller	Wolpe	Shoben
1. . . .	. . .	. . .
2. Empathy	Empathy	Understanding
3. Acceptance Positive Outlook	Respectful Seriousness	Warmth . . .
4. . . .	. . .	Nonretaliatory Permissiveness
5. Mental Freedom Restraint	Communicate Desire to Serve	Honesty of Communication

Van Kaam	Dreyfus	May
1. Sincerity	Openness	Encounter
2. Acceptance	Understanding	Empathy
3. Gentleness	. . .	. . .
4. Nonjudgmental	Letting-Be	Nonthreatening Atmosphere
5. Creativity	. . .	. . .

Fiedler's Study	Truax's Study	Carkhuff and Berenson
1. . . .	Genuineness	Genuineness
2. Understanding	Accurate Empathy	Empathy
3. Warm Interest	. . .	Positive Regard
4. . . .	Nonpossessive Warmth	. . .
5. . . .	. . .	Concreteness

is actually called countertransference. They may also include behaviors based on conscious deliberations and also on his spontaneous, idiosyncratic attitudes. Therefore, although Alexander does not state that being one's self in the interview is necessary, he is aware that it frequently occurs. He also talks about the conditions of understanding the client and providing friendly interest.

LEARNING THEORISTS

Three learning-theory orientations are included in the chart. Dollard and Miller (1950) believe that the client finds in the counselor someone with prestige who pays favorable attention and listens sympathetically, thereby giving the client faith of some help. The counselor shows excess permissiveness and encourages the client to express feelings. He does not condemn and tolerates discussions of matter that has caused the client's friends to show anxiety and disgust. The counselor's composure tends to be imitated by the anxious client, which is reassuring for him. When the client has always received severe disapproval, the counselor's calm, accepting manner is experienced as a great relief and a striking intervention. "It may be worthwhile to name four attributes of the therapist as a teacher in the situation of psychotherapy: we suggest that the therapist should be mentally free, empathic, restrained, and positive."

Although Miller and Dollard do not list acceptance specifically, from their writings it is apparent that they expect the counselor to be accepting of the client. Their description of the counselor as being calm and accepting and not condemning may not include unconditional positive regard but at least must include a concept of positive regard for the client. The attribute of a positive outlook really means that the counselor has faith in the client and that he will be able to solve his problem and eliminate the conflicts. Dollard and Miller believe that by being mentally free, the counselor must have much less anxiety than the client about the worst things that bother clients. He must be able to work with what the client says without anxiety. The counselor must also use some restraint and resist the strong tendency to conduct the interview as a conversation. He must subordinate himself to the strategy of cure and say nothing that does not further this strategy. This idea of restraint may inhibit the counselor from really being congruent or genuine in the relationship.

The action-oriented counselors who use conditioning approaches in their counseling are frequently perceived as cold and inhuman. However, Wolpe (1966) describes relationship variables that are quite similar to those of other approaches to counseling. He states that, whatever else the counselor may do, it is of first importance to display empathy and establish a trustful relationship. The client must feel fully accepted as a human being and not less worthy or less fortunate than the counselor. Wolpe believes that the specific techniques used in therapy must be administered by persons who are able to treat their clients with respectful seriousness and who can communicate a sincere desire to be of service.

Shoben (1956) discusses similar variables for the counseling relationship. He believes the counselor should express a genuine concern for the client as a human being and devote his entire attention during the interview to understanding the client's feelings as fully as possible. The counselor should communicate his friendliness or warmth to the client without condemnation. The counselor will also interpret the feelings of the client. In this area Shoben talks about honesty of communication. He uses the term "nonretaliatory permissiveness" in a way that is very similar to unconditional positive regard. He states that the client should be free to discuss any subject he desires and is never rejected or criticized for his beliefs or feelings.

EXISTENTIAL THEORISTS

Three existential counselors are presented in the chart. Van Kaam (1966) describes the relationship as including sincerity, acceptance, gentleness, and flexibility. His use of the term "sincerity" is very similar to Rogers' term of congruence. Van Kaam believes the counselor should develop sincerity in the depth of his being; his attitude should be straightforward, honest, and truthful. His use of the word acceptance is a very broad concept. He believes that the attitude will generate in the client an experience of really feeling understood in his uniqueness and in his personal world. The acceptance of the client does not imply personal agreement with his strivings and decisions, but a co-experience and a nonjudgmental attitude. The counselor's special function is not to judge how far the client is personally responsible for the attitudes and the feelings, but to understand the region of their existence that they reveal. Under the terminology of acceptance, then, Van Kaam really includes understanding, which is quite similar to empathy, and also a nonjudgmental attitude similar to unconditional positive regard.

He describes gentleness as an attribute in the relationship that is similar to a positive regard for the client. Gentleness is a basic orientation which reveals itself in respectful, sensitive, considerate, and tolerant modes of existence. He believes the counselor respects the client because the nature is a gift of being which is fundamentally good and, therefore, lovable no matter how it may be overgrown or veiled by attitudes and feelings with which the counselor may not agree. Van Kaam uses the word "flexibility" in the same manner that he termed the quality creativity. He states that the counselor should be flexible, that counseling should not be a rigid observation of rules that have been learned, but that the counselor should be convinced that every client is in some way unique and that everything the counselor says or does is a creative outgrowth of his participation in the unique experience of the here and now.

Dreyfus (1962) talks about the counselor's being human or open, understanding, and having an attitude of "letting be." He believes the counselor is trying to understand the client's being-in-the-world, the way the client perceives himself, his environment, and his reaction to both. It is through understanding by the counselor that the client understands himself. The term, "letting be," means the affirmation of the other person. It constitutes an attitude that permits the free emergence of the inherited creative potentialities of the other person. The counselor does not evaluate, judge, or condemn. When the counselor allows himself to be open to the client without trying to treat him as an object, he will then be able to understand the client.

May (1967) states that empathy is the key to the counseling process. He describes empathy as "feeling into" another person; that is, the feeling of the counselor into the client's personality until some state of identification is achieved. It is through this process that real understanding occurs—and it is understanding the client's unique pattern that is the major goal. He suggests that both the client and counselor become merged into a common psychic entity to work on the client's problem. He also believes the encounter is a real here-and-now relationship, and that the counselor must be wholly present in the relationship. This encounter means the presence of the counselor and client in a relationship where both are somehow changed. May (1961) also believes this type of relationship can exist only in a nonthreatening atmosphere in which the client experiences his existence.

RESEARCH

Two research studies are also shown in the chart. The much quoted Fiedler studies from the 1950's are usually noted because of the comparison of experts with non-experts. The conclusion is that the experts from different theoretical orientations provide a similar relationship, while the non-experts from different points of view are quite different. In examining the relationship, Fiedler believes his investigation supports the "theory that relationship is therapy, that the goodness of therapy is a function of the goodness of therapeutic relationship." He stated that the expert counselors of any of the three orientations created a relationship more closely approximating the ideal therapeutic relationship than relationships created by nonexperts. The variables that differentiate the relationships formed by the counselors include an ability to understand the client's meanings and feelings, a sensitivity to the client's attitudes, a warm interest without an emotional over-involvement. Fiedler concludes that the ability to understand the client is the most important of the criteria of a counselor's expertness.

One of the most significant research studies in the field of counseling was reported by Truax (1963), when he concluded that counseling can be for better or for worse. He reported that counselors who provided high levels of accurate empathy, understanding, nonpossessive warmth, and genuineness induced greater self-exploration throughout the process of counseling and also produced constructive behavioral and personality change in the clients. He also reported that low levels of these factors led to client deterioration so that counseling could be detrimental as well as beneficial for the client. Truax stated that genuineness implies the counselor's being himself in the moment rather than presenting a professional facade. This simply means that, at the moment, the counselor is really whatever his response denotes. Truax described accurate empathy rather than just empathic understanding. Accurate empathy involves more than just the ability of the counselor to sense the client's private world as if it were his own. It also involves more than just his ability to know what the client means. Accurate empathy involves the counselor's sensitivity to the current feelings, and his verbal facility to communicate this understanding in a language attuned to the client's feelings. The dimension of nonpossessive warmth or unconditional positive regard ranges from a high level, where the counselor warmly accepts the client experience without imposing any conditions, to a lower level, where the therapist would evaluate the client or his feelings in a selective and evaluative way.

The last column on the chart presents the facilitative conditions that Carkhuff and Berenson (1967) have developed from their research into an eclectic approach to counseling. Although these concepts grew out of the client-centered orientation, they have been refined, extended, and researched to the point that Carkhuff and Berenson have established a model for counseling. They describe this as a comprehensive model of facilitative processes. They employ the same conditions of empathy, respect, and genuineness and also include a new condition called concreteness..

Carkhuff (1967) developed a five-point scale to assess the level of facilitative dimensions that are related to an improved functioning in all interpersonal processes. On all scales, Level 3 is defined as a minimally facilitative level of interpersonal function. At Level 3, the counselor's response of empathic understanding is essentially interchangeable with that of the client in that both express essentially the same affect and meaning. The positive respect and communication for the client's feelings, experiences, and potentials are communicated. The counselor provides no discrepancies between what he verbally states and what other cues indicate he is feeling. His response to the personally relevant concreteness of the client is defined as the counselor's enabling the client to discuss personally relevant material in a specific and concrete terminology.

Below Level 3 the responses of the counselor detract from those of the client. Thus at Level 2, while the counselor does respond to expressed feelings of the client, he does so in such a way that he subtracts noticeably from the affective communication of the client. The counselor's response to the client is made in such a way that he communicates little respect and concern for the feelings and experiences of the client and there are indications that the counselor's responses are slightly interrelated to what other cues indicate he is feeling at the moment. The counselor frequently leads or allows the discussion of material that is relevant to the client to be dealt with on a somewhat vague and abstract level. At the lowest level, Level 1, there is communication of a clear lack of respect or negative regard for the client. The counselor's expressions are clearly unrelated to other cues which indicate what he is feeling at the moment, and his general responses are negative in regard to the client's. At Level 1 the counselor's responses either do not attend to or distract significantly from the expression of the client in such a way as to communicate that the counselor does not understand the client. He leads or allows all discussions with the client to deal only with vague and anonymous generalizations.

Above Level 3, the counselor's responses are additive in nature so that, at Level 4, the responses of the counselor add noticeably to the expression of the client in such a way as to express feelings at a deeper level than the client is expressing himself. The counselor's communications create a deep respect and concern for the client and he presents positive cues, indicating a human response, whether positive or negative, in a nondestructive manner to the client. The counselor is frequently helpful in enabling the client to develop fully in concrete and specific words almost all instances of concern.

The fifth level characterizes counselor responses that add significantly to the feelings and meanings of the client in such a way as to express accurate feelings beyond what the person is able to express. The counselor communicates the very deepest respect for the client's worth as a person and his potential as a free individual, and his expressions indicate that he is freely and deeply himself in the relationship with the client. He is completely spontaneous in his interaction and open to all of his experiences. The counselor's communications are always helpful in guiding discussion so the client may discuss fluently, directly, and completely specific feelings and experiences.

CONCLUSION

It is apparent that the facilitative conditions of empathic understanding, respect for the client, and the counselor's honestly communicating as a person with the client have been important variables across all counseling approaches. One is able to see a time dimension in the chart. The Freudian orientation did not picture the counselor as functioning in a personal way similar to the concept of being genuine or congruent, but did use the idea of friendly interest with the client as well as understanding him. The learning theorists also have relied most heavily on accepting the client and understanding him, and have been less concerned with the counselor as a person in their relationship. In more recent years with the writing of Rogers, the existential orientation, and research on the relationship variables, the concept of the counselor as a person in the relationship has come into prominence. There is an ever-growing body of research on these facilitative relationship variables that supports the idea that higher levels of these conditions do lead to clients' depth of exploration and to change in both insight and behavior. One can conclude that these facilitative conditions are the base of the counseling relationship and that these relationship variables supersede the theory or techniques a counselor might use.

DIMENSIONS OF THE RELATIONSHIP

Although the facilitative conditions are a foundation, there are numerous other dimensions that make up a counseling relationship. The interpersonal interaction involves variables that are, in ways, intangible but nevertheless the real process of counseling. Attitudes, thoughts, feelings, and perceptions between the people, as well as within each person, are an integral part of the process. Such dimensions as the ambiguity in the situation, the expression of feelings and thoughts, the transference and countertransference attitudes, resistance feelings, and the confrontations between the two people are frequently involved in counseling relationships. Certainly these variables are handled through verbal and nonverbal communication. Instead of thinking about the counselor's using counseling techniques, it seems more appropriate to conceptualize counseling as a relationship in which the two people interact to help the client understand himself, his situation, and to learn to behave effectively. It is important that a counselor be familiar with some of the more significant dimensions existing in varying degrees in most interviews.

AMBIGUITY IN THE RELATIONSHIP

The degree of ambiguity ranges from a stimulus situation that is so incomplete and vague that no clear-cut response is predetermined to one with definite guidelines. In counseling, this concerns the degree to which the counselor gives structure to the counseling situation for the client. The degree of ambiguity in the relationship is controlled by the counselor by the way he defines himself and the situation. Part of this may be done directly but, frequently, the definition is more indirect. Bordin (1968) conceives three areas in which the counselor communicates the degree of ambiguity: "(a) the topic he considers appropriate for the client to discuss; (b) the closeness and other characteristics of the relationship expected; and (c) the counselor's values in terms of the goal he sets up toward which he and the client should work as well as his values in general." The counselor may structure the relationship with different degrees of clarity among these areas; that is, one or two may be clearly defined while the others are left vague.

What is the function of ambiguity in the counseling relationship? It is assumed that an individual's reaction to a stimulus situation is the result of a larger motivational organization. Thus, when a client reacts to the counselor in the counseling relationship, it is usually an exemplification of the client's needs. This behavior becomes a basis for inferences about the client's personality. The counselor can highlight the inner determinants of the client's actions by weakening the external demands. This is most clearly seen in the theory of projective techniques.

The control of ambiguity in counseling rests on the principle that people invest into ambiguous stimuli those responses that are most heavily laden with the unique aspects of their life history. This permits the client to bring out his major conflicted feelings, no matter how unaware of them he may be. It is also assumed that this investment of the client's motivational and emotional structure into the relationship enables the counselor to understand more fully and deeply the core of the client's actions. Therefore, inferences about the nature of the client's defenses can be made from his reactions to the ambiguity situation. From the content and sequence of his responses, one can obtain understanding of the client's conflicts and the types of relationships he has with other people. An ambiguous situation may also provide a background for the client's irrational feelings to be brought into awareness.

Ambiguity in the counseling relationship can be very useful; however, it must be controlled. It is not a case of "if a little bit is good, more will be better." When using ambiguity, there are several reasons why it needs to be controlled. First, ambiguity produces anxiety. Although anxiety is an important part of effective therapy, there is an optimal level that each person can tolerate. If anxiety exceeds this point, the person will be so overwhelmed by his anxiety that all of his energies will be used in self-preservation efforts, leaving no energy for therapeutic movement. The counselor must relate the degree of ambiguity to the level of anxiety to create an optimal situation for the particular client. Secondly, a person with schizoid tendencies needs less ambiguity since he is trying to maintain contact with reality; hence a more structural situation is called for. Thirdly, a relatively adjusted person who comes to counseling primarily for positive consultation has not made the decision to place his entire welfare into the counselor's hands. The amount of ambiguity the counselor can interject into the relationship is extremely limited. Fourthly, the counselor is subject to anxiety produced by ambiguity. There is less certainty and less control of the client's reactions in an ambiguous counseling relationship. Ambiguity can lead to increased anxiety or to a greater expression of feelings by the client. A direct expression of feelings toward the counselor is also possible. Finally, a counselor can use ambiguity to serve his own needs rather than his client's needs. This can be in the form of avoiding the revelation of himself as a person to the client or, in the case of an inexperienced counselor, expressing uncertainty and fear of making a wrong move.

While ambiguity is a powerful tool in the relationship, it can lead to incorrect inferences. Epstein's (1966) writings apply primarily to the use of ambiguity in projective testing, but his results are just as applicable to the counseling situation. It is assumed that the greater the ambiguity, the more revealing is the information about the personality. This assumption fails to consider that individual differences can reflect random, inconsequential information as well as significant personality material. Most drives and responses are latent, awaiting appropriate stimuli to arouse them. Thus, the more a stimulus is ambiguous, the greater is the likelihood that it will bypass ego defenses and allow an opportunity for all drives to be expressed. Also, the more ambiguous the stimulus, the less its potency for activating specific drives. An unresponsive client is often assumed to be defensive when there is the possibility that he hasn't been aroused in the first place.

The "blank screen" hypothesis, which states that reactions to a specific stimulus can be generalized to all stimuli, can be refuted. A highly ambiguous stimulus may not arouse specific drives but nevertheless have stimulating characteristics of its own. The nature of the stimulus may vary from person to person. For example, some people fear the loss of control that an unstructured stimulus provides, while others welcome the opportunity to let their imaginations loose.

Finally, as Bordin also warns, the more ambiguous the stimulus, the more the counselor as well as the client can lose control of it, making for problems in interpretation. Epstein also agrees with Bordin that the most effective level of ambiguity should be stressed rather than resting on the conclusion that because ambiguity is good, use more of it.

THE COGNITIVE-CONATIVE DIMENSIONS

Bordin (1968) discussed the cognitive-conative balance that exists in the relationship. The conative aspects of behavior include a person's feelings, strivings, and emotions, while the cognitive aspects of behavior include the conceptual, perceptual, and motor processes. The affective aspects of behavior are generally related to the release of energy. The infant's release of energy involves disorganized and unintegrated motor discharge. As he develops perceptual and motor skills, his energy is released in a more organized manner to express his needs. Therefore, the cognitive processes are particularly important in modifying and controlling most complex and meaningful behavior.

Bordin (1968) suggests that the cognitive process serves two purposes in the cognitive-conative balance of behavior. "The cognitive aspects may either serve the purpose of controlling affect in the sense of leading to less or no expression, or may serve a truly instrumental function through the fullest possible successful expression of the affect." Therefore, cognitive processes function to control and organize energy. In order to fully understand the client, it is necessary to understand both the cognitive and conative aspects of the client's communications. The counselor must apply his own cognitive and conative capacities in understanding the client. Achieving a deep understanding of the client is essential for effective counseling.

There is a cognitive-conative balance in the counseling relationship. The counselor can control this balance by his actions and communications toward the client. To do this effectively, the counselor must understand his client and encourage the expression of emotion or help conceptualize the affect. For example, a client who expresses his emotions by an over-intellec-tual or over-rational examination of them needs to be encouraged to ex-press his feelings more freely and to relax his efforts at controlling them. On the other hand, a client who freely expresses his feelings needs to be encouraged to introduce more conceptual aspects into his communica-tions.

A major assumption in counseling involves insight leading to changed behavior. The counselor's role is to help the client explore his affective re-gions, to gain cognition of the relationship between his feelings and actions and, with this new conception, change his behavior to more appropriately meet his goals. When the counselor gives cognition to the client, it is usually an interpretation. When applying cognition to an interpretation, there are two things to keep in mind. First, before defenses are loosened, interpreta-tion, whether accepted or rejected, will be ineffective. Secondly, the amount of emphasis placed on the cognitive aspects of the interaction should be re-lated to the intensity of the affect the client expresses. The greater the client's affective expression, the more cognitively the counselor can respond. Thus, interpretation is not necessarily of therapeutic value. It can be of use only when the client is ready for it.

Cognition, or the giving of information and calling attention to particu-lar behaviors, will be most effective when introduced during a period of low resistance. It is best for the client to make the final interpretation, with the counselor leading up to but not stating it. However, if the client is defensive and fearful, any effort to introduce cognitions that are not specifically re-lated to the avoidance will be seen and distorted by the defenses. When feel-ings are built up and the reasons for avoidance are near the surface, then the interpretation of resistance may be made.

As the client begins to see case after case in which his defenses have pro-tected him, he begins to achieve an awareness of his distorted actions. This process has been called "working through" and refers to the repetitive proc-ess of rediscovery. The client finds in different incidents his need to defend himself and how this affects his interpersonal relationships. The amount of times that the counselor must work through incidents with his client de-pends on how well integrated the client is. Some people understand with the awareness of one or two experiences; other people need more examples.

The counselor must also be aware of his own needs and careful not to press upon the client certain interpretations and cognitions that are not rele-vant to the client's problems. These interpretations may be part of the coun-selor's defenses against the particular conflict. Finally, counselors seem to overemphasize the use of verbal reasoning and should remember that interpretation can advance the therapeutic process only at times when it is relevant to the client's needs.

TRANSFERENCE IN THE RELATIONSHIP

Freud found that when a client in analysis proceeded to a successful outcome, there was a time of intense personal attachment to the therapist. Because of the analytical situation, the client never really knew his therapist as a person. He lay on a couch and did not see the therapist. Between hours he had no other contact with him. With such an unstructured "blank screen" on which to picture his therapist, the client reacted during therapy in the way he reacted to most significant persons in his past life. He transferred his whole relaionship to the therapist and was able to reenact earlier struggles, many of which he had no clear memory of. According to Freud, it was this experience that made possible profound personality reorganization. This process of transference permitted the client to relive the developmental periods in which the basic personality patterns were established and modify these patterns through this new emotional experience.

It was this experience that was frequently termed "transference neurosis." The resolution of this neurotic attachment to the counselor was of major importance. The working-through process is another aspect of the transference that has become prominent. The insights achieved in therapy do not automatically transfer to all areas of the client's life. There is much to discuss even after significant unconscious material has been brought to light. It takes considerable time to resolve a deep transference to the analyst and also to translate this to other relationships with significant persons (Sunberg and Tyler, 1962).

There are other conceptions of transference. Dollard and Miller (1950) would equate the words "to transfer" with the idea "to generalize." Transference as a noun suggests that "something" is transferred. In psychoanalytic theory it is not always clear what that is, although most frequently it seems to be a feeling or an emotion. The concept of generalization implies that any of a variety of similar stimuli may evoke the same response even though the response has been habitually associated with only one of these stimuli.

Transference is viewed as "the degree of involvement the client feels with the therapist" (Rotter, 1954). From the social learning point of view, the degree of involvement is a direct function of the amount of direct reinforcement the client has received from the counselor or expects to receive, and is also a function of the degree to which the client sees his future satisfactions as dependent upon the counselor's behavior. Rotter implies that transference and countertransference are natural and helpful to the relationship so long as the counselor and client are aware of their existence.

Existential therapists believe that the client does not really transfer his feeling to the therapist but ". . . the neurotic is one who in certain areas never developed beyond the limited and restricted forms of experience characteristic of the infant. Hence in later years he perceives wife or therapist through the same restricted, distorted 'spectacles' as he perceived father or mother" (May, Angel, and Ellenberger, 1968).

Rogers (1951) admits that transference occurs in a majority of client-centered relationships. "If one's definition of transference includes all affect toward others, then transference is obviously present in the relationship, if the definition is being used in the transfer of infantile attitudes to a present relationship, and very little if any transference is present." How is such transference to be handled? Rogers suggests that the client-centered counselor's reaction to transference is the same as any other attitude to the client; he endeavors to understand and accept. Such acceptance will lead the client to perceive the transferred attitudes as coming from within him and not from the counselor. Rogers also suggests that the transference does not become a problem because of the interpersonal nature of the therapeutic relationship. "The whole relationship is composed of the self of the client, the counselor being depersonalized for the purpose of therapy into being the client's other self."

Although they do not talk about transference as such, Kell and Mueller (1967) talk about the transfer of feelings. They believe that when the client is under stress and the relationship becomes intense, the client may choose events out of his past and symbolically present them to the counselor as a means of communicating some of the feelings he is having about the current relationships and, possibly, some doubts about the counselor's adequacy to meet his needs. At one level the client may communicate his faith and confidence in the counselor's ability to satisfy his needs, but at another level he may also communicate fears, concerns, and doubts. "A client may assure the counselor, for example, that he is succeeding in helping him, but at the same time the client may talk about how weak his father is. We believe that at such times, the counselor should consider the probability that the client is also concerned about the counselor's weakness."

Brammer and Shostrom (1968) view transference as a concept midway between the classical Freudian view, with emphasis on the past, and the position that all feelings currently expressed toward the counselor are transference. They view transference as a type of projection of a client's past or present unresolved and unrecognized attitudes toward authority figures and love objects. This projection is done in such a way that the client responds

to the counselor in a manner similar to the way he responds to other significant persons. The client builds certain expectations of the counselor and his
role through this transference process. Transference therefore is a term describing how the client construes the counselor and how he behaves toward
the counselor. It is a largely irrational part of the counseling relationship
in which the client projects onto the counselor self-regarding attitudes and
unresolved feelings from earlier relationships. The intensity of transference
is a function of the type of client involved, the setting, length of counseling, extent of emotional involvement, counselor personality, and counselor
technique.

Holland (1965) assumes that the client has a problem or is functioning
unsatisfactorily because some of the conditions required for his development were inadequately or improperly supplied. He has not been able to
understand the nature of his deficiency or, if he has done so, he has not
been able to find conditions that would enable him to complete or correct
his inadequate development. Therefore, he comes to a counselor hoping to
complete or improve his confidence in obtaining satisfaction. The client's
need for help and his selection of a counselor as his helper automatically
places the counselor *in loco parentis*. The cognitive and emotional responses to the counselor, therefore, frequently take up at a point where previous helping relationships have left off.

Holland believes that transference is related to the client's level of maturity and that the extent to which transference responses create problems
in the therapeutic relationship is determined by the developmental status of
the client. If the client is relatively mature and relatively competent, the
distortion involved in the perception of the counselor may be slight. The
transference problems of such a client are not likely to involve intense
feelings but, possibly, the ambivalence created by the desire for assistance as well as a reluctance to accept a dependent role relative to the
counselor.

In this developmental concept of transference, the client may look at the
counselor as "the good parent." The immature client would resist many parts
of the working relationship in counseling. He may resist recognizing the
reality of his demands on the counselor; he might expect the "good counselor" not to require him to grow or to develop competence in order to insure continuation of the relationship. When the client anticipates direct emotional gratification that the counselor does not provide, he may also be
frustrated and angry.

Handling Transference

An analyst uses transference feelings to help his patient recognize what he
is trying to do in the relationship to the therapist. The client's transference

helps the therapist understand him and provides valuable clues for later interpretation on the quality of his interpersonal relationship.

The counselor recognizes that he does not depend upon the transference relationship for effective therapy; however, he is aware that transference feelings are present in varying amounts. In brief forms of counseling, the counselor would rarely attempt to interpret transference feelings. He would not try to analyze the deep feelings his client has in the manner in which he manipulates his life relationships. The counselor would reflect the feelings and accept the client in an attempt to aid him in seeing that the transference feelings reside within his own inadequate perceptions. The counselor should regard expressions of negativism and hostility more as resistance in an incomplete growing-up process.

Holland (1965) states that the client will persist in believing in these attributes so long as he "needs" to believe in them to allay his own anxieties and feelings of inadequacy. He suggests that the usual way of handling the situation is to accept the client's transference initially and to use it to help the client develop his own competence and confidence. If the counselor is successful in this endeavor, the client will more or less spontaneously relinquish his illusions about the counselor and accept him as just another human being, although often with a feeling of gratitude for the valuable services performed.

Kell and Mueller (1966) suggest that when the client begins to speak in metaphorical or symbolic ways about experiences that seem to be related to the present relationship, the counselor may find it necessary to expose the underlying implications to enter the experiences more meaningfully within the current counseling relationship. The counselor's response should be designed to release the client so that he can continue the feelings that are related to the basic conflict. If, for example, the client repeatedly expresses doubt about others, and the counselor suggests "perhaps you are doubtful of me," the dynamism underlying the counselor's response is that he is not fearful of the client's feelings but is perceptive and not punishing. Kell and Mueller go on to say that a counselor's adequacy is a function of the ability to recognize and respond directly to feelings, no matter what the feelings are.

Holland (1965) uses the term "cognitive transference" to refer to the client's tendency to think about the counselor as having the same characteristics as persons he has known previously. He uses the term "emotional transference" to refer to the feeling qualities of the cognitive responses plus the corresponding behavioral tendencies that are generalized from previous to new relationships. The term "working through transference" is found frequently in the psychoanalytic literature; however, the meaning is not very clear. The concept may be viewed as the extent to which the client perceives and thinks about the counselor in terms of his actual characteristics and the extent to which his feelings toward the counselor represent a reasonable response to the counselor's actual behavior. The term "working through transference," therefore, would not be so much a general description of the counselor's efforts as it would be a description of the ultimate goal. Because feelings and thoughts may be generalized to many people, the ultimate goal of counseling would be to have the client adequately and realistically handle all his relationships in terms of the individual.

Brammer and Shostrom (1968) suggested that while transferences may complicate the counselor's task, they do serve significant functions for the client. Transference helps build the relationship by allowing the client to express his distorted feelings without the usual counter-defensive responses. In other words, when he gets irritated with the counselor, the counselor accepts these feelings rather than countering with his irritation. Another function of transference is to promote the client's confidence in the counselor through his handling of these transference feelings. A third function of transference permits the client to become aware of the origin and the significance of his feelings in his present life through the interpretation of the transference feelings.

Brammer and Shostrom (1968) also suggested that the counselor's main task in regard to transference is to encourage free expression of feeling while keeping the transference attitudes from developing into a deep transference relationship. They give several suggestions for handling and resolving transference feelings at various depths.

1. The usual technique for resolving transference is one of simple acceptance, which permits the client to live out his projected feelings and to feel free in the interview.

2. The counselor may ask clarifying questions about the forms of anxiety the client seems to be manifesting.

3. The counselor may reflect the client's feeling level.

4. A stronger technique will exist when the counselor interprets the transference feeling directly. An interpretation involves communicating information to the client that he has not already stated himself and, therefore, may be rejected.

5. The counselor may focus on what is going on presently with the client's feelings rather than why he is having these feelings.

6. Frequently, calling attention to the feelings causes the client to react in the opposite manner; therefore, a counselor may want to call attention to negative feelings but not to the positive transference.

7. The counselor may test the idea that the client is projecting feelings by

asking him to reverse the projection and may encourage repetition until the statement is felt by the client as that which he is really feeling.

8. The counselor may interpret transference feelings as an expression of "being deficiency" in which the client is seeking environmental support, rather than viewing the feeling as a transference from the past to the counselor.

9. The last suggestion is that the counselor may refer the client to a counselor more qualified to give intensive psychotherapy when their relationship develops to an intensity that is beyond the competence of the counselor.

COUNTERTRANSFERENCE

Countertransference refers to the emotional reactions and projections of the counselor toward the client. Countertransference may include conscious as well as unconscious attitudes of the counselor toward real or imagined client attitudes and behavior. It may be caused by an anxiety within the counselor, and these anxiety patterns may be classified into three types: unresolved personal problems, situational pressures, and the communication of the client's feelings to the counselor by empathic means. The counselor's unresolved personal problems need to be resolved by working them out with another counselor. Many times, a counselor may carry over feelings to the client that really grow out of the situation. Situational pressures involve the counselor's feeling responsible for the client's improvement or that his professional reputation is involved in the client's success. In the latter case, he may try too hard and defeat his purposes. Countertransference may also come from the communication of a client's feelings to the counselor. The counselor may respond overly sympathetically in response to the client's need for sympathy or he may become angry, having been provoked by the client.

A discussion of countertransference should include the counselor's value structure. Obviously a counselor is going to communicate some of his values even in the most objective relationship. The counselor generally conveys values of how the client should live in general as well as those concerned with how he should behave in counseling.

Handling Countertransference Feelings

Brammer and Shostrom (1968) offer several methods for handling countertransference feelings. First of all, the counselor must be aware that he has the feelings and begin looking for the reasons why. The counselor may need some supervisory assistance to help him locate these sources of feelings and resolve them. By discussing the problems in a supervisory relationship with his supervisor, the counselor may resolve his own feelings. A major source of countertransference awareness may be found in audio and videotape recordings. The counselor can listen to himself and locate many of the attitudes there. This may also be a base for supervisory discussions. Another approach to dealing with countertransference feelings is a discussion about them with the client. A mild reassuring interpretative reference occasionally may be helpful in relieving the anxiety in both the client and the counselor. Obviously, the existential idea of the encounter would permit the counselor to express and interject his own feelings of anger and frustration as an open model of humanness and expression. Certainly the counselor can use his awareness of himself to enhance his own growth and to resolve his own difficulties, hence making him more effective in his personal life as well as in his professional relationships.

RESISTANCE IN THE RELATIONSHIP

Resistance refers to the characteristic of a client's defenses that opposes the purposes of counseling and must be dealt with in building and maintaining an effective relationship. The psychoanalytic concept of resistance is used to indicate the unconscious opposition toward bringing unconscious material to consciousness and, therefore, mobilizes the repressive and protective function of the ego. Resistance in the traditional psychoanalytic interview is related to the idea of free association. The analyst assumes that the client's free association will not be free in that the client's desire to change will motivate him to talk about areas of importance but, when he approaches strongly defended areas, he will block or distort his communication. Resistance, then, is the client's inability to deal directly and constructively with his impulses as they appear in the process of therapy. Resistance is also associated with the transference feelings of the client because, as he directs some of his impulses toward the counselor, he also will defend against these impulses. Therefore, the reactions to the therapist are interwoven with the resistance process (Bordin, 1968).

In counseling, resistance generally arises when the client perceives that the topic or the situation is threatening and, because there is a threat to the client, he is compelled to defend himself against further anxiety. The client may feel anxious about examining patterns of behavior or his personality structure, fearing that he is going to grow and not wishing to change himself. The client sometimes fears that by saying the things he is feeling, it will make the condition real; that is, he is reluctant to talk about death or losing love.

One view of resistance as coming from within the client is that, as he approaches a topic that causes anxiety, he defends himself by avoiding the topic or, possibly, the whole counseling situation. Another view of resistance assumes that it is caused by an external threat, such as the counselor's interpreting material before the client is prepared to handle it. Rogers (1942) states that resistance is not necessarily a part of counseling and assumes that it is present because of the counselor's behavior. He suggests that attempts to accelerate or cut short the counseling process may cause resistance in the client. The counselor's suggestion to a client may make him feel anxious about carrying out this suggestion and he may resist being drawn into such a situation. Where a therapist may analyze the resistance in a similar way to the transference of the client, a counselor uses resistance as interfering with progress and problem solving, and attempts to reduce the resistance.

Resistance probably exists in all interviews in varying degrees and may be viewed as the opposite end of a continuum from coping emotional expression. Resistance varies from the rejection of counseling to more subtle forms of inattention. Although it is present to some degree in all interviews, the client usually does not recognize it. Therefore, it is mostly an unconscious phenomenon. It is an ambivalent attitude toward counseling in that the client wants help and yet resists it. Brammer and Shostrom (1968) suggest "this ambivalent client attitude is one of the most baffling situations confronting the inexperienced counselor. Even experienced counselors occasionally cite resistance as an excuse for not establishing an effective relationship."

Handling Resistance

Bordin (1968) sees two types of reactions that are called resistance. One type of resistance is the client's unwillingness to give up his autonomy or living up to the social standard of acting independently. The other type of resistance refers to the client's defenses against his inner conflicts when the nature of the counseling relationship tempts him to express conflicting impulses. Obviously, both types of resistance are significant for the counselor in the relationship. In the first type of resistance the counselor must avoid encroaching on the client's feelings of independence. He must learn to see his desire to differentiate himself as a positive development in the client rather than a problem in their relationship. When the client is resisting his internal conflicts, the counselor should try to reduce the self-defeating behavior, hoping that he is providing a relationship where the client can be free to explore himself. If the second type of resistance does appear, the counselor must examine his behavior to see if he has aligned himself with the client to prevent the expression of impulses that underlie the difficulty.

Brammer and Shostrom (1968) offer five approaches to handling resistance. They examine these five techniques according to different levels of resistance in the client. Obviously, before handling resistance, the counlor must be aware of any of the external causes in himself and the situation that may be contributing to the resistance. He must also be aware of the influence of his techniques. The first type of technique includes being alert to the resistance of the client but not responding to it. Because the client is experiencing a mild resistance does not indicate the counselor must do something about it. The counselor recognizes that this level of resistance is natural in counseling and concentrates on understanding the unique defensive style of the client.

When the client shows a more pronounced disinterest in counseling by giving short answers or not hearing or seeing certain things, the counselor may feel he must do something actively to reduce the client's resistance. There are some minor adaptations to reduce the client's defensiveness and keep him exploring his problem further. One adaptation would be to lessen the emotional impact of the discussion by moving to a more intellectual level, thereby reducing the pressure on the client. Another technique may be to change the pace of the interview in terms of shortening the degree of lead or just shifting the physical position; possibly a judicious use of mild humor could ease the tension. If a good relationship exists between the counselor and the client, supportive and accepting techniques may help clarify the situation and reduce the resistance.

If the resistance is stronger, the counselor may wish to redirect the interview to a less threatening area for the client. This temporary diversion technique will take the pressure off the client and reduce the intensity of the interview by gently changing the subject. When the client appears to be aware of his resistance and a good working relationship exists, the counselor may wish to use some direct manipulation techniques. The counselor may offer an explanation of what the client is doing. This interpretation may help the client develop a tolerance and acceptance of his own resistance as well as an intellectual understanding of what he is doing. A reflection of the feelings of resistance is also an effective technique, particularly in earlier interviews where the relationship is not as well established. The strongest technique in dealing with resistance is a direct confrontation of questioning around the resistance theme.

If the counselor assesses his own confidence and examines the defenses of a highly resistant client, he may wish to refer this person to another counselor who can remove the source of external resistance that has been inhibiting their relationship.

CONFRONTATION IN COUNSELING

Confrontation may be defined as the counselor's pointing out a discrepancy between his own and the client's way of viewing reality (Anderson, 1968). By pointing out a discrepancy in their views, he is causing the client to face or to meet this situation. Discrepancies in client thinking and actions appear most frequently in three areas: between his ideal and real self; between his insight and his actions; and between reality and illusions. "The purpose of confrontation is to reduce the ambiguity and incongruencies in the client's experiencing and communication. In effect, it is a challenge to the client to become integrated; that is, at one with his own experience" (Carkhuff and Berenson, 1967). The term "confrontation" frequently conjures the idea of a hostile act. However, this need not be true. Confrontation is hostile to the unhealthy patterns the client has developed, but the challenge can be considered healthy rather than destructive.

Berenson (1968) outlined five types of confrontation as experiential, didactic, strength, weakness, and encouragement to action. Experiential confrontation is the counselor's response to any discrepancy between what the client said about himself and how the counselor experiences the client. A didactic confrontation is the counselor's response to a client's misinformation, lack of information, or need for information regarding the educational, vocational, or social areas as well as the counseling process. Confrontation of strength occurs when the counselor focuses on the client's constructive resources; weakness when the counselor emphasizes the client's liabilities or pathology. Encouragement occurs when the counselor presses the client to act in life in some constructive manner or discourages his passive stance.

> Confrontation may range from a light challenge to a direct collision between the therapist and client. It constitutes a challenge to the client to mobilize his resources to take another step toward deeper self-recognition or constructive action on his own behalf. Frequently, it will precipitate a crisis that disturbs, at least temporarily, the client's personal and social equilibrium. Again, crises are viewed as the very fabric of growth, invoking new responses and charting new developments. Growth is viewed as a series of endless self-confrontations. Confrontation is a vehicle that ultimately translates awareness and insight into action, directionality, wholeness, and meaning in the client's life. A life without confrontation is directionless, passive, and impotent (Carkhuff and Berenson, 1967).

A client may feel that he is powerless to do something for himself and feel that whatever happens to him is under someone else's control. He frequently searches for someone who will do something for him and waits for the magical moment when someone gives him directionality or meaning for life. He often knows that the life he is leading is miserable and reacts to it but feels that there is nothing he can do to change it. He continues a passive-reactive stance and lives in an illusion. By the use of confrontation, the counselor forces the client to choose between continuing life as it is and becoming an active force in the creation of a new life.

There are a number of potentially beneficial effects of confrontation. It provides the counselor with a vehicle for expressing his real thoughts and feelings. It also provides a model to help the client learn to accept and express his thoughts and feelings and to test his perceptions against another person's reality. The client learns that there are more ways of viewing a person or a situation and that the two people may disagree without harboring hostile feelings for each other. A constructive confrontation gives a client an honest and immediate experience of himself. Through becoming aware of the impact he has on another person, he begins to realize his impact on himself—a move toward self-confrontation and the ability to face oneself honestly. Confrontation may also indicate to the client a measure of respect for his capacity for self-determination. The counselor is not handling him with kid gloves for fear of overwhelming or hurting him. By directly communicating his own position to the client, the counselor allows the client to make his own stand clear and evaluate it. By checking and comparing his views with those of another person, the client is learning to recognize and face the inter- and intra-personal discrepancies that are inevitably a part of life (Anderson, 1968).

Counseling can be for better or for worse. The counselor must question how he can be sure that the awareness of the crisis he creates for the use of confrontation will be resolved to the benefit of the client. Confrontation is intended to be used in conjunction with the other elements of a good therapeutic relationship. When rapport has been established and appropriate levels of empathy, positive regard, concreteness, and self-disclosure are reached, then confrontation can be introduced.

Anderson (1968) reports a study of the effects of confrontation by high and low facilitative counselors. The high facilitative counselors were rated 3 or above and the low counselors were rated below 3 on the five-point scale of facilitative conditions. There were four high-functioning counselors and 16 lower-functioning counselors in the study, which reported a total of 50 confrontations: 41 initiated by the high counselors and nine by the low counselors. There was an obvious difference in the frequency of confrontations between the high- and low-functioning counselors. Further, Anderson found that the high-functioning counselors confronted their clients more often with their resources, while the low-functioning counselors, when they confronted the client, did so more often with their limitations. Therefore, when confrontation was used by the high-functioning counselors, it led to an increased level of client self-exploration.

Berenson (1968) reported confirmation of Anderson's results and stated that the high-functioning counselor employed confrontation more often, regardless of the client's level of self-exploration. He also found that high-functioning counselors confronted strengths and confronted more often, while low-functioning counselors confronted weakness and confronted less often. It is suggested that when confrontation is made, the client will reach greater levels of self-exploration. "Thus, with the kind of confrontation which typifies the activities of the high-level therapist, the client becomes more deeply involved in the constructive therapeutic process movement with all of the intensity, extensiveness, and immediacy that this implies" (Carkhuff and Berenson, 1967).

Bailey and Sower (1970) have reviewed the literature on self-confrontation with emphasis on audio and video playback techniques. Their review of the literature reveals that the different playback techniques counselors have used reportedly aided in overcoming resistance and lifting repressions, and promoted insight, self-awareness, and realistic confrontation with self-contradictions. Clients have consequently become more objective and realistic in their self-evaluations. Every type of clientele discussed in the literature reported salutary effects from their self-confrontation process. All of the reports indicate beneficial results from exposure to the playback situation.

How can the counselor be sure that the crisis he creates to use confrontation will be resolved to the benefit of the client? He can never be sure. The crisis and the decision for handling it are the client's. The research quoted above, though not conclusive, demonstrates that the counselors who use confrontation to precipitate a crisis are probably best able to help the client successfully resolve it.

COMMUNICATION

We have described the counseling process as more of a relationship between the two people rather than the counselor's using techniques to solve the client's problem. However, in part of this relationship, the counselor does use some techniques to help the client understand himself and the environment and to reach decisions for effective behavior. These techniques have been extracted from various ways of conversing about problems and steps taken by clients between interviews. The techniques of counseling involve the counselor's sensitivity and skill in receiving communication from the client as well as his skill in communicating with the client. If we examine the previous dimensions of the relationship, it is obvious that each one requires communication between the counselor and client.

Williamson (1959) reviews several possible modes of communication between the counselor and the client: the counselor's manner, rational use of language, and intuition. The comment from Emerson that "what you are speaks so loudly that I can't hear what you say" pertains to the counselor's habitual and natural manner of behaving. The counselor's behavior will indicate his own belief system. Certainly, the counselor believes that he will be more effective if he acts in one way rather than another. Williamson assumes that the counselor's values will determine his behavior and that this behavior is part of the best way of communicating to the client that his problems and welfare are of primary consideration to the counselor.

The use of spoken language as a mode of communication is what is most generally practiced. Through language, the counselor attempts to communicate to the client concerning an alternative consideration for his choice. Through the conversation, the client will review his present state of behavior, organize his own difficulties and, through the interchange, begin to see more clearly what was once confusing. The use of language is an objective way of helping the client identify his problem areas, interpret facts about the situation and himself, and thereby gain a better orientation to controlling himself. It is assumed that in a facilitative interview, the client may come to accept himself when he clearly perceives those value options that are open to him and he chooses those that are productive of self-fulfillment.

Robinson (1950) has made a major contribution to counseling literature by focusing on the social psychology of the counselor-client interaction. Over the years he and his colleagues have examined the optimum means of communicating the counselor orientations that help a client to discover insights into his problem and move forward. He has also discussed the optimum means of giving treatment so that clients are able to understand and carry out decisions. This involves the counselor's skill in expressing attitudes and ideas in light of the client's characteristics as he enters the interview, as well as the dynamics of the interaction as it progresses. Robinson has been concerned with examining the communication that goes on during the interview; that is, the listening, giving of information, interpreting, and various degrees of leading. Early studies in this communication approach indicate that each counselor has a definite pattern of responses as he moves from one client to another, but that various counselors have considerably different patterns of responding to clients. Other studies suggest that counselors change their style of communication as they move from responding to adjustment problems to skill problems with their clients.

This concern with communication involves the ways in which the counselor varies his procedures to fit sensitively with the characteristics of the client. Although Robinson talks about the arrangement of the office and the counselor's own dress and manner, he focuses much more on the manner of speaking. There are four general dimensions of counselor response that have been emphasized in examining the counselor's speech—i.e., an acceptance attitude, a division of responsibility, a response to the core of the client's statement, and the degree of lead in the counselor's response. The counselor's communication of an accepting attitude has already been discussed with similar concepts of acceptance or respect for the client as one of the main facilitative conditions in counseling. The concept of responding to the core of what the client says is similar to the concreteness of communication Carkhuff and Berenson have suggested. This term means that the counselor responds to the central meaning that the client is communicating, whether this is in content or in feeling. If the counselor responds to something more extraneous in the client's response or if the counselor introduces new material himself, he is really not communicating that he understands the client or respects what he is talking about.

There will be a varying degree of responsibility in the interview, depending upon the type of problem and the client's stage in attacking his problem. The division of responsibility focuses on the amount of time the client is talking, either in describing his situation or in reaching his decision, and the time in which the counselor is responding to the client. Therefore, it is a verbal division of responsibility. The techniques of communication that have been described by Robinson involve a continuum on the degree of lead. It is believed that counselors can be trained to be more effective in using various degrees of lead as they respond to their clients.

The counselor communicates in terms of what the client has been saying or thinking so that he will be stimulated to move toward effective adjustment. The counselor's remarks move the client from his immediate statements toward his desired goal. The amount of leading at any given time will be determined by the background of the client and the amount of defensiveness or resistance such a remark might arouse. The amount of lead may vary greatly from topic to topic or from moment to moment in the interview. The counselor's lead should move the client toward the next stage in his thinking. Robinson suggests the concept of a counseling ladder in which the counselor's response would be relevant to the client's needs and interests. This response would be at the next rung above the client's thinking so as to stimulate his development and lead to further insight, but this next level should be close enough to be easily understood and accepted without arousing defensive reactions. The counselor may lead too little as well as too much. If the counselor is too passive in the interview, the client may resent the counselor's use of only acceptance remarks and his refusal to participate with the client in resolving his problem.

Degrees of Lead in Communication

The counselor can vary the degree to which his response leads the client toward solving his problem or developing insight. Some of the earlier research indicates that counselors' verbal techniques tend to fall into definite categories. An awareness of the different degrees of lead will permit a counselor to enlarge his repertoire of techniques and make him aware of his pattern of responses.

The categories of responses can be labeled and laid out on a continuum of leading. Some of the responses are quite similar and can be grouped together. The group of responses with the least degree of lead include silence, acceptance, restatement, clarification and summary clarification. The counselor communicates that he understands and accepts what the client is saying and hopefully communicates that the client should continue in the same vein. The counselor does not interject much of himself or any of his ideas but merely communicates that he is with the client and encourages him to continue.

By remaining silent when the client pauses, the counselor can communicate that he understands the client and is permitting him to think and continue to talk. When the counselor wishes to communicate verbally that he understands what the client is saying, and yet not really interrupt the client's momentum, he may make an acceptance remark such as "uh-um," which will communicate he accepts what the client is saying while permitting him to continue. The counselor may restate in nearly the same words the content or feeling that was communicated, thereby reflecting for the client and permitting him to hear what has just come out of him. With this type of reflection, the counselor does not interpret or interject anything of himself. At times, the counselor may wish to clarify the client's rambling comments or feelings and make a more precise statement as to the problem or the client's feelings. A clarification comment should illuminate what the client has been communicating but not push him in any direction. A summary clarification is used at the end of a series of comments on a topic when the counselor wishes to tie together several aspects that the client has been rambling through.

A greater degree of lead is involved when the counselor uses a general lead. The counselor may wish to have more information from the client or to have the client go deeper into his problem. By saying, "How do you feel about that?" or, "Can you tell me a little more about that?", he can lead the client into the content or affective areas without developing resistance in the client, since the client is still able to control what he says.

Much greater leading techniques include the tentative analysis, interpretation, and urging. With these techniques the counselor not only communicates that he understands what the client has been saying, but that he wants to introduce some new ideas. The counselor, then, is going beyond the client's present communication and putting across additional ideas. When the counselor wishes to present a new look at the problem or a new approach, he may do so in a very tentative manner, thereby leaving the client free to accept, modify, or reject this communication. The counselor may say "do you suppose . . . ," or "correct me if I'm wrong . . . ," or "what would you think about . . ." The counselor makes an interpretation when he states something that is inferred from the client's communication but which the client has not specifically said. "Intepretation speeds insight and causes little difficulty if the client is just about to state the idea anyway, would have presented the idea if he had thought of it, or if it fits a need which he has expressed" (Robinson, 1950). However, an interpretation may cause resistance in the client if the lead is too far ahead of the client's present thinking or has negative implications for him. An urging comment would suggest a solution for the client's problems and would certainly involve the counselor's own values. Urging the client to make a certain decision may lead to a successful outcome for him or it may not, but the decision is the counselor's and not the client's.

Robinson suggests that techniques such as depth interpretation, rejection, assurance, and introducing an unrelated aspect of the subject provide the greatest degree of lead and are frequently detrimental to the counseling relationship. A depth interpretation is made from some theory of personality dynamics and is a lead far beyond the client's present thinking, frequently touching sensitive areas in the client's unconscious. Although the counselor feels that the client may be wrong in his attitudes or decision, a rejection of his view may only hurt the client, or at least increase his resistance. It should be more effective to work with the client to gradually bring about change in his views. Assurance may have the same effect as rejection, because the counselor tends to belittle the client's view of the problem. By saying, "I'm sure everything will work out," the counselor really denies that the client has anything to worry about and his feelings are not real. Also, if the counselor introduces a new and apparently unrelated topic, the client may also feel that what he is interested in is being rejected. This certainly is not a response to the core of what the client is talking about, let alone feeling, and certainly would not be considered a concrete statement, all of which leads to a low level of facilitation for the client.

NONVERBAL COMMUNICATION

Varieties of Nonverbal Language

Smith (1966) describes the expressive levels of speech as the other vocal phenomena that accompany language. These can be systematically analyzed as qualities and noises separable from language itself. In considering the following phenomena, it should be understood that while they contribute to the overall meaning of the communication, by themselves they have no referential meaning. Among these are six vocal qualifiers, which are established on a level or baseline of any spoken communication. The six vocal qualifiers follow.

1. Intensity or the increasing of loudness or softness. The part of the utterance having the increasing loudness or softness may be a single syllable or a whole sentence or more. Increasing loudness is usually used to display alarm or annoyance. while increasing softness might display displeasure or disappointment.
2. Pitch range overall or the raising or lowering of pitch. Raising of pitch is usually used in context of annoyance or alarm, while lowering of pitch might be used for various kinds of emphasis, including incredulity.
3. Spread register and squeezed register. Respectively, these are the "stretching" and compressing of the usual interval between the pitch phonemes in the utterance.
4. Rasp and openness. These have to do physiologically with the amount of muscular tension under which the laryngeal apparatus is held. The more tension, the more the strained or rasping effect. With openness or looseness, a sort of hollow, booming, authoritative impression results.
5. Drawl and clipping. These have to do with the tempo of the individual syllables.
6. Increased tempo and decreased tempo. In contrast to drawl and clipping, these are used to describe longer utterances. In many contexts, increased tempo signals annoyance or anxiety, while decreased tempo signals uncertainty.

When the aforementioned elements are used in differing amounts than "normal" or in unusual contexts, it is this event that is figuratively perceived by the skilled listener's "third ear."

Another set of vocal phenomena, termed vocal differentiators, include laughing, crying, and breaking. Laughing and crying are commonly used and are self-evident. Breaking is characterized by special muscular phenomena of the laryngeal machinery. There is a rigid and intermittent tension and relaxation of the vocal cords such that the voice is broken with a tremulous interruption of tone. It is used to signify great or deep emotional involvement on the part of the speaker.

Vocal identifiers are considered to be another significant set of vocal phenomena, although so far only one has been described in the communication systems. This is the interruption of a word by a glottal stop and pause, usually signifying that all or part of the utterance is negated or changed by a suddenly perceived contrasting thought or insight.

Certain other phenomena may be usefully termed voice quality and voice set. These are aspects of voice that seem to transcend the overall communication interchange and signify the general emotional state of the organism. Such things as an anxious voice or a hostile voice are termed as voice quality, while a thin voice, an immature voice, an aged voice, or a dispirited voice are termed as voice set. Although these are clearly separable phenomena, they are not yet as systematically describable as the vocal modifiers. Need of further research is indicated.

The patterns of use for the various elements of all the vocal phenomena, taken singly or in combinations, are recognizable as culturally, institutionally, and personally determined. Variations on individual and/or group levels can be studied.

A great deal of communication takes place without sound. We communicate with others through gestures, peculiarities in gait and dress, a sense of touch while shaking hands, mannerisms of a glance or look, the condition and texture of the skin, body build, and a multitude of similar bodily characteristics (Barbara, 1956).

Facial Expressions of Emotions

In the personal relations of everyday life, the face is the primary locus of regard in identifying the nature of emotional responses (Kline and Johannsen, 1935). In the counseling process, as in any interpersonal interaction, the emotions, as expressed through facial expressions, frequently determine the direction of the interaction. For example, a client who enters a counselor's office with apparent signs of despair or torment does not wish, at least at that moment, to discuss the fact that his favorite basketball team won the game the night before. In all likelihood, he wishes to discuss the problem that presently has brought him to the counseling interview—a problem that may be easily and, at times, not so easily detected by his facial expression. Throughout the counseling interview, the facial expressions change many times. It is very important to be able to detect facial changes in emotion so that the counselor can lead the interview in the appropriate direction. If the counselor pays close attention to verbal communications only, the original problem that the client came to the interview with may go completely undetected.

If people in general, and counselors in particular, are able to detect accurately the emotions displayed through facial expressions, better understanding and insight into the person's particular problem can come about. Verbal communication to the client of his emotion as expressed by verbal expression can convince the client that the counselor does understand his problem—that the counselor can truly empathize with his client. True empathy by the counselor does not take the form of a verbal communication only. Verbal remarks can sound very artificial in the counselor's tone of voice. If the client is able both to hear an empathic expression, and to have it compounded by a truly empathic facial expression on the part of the counselor, the client can feel that the counselor really does understand the specific situation and, because of this understanding, he may be able to help.

Kinesics

Although the face is the primary area of regard in identifying the nature of emotional responses, the body, limbs, and hands play an important role in communication. Kinesics may be described as the way people communicate through body movements and gestures. The phonetic signals of speech are sounds we hear, while the kinesic signals are motions we see and feel. Kinesics are not instinctive human nature but are learned systems of behavior that are culturally influenced and learned informally by imitation of role models (Knapp, 1963). Most of this behavior is learned out of awareness and, because of this, most people remain unaware of their participation in an elaborate system of bodily gestures and motions (Smith, 1966).

Nonverbal physical movements of expression include gestures and bodily postures. Ruesch and Kees (1956) emphasize that gestures are used to illustrate, emphasize, point, explain or interrupt and, therefore, cannot be isolated from verbal communication. Gestures are determined by the way the human body is constructed but are elaborated in interpersonal and social relationships. Consequently, expressions of amazement, desperation, anger, anxiety, pleasure and indignation are similar to a degree in all countries and cultures. On the other hand, the understanding of their meaning is dependent upon being familiar with the communication system of a given culture. Gestures are necessary when verbalization is impossible, as when language barriers or hearing difficulties are present. Gestures are frequently used when verbal expression would be considered socially unacceptable. Quite different impressions are communicated by those burdened with diseases that result in involuntary movements or gestures.

An anxious person frequently will exhibit rapid, restless movements of his limbs and tremors of the hands. A depressed person moves very slowly as if every action is a great effort for him. An important observation with regard to body movements is the physical distance maintained by the person between himself and other people in his environment. The person who is withdrawn keeps his arms in close contact with his body and his head lowered. As Hahn and MacLean state, "bodily postures, tension and relaxation of the muscular systems, gestures with head, hands and feet all have accepted symbolic values as communicated in our culture" (Hahn and MacLean, 1955).

Ekman (1965) found that head and body nonverbal cues provide different affective information. Head cues carry information primarily about what particular effect is being experienced, and relatively little about the intensity of affect or level of arousal. Body cues reverse this pattern, communicating information primarily about level of arousal or degree of intensity in an affective experience, but relatively little about what particular affect is being experienced.

The counselor should have a working knowledge of nonverbal communication so that he might perceive the myriad of messages that come to him from his client via this avenue, and be aware of the messages he is sending out to his client via this same avenue that might facilitate understanding and support, or lack thereof.

The correct identification of expression is very important for the counseling situation, for counseling is a communicative process, and nonverbal expressions are a part of it. The variables in the complexity of the process are dealt with primarily by participants through verbal and nonverbal communicative means.

Several studies have investigated counselor sensitivity to nonverbal cues. Delaney and Heimann (1966) found that emotions are not always accurately perceived by another. It appears that for counselors to correctly identify emotions in a client, there needs to be a period of training and practice. Cullen (1967) developed a paradigm to show the complex relationship between the client and counselor when a nonverbal cue is emitted. She points out that the counselor must perceive the cue and then must decode it. She concludes that careful decoding is indicative of training while careless decoding is not. She supports the concept of training counselors to sensitively perceive and utilize nonverbal cues.

In a study on postural movements in a counseling dyad, Fretz (1966) concluded that:

1. Clients who perceive a highly favorable relationship with counselors use fewer negative nods and tend to lean forward and back more than those who perceive an unfavorable relationship.
2. Counselors who perceive a highly favorable relationship with the client use more hand movements and more smiles and laughs than those who perceive an unfavorable relationship.
3. Counselors in approval-seeking conditions use more positive nods and more smiles and laughs than those in non-approval-seeking conditions.

This valuable information can be used by the counselor not only to study his own behavior in a counseling situation, but, more important, as a means of improving his sensitivity to client characteristics, emotional states, and feelings about the relationship.

Scheflen (1964) adds emphasis to the importance of sensitizing counselors to nonverbal cues when he states, "Configurations of posture or body positioning indicate at a glance a great deal about what is going on in an interaction. A conscious knowledge of these postural functions is of great value in research in human behavior and in studying or conducting a psychotherapy session informedly." He feels that postures are characteristic, standard configurations, whose common recognizability is the basis of their value in communication. Scheflen found that all psychotherapy is strikingly similar in basic configurations, regardless of the identity of the therapist or the school of psychotherapy that he espouses, and suggests typical postures and movements in a counseling setting.

CONCLUSION

Counseling has been viewed as a relationship between the counselor and client. This chapter has presented the facilitative conditions of empathy, congruence, positive regard and specificity of communication as a base for the relationships. It was suggested that these concepts cut across all counseling theories. Several other dimensions that appear in the relationship were explored. The significance of verbal and nonverbal communication in counseling was presented as well as a review of communication techniques.

REFERENCES

Adler, A. *The Practice and Theory of Individual Psychology*. New York: Harcourt, Brace, 1924.

Alexander, F. *Fundamentals of Psychoanalysis*. New York: Norton, 1963.

Anderson, Susan. "Effects of Confrontation by High-and-Low-Functioning Therapists." *Journal of Counseling Psychology* 15:411–416.

Bailey, K. G., and Sower, W. T. "Audio Tape and Video Tape Self-Confrontation in Psychotherapy." *Psychological Bulletin* 74:127–137.

Barbara, D. "The Value of Non-Verbal Communication in Personality Understanding." *Journal of Nervous and Mental Disease* 123:286–291.

Berenson, B. G.; Mitchell, K. M.; and Moraver, J. A. "Level of Therapist Functioning, Patient Depth of Self-Exploration, and Type of Confrontation." *Journal of Counseling Psychology* 15:136–139.

Bordin, E. *Psychological Counseling.* New York: Appleton-Century-Crofts, 1968.

Brammer, L., and Shostrom, E. *Therapeutic Psychology.* Englewood Cliffs: Prentice-Hall, Inc., 1968.

Carkhuff, R. "Toward a Comprehensive Model of Facilitative Interpersonal Processes." *Journal of Counseling Psychology* 14:67–72.

Carkhuff, R., and Berenson, B. *Beyond Counseling and Therapy.* New York: Holt, Rinehart and Winston, Inc., 1967.

Cullen, Lola F. "Nonverbal Communication in Counseling: An Exploratory Study." *Dissertation Abstracts* 27:2047.

Delaney, D. J., and Heimann, R. A. "Effectiveness of Sensitivity Training on the Perception on Nonverbal Communications." *Journal of Counseling Psychology* 13:436–440.

Dollard, J., and Miller, N. *Personality and Psychotherapy.* New York: McGraw-Hill Co., 1950.

Dreyfus, E. "Counseling and Existentialism." *Journal of Counseling Psychology* 9:128–132.

Ekman, P. "Differential Communication of Affect by Head and Body Cues." *Journal of Personality and Social Psychology* 2:726–735.

Epstein, S. "Some Theoretical Considerations on the Nature of Ambiguity and the Use of Stimulus Dimensions in Projective Techniques." *Journal of Consulting Psychology* 30:183–192.

Fretz, B. "Postural Movements in a Counseling Dyad." *Journal of Counseling Psychology* 13:367–371.

Fiedler, F. "The Concept of an Ideal Therapeutic Relationship." *Journal of Consulting Psychology* 14:339–345.

Hahn, M., and MacLean, M. *Counseling Psychology.* New York: McGraw-Hill Book Co., Inc., 1955.

Holland, G. *Fundamentals of Psychotherapy.* New York: Holt, Rinehart and Winston, 1965.

Horney, Karen. *Self Analysis.* New York: W. W. Norton and Co., 1942.

Kell, B., and Mueller, W. *Impact and Change.* New York: Appleton-Century-Crofts, 1966.

Kline, L. W., and Johannsen, Dorothea E. "Comparative Role of the Face and of the Face-Body-Hands as Aids in Identifying Emotions." *Journal of Abnormal and Social Psychology* 29:415.

Knapp, P. H. *Expression of the Emotions in Man.* New York: International Universities Press, Inc., 1963.

May, R. (ed.) *Existential Psychology.* New York: Random House, 1961.

May, R. *The Art of Counseling.* New York: Abingdon Press, 1967.

May, R.; Angel, E.; and Ellenberger, H. *Existence.* New York: Basic Books, 1958.

Robinson, F. *Principles and Procedures in Student Counseling.* New York: Harper and Brothers Publishers, 1950.

Rogers, C. *Counseling and Psychotherapy.* Boston: Houghton Mifflin Co., 1942.

Rogers, C. *Client-Centered Therapy.* Boston: Houghton Mifflin Co.. 1951.

Rogers, C. "The Necessary and Sufficient Conditions of Therapeutic Personality Change." *Journal of Counseling Psychology* 21:95–103.

Rotter, J. *Social Learning and Clinical Psychology.* Englewood Cliffs: Prentice-Hall, 1954.

Ruesch, J., and Kees, W. *Nonverbal Communication.* Berkeley: University of California Press, 1956.

Scheflen, A. "The Significance of Posture in Communication Systems." *Psychiatry* 27:316.

Shaffer, L., and Shoben, E. *The Psychology of Adjustment.* Boston: Houghton Mifflin Co., 1956.

Smith, A. *Communication and Culture.* New York: Holt, Rinehart and Winston, 1966.

Sullivan, H. *The Psychiatric Interview.* New York: Norton, 1954.

Sunberg, N., and Tyler, Leona. *Clinical Psychology.* New York: Appleton-Century-Crofts, 1962.

Truax, C. "Effective Ingredients in Psychotherapy." *Journal of Counseling Psychology* 10:256–263.

Van Kaam, A. *The Art of Existential Counseling.* Wilkes-Barre: Dimension Books, 1966.

Williamson, E. G. "The Meaning of Communication in Counseling." *Personnel and Guidance Journal* 38:6–14.

Wolpe, J., and Lazarus, M. *Behavior Therapy Techniques.* New York: Pergamon Press, 1966.

10

Continuing
the Relationship

The counseling relationship evolves through various phases as the client explores himself, gains understanding, and works through this understanding and trying of new behaviors to a point of termination. This chapter presents a model of a continuing counseling relationship. Not all counseling will follow this model exactly, but it explores the developmental stages of the counseling process. An understanding of these phases in the relationship can help the counselor place a single event in perspective.

This model may be more appropriate for counseling with personal-social problems than educational-vocational decision-making interviews. Obviously, there is no clear-cut difference. There is considerable emotional involvement in making vocational decisions and many decisions are made to resolve personal problems. Therefore, many of the concepts presented here can be integrated with the chapter on decision-making interviews.

A number of social scientists have described certain developmental changes in the continuing counseling relationship. Each phase of this model is a composite of the models presented in the literature. A consensus of the literature establishes phases of initiating counseling and establishing a relationship, exploration of self, deeper exploration, and working through, which lead to termination of the counseling relationship.

The process presented in this model does not always move in sequence through the phases, but may move backward and forward with a general

266

forward movement. The phases are not separate and discrete and there is no time dimension presented. Some clients will move quickly into the self-exploration phase while others will experience more difficulty overcoming their resistances. Many clients will not delve into the deeper exploration of themselves involved in the third phase but can move to the working through aspects of the process. The process of understanding one's self and trying new behaviors will certainly vary with each client.

PHASE 1: INITIATING COUNSELING AND ESTABLISHING A RELATIONSHIP

The first step in the counseling relationship must involve the client's recognizing that he has a problem and being motivated enough to work with the counselor toward a solution. Certainly, it is a better situation if the client recognizes this situation and voluntarily sees the counselor. If he is referred by someone else who recognizes a problem in the client, the client must feel that he wants to work toward a resolution. If he is unaware or unwilling to recognize the problem area, he will not be sufficiently motivated to work in the counseling process.

Frequently, clients come to the counselor with a rather vague feeling that something is wrong, but are unable to really put it into words. It is not uncommon for clients to talk about "it." Rogers (1958) describes the client's fixity and the remoteness of his feelings when he comes to the interview, claiming there is a great deal of blockage of internal communication so that the clients cannot accurately describe it. Frequently, the client does not recognize many of his feelings and many aspects of the problem are not apparent to him. It is not unusual for the client to be unwilling to communicate about himself at this point in that he describes external situations that impinge upon him rather than talking about himself. Rogers also suggests there is no desire for change—the person wants the problem solved but really does not want to risk changing himself.

The reader may recall that Tom's early statement of his problem was similar to this description.

S   Well I'm not really sure you know what, what it is, what's been happening. I've just been—I suppose some of the teachers have told you—I've been having some trouble—and my work isn't good—I've been in trouble in some of the classes. I don't really know, you know, what's, what's wrong for that matter. They told me I'd better come and see you—I'm not sure exactly what it is.

C You sound a little bit confused—uh—maybe about what's going on inside of you and what's therefore led to the kind of behavior you're having—that other people are saying—

S (interrupting) yeah—I don't—in other words I seem to be having a problem—but I'm not sure why—I just don't know what's happened Ah-h-h school, everything seems different just over the—probably nothing I can put my finger on, you know what I mean—but school just doesn't interest me that much any more and I find it kind of boring—I just can't put myself into it.

C It sounds like everything has just sort of lost meaning for you.

S That meaning's a good—a good word, yeah because it doesn't make sense, I guess meaning and sense are the same thing. . . .

GOALS

The primary goal for the first phase of counseling is to establish a relationship with the client. Chapter 8 has already discussed the facilitative conditions of positive regard, empathy, and congruence as being important in establishing this relationship. The client needs to feel accepted and to have mutual liking and trust the counselor. Brammer and Shostrom (1968) describe this as building a pipeline between the two individuals in which they develop a relationship. The client is able to experience trust in the strength of the counselor and he will be able to feel safe to investigate aspects of his own feelings and behavior. This does not deny the strength and potential for growth within the client, but does give him comfort and security with this new person in his life.

May (1967) considers the first phase of the interview to be taken up with establishing rapport. Rapport depends upon both the client and the counselor being at ease. This is probably best facilitated by the counselor's being comfortable and showing it. The relaxation will help break the psychological tension that the client may feel. May suggests that the counselor's attitude must be a balance between sensitivity and robustness. Sensitivity is a communication of understanding the client but not letting one's sensitivity appear too obvious. When the counselor becomes too obvious with his concern, the client may feel that he is not genuine and thereby withhold his confidence. May's term "robustness" deals with the quality of a hearty voice and a good sense of humor. Both of these are used to communicate the humanness in the counselor. It is not easy to establish the balance between sensitivity and robustness and certainly it would vary with different clients. And, as May suggests, one must be sensitive enough to know when to be robust.

The counselor's professional manner could interfere with establishing rapport. If the counselor is more of a "role of the counselor" than a real person, it will communicate a separation in the levels between the two people. Holland (1965) talks about two kinds of relationships that are apparent in this early phase of counseling: one ostensible and one hidden. He states that the ostensible relationship is one of equality between the counselor and client in which the inadequate self-concept of the client is defended by both. This equality means that they are both equal as human beings and the counselor is not superior because the client is dealing with his problem. The counselor may have certain information or skills to help the client solve his problem, but this does not make him a superior human being. To offer an analogy, the counselor may have car difficulty on his way home and require the services of a mechanic. The counselor is no less a person than a mechanic, even though he needs his assistance in solving the problem. The hidden aspect of the interview is that the client does have a problem and may feel that he is not equal or he would not be seeking the help. Generally, the client does have a dependent position.

Another set of goals in the early phase of counseling concerns the client's expression of feeling about his problem. The goal at this point is to have the client maintain his expression of feelings, to confront himself regarding his feelings and behaviors, and to help him clarify his problem. At this time, the counselor is able to begin formulating hypotheses about the client's problem area and his patterns of behavior.

The reader may wish to examine the beginning of the relationship with Tom in Chapter 12. Did the counselor meet these early goals?

PROCESS

Early communication relates to the discrepancy between the apparent and hidden aspects of the relationship (Holland, 1965). If the counselor dominates the interview, the client may retreat even more deeply into his feeling of inadequacy and, if the counselor is too passive, the client may feel he is not getting any help. Therefore, there must be an appropriate sharing of responsibility in this early phase of counseling. The counselor wants to encourage the client to talk and to permit him to control the interview and the depth of exploration of himself. Counselor responses will generally be restricted to acceptance, reflection, and clarification remarks. These are the least leading responses and permit the counselor to check his accuracy in understanding the client. They also serve to clarify the problem area for the client.

PHASE 2: EXPLORATION OF SELF

The second phase of counseling will begin when the person feels a minimal level of acceptance. Rogers (1958) describes this as the point when the client feels fully received. When the relationship is secure for the client, there will be a loosening and a flowing of expression from the client. This phase may occur in the first interview or it may take more than one. In the beginning, the client's expression starts to flow more readily but in regard to non-self topics. He still describes problems as external to himself and there is little sense of personal responsibility for the problem. Feelings are expressed but usually talked about rather than experienced. The differentiating of personal meaning and feelings is somewhat limited and global. Although the person may express some contradictions, there is little recognition of them as contradictions.

GOALS

The counselor wants to bring out and determine the client's evaluation of himself. He wants the client to be aware of the various feelings about himself and to be aware of how these feelings and attitudes affect his behavior. The main objective of this phase of counseling is to gain a more clear and complete delineation of the various aspects of the person's self-concept. Holland (1965) suggests that there are usually three different self-concepts that emerge from the client. The client frequently depreciates himself by pointing out his bad characteristics, how inferior he is in the areas in which he is inadequate. This depreciated self-concept is one aspect of the client's evaluation of himself. Closely related to this concept is a second conception of the self representing compensatory fantasies. These positive feelings tend to compensate for the negative feelings that the person uses to describe himself. The third concept of the self includes his contemporary attributes that constitute a more or less realistic image and an evaluation of himself by reasonable standards.

PROCESS

May (1967) calls this stage of counseling the confession and assumes that two-thirds of every hour will be taken up with the client's "talking it out." It is important that the client talk about his problem with some degree of thoroughness in order to reach the basics of his problem. May feels that if the client does not do most of the talking in the interview, something is wrong with the counseling procedure. He assumes that every word the counselor utters must have a purpose.

The counselor should not indicate that he is shocked or offended by anything the client says. Emotional upsets must be a part of this period; clients become upset because they are expressing their ideas and fears and frequently suppress materials they may not have told to anyone before. The client may cry, in which case the counselor must exercise his skill in remaining calm and making sure that his calm and empathy are communicated to the client. It is at this point that one can clearly discriminate between empathy and sympathy. Giving sympathy to the client at this point would be an augment to emotional upsets; empathy is more objective and valuable.

Brammer and Shostrom (1968) talk about this phase of counseling as a catharsis, and point out that there are positive and negative aspects of a catharsis. First of all, there is a strong physiological relief from the tension that the person has been carrying. This is experienced as the relaxation one may feel after crying. There is also a feeling of satisfaction that comes from the control of verbalizing the material. The client feels that by gaining control of his problem verbally, he does have a certain amount of security and control over the problem. There is also a release of emotional energy now, which the client has previously used to defend himself, and now he may feel considerably better.

May (1967) comments on the cathartic value in confession, stating the mere fact that the client has talked about his problem will make him psychologically healthier. It will relieve some of his inhibitions, make it possible for a more ready flow of his internal feelings, and help him see his problems in their clarifying objectivity. A skillful counselor helps focus the client's confession to the core of his problems. This indicates that skill and sensitivity are required on the part of the counselor to perceive the feelings beneath the client's statements.

One of the limitations of the catharsis involves this feeling of control and the feeling of exhilaration with new energy because the client sometimes makes a "flight into health," believing that he has solved his problem. In many cases he has dealt with some aspects of the problem but needs further understanding and change in behavior before the problem is solved. Frequently, a catharsis only includes material at a somewhat intellectual level in that the client is really presented material he has already been able to think out himself, while other material is still being defended. Holland (1965) points out that the client feels defensive when he has communicated all that he knows or is willing to tell about himself, but is aware that this is not sufficient. This defensive period usually follows one or a combination of three patterns: the avoidance of discussing one's self while directing the counselor's attention to externals, denying weaknesses and inadequacies in one's self, or exposing one's own concept and evaluation of his problem.

A CRITICAL POINT

This is a critical point in counseling and the client may be so threatened by his lack of understanding and lack of control that he could drop out of counseling. The client has made a deeper exploration of his feeling and this is not a pleasant experience. He feels less secure and comfortable and may not be sure if the pain involved to work through the process is something he wishes to endure. He may be aware of other aspects of his problem, as his defense system is open enough for him to see things that he has denied before. He may recognize that things may get worse before they get better. It is important that the counselor be able to support and encourage the client at this point. Frequently, if he is able to explain to the client that these anxieties occur in many clients and, although there may be a fear of exposing too much of himself, he will be able to carry himself through this critical point (Brammer and Shostrom, 1968).

TRANSITION

There may be a transition stage in this phase of counseling. The client becomes aware that he cannot account for his behavior through what he knows about himself and the logic of his behavior does not always lead to understanding. Therefore, he relaxes some of his defenses and the counselor becomes more actively involved. Obviously, the counselor is gentle and uses short leading techniques.

Holland (1965) suggests that there may be strong resistance to dealing with feelings about himself. The client will reach a point of avoiding discussion of his depreciated self and may be reluctant to evaluate his compensatory fantasies. His real self-concept is not strong enough to give him security. The client has several needs that the counselor will have to fulfill during this period. Because he is unable to do so, the client needs the counselor to see some of the negative aspects of the depreciated self he avoids. He may solve it with very little help from the counselor. The counselor also wants to see how much the client can handle. It is important to let the client know that the counselor trusts him and will enter more actively only when he is needed.

S   I can't—ah—I just don't—I don't have interest in anything— ah, I don't know—it's almost like rather than start something and get involved in it—it just seems easier to say the hell with it and not—ah—and not get involved in it.

C   I guess I feel—though it's sort of early today—that you're almost having the same attitude about our session—that it's just pretty hard to get into this also.

S   Yeah, maybe.

C   It's easier not to get in it—you've been round and round with yourself, you might be thinking it's going to be round and round here.

S   I guess I hadn't thought of it like that but I didn't—you know—I didn't really—huh—I almost didn't come back 'cause maybe for what you just said, I just didn't want to get involved in it—I didn't think it was going to go any place. Just seems like just—I don't know I can't—I can't—I don't want to do any (laugh) I don't know—I just don't like—don't—don't feel like ah doing—I guess—I don't know.

C   You seem to be asking or looking for reasons—you say you don't understand why, ah—would you want to try and start by exploring some reasons of why you feel this way—of—taking a look at what's happened to you before now that's led you this way.

S   You mean like what what is it that's ah—you know—why me (laugh) why (laugh) what's happened to me that that ah I feel this way.

C   Uh-huh.

S   You know when you say that I just draw a blank uhm.

C   You said last week that you at one time sort of accepted goals like what your family did and general societal kinds of goal-oriented behavior but, but you've ah changed from that and part of this may have been because of the maturation type thing.

S   Uh-huh. Yeah, that's, a that's for sure—what a—now that I can't —ah—I don't know I guess.

C   Maybe you can talk about how you feel about yourself.

S   Huh—I was—I was going to—you know—sort of respond to what—how I felt about my parents and I guess—you know—how I feel about myself is pretty much involved with how I feel about them. Got a my par—I've always been—my parents have always taken very good care of me and ah I've never had to—to worry about anything in any sense I've always had everything in a sense you know—on a silver platter—and—I don't know I'm really that's what I can't understand about myself 'cause I didn't use to be like this—I really used to—ah—to really have everything I wanted and—ah—my parents have always really taken—ah given me anything. I was ah I was kind of sick when I was when I was young and so my mother and my grandmother who was home a lot I think always paid special attention to me and I always I don't know (chuckle) when I look back it seems pretty rosy I always had everything that ah I could that I could want.

C   Your parents haven't rejected you lately either have they? You could—you could still—

S   It's not—they don't—not at all, that's in fact, if anything it's the other way around—you know—they still treat me like in a sense like I was still the the I don't know baby—I hate to say—baby but they still treat me like I was the baby and uhm I don't know—I kind of resent but I don't—I resent it but I don't because I know that they—you know—that they love me and everything yet I resent being treated like that and whenever you see I have asthma pretty badly and when I get an asthma attack ah I'm usually pretty sick for a couple of days—and I don't know they treat me they—ah specially my mother keeps keeps that—you know she doesn't like me to do too much a-a-a—

C   Sometimes they still treat you like they did when when you were a child when you were sick as a child.

S   Specially my mother and my grandmother they ah and it's in lots of little ways little things that they do they don't almost like they don't want me to to grow up not grow up but they don't want me to be independent of them and they like they they like to take of me it's important to them to be able to take care of me so they like they keep this idea that I've that I'm have asthma and that I should stay at home and I shouldn't do some of the things that other kids do um-m-m—

C   Now you're at the point where you sort of resent this kind of ah treatment. In a way though it sounds at times it's sort of comforting—possibly kind of tough to give up at other times huh?

S   (laugh) Yeah but I hate to admit that but sometimes you know and that's the thing I like it and I don't like it.

C   It builds up conflicting feelings in you.

S   At home sometimes—you know—I like to go home and I know that they they'll just do anything for me. I mean I still when I get up in the morning my mother gets up and makes breakfast for me and things like that—ah—they do—any money that I need—anything like that—ah they give to me and ah at the same time I resent it because they don't—I don't know—I don't have a sense of independence I don't have a sense—I don't know—I just—I guess I'm pretty confused. (half laugh)

C   Yeah, it sounds like you would like to have the independence—
    there's some comfort to the other, but you don't want to hurt your
    parents' feelings as you point out, it's important to them to have
    this kind of relationship.

S   Uh-huh.

C   It certainly slows down your personal independence.

S   Yeah.

During these early interviews the client is communicating about his inadequacies and wants help from the counselor. The counselor should communicate recognition of this desire to gain something from him. Holland
(1965) suggests the counselor may indicate some progress is being made
and that the client has been largely responsible for this progress. This
communicates that the counselor regards him as functioning adequately.
The counselor may also wish to communicate they are both personally involved in the process by trying to make this evaluation. There may also be
plans of action being developed and the counselor may be able to indicate
some of these to the client. Tom's counselor communicates this nicely near
the end of the initial interview. In a later interview the counselor adds another.

C   In the next—in the next week before we meet again why don't you
    try looking at several places in which you can develop more in-
    dependence and at least I think we may be aware now that you,
    that you've sort of seen some differences in your behavior pat-
    tern for what might come. Obviously as you're already aware it's
    not an easy thing to make an immediate change—so it's a—it's
    a process. I think we've reached one step in it and ah let's take
    this step and examine where we're going to go from there.

The counselor should permit the client to maintain control of himself in
the interview as long as possible. If the client is effective in handling his
problems and if the problems are not too difficult, he also needs the counselor to teach him the labels to put on the feelings he has about himself. It
is apparent that his expression of behaviors and feelings is loosening and
there is some freedom in terms of his internal communication, but he still
may be having difficulties tapping the spontaneousness of his feelings. The
counselor will help the client by pointing out some relationships between
the various self-concepts and his behavior pattern. Certainly, the client
needs the acceptance, approval, and support of the counselor as he looks
at these various self-concepts that he would rather avoid.

Holland suggests that the counselor may become more active in the later part of this phase and be viewed as using a more controlling role; therefore, he appears to be more authoritarian. If the counselor is more controlling of the communication at this point in the relationship, the client will have the greatest need for the counselor's acceptance and help. Otherwise, the client's strong feelings about being controlled would interfere with the progress of counseling. It is important that the counselor be gentle and provide acceptance and support for the client.

In addition to the reflection and clarification techniques, the counselor will probably be sharing information and ideas and providing some interpretation for the client. The sharing that takes place involves the client's acceptance of the counselor as a real person rather than using his projections about the counselor. As the counselor gives information to the client, it is not forced upon him but is presented for him to use. The interpretation is one further step in leading in which the counselor presents some hypotheses to the client.

May (1967) states that after the client has talked out his problem, interpretation will take place. Both the client and counselor survey the facts that have been brought to light and discover through them the pattern of the client's behavior. "Interpretation is a function of both the counselor and the counselee working together." It is not a matter of the counselor diagnosing the pattern and then presenting it to the client. The counselor may make some tentative analysis or some tentative suggestions. May points out that the counselor suggests interpretations rather than stating them dogmatically.

C   It sounds like you may be sort of—I'm not sure you resent their behavior as much as you resent yourself behaving that way. Why —why can't you love your parents and still and still break out of this mould?

S   Hm-m-m—never—thought of that—in a sense—you know—what the hell's wrong with me that I can't stand on my own two feet— yeah—I'm too quick to run home—I'm afraid—to ah—to try sometimes—it's too say just to ah I guess that's that's it it's too easy just to let things go the way they are—why get involved in something when things have been so easy like that.

C   Yeah but underneath it sounds like sort of a fear that—"Hey, if I'm not able to do this—am I ever—am I ever going to be a man? Am I always going to simply rely on the comfort of mother?" You talk about not having any meaning or or power or control over your your future. Part of it may be the fact that you haven't really had much in the past, much of this has been controlled by your family.

S (pause) Yeah, you mean—ah—maybe that some of the ways—in other words the way that I was—would react at home or the way that I've been brought up at home (pause)—I see what you mean. It's just like I been I haven't I've just been taken care of at home rather than stand up and do anything I've just let them take care of me and the point is that I've liked it more than try to do any-thing. (pause) It's so easy—so easy just to let them do that—I guess I can understand that—but still—

It is important for the counselor to read the meaning of the client's reac-tions to the interpretations or suggestions. If the client is indifferent, and the suggestions do not seem to make any difference to him, the counselor may assume that the idea was not very important. If the client rejects the suggestion or the interpretation violently, protesting strongly that it is un-true, the counselor may tentatively assume that the interpretation is close enough to have struck a cord. It is similar to the old saying "methinks the lady protests too strongly." However, the counselor must be careful not to make this assumption for sure because it may in fact be inaccurate and the rejection appropriate. If the client accepts the suggestion or interpretation and agrees with it, both the counselor and client can accept it for the time being. Whether or not it is accurate and meaningful may not be known until the client continues to work further on his problem and a solution. The client could have just accepted the interpretation rather than reject-ing it.

Many clients' problems will move from this point to a stage of working through the behavior problems and the insight that leads to behavior change. These clients would not experience Phase 3 in this model of the counseling process. However, some clients will go into a deeper explora-tion of feelings prior to that stage.

PHASE 3: DEEPER EXPLORATION

Some clients need more therapeutic counseling in order to tap in on those feelings that will lead them to a better understanding. This type of client will be involved in a deeper exploration of feelings and attitudes. Most counselors are not equipped to deal with the intense feelings and in-tricate problems involved in personality reorganization as they may occur at this depth of counseling. Most counselors who work in agencies, schools, or colleges will probably not have sufficient time to work through this phase of counseling.

GOALS

The counselor attempts to eliminate depreciated and fantasy concepts as determinants of client behavior. At the same time, there is an attempt to complete his awareness of the real self-concept and establish reasonable standards to evaluate it. It is apparent that part of the depreciated self-concept may have been true at one time but, since it is no longer true, it must be re-evaluated in terms of reasonable standards being developed for the real self. As this occurs, there will be a reduction in the client's need for fantasies to compensate. He may find, however, that part of the compensated fantasies coincide with some of the actual attributes that he has (Holland, 1965).

During this time the client's feelings will be expressed more freely in the present. Feelings will bubble up even though the person may fear and distrust what he feels. There is a beginning tendency to realize that what he is feeling involves a direct referent. There is frequently surprise as well as fright at the feeling that bubbles up. There is increasingly freer communication within the individual and increasing ownership of the feelings as a part of himself (Rogers, 1958).

As the client becomes aware of himself and his own uniqueness, he should establish reasonable personal standards. Such standards can be relative standards that are indicative of behaviors and achievements of other persons comparable to himself. Instead of global evaluations, the client should break these down and examine smaller parts of the whole. This process is one of helping to fill in the details of the self-concept and the person's cognitive structure.

PROCESS

The counselor, either directly or indirectly, communicates what he considers to be inaccurate or inadequate in the client's thinking process. This means that he is fairly active in the interview and exerts some control because he is involved with active emotional resistance. It always seems to amaze beginning counselors that, when they are trying to help a client, he is resisting the help. Clients continue to deceive themselves in part, and attempt deception of the counselor. Holland (1965) offers four reasons for this level of resistance. There may be a generalization of hostile feelings toward people who exert some control over persons' lives. There are possible negative feelings about giving up the various self-concepts. There are anxieties associated with depending upon a new self-concept that is not yet reliable outside the counseling situation. There may be negative feelings regarding the efforts and risks involved with living this new self-concept. It is this aspect that the client needs to change in order to use new behavior patterns.

Because of these feelings, the client is not a passive recipient of the counselor's communication. In order to meet the objectives of this phase, the counselor may need to become involved in persuasion with the client. The term "persuasion" generally has a negative connotation in that it sounds as though the counselor were pushing the client into something. This would be true if the counselor had his values involved and was persuading the client to do something to meet the counselor's needs. Actually, the counselor is using it to meet the objectives that the client has established when less controlling techniques have not worked. Much of the persuasive efforts should be directed toward what the client thinks, thereby letting the behavioral responses remain up to his decision. The confrontation at this point is focusing on the client's avoidance tendencies and the lack of tying things together. The counselor is trying to persuade the client to give up his self-defeating and self-deceptive ways of thinking. The counselor must be careful not to be too controlling in this endeavor and not to enter into persuasion too early with clients.

CRITICAL POINT

A second critical point in the counseling relationship occurs during this deeper exploration process. The client may become aware of the inadequacy of his defense mechanisms. They may no longer give him the protection from the awareness of his deeper feelings. A sudden awareness of too many impulses, thoughts, or feelings may be quite traumatic. The counselor should control the relationship to enable the client to explore these slowly. If the client experiences too much pain at this point, he may be frightened of his lack of control and withdraw from counseling.

PHASE 4: WORKING THROUGH

A significant part of changing one's behavior to be consistent with the new insights is involved in the process called "working through." The original concept of working through was used by Freud and generally meant the breaking down of the network of resistance. A broader concept of the term today refers to the client's becoming aware of the meaning of past experiences and present feelings. The client develops an awareness of his inner feelings as well as the external world. He gains a rational type of understanding of his problems, feelings, and behaviors, and this depth of understanding can lead to further behavior change.

May (1967) considers the final stage of the counseling process and the goal of the whole process the transforming of the client's personality. Although the terminology is different, the concept is very similar to the working-through phase. He assumes that during the confession-interpretation stages, the client has identified the tensions involved in his problems, has been able to see the relationship between his mistaken attitudes and his behavior. He considers this phase transforming because the person now learns a new form in terms of his tensions and behaviors.

GOALS

The goals for this phase of counseling would include the client's clarification and acceptance of his present feelings and defense manipulations. The client will rationally understand the historical roots of his problems and will work out the problems in terms of the relationship of past events and present experiencing in the relationship with the counselor. The culmination of this phase is to elicit and establish behavioral responses that are consistent with a valid self-concept of the client (Brammer and Shostrom, 1968).

Feelings and experiences need to be worked out in all areas before the person is able to integrate his feelings and behavior patterns. The working-through process means that the conflicts must be worked out from many vantage points, possibly described in different words with varying degrees of insight before reaching a final integration.

INSIGHT

The client has an increasingly clear ability to face the contradictions and incongruencies that he finds within himself. His feelings are much more in the present rather than postponing and thinking about them. He has an increasing ownership of his feelings and he has a freer dialogue within himself. There is an increasing ability to accept responsibility for the problems being faced and a concern as to how he has contributed to the problems (Rogers, 1958).

As greater depth of insight occurs, the feelings that have previously been inhibited are now released and experienced with immediacy and the feelings seem to flow within the individual. The individual has an immediacy of experiencing in that he is then living his feelings subjectively rather than feeling about them. He is now gaining a trust in his feelings and the momentary changing of his feelings.

In the process of self-exploration, the client develops insight or becomes aware of other facets of his feelings that affect his behaviors. The majority of counseling approaches are insight oriented. The assumption is made that as the client gains insight or self-knowledge, he will therefore see alternate behaviors and this new insight will lead to behavior change. Obviously, the case is not so simple that, when insight is achieved, the problem automatically disappears. Even so, most counseling is still based on the concept that it is important for the client to have insight or an understanding of himself to meet the behavior change. The idea of insight frequently conjures up the idea of the "ah-hah" effect or the light bulb suddenly going on. Although this occurs at times in counseling, quite frequently it is a series of insights that are involved with the slow changing of behavior that occurs during this working-through process. These insights and changed perceptions of one's self become integrated into a new behavior pattern. There is a deepening in the awareness of what is going on both objectively and subjectively within the client. He is able to see relationships that he has not been aware of previously. The person is able to give up his former defensive patterns and have a freer self-confidence.

A CRITICAL POINT

A third critical point in counseling may occur in this phase of the relationship (Brammer and Shostrom, 1968). It is another type of flight into health. After the client has explored some of his present feelings and understands them in terms of previous experiences, he may have a feeling of wellbeing. With his new-found insight, the client may think that he is ready to terminate counseling. It may be that the client has the insight but is lacking in the commitment to action. In addition, as part of the working-through process, the client may run into difficulty carrying out his decision in his everyday life. Just because he has new insights is no sign that other people will change in the way they relate to him. All of this may lead to the client's terminating counseling prematurely. This is a judgment similar to that of the person getting up from bed too soon after having the flu. He may experience a relapse. The counselor must be careful not to keep the client in counseling longer than the client desires but must be careful not to terminate prematurely. It is a fine line for a decision.

THE PROCESS

The working-through phase involves putting the insight into action. The client gains little good in the long run from an intellectual understanding of his problem unless he is able to try out new methods of behaving. Prior to this point the client has been behaving according to the various concepts of himself; giving up those behavior patterns to adjust to the new self-concept may be quite difficult. Holland (1965) points out that a part of this aspect of counseling involves a behavioral retraining that includes giving up the undesirable responses and trying out some new ones. With many clients much of this working through the understanding, gaining insight, and adapting behaviors will be carried out by themselves. With other clients the counselor may need to play a more active role.

One variable that May (1967) suggests in changing the client is the utilization of his suffering. The counselor should channel the suffering of the client to furnish power to bring about this change. An individual will not change his pattern until he is forced to do so by his own suffering. Many individuals prefer to endure the misery of their situation rather than risk the uncertainty of what would come with change. May believes that the counselor should not relieve the client's suffering but rather redirect this suffering into constructive channels. The client may leave the interview more courageous, but more courageous with the realization that he must change his behavior. If the counseling is more than just superficial, the client may feel shaken and probably unhappy with his present situation. Part of what the counselor does then is to indicate the individual is suffering with his inappropriate attitudes and behaviors.

It is at this point in counseling that the client may have to look at a variety of alternative responses. He may look at a given situation and recognize that there are several different behavioral responses he can make. He may look at what would happen if he followed a particular behavioral response versus a second alternative versus a third alternative, and think through these kinds of behavior. In situations where the client is unable to generate such alternative responses, the counselor may become involved in a type of teaching process in which he aspires to help the client by suggesting several alternatives. By offering more than one alternative, the counselor is not making a suggestion of a specific behavior for the client but continues to help the client think through various alternatives. May (1967) claims that suggestion is often condemned as a technique because it is misconceived. It is not advice. The counselor may not be able to escape using suggestions in some forms but should be intelligent about using them. The suggestions may be alternatives for the client to consider. Possibly the most useful function for the counselor is to lay all the constructive alternatives before the client. From these alternatives he may select the one that will best meet his needs.

We can again observe Tom as he reaches this point. This excerpt clearly illustrates that the phases in counseling are not discretely separate nor do they move in a sequence. Although Tom has explored part of himself and his problem to the point of intellectual insight, there is still resistance and the need for further understanding. The working through involves trying out some of his insights by trying to be independent in different situations.

C   This may be one of the points in your life for the first time—you know, of leaving home in a way, when you've really been given an opportunity to have control over part of your life—or—sufficient power now to carry it out.

S   Hum—rather than go to college I'd just rather stay home. But what am I afraid of? Why am I—hum—seems like I'm just afraid to leave home in a sense.

C   That's probably the—the simple look at it—there may be more complex variables behind a simple answer. It may be something like that uh-h-h—it really means truly developing a certain amount of individual behavior.
(Long pause)

S   I guess I can understand that but I'm not—I don't know what to do uh—(laugh)

C   Yes (so) you can understand it intellectually it's pretty hard to accept it and carry it out.

S   I think for sure that—for sure it is—I've been—I've just leaned on my family and let them take care of me and I think what happened is I don't dare—I—when something challenges me I'd rather just drop out of it than do it—get out before I really have to do something—so—go home and—I don't like to think about it.

C   You're sorta having the same kind of feelings right now—but by doing all that it leaves you with a sort of a—feeling of not knowing what you want to do or why you want to do—nothing seems to have meaning then—all in sort of a—running away thing. What do we—just look at a few areas in which you do have some decisions that are within your means of control and and that you can carry out—what are—what are a few things that we look at now in terms of development of this?

S   I think probably the most immediate thing the thing that I've been thinking about the most is in how going to college next year'n like over the last couple of weeks—it's pretty—it's time now that you have to be applying and I haven't I haven't even thought about where I want to go let alone what I'd major in or anything like that. I know I could—I could still get in if I applied—I'd pretty well decided that I wouldn't even apply. (pause) Ya know I'd told my parents 'n they think I should stay at home and just go and maybe go to a community college or something like that. I don't want to do that. (laugh) But I don't—you know —I've never really been away from home. It's not—don't think I'm not afraid to go away from home.

C   You're not ready to make a final decision about going away to college yet either—but it may be something we can explore in terms of different places you might want to go, or, if not to college to take a job which might permit you to live away from home —maybe not a long way where you still have a certain kind of security. Short of that, you may want to talk with your parents about certain areas in which you are developing some individuality. You can develop some independence yourself there.

S   It all seems so kind of—seems kind of abstract and far away from me right now—you know—but somehow I know that—somehow I know that I have to—'n—what makes it so hard is—you know —my parents are so good to me but somehow I have—I've gotta actually, physically leave them.

C   It's going to be hard on both of you.

S   I think it's going to be harder on them than it is on me, almost— but I can see that—that I can't stay there—the way—as long as I stay there I'm just a little boy—you know—and I'm—I don't know maybe it's like that with everything—I'm just—anything that's going to involve *me* having to make a decision—and—and stand up for myself and do the work—almost seems as if everything like that I've just backed away from—I've never had—I never had to do it at home.

C   Sorta what I meant about the school work in that, maybe you've developed this pattern of dependency. Now's the time to start working at various areas of independence.

S   I guess maybe I—I guess maybe I know that that's what I have to do and I don't—really still don't—it all seems so simple but when you come down—like when I walk out of the office now— I'll understand everything we talked about but I won't know where to start—what to do.

C   Yeah—that's the tough part. It's too easy to go back into the old pattern instead of learning a new one.

S   I know, I—huh—I just—I've worked into a point now where everything—I can see that everything that I was doing I'm not
happy with anymore but I can't seem to make a step towards doing what I want to do now, and maybe like—you know—I've always (pause) I guess maybe college—I *do* want to go to college.

It is clear from this excerpt that although he has some insight, Tom is
not ready for termination. He must work through integrating the insight
into new behaviors. Obviously, the most important part of this integrative
work comes from the client's trying out these new insights and behaviors in
his everyday life. The personal conceptions are tentatively reformulated to
be validated against further experience, but even then held more loosely.
The counselor encourages the client to live out his insights by trying new
behaviors. It is the success of these experiences that will reinforce new behavior patterns. Should setbacks occur, they are worked through in the
later sessions, and the client tries out new insights and behaviors.

TERMINATION

Termination of the counseling process may be complicated. There may
be feelings of ambivalence about it. Just as an adolescent desires to be free
and leave home, he is anxious about really leaving. Frequently, the client
will recognize that he is handling his situation adequately and tends to
consider termination. The counselor can discuss the idea with the client to
help him prepare for termination. This communicates that the counselor
has confidence in him and removes any concern he might have about the
counselor's feeling rejected by his move toward independence. Actually the
relationship is never over, as it may be renewed if the client desires.

TERMINATION IN COUNSELING

Termination is an important aspect of the continuing process of counseling. In each counseling session and series of counseling sessions there is
a need to bring closure to what has been occurring in the counselor-client
interaction. Termination can occur at three rather specific points: the conclusion of a discussion unit within an interview, the conclusion of each interview, and the conclusion of the counseling process (Brammer and Shostrom, 1968).

Discussion Units

The first type of termination is that which is necessary following the discussion of a specific client concern. Although some counselors seem to want to keep the client talking without clearly delineating or dealing with his concerns, most often the counselor-client interaction can be seen as a series of mini-sessions that occur in a particular block of time. It is not always possible or meaningful to close off these segments but, when it is possible, there are several techniques that can be of value.

This unit or mini-session can be terminated by a summary statement by either the client or counselor. The intent here is to draw together what has been said during the unit and to help the client see what progress has been made. Obviously, the client must then decide whether to move on to further areas or to continue in the present discussion. The latter decision suggests that the summary or closure by the counselor was premature. The counselor must be sensitive to the client's needs in order to really use the summary termination effectively. He must also convey to the client that continuation of the topic is possible even though, in his own mind, the discussion has been fairly completely developed.

A second method is a more direct method of stopping discussion on a topic. The counselor chooses to suggest directly that the discussion may not be as meaningful at the particular time due to client psychological condition, counselor skill, or other inner or outer related factors. The counselor does not shut off the possibility of returning to the topic. What he suggests is that further discussion may be inappropriate or non-rewarding and that, when certain other factors are present, the topic can be reintroduced. The counselor will have to explain this action at times because he is really interpreting something in the client, the relationship, the environment, or himself that may not be so apparent to the client. The crucial variable here is communication of what is happening and why it is happening.

A third termination technique falls somewhere between these two methods. This intermediate method is designed to shut off the particular topic without stopping client progress and client involvement. Several techniques can be used. The counselor may choose to alter the subject slightly so that the direction is unaltered but the intensity of feelings exhibited by the client is reduced. This is done when a client is deep in self-exploration and the counselor wants to bring him up and cap off that emotion for the present time. Old topics can be reintroduced or new topics of some interrelationship introduced. The counselor can use other counseling techniques to accomplish these goals. He can react to different parts of client statements, thus leading the client into a different topical area. He can increase the number and direction of pauses so that the interview slows down in speed and intensity of effect. Again it is important to understand the effect of this type of activity on the client. Any action of the counselor that "shuts off" the client's communication has an undesirable effect and should be avoided.

TERMINATING AN INTERVIEW

A second type of termination is that which relates to ending an interview. Many counselors, especially those in the early part of their professional career, report that the client really begins to bring up important material right at the end of the allotted interview time. They are obviously hesitant to terminate at what appears to be a crucial point in the counseling session. Yet, time constraints and the need to keep counseling within some reasonable boundaries forces the issue. Often it is of considerable value to examine two aspects in this situation. What, if any, aspects of the counselor's "modus operandi" precluded earlier client "meaningful" involvement and what, if anything, stimulated the client to move at the end of the session? This means a close examination by the counselor of his own motivations as well as an understanding of the client. Assuming that this particular area, albeit important, can be understood and any necessary corrective steps taken, the techniques of termination become important.

The counselor should establish with the client a time limit in which the counseling is to take place. If the client has a prearranged appointment, he should know that he will be with the counselor from a specific time to a specific time. The counselor only need refer to the time factors to effect a termination under most situations. However, simply saying "your time is up" will probably not satisfy the client. Someone needs to summarize what has occurred, what has been discussed during the session, and what might be the next steps. Often, the counselor is likely to take the responsibility of summarizing. He should, at least, consider the possibility of including the client. Having the client suggest what might be done also is a valuable tool. Setting up the time and date for the next meeting, as well as some of the potential discussion topics, makes the termination of the interview smooth and does not leave the client dangling without any sense of direction or accomplishment.

With some clients, summarizing is not enough. They still wish to sit and talk. The counselor often needs to stand up and move toward the door or toward assisting the client to get his coat and thus leave the situation. The counselor may use some subtle devices to suggest that the time has arrived to end the particular interview. He can move his chair or place his hands on the arms of the chair as if to rise, and so forth. Actually, these devices or techniques are usually accepted by the client without any particular stress or strain. The more nervous the counselor is about using them, the more likely that client resistance to the action will occur.

Depending upon the type of counseling approach one might utilize, there are some other fairly meaningful ways to end the interview. Assigning some task to the client is one example of a general method. Obviously, the counselor can phrase the instructions in such a way that the intent to end the session is communicated. For example, he might say "Now that we are finished for today, I would like to suggest some questions that both of us should consider for next time." A related approach would be to arrange for any tests or reading that may have been determined during the session.

There are two or three limitations that should be included in our discussion. The counselor must avoid, as much as possible, leaving the client in an ambiguous situation. The more hesitancy, unsureness, or uneasiness the counselor exhibits, the less likely the client is to be able to understand or accept what is occurring.

The counselor may wish to provide extra counseling time when he senses that there is a need for the client to continue. This simply suggests that the counselor should have some flexibility to provide additional assistance when the client seems to need it. A caution is necessary; namely, that certain clients may use this as a manipulative device to meet their own needs and continue to waste the first counseling "hour" in order to effect some control or manipulation over the counselor. This obviously calls for a great deal of counselor self-examination and understanding.

Regardless of the method the counselor uses, he should make sure that the client leaves with the most positive feeling possible about what occurs in the session and what the future activities might be. The counselor should have a tentative plan and some activities in mind to effect termination.

TERMINATION OF THE RELATIONSHIP

The final type of termination is that which relates to the closing of a case. Since two persons, the counselor and client, are involved, both have potential for terminating. We shall be less concerned with the client's reasons, for these can be numerous and varied and there is often nothing that can be done about it. Beginning counselors often feel rejected and less than competent as a counselor when a client fails to return. There is a fine line between letting this affect his future counseling contacts with other clients or, indeed, the same client, and a feeling of "sour grapes" or a hardened psychological set that "I have plenty of other people to work with—who needs him?" We would hope that any preparation program would help the potential counselor deal with both extremes of this continuum.

The counselor's case termination skills and activities are important. Several factors may lead to the need for the counselor to terminate future contact. Time restraints or change of position may cause the counselor to prematurely end his relationship with a client. Hopefully, most of the conditions are known several weeks prior to occurrence and can be programmed into the counseling session prior to a fixed termination date. It would be necessary for the counselor to arrange for referral of those persons who may desire further assistance. This process is discussed in another section.

Dependency activities on the client's part may be a clue to termination. One counseling goal must be to help the client function more adequately in his own personal life and to begin to be an independent person. When these do not seem to be occurring, the counselor is not being honest in continuing the relationship as constituted. Since the counselor may not be able to alter his style that much, it would appear that termination and/or referral are called for.

The usual termination comes when the client feels he has made the decision, has the information, or is coping adequately with his problem. He may give clues that he does not need the counseling any longer. It is not uncommon for a feeling of friendship and good will to develop between the two people. After talking through some meaningful things in your life with another person, it is difficult to separate.

The methods or steps in closure of a series of counseling sessions are somewhat parallel to those used in unit and session termination. First, some preparatory steps should be taken. This has already been alluded to and simply means that the counselor does not wait until the last minute to indicate that he cannot continue the relationship. Whatever the reasons for termination, they seldom wait to pop up until the middle of the final interview. The counselor should provide or encourage the client to provide an overall summarization of what has occurred. It may well be that, due to the nature of an extended series of meetings, both must be involved and considerable clarification may be necessary.

It is of some importance that the same conditions exist when case termination occurs as when session termination takes place. The counselor must avoid leaving the client in an ambiguous or defenseless position. He must be certain that either the client can function in his society or some further assistance is necessary. In any case, the counselor, regardless of his orientation, must be able to understand the situation the client faces, understand his own situation, weigh the values, and make a decision.

REFERRAL IN COUNSELING

At any point in the counseling process, the counselor may recognize that the client would profit from working with a different professional person. Successful counseling is often related to the utilization of various resource personnel. A counselor cannot be expected to be able to meet the needs of all clients. He must rely upon others to assist him or, more particularly, the client, to better resolve his problems or concerns. The process of referral is of considerable importance and deserves the attention of the counselor or counseling staff.

Several dimensions regarding referral can be identified. These dimensions can be related to the process of referral, the effect upon the counselor and client, and follow-up of the referral. It becomes obvious that the referral process should be considered an integral part of the counselor's preparation, role, and personal concern.

Each counselor will eventually find himself in the position of needing to call upon outside assistance for his client. The reasons for this action frequently revolve around client-presented problems beyond or outside the present functional level of the counselor. Another reason may be related to a long-term involvement which the counselor cannot provide. It is important that the counselor understand and be prepared for the referral process. A number of factors must be considered, not the least of which is the counselor himself.

THE COUNSELOR

Whenever a person is involved as a counselor with a client, there is a certain amount of ego involvement present. The counselor must feel that he is able to function effectively, yet he must be open to the possibility of someone else helping the client more. A counselor could feel a personal weakness or inadequacy when he cannot meet the task and so needs to refer a client. The counselor must maintain a proper balance of confidence and know when to refer.

There are several ways by which the counselor may come to this balance. First, he needs to know himself. He must be aware of what kind of assistance he can provide and, to the degree possible, the kinds of client help that are beyond his scope. Of course, it is hoped that during his education the counselor will have had the opportunity to examine his strengths and weaknesses and to improve those areas that may be potential problems.

We are not suggesting any special type of activity for counselor self-understanding. Various methods are employed and produce the desired outcomes of self-understanding, improved interrelationships, decrease in defensiveness, and more adequate counseling practice. These methods include personal counseling, group seminars or sensitivity training, and supervision. Even after the formal education ends, the practicing counselor profits from continued supervision. A portion of the supervisory period is given to personal matters that might affect the performance of the counselor. This is a mild form of counseling, perhaps the chief difference revolving around the intensity of the counselor's effort to change his behavior. Often the supervisor helps the counselor become aware of the behavior and the assumption is made that change will take place.

THE CLIENT

The client represents another important factor in the referral process. For some clients it will be difficult to accept a change of counselors. This may be true for several reasons, some of which reside within the client and some of which are outside the client's personal situation but, nonetheless, potent aspects that inhibit accepting referral.

Often the client is unable to accept the referral because of lack of mobility, time difficulties, monetary problems, or other such factors that are, in effect, beyond his control. The person who has no transportation has a difficult time going across town to meet with a more appropriate helper. Similarly, when fees are involved, some clients do not have the support to take advantage of the referral agency's services. Finally, the client may not be able to go when the referral agent is available. All of these, plus any other external variable, need to be considered by the counselor and client whenever a referral is suggested. They are not insurmountable but must be dealt with to insure a meaningful referral.

The internal inhibitors that affect the client's potential for referral are more critical and crucial. He may resist referral because of a dependency relationship that exists between him and the counselor. Because the counselor has established a relationship, the client may feel more secure with him and not wish to move. Obviously, the fear of a new situation may also be involved in the rejection of a referral by the client. Although he may be aware that his present counselor cannot help him, he may be reluctant to go into a new situation due simply to the unknown quality of the new counselor. Referral suggests that the problem or concern of the client is worse than originally conceived. Although this may not be the case at all, the client quite naturally may feel that the degree of difficulty he is experiencing is worse than he once thought. He may realize that it is essential to seek more competent assistance and will often feel some reluctance to actually accept the additional help. Many of these anxieties can be handled by the counselor's preparing the client for the referral. If the counselor is leaving his position or the client needs additional assistance, he will know this in time to prepare the client. If the client understands the reason for the referral and participates in the process, it will proceed more smoothly.

The Process

The counselor can aid the smooth transition by giving the client two or more equally meaningful possibilities for additional assistance. Thus, the client is not placed in the position of feeling shunted from one person to another with little input or control of the situation. It is assumed that the counselor knows the referral source and that he promotes the best possible fit for client and agency or client and other helper. In this light, the counselor can be of assistance to the agency to which the client is referred by providing information within the limits of confidentiality and of helping the agency better mobilize its resources to meet the needs of the client.

Finally, the counselor ought to have some sort of a check list to insure that the referral is necessary and the referral agency is the most appropriate for the client. The following points may be valuable in preparing this check list.

1. List the various resources of the school or agency to be sure that all within-agency resources have been utilized to meet the client's needs. Often counselors are reluctant to use the other personnel in the agency when, in fact, these people might have the skill to provide quite meaningful assistance.

2. Be attuned to the ongoing dynamics of the counseling situation so that referable necessities might be identified and discussions with the agency, both for technical assistance and perhaps eventual referral, are developed.

3. Be as involved as possible in identifying those already a part of the problem-treatment situation. This would include knowing where other family members fit in, and what agencies are already involved so that minimal overlap exists and personal feelings are not strained.

4. Understand the agency, its limitations and strengths, and be particularly careful in communicating these to the client and others involved with the client.

5. Be certain that a balance exists between dependency of the client on you to do everything and the real needs of the client for assistance in accepting the referral.

6. Develop communication lines with the agency so that both the referring counselor and the person in the agency have contact possibilities. Obviously, some involvement of the client and his family may be included in this step, but the counselor should avoid coaching or supporting illicit methods of obtaining services.

SUMMARY

This chapter has presented a descriptive model of a continuing counseling relationship. Not all relationships, and probably no single one, would follow this model exactly. However, it is a guide to the various stages that have been observed. Clients frequently enter counseling with apprehensions and talk *about* their problem, move to some exploration of themselves, gain some understanding of themselves and the problem, work through the understanding and trying of new behaviors, and terminate counseling. The process does not move in sequence but with stops, starts, and regressions through the various phases. The various aspects of termination occur through the process and provide closure of the various points in time. Because a counselor may not be able to help a client through the entire process, referral is a part of the continuing relationship.

REFERENCES

Brammer, L., and Shostrom, E. *Therapeutic Psychology*. Englewood Cliffs: Prentice-Hall, Inc., 1968.

Holland, G. *Fundamentals of Psychology*. New York: Holt, Rinehart and Winston, 1965.

May, R. *The Art of Counseling*. New York: Abingdon Press, 1967.

Rogers, C. "A Process Conception of Psychotherapy." *American Psychologist* 13:142–149.

11

Decision Making
in Counseling

Counseling is often a means for aiding a client in making decisions. The assumption must consistently be made that each decision which is of enough significance to the client to bring him to the counselor's office is important enough to demand the counselor's full efforts and attention. Additionally, the skill necessary for decision making can be learned and the counseling process offers an ideal situation for the counselor to aid in the learning process. This suggests that the counselor knows something of decision making himself so that he can aid the client in learning. It should be clear that the ultimate decision must be made by the client. The counselor creates the decision-making environment and assists in learning the process.

There are various types of decisions that are made and for which the counseling situation offers an ideal setting. Generally, these may be differentiated into educational decisions, vocational decisions, and personal decisions. Of course it is not as easy to delineate these areas in the actual counseling setting, as they are generally intermingled.

GENERAL NOTIONS OF DECISION MAKING

There are some overarching aspects that apply to the decision-making interview. First, the client needs to develop the general direction in which he

294

wishes to move. He must have rather definite ideas about the purposes that the decision may serve for him. Second, the client must be able to consider the parameters of his free-choice situation. These may be external or internal in nature. Normally, they serve the purpose of restricting the range of possibilities and thus diminishing the amount of confusion. It may well be that understanding the parameters is really understanding what one cannot do, leaving only positive actions from which the selection is made.

Third, the client needs to understand himself as a person. We sometimes assume that the client has the ability to gain this understanding outside of the counseling situation. Counselors are prone to "accept" certain statements the client ascribes to himself. Often, subsequent information suggests that the understanding the client had was partial at best. Thus, the decision maker may need help in gaining further understanding of his own abilities, needs, goals, and potentials, among other aspects, in order to move toward the decision.

Decision making has some identifiable facets that should be considered. Although Hansen (1965) relates these to college choice, they are probably attributes of all decision making. Decisions are continuous, tentative, and psychological. In almost any situation there are prior factors or antecedent conditions that are related to the decision. Educational preparation is often highly related to vocational choices. The antecedent choice of a specific educational choice relates in a continuing way to the possible choices available.

Fortunately, many of the decisions made are tentative and can be altered to a degree sometime afterward. It is of some importance to remember that there is a degree of irreversibility in any decision, so that some avenues may be closed by the decision. However, the client should realize that the decision he is called upon to make does not bind him forever to the outcomes of the activity he has chosen.

Very often, outside factors become more deeply enmeshed in the decision than is apparent from a surface examination. Hoppock's (1957) description of a man choosing a particular occupation well below the level of his abilities is an example in that the moral factor of providing for his family was an unknown but very potent aspect of the life of the chooser. Other examples of a rational or irrational nature can be given but, suffice it to say, outside or inside psychological factors are highly related to the decision-making process.

MODELS OF DECISION MAKING

There are several models that have been developed for understanding the decision-making process. The value of a model is that it can help the client and the counselor conceptualize the steps that need to be accomplished and the necessary informational input related to the decision making.

Authoritarian Model

The authoritarian model of decision making posits a situation where an expert advises the decision maker. The resultant decision is fairly predictable and, in some cases, is insured by the authoritarian. For example, a young child about to cross the street may be given the important facts of the situation. Watch for the green light because this means you have the right-of-way. Look out for cars, and so forth. Many of the elements can be described but, even more important, the child can be forced into the "right" decision by the physical intervention of the parent. This is not to suggest that the authoritarian model always ends up with physical intervention. On the contrary, the expectation is that the individual will act reasonably or decide reasonably when the facts are known.

Laissez Faire Model

On the other side of the decision-making continuum is the laissez faire model, in which very little information or direction is given by the counselor or teacher. The decision maker is expected to sort out the important factors by himself and to move in reasonable ways because of his ability to do this. Obviously, some undesirable alternatives can occur. The model is one of little involvement on the part of the advisor.

Mathematics Model

Another type of model is the mathematical model. In this case, the decision is seen in light of probabilities. Perhaps the most illustrative model of this type is presented by Katz (1966) (Fig. 11-1).

In this model two factors are important: values and options. The individual determines three aspects of values for himself. He must first identify the dimensions that are important to him. These could be money, power, authority and so on. Since these may be multifaceted, a second identification is made concerning the magnitude of the dimension where various incomes can be delineated. Finally, the client assigns a level of importance to the dimension with an arbitrary sum. Since these numbers can be altered from the original assignment, the only criterion is that they are manageable.

A second factor that the client must select is a series of options. In this

VALUES			OPTIONS — Strength of Return							
			W		X		Y		Z	
Dimension	Magnitude	Importance (Sum = 100)	Coefficient	Product	Coefficient	Product	Coefficient	Product	Coefficient	Product
A	A_1 A_2 A_3 A_4 A_5	30	5	150	2	60	4	120	2	60
B	B_1 B_2 B_3	20	4	80	5	100	5	100	3	60
C	C_1 C_2	10	5	50	1	10	3	30	1	10
D	D_1 D_2	5	5	25	3	15	1	5	1	5
E	E_1 E_2 E_3 E_4	35	3	105	2	70	3	105	4	140
Sum of value returns				410		255		360		275
Joe's probability of success				0.7		0.8		0.7		0.5
Expected value				287		204		252		137.5

FIGURE 11-1. MODEL OF GUIDANCE FOR DECISION-MAKING. ILLUS-TRATIVE CHART FOR JOE DOE. Martin Katz, "A model of guidance for career decision-making," *Vocational Guidance Quarterly*, 1966, 15, 2–10. By permission.

case, options mean the possibilities within a given situation, or a series of possibilities that may or may not be related. The client might list the curricular offerings at a particular high school or he may want to examine a variety of jobs available to him. The coefficient listed in the chart may be calculated according to some pattern of value magnitude. For example, the percentage of persons earning a particular amount of money can provide the coefficient. In other cases the coefficient may result from an educated guess by the counselor concerning the probability of a certain percentage of persons attaining a particular level of operation.

One further aspect must be determined—i.e., the probability of the client's success in the option. This figure is derived from expectancy tables, tests, and characteristics studies. The counselor may not always have as complete prediction information as he would like and soft data—e.g., counselor impressions—might be necessary.

The client performs the mathematical computations called for and has available to him an expected value or success outcome. These numbers, while transitory, do provide information for the decision maker concerning continued exploration, change in values, greater self-understanding, or for the actual decision.

The reader should note that when hard data are available and used, the model is a bit more accurate than when soft data are used. The desired outcome is to promote the deliberation of the decision maker through acquiring and processing relevant information. Katz (1966) suggests "this model of guidance for career decision-making first assists the student in taking full cognizance of the range of values in the culture and encourages him to make his own values explicit."

GELATT'S SEQUENTIAL MODEL

Gelatt (1962) proposes a decision-making framework in which objectives are defined, data are collected and analyzed, possible alternatives are studied, and consequences are evaluated. He frames his decision making in the following schematic way.

The reader will note that the four steps listed above are contained in the schema. First, a purpose or objective is established. Data are gathered from various sources. This leads the client into a strategy that includes a prediction system, a value system, and the criterion for evaluating or selecting a decision. This process leads to a decision that may be tentative or final. In either case, a recycling may occur.

The importance of the Gelatt model is that it delineates possible involvement of a counselor. The counselor can provide specific assistance at each of the levels. Obviously, he avoids making the decision or framing his input to lead to a specific decision.

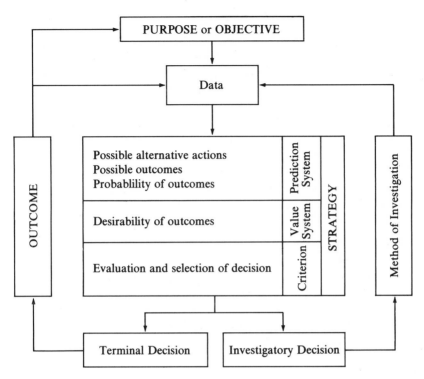

FIGURE 11-2. THE SEQUENTIAL DECISION-MAKING PROCESS. *The Sequential Decision-Making Process.* H. B. Gelatt, "Decision-Making A Conceptual Frame of Reference for Counseling," *Journal of Counseling Psychology*, 1962, 9, 240–245. By permission.

STOCHASTIC MODEL

The concept of a stochastic model presumes that, following a decision, there are two separate and independent paths to be followed. A decision to follow one course denies the facts or probability of the other. Reversibility is not possible. This seems to be the type of situation most of us would prefer; namely, that we could clearly delineate the various facets of the paths to be followed and make our decision on the basis of knowing with clarity just what to expect. However, this is not usually the case. Because we are dealing with humans and future behavior, it is difficult to ever be certain. There is usually an element of risk involved and, thus, the counselor and student must deal with this risk factor.

Trait and Factor Model

The trait and factor model of choice presumes that each individual has certain traits or characteristics. The choices available to the individual have certain identifiable factors or requirements. When these choices are known, the individual, with some compromise, can match his traits with the job requirements. This essentially is the earliest model of vocational choice espoused by Parsons (1909) and, although of some help to the potential decider, contains some major points of weakness. First, it describes a generally static process in which neither the individual nor choice can change. Second, as importantly, perhaps even admitting that change can occur, the model does not effectively handle out-of-date material which in our present society is usually the case rather than the exception.

Other Decision-Making Models

Other decision-making models involve specific factors that override other facts of the choice. Included here are the maximum-gain–maximum-loss posssibility and cultural models. The maximum-gain decision is most affected by the possible personal gain that will accrue to the individual. A most obvious gain would be money, but this is not the only factor. This model ignores several meaningful and important factors while concentrating only on gain.

The social background or, more specifically, limitations imposed by the cultural and environmental aspects of the individual's existence often affect a decision. This model is used most often by culturally different individuals who have neither the background nor assistance necessary to deal with a broader range of possibilities. Choices are made in a restrictive area which is not at all indicative of the true possibilities available to the individual.

Decisions are often made and supported on an after-the-fact basis. In this case a decision—good or bad—is forced, and the individual then develops a rationale to support his decision. This may be necessary for mental health but it also has been the foundation of some fairly poor choices on the part of individuals.

Finally, one might attempt to subsume the important or major elements of the previous models and build an overarching model for choice making. Thus the trait and factor approach provides valuable information but needs constant reappraisal from some source. The counselor might at least provide some assistance here. Obviously the characteristics of the maximum-gain model—i.e., outcomes—are important and should be included in any decision-making process. It provides extra information which should be considered. The individual who is forced into a rather narrow frame of reference can be aided to build both horizontally and vertically from the foundation that he presently understands. Finally, the ability to make decisions implied in the after-the-fact model is important but must be reappraised and restructured to be effective. The decision-making paradigm must include knowledge of self, traits, social, personal, and environmental background and a rather comprehensive but manageable array of choices so that the final decision can be relevant to the needs of the individual as well as to society.

THE PROCESS OF DECISION MAKING

The process of decision making poses an interesting dilemma at times since it is possible to make a decision with little or no consideration of the process. For example, a housewife shopping for vegetables in a supermarket selects a particular package of carrots. She has made a decision, but it could have been accomplished via a wide variety of processes. She could have just picked up the package without applying any criterion for selection. She could have had negative criteria and thus rejected certain packages. She could have had positive criteria and thus picked the package that most closely met the criteria she had in mind. In all probability she could not have specified which of the three possibilities she had chosen. Yet, over a period of time she is probably consistent in the way she chooses packages of carrots.

The above illustration presents some of the major considerations in the decision-making process. First, there was the suggestion that decision making can be accidental. Second, there was the possibility of negative decisions. Third, there was the implicit development of selection criteria to guide the choice. Finally, although not specifically discussed, there was the differentiation of no-risk versus risk decisions. In the illustration the housewife probably was in a no-risk situation. It really did not make that much difference which package she chose since all were approximately alike. There was probably a guarantee that, if she did not like the purchase, it could be returned.

Accidental Decisions

When one examines the many decisions that are made each day, he finds that a large percentage falls into the accidental category. We are faced with the need to decide something and we decide. We choose particular clothes to wear simply because they were the first ones we saw. Much of our daily life is filled with this type of decision; perhaps the most effective way is the existential—do whatever seems right. It is possible to utilize this process at wrong moments in time. When this occurs, the need to gain a clearer understanding of the process becomes more apparent.

NEGATIVE CRITERIA

Often decisions are based upon negative criteria. In effect certain choices are ruled out and thus greatly restrict what is actually available. Suppose a person is in a restaurant looking at the menu. He must make a decision about what to order. Some would begin first by eliminating those items that are perceived negatively: "I don't like seafood." "The roast duck costs too much." In short, although not verbalized, the individual is narrowing the list of possibilities available to him. His final choice may be made for him by the elimination process or by reducing the list to a number of equally attractive items. He has negatively moved toward his selection for the evening.

POSITIVE CRITERIA

An individual often uses positive criteria to choose between equally attractive items. He may say, "I like item X because I've had it before." He may say, "I think I will try item Y because I've heard others say how good it is." He is implicitly establishing criteria for selection. He is going to choose that item which has most positive value for him. It would have been possible to do this in the first place—i.e., he could have decided to select a particular item because it was the most positive item—without regard to any negative feelings about the remainder of the items.

NO–RISK VERSUS RISK DECISION MAKING

If the decision we are called upon to make presents no risk to us, then perhaps we need not have much concern. If it really does not make any difference, then working through the process might be unnecessary as well as a time waster. However, when risk is involved, we must be aware of probable outcomes. We need to know the information necessary to examine alternatives. We may need outside assistance to bring all the critical elements to bear upon the decision. Perhaps no-risk decisions can be valuable to us as learning devices for the later, more important risk decisions that each person faces.

RISK TAKING

Risk taking deserves a bit of extra attention in our discussion of decision making. By definition, any decision that one must make has inherent in it two aspects that client and counselor must understand: a lack of certainty and the prospect of loss or failure resulting from the decision. Although this is most easily illustrated by gambling or stock market activity, Kogan and Wallach (1967) point out:

> Risk taking refers to behavior in situations where there is a desirable goal and a lack of certainty that it can be attained. The situations may take the form of requiring a choice between more or less desirable goals, with the former having a lower probability of attainment than the latter. A further possible but unnecessary characteristic of such situations is the threat of negative consequences for failure, so that the individual at the post-decisional stage might find himself worse off than he was before having made his decision.

Part of the need in counseling is to develop accurate predictors upon which clients can base relevant decisions. Many models for prediction deal with some sort of mathematical probability. We have discussed these in another portion of this chapter. We have also alluded to the need of understanding the risk-taking propensity of the client. Less information is available in this area; thus, the counselor is forced to develop a method of determining the client's level and, more importantly, the meaning that taking the risk has to the client.

It is important at this point to understand the difference between chance and skill outcomes. When the prediction is toward a chance type of situation—for example, gambling—there is a different set of dimensions than when some specific or learned skill can affect the outcome. The individual will react differently when he can have some manipulative relationship to success than when chance is at issue. The problem is that we may have difficulty specifying the direction of this response. Some clients are gamblers and thus will take chances whereas others are more certain that the skills they possess are most important and are more willing to take the skill chance.

We can identify several situational and personal factors related to risk taking, thus related to decision making. We have already listed the chance versus skill factor. In general, Kogan and Wallach (1967) suggest that the skill context appears to stimulate a moderate level of risk taking whereas a chance context seems to induce an avoidance of intermediate in favor of extremely risky or conservative strategies.

A second factor related to risk taking deals with the type and extent of information available to the decider. The amount of information available and the degree of importance of the decision combine to determine the choice that is made. A purchase in the supermarket causes less dilemma than buying a house. Again the problem might be that decisions are not as simply differentiated as the above example and the counselor may be called upon to provide information and promote the decision. Probably more individual difference is involved in the information-seeking factor than in other areas. However, it may be true that interrelated material is seen as more valuable than that data which seem to have little internal consistency. Most likely, it is also true that the pattern of each individual is rather consistent so that once the client has given an indication of his proclivities, the counselor will have a substantial base upon which to build.

A third determinant is that of gain or cost. We have already listed this as an important determinant in decision making. It is also related to the risk-taking level of the individual. In general the greater the value of the goal, the greater the potential risk-taking behavior. As gain increases in value, to the point of dominance over costs, the risk taking increases. The converse is also true. Again there will be great individual differences that indicate the need for counselor attention to the client's mode of action.

A fourth aspect deals with real incentives. Obviously it is easy to deal with hypothetical situations and to make all sorts of "decisions." When real outcomes are involved, however, a different behavior is usually exhibited. Conservatism in risk taking should be expected when real incentives are offered.

Finally, there is some evidence concerning the relationship of previous gains or losses to the individual's risk taking. One would assume that prior successes with various models would lead the individual to the utilization of a similar model for decisions. The evidence is not all that clear since in some gambling situations previous losses seem to have obverse effect upon present and future betting. Again the individual's reaction to prior losses or gains will be important data for the counselor and client to understand. There is no suggestion that the counselor force a method of risk taking or decision making. Previous methods which are understood can be built upon or altered to lead to a more appropriate strategy.

It might be of some value to understand some general personal characteristics about risk takers. The following factors seem to be logical areas of investigation.

Sex of the individual does not appear to be related to the general level of risk taking. Men and women are not differentiated by most methods of determining risk-taking behavior. When age is the variable, the older person seems to become more conservative. When social class is the variable, two conjectures are possible. On a financial basis persons with higher status can afford greater risks than those with lower status. However, the person with lower status has less to lose in many cases and thus may be willing to assume rather great risks. Little is known about which, if either, is true.

Some other factors have been identified through personality measures. Motivation toward achievement, inner directedness, and independence have been studied with less than desired results. Although these factors seem to have a logical relationship to the risk-taking stance of an individual, there is little collaborative information available.

The purpose of this section was to provide a background in the area of risk taking since this is related to decision making. Although, in general, little substantive evidence is available concerning relationships between these variables and risk taking, it is important that, for certain decisions, the client understand the variable as well as his inclination toward the variable. Obviously the counselor needs to know something of the risk-taking area so that he can intelligently provide meaningful assistance to the client.

SEQUENTIAL NATURE

Many decisions are sequential in nature. The process extends over a period of time, and previous experiences and decisions influence and direct the outcome. In some cases previous experiences and decisions are linked to irreversibility of direction. The vocational theory of Ginzberg et al. (1951) is illustrative of this point.

The important aspect to be considered here is that the client should be aware that the decisions he is called upon to make are for the most part not single events but rather a series of events that occur across a period of time. If we now relate this to stages of analyzing, organizing, and synthesizing (Gelatt, 1962), we can see the need for information input at each point along the way. In addition, there is a need for the counselor to provide assistance in monitoring the analyzing, organizing, and synthesizing processes. Several other aspects of the decision-making process need to be considered. These generally fall under the categories of alternatives, outcomes, probabilities, and personal preferences.

INFORMATION IN DECISION MAKING

A prime factor in understanding decision making involves an understanding of the role of information in the process. The decision maker must utilize various types of information in the decision process. This may be at a minimal level or at a level where much information, feedback, and prognosis occur.

This process has been described by Hollis and Hollis (1969) as personalizing information. The individual internalizes the information available to him in order for it to be usable. The counselor helps the individual pick and choose that information which is most relevant to him as a person.

Another important factor in the decision process is that of continuous information. The decider must understand that most decisions are only avenues to later, more difficult decisions. Information available and used at one point may be far from adequate for future decisions. In addition there is a need to make sure that the information is up to date so that decisions are made as accurately as possible.

It is of some interest to note that many decisions that individuals are asked to make relate most closely to activities of several years hence. One might argue the value of a junior high school student choosing between one type of high school curriculum and another, but the fact is that in all too many cases this is exactly what is required. The decision made at the eighth- or ninth-grade level is related to college plans, type of occupation which one wishes to enter, and so forth; and, the information necessary to help the individual make the decision is based upon present-day status. At present the eighth- or ninth-grade boy may need some information concerning the draft situation if he is called upon to decide whether to aim at college or at an occupation immediately after high school. It is difficult to know what the situation will actually be when the individual graduates. Information must be continuously updated, and the client may need to review on a regular basis the decision that he has made. Some decisions are really not decisions. If the decision is a foregone conclusion, there is little value in playing the game. If a decision must be made and the client seeks the aid of a counselor, it is safe to assume that either the individual does not know what information he needs, does not have the information he wants, or is unable to use the information available to him.

PERSONAL PREFERENCE

The individual needs to have an understanding of his own personal preferences so that his final decision will be one that both moves him toward a goal and fosters a feeling of meeting his needs. The value factor becomes important in any decision-making process. In retrospect it often helps us to understand why certain things were done by people when in the cold light of reality the decision did not make any sense. In order to reach a meaningful personal decision, the client must understand something of the personal value attached to any possible outcome.

VALUES

Decisions are affected by the values held by the individual. He may not be able to accurately verbalize these values. However, they will have input into the decision made by the client. The counselor's job may include helping the client be more aware of and thus better able to understand his values as these relate to the decision-making process.

Patterson (1959) suggests that values are "standards, or criteria, which are non-objective, in the sense that they represent preferences, which are in part socially or culturally determined" (p. 55). Values also are seen as representing a desirable condition. Interests, preferences, attitudes, and opinions contribute to the value structure of the individual.

Much has been written concerning the value structure of the counselor as it relates to the values held by the client. At times the counselor is told that he should not indicate his own values in an interview. At other times the counselor is told that he should put his value structure on the line so that the client knows where the counselor stands. The client may either reject the values and/or counselor or work within a known framework. The problem thus identified is how the counselor deals with his own values as well as those of the client in helping the client reach a meaningful decision.

For a successful counseling relationship, we believe that it is essential for the counselor to understand his own as well as his client's value structure. Hopefully, the counselor will have had the opportunity to examine his own values during the preparation period. It also follows that the counselor needs an opportunity for learning methods of identifying the client's values and attempt to bring these together in a counseling relationship.

Values or beliefs are very personal matters, and the client probably will not be immediately willing to discuss these openly. He will test the counselor to see if it is safe to talk about values or beliefs, to see if confidentiality is maintained. Most decisions will emerge from the interaction of the decider with various elements in his environment: values, significant persons, and meaningfulness of alternatives, among other aspects. The process usually means that the client is exposing himself to a change of values or beliefs, to a changed style of life, or to the possibility of loss as well as gain. The counselor's job is to help the student deal effectively with the wide array of factors involved and to make a decision and follow through on what is decided.

ALTERNATIVES

Various alternatives exist, and the client must identify and sort through these alternatives to eventually reach his own decision. As an example, the high school student is faced with the need to decide which colleges he should apply to, and eventually which college is the best for him. He may use various methods of eliminating colleges, but in the end he develops a list of several colleges that are reasonable choices. He has to decide which of the several colleges is the one he should attend. He should go through a process of weighing the characteristics of the colleges and his own strengths and weaknesses to reach his decision. In this process he may identify certain factors about more than one college which are within his acceptable alternatives. Thus, the alternatives become clear. He may like the breadth of academia at a particular college, but not the size of its student population. Or, he may like the size of the institution but be concerned that his potential courses of action are limited. Perhaps he can afford college Z, but is concerned over its academic reputation. All are alternatives, and the decider wants to select that college which is the most appropriate for him.

Another factor comes into play in the decision-making process. This might be called the control of the decision-making process by someone else. As an example, college choice is not a one-way street. The college exercises a significant influence in the final choice. This is also true of other types of decisions that we are called upon to make and contributes to a compromise factor. Compromise is important enough that it is discussed at length in a subsequent section. The counselor should provide help to the client in understanding the factor of outside control. Although this seems evident, practicing counselors realize the disregard that clients have for the input of institutions and other persons in the decision process.

PROBABILITIES

The client must understand the probabilities of success if certain actions are taken or omitted. Thus, there may be a certain degree of risk involved in some decisions. When this risk is present, the notion of probability becomes important. Much information is available for the understanding of probability. Many school counselors, for example, have data available to them concerning the probability of the student to succeed in certain courses. Expectancy tables provide data which the client can use as aids in making his decision. This same type of information is often available for college selection and job potential. The college boards and ACT programs provide basic probability information for potential students. The employment service often has information about the relationship of the client's performance to his characteristics, tested and otherwise. These are meant to be applied with some leeway. Expectancy tables provide additional probability data for the student to analyze, organize, and synthesize for the final decision.

COMPROMISE

Basic to any decision is the idea of compromise. The ability to conceive of various levels of value or meaning is important. Super's (1957) third proposition suggests that vocational development, including choice, involves a compromise between personal and social factors, self-concept and reality, newly learned responses, and existing patterns of reacting. It is difficult to conceive of any important decision fulfilling every possible value and personal need of the individual. Thus the need for compromise.

The counselor provides an opportunity for the client to consider the various facets of the alternatives available to him. For example, a student may be interested in attending a state college or university, although his first choice may be a local university. His own values, parents' desires, and other factors may preclude the possibility of choosing the local school. On the other hand, the small student population, ratio of instructors to students, and location of a private college may also fit the student's value outcome. However, cost may preclude this choice, and the process of compromise may lead the student to locating another college that comes close to both values but does not meet either completely.

Today, there is within society a feeling about compromise which puts it into a negative category. The general feeling is that compromise is giving in to the system and that this is an undesirable action. Counselor as well as client should understand the reality of this point of view and, when necessary, may need to spend some counseling time discussing the meaning which the client ascribes to compromise. We are prone to identify certain areas in which the actions we take are no longer acceptable. Giving in to the establishment is one of these and poses a potential dilemma for the counselor who must help the client deal with his personal feelings about compromise in addition to the actual compromise itself.

Other meaningful persons in the client's life are not excluded from this problem since quite often the preferences of these persons are interjected into the decision-making process. The counselor should realize that the process of selection involves more than one person in terms of values and attitudes as well as the actual decision itself. In these cases it is necessary to include these people, either directly or indirectly, in the decision-making process.

OUTCOMES

Any decision is made to move a person toward desirable outcomes. In many instances previous experiences—in effect, decisions—play an important part in the outcome. For example, the student who earned top scholastic marks in high school has open to him many potential outcomes that the average student does not have. His "decision" to work hard enough to earn good grades has contributed to potential outcomes.

It may be important for the client to deal with sub-outcomes or outcomes of a lesser magnitude than the ultimate one. This relates to the need of people to have some points of reinforcement along the way to the desired outcome. It is difficult to maintain one's direction if the goal is so faraway as to be meaningless. Sub-goals may be necessary to keep the person moving steadily toward the final goal.

THE DECISION

It is important to realize that the final decision must be the responsibility of the client. The counselor's responsibility is to foster an investigation of alternatives, to bring relevant information to bear upon the problem, and to involve the various people who are interrelated to the client. Nonetheless, the final decision is the counselee's to make.

In some cases the counselor's most difficult job is to get the individual to accept responsibility for the decision. Many persons' perception of the counseling process is that the counselor, in some magical way, can force or coerce the client to move in different directions than he would move by himself. Although it may be possible to help the client move in different directions, the probability is that the student has greater insight into his own behavior and can be helped to see new and more meaningful directions in which to go. This is not accomplished in a short period of time and, with some minor exceptions, does not come about because the counselor has told the client to change. Rather it is a process of close interaction and involvement by counselor and client to reach a point of meaning to the client.

THE COUNSELING SITUATION

The counseling setting offers an ideal situation in which facilitation of decision-making skills may occur. All principles of counseling relationship—the value system of the counselor and his activity or inactivities—are (still) important. There is a general list of important principles which cuts across counseling regardless of the specific purposes for which the counseling is undertaken. The counseling setting should be as free from threat as possible. This especially relates to the counselor as he attempts to deal with himself and his concern. Any action on the part of the counselor which demeans the client must inevitably reduce the effective outcomes that are possible. The counselor should respect the client, his feelings, and his values, and he must like the client as a fellow human being even though he may not like some facets of his personality. The attitudes which the client brings with him to the session must be recognized, accepted, and understood to the highest degree possible and clarified when appropriate.

There are some unique aspects of the decision-making relationship. It is necessary to know whether a decision has been made. This may involve distinguishing between real and unreal decisions. The differentiation here represents skill on the part of the counselor which is necessarily improved during his training as well as his practice. The counselor must be very careful that he does not accept the "decision" when, in fact, it either has not been made or has been made to get "someone," perhaps the counselor, off the client's back.

An example might help to clarify this situation. A student comes to the counselor and states that he wishes to go to college. The counselor asks certain questions to determine whether this is really the case and then decides that the client does indeed want to go to college. When this is settled, the counselor moves on to more important areas—namely, what type of college, college requirements, and so on. But in the midst of deciding between state colleges and private colleges, the client suggests that he is not really sure that he wants to go to college, rather that it just seems to be the thing to do. Obviously, this is a very simplistic example. However, two important aspects are illustrated. First, a premature decision on the part of the counselor is not particularly wise. The counselor hears certain cue words and then begins to react like a computer spewing out all sorts of information. Usually premature decisions relate more to the counselor's needs and are of little value to the client. Second, even after a tentative decision is made, the counselor must continue to listen for cues that support or refute the earlier position. The one hope that counselors seem to have is suggested by Kell and Mueller (1966), who feel that important topics will be raised several times by the client in the face of counselor avoidance or missing of the cue.

It may be essential for the counselor to deal with this type of behavior—namely, indecisiveness or inability to make a decision. The counselor should be willing to aid the client in his examination of some of the causes for his behavior, especially when the reasons for this inability surface. In a non-evaluative light this type of examination by counselor-client can often move the client toward more productive activity.

THE DECISION–MAKING PROCESS

Much counseling is concerned with deciding on a course of action that is appropriate to the client. While it is possible to envision a rather simplistic model of how this occurs, it is apparent that the client as well as the counselor be related to the process. Thus, aspirations, self-understanding, interests, and values are interrelated with the rational process or sequence of decision making.

Quite often the decision to be made is related to a vocational or educational choice. Although this type of topic often occurs in counseling, most counselors have never responded as professionally to vocational or educational choice making as they have to more personal problems presented by their clients. In many cases the model used would be selected for ease of completing the task rather than for meaningfulness to the client. We are proposing a model that should allow the decision-making process to proceed, at the same time taking into consideration the dynamics of the self. The model is presented in outline form below.

1. Establishing the relationship.
2. Statement and development of the decision.
3. Data gathering from the client and other relevant sources.
4. Interpretation and assistance in integration of data for the client.
5. Synthesis of personal and vocational data into a tentative plan of action.
6. Choice making—the decision.
7. Follow-up with change in action when appropriate.

Establishing the Relationship

The need for establishing a working relationship with the client is obvious. The methods for accomplishing this goal are discussed in Chapter 9.

Since the decision(s) which the client is going to make may be related to vocation or education, there may be a tendency to assign less emphasis to the need for the relationship than when one is talking about some personal type of counseling. The counselor must be aware that the value of the relationship is equivalent throughout various types of counseling. Unless this is clearly established, the chances of working through the subsequent steps of the process toward successful outcomes are decreased.

STATEMENT AND DEVELOPMENT OF THE DECISION

The second step in a decision-making counseling interview involves the statement and exploration of the particular decision(s) with which the client might be concerned. The counselor should be concerned with helping his client delineate the particular needs that he might have and determine what the specifics of the decision might be. He provides clarification statements to help the client make as clear a statement as possible about the possibilities facing him. This may result in one or more specific statements of the decisions which the client sees as being relevant to him.

DATA GATHERING

The counselor begins to aid the client in collecting data about the relevant factors concerning the decision and the client's relationship to that decision. The counselor uses this information in at least two ways. First, he begins to develop predictions about the client's probabilities of success in the various alternatives of the decision. The second use is to aid the client toward a better understanding of himself and the probabilities that exist (Brammer and Shostrom, 1968). Hopefully, the two aspects will be somewhat congruent so that the kinds of probabilities emerging from the counselor's examination of data are roughly equivalent to the client's examination. If these are too divergent, the decision-making process may have to stop until resolution of this discrepancy is achieved.

INTERPRETATION AND ASSISTANCE IN INTEGRATION OF DATA

In normal situations, this step merges quite closely with the preceding one. Thus, when the data are gathered and examined for the relationship between client characteristics and existing probabilities, the counselor begins to provide assistance in the interpretative aspect. He aids the client to understand the various aspects of the decision and data which are not readily understood. He begins the process of integrating client data, outside information, and client characteristics.

SYNTHESIS

The next step translates the previous integration into a tentative plan of action. In this step it would be possible to provide some practical experience for the client. This might take the form of role laying, actual experience, simulation, or some mechanical manipulation of the factors that have been identified. Part of this decision depends upon the general model being used by the counselor. Models were discussed earlier. The reader will note that if one were to use the process proposed by Katz, the possibilities for manipulation of data toward a tentative plan of action could be manifold.

CHOICE MAKING

The next step is for the client to make the decision. It is important that the client be the one who actually makes the decision. This must be, as the client eventually takes the responsibility for whatever consequences might occur. It is also valuable to learn the process for future and more critical or intricate decisions.

FOLLOW-UP

Quite often the process stops after a decision is made. The counselor should indicate that he is interested in what occurs. He will be available to review the outcomes at some not-too-distant time. He would be able to provide assistance in a change of direction when appropriate. This poses some difficulty for the counselor, since he will have many clients and follow-up demands time that he may not have. He may also find that the client is manipulating him at times and react negatively to this. Thus, the client simply pressures the counselor to rearrange things so that a previous less-than-adequate decision can be wiped out and something else substituted. If this occurs the counselor should begin to deal with this aspect before any further decisions are allowed or fostered.

SUMMARY

Decision making offers counselor and client an important milieu for counseling. The counseling process involves a situation in which the client can examine himself and the possibilities open to him. There is a need to understand such personal variables as risk-taking propensity. There is also a need to have as much accurate information as possible about the alternatives which exist so that the best decision possible is made. The counselor should be a potent contributor to the client's decision making.

REFERENCES

Brammer, L. M., and Shostrom, E. L. *Therapeutic Psychology* (2nd ed.) Englewood Cliffs, N. J.: Prentice-Hall Inc., 1968.

Gelatt, H. B. "Decision-Making: A Conceptual Frame of Reference for Counseling." *Journal of Counseling Psychology 1962* 9, 240–245.

Ginzberg, E., Ginsberg, S. W., Axelrad, S., and Herma, J. L. *Occupational Choice.* New York: Columbia University Press, 1951.

Hansen, Lorraine S. "How Do They Choose a College?" *College Board Review 1965* 57, 35–37.

Hollis, J. W., and Hollis, Lucile V. *Personalizing Informational Processes.* New York: Macmillan, 1969.

Hoppock, Robert. *Occupational Information.* New York: McGraw-Hill, 1957.

Katz, Martin. "A Model of Guidance for Career Decision-Making." *Vocational Guidance Quarterly 1966* 15, 2–10.

Kell, B. L., and Mueller, W. J. *Impact and Change: A Study of Counseling Relationships.* New York: Appleton-Century-Crofts, 1966.

Kogan, N., and Wallach, M. A. "Risk Taking as a Function of the Situation, the Person, and the Group." In Mandler, G., Mussen, P., Kogan N., and Wallach, M. A. *New Directions in Psychology II.* New York: Holt, Rinehart and Winston, Inc., 1967.

Parsons, F. *Choosing a Vocation.* Boston: Houghton Mifflin Co., 1909.

Patterson, C. H. *Counseling and Psychotherapy: Theory and Practice.* New York: Harper and Brothers, 1959.

Super, D. *The Psychology of Careers.* New York: Harper and Row, 1957.

12

Using Tests
in Counseling

Counseling is generally assumed to be a situation in which the client is aided by the counselor to have a better understanding of himself, greater self-direction, improved functioning, or stronger decision-making abilities. To this end there is often a need to provide informational assistance to the client. One type of information is test data. The integration of data from tests into the informational system of the client is important.

Tests are designed to provide samples of performance in given areas. As samples they are representative of performance but are also inadequate in many ways. It is important to understand the strengths and weaknesses of tests so that accurate selection as well as interpretation may result. It is also important to realize that test results refer to groups of people and that individual interpretation must be done carefully or very inaccurate results may occur. This is illustrated in any prediction or actuarial table. One can say with a relatively high degree of certainty that nine of ten people will live to be 60 years old. One cannot say with equal certainty which nine will live or which one will die. Any test data that are developed must be utilized as group data which provide information for the individual, but may not provide as accurate predictive power as the client might want.

Testing can be used in any of several ways. In most cases these are special cases of the prediction power of the test. We may use tests as one part of a selection package. In truth we are only making a positive or negative prediction about the person's ability to complete a given sequence of activities. This point needs to be included when tests are used to aid the client during counseling. The data provide increased input into the predictive sequence for the client. When understood from this framework, test data can be more valuable.

TEST TERMINOLOGY

The individual counselor and client need certain basic information about tests in order to better utilize them. The following brief discussion points out the important areas. If the reader is unfamiliar with some of the terminology, he would be well advised to review his test and measurement information.

Measures of Central Tendency

The most frequently reported central tendency score is the mean. This is the arithmetic average of all scores in a given set. It is represented in most test manuals as $\bar{X}$ or M. The mean or average score usually falls near the midpoint of the sequence of scores although at times, depending upon the scores, this is not true.

Other central tendency measures are the median and mode. One-half the cases fall above and below the median score. The median is determined after the scores are arranged in sequence from highest to lowest. The mode is that score which appears most frequently in the distribution or set of scores. Very often, more than one score appears equal numbers of times and thus there is a possibility of multiple modes in any set of scores. This circumstance limits the utility of the mode as a statistical unit for testing.

Measures of Variability

Since it is possible to have similar central tendency scores from highly dissimilar sets of scores, there is a need to include other types of measures to understand the set of scores—or, more to the point, one score in a sequence of scores. The concepts providing this information are measures of variability.

The difference between the highest and lowest score in a sequence is the range. Although not as potent a measure as some to be described later, the range does provide information about the spread of scores in a set. One would interpret a score of 99 within a sequence of scores 98–100 differently than a 99 in a sequence of scores 50–150. In the first case, nearly everyone scored very near 99 and little differentiation is possible. The second 99 could be widely separated from the remaining scores and permits a different kind of interpretation.

A second type of variability score, and one that is used more often and more potently, is the standard deviation. This is defined as the average variation of scores from the mean. When used with the normal curve shown, the test interpreter is provided with quite meaningful information.

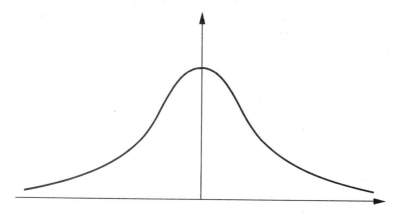

The reasoning here is that the standard deviation defines certain limits within the population and can aid in the placement of one score in a total set of scores. When one knows the mean and standard deviation, he can have greater insight as to where the client's test score places him within the following parameters.

One standard deviation above and below the mean contains approximately 68 percent of the cases. A score somewhere between these two limits places the individual in the slightly above or slightly below average category. A score in the second standard deviation above or below the mean suggests that the person is either in the top 16 percent or bottom 16 percent of the set. A score somewhere in either of these areas indicates a different type of performance than the score within the first standard deviation. When these data—i.e., mean and standard deviation—are available, the counselor can provide much more usable information for the client.

There is also a variation in the score which an individual has over a multiple administration of the test. Although it is not practical to give the same test several times, we can say with some certainty that the score which an individual receives on a test represents an approximate score. The concept of a standard error of measurement provides data for more precision in determining the score of the individual. In simple form the suggestion is made that the real score of the individual is not the precise score on the test but rather falls somewhere between two points determined by the reliability of the test and the score which individuals have on the single administration of the test. The standard error of measurement is interpreted as follows. The chances are two out of three that the test taker's real score lies somewhere between 1 standard error $\pm$ his recorded score. As one adds standard errors the probability of the score being included within the range increases. In general, a high reported standard error makes the test more suspect than a low standard error.

MEASURES OF COMPARISON

In a later section we shall deal with some of the specifics of comparison of data. For our purposes in this section the following concepts are included: correlation and significance level. Correlation refers to the degree of relationship between the same individual's scores on two measures. Correlations range from a $+1.00$ to a -1.00 and are interpreted to suggest that the closer one gets to the extremes the more confident one can be about the predictive relationship that exists. Negativeness or positiveness relates to the direction of prediction of one score from another. A correlation in the middle reduces this relationship and means that the data are not as useful.

Significance may be used to provide data about the difference that exists between sets of scores. Since the mean and standard deviation are the measures used, there is no need to match scores as in correlation. Any significant level, usually reported as .05 or .01, means that some difference exists in the groups being examined. Although infrequently reported in test manuals, the counselor needs to realize how significance might be interpreted in the counseling relationship.

VALIDITY OF TESTS

It is essential for the counselor to know what tests measure. He should know the technical data provided for the test by the publisher and realize that the more available research material the better the test. For this reason, Tyler (1969) suggests that the older the test is, the better it may be for counseling purposes.

In a measurement usage, validity refers to the extent to which a test measures what it purports to measure. A valid intelligence test measures intelligence with some accuracy. A construct such as intelligence poses a difficult measurement problem—i.e., Are we really tapping the person's intellectual capacity, or are we measuring some other factor and calling it intelligence? There will be no attempt to resolve this type of dilemma for all kinds of tests. The reader is cautioned that he should find out what the author(s) say the test is measuring to be certain that the goals of the counselor and counselee in using the test are compatible.

It has been common practice to deal with four types of validity: content, concurrent, predictive, and construct. Content validity refers to the degree to which the items on the test constitute a sample of the generally agreed upon content area to be measured. A simple example is that any mathematics test which purports to measure some sort of multiplication skills should include multiplication items. If a variety of types of multiplication items are included, there would be a relatively high content validity for the test. Some universes of content have greater agreement than others, so not all content validities can be easily established. However, the content validity of achievement tests in subject matter areas ought to be high and related to the subject matter included in the course itself, rather than from a larger sampling that a standardized achievement test might offer.

The second type of validity is concurrent validity. Basically, concurrent validity relates to the degree in which a shorter, more economical test provides similar results to a larger and perhaps more expensive test. An example would be using part of a test rather than a whole test when time limitations prohibit using an entire test. Another example is the use of a group test when it is impossible to administer individual tests. A third example would be substituting easily scored objective items for essay items which are not as easily scored. Concurrent validity is determined by administering two tests to similar populations and computing the degree of similarity of scores. It is generally necessary to obtain a .80 and above correlation to justify the substitution of the specific test under investigation. Adams (1964) suggests that the test user be alert to the possible interchange of concurrent validity with predictive validity. This may occur since many test publishers do not follow students on a longitudinal basis to determine whether, in fact, the test with strong concurrent validity really does help in predicting future success or whatever other outcome variable exists.

Predictive validity refers to the relationship between test scores and success in some specific area. Any test with sufficient longitudinal data can be predictive. Many tests are designed for this purpose and usually have predictive data available. These data generally support the value of the test for prediction. The college boards are typical of this type of test, for the publishers have acquired and processed large amounts of data which provide estimates of a particular type of individual's chance of success in various types of colleges. Readiness tests at the kindergarten and elementary school level also purport to serve this need. The establishment of the predictive validity is a correlation of the test scores of persons with some measurable outcome criterion of a future nature. Quite often the data are presented in the form of expectancy tables, which again are group data but can be helpful in providing additional information for the client. Later, we shall speak about some of the specifics that should be considered by a counselor as he uses tests in the counseling process.

The final type of validity is construct validity. This is defined as analysis of test data—i.e., scores, usually—in terms of a specific psychological trait or construct. In some tests the authors suggest that the test measures a particular construct or trait. If, as test users, we are interested in the particular construct, it is essential to know the validity of the test as related to the construct. Usually esoteric statistical processes are used to determine the construct validity, and any description of these processes is beyond the scope of this book. In counseling, it is of some importance that the counselor know what construct the test is measuring and the degree to which this has occurred. Without data the test value is limited more with construct validity use than the other three, since logic often is not involved in the process. Construct validity often has the least input into counseling sessions. The client wishing to deal with various constructs—e.g., shyness or anxiety—usually can be aided more effectively by intensive personal counseling than by administering a test that generally measures what the client may be already willing to admit. He needs assistance in resolving the concern, not more data confirming the rightness of the diagnosis.

Some Concerns About Validity

It is of little value for most clients to know where they stand in a large universe of data. What they need are the most specific data possible. This means that the counselor cannot depend upon others to develop all the normative or population data which he needs. Local research and data gathering are essential. Obviously, the client may need both local and the larger geographical area data. One without the other is often valueless. The data for larger settings will be available from the test publisher. Data, especially predictive data, should be obtained locally. As a specified example, it is of little value for a freshman to realize that most people who take a particular placement test score higher or lower than he. What is important for his decision making is that which others like him in the local school situation have done in specific courses of study.

Related to the above concern is the lack of data which occurs with predictive tests. Whenever cut-off scores are used, and this is the rule rather than the exception, some people are eliminated from the eventual data bank. When a student applies to a particular program and his test scores, one factor often used for selection, are below the established norm, he is not allowed to even attempt the program. Any prediction that is done is based upon a select sample. Although this may not pose a problem in many cases, since we generally "counsel" students out by saying that the competition might be too difficult or some similar statement, the fact is that we really do not know how he or others like him might do. There are some instances where interpolation might help, but usually predictive data are not linear data and some loopholes exist. If the ideal existed, the individual would still be able to enter the course. This would be the exception to the rule in many educational and vocational institutions with which the authors are familiar.

It should be apparent that a test's validity is validity for a purpose. The validity of a test is really the test's value for providing data to make judgments and for input into the decision-making process—in short, to measure something that can be used by the client in a meaningful way to further his own growth. The professional counselor will understand the various types of validity and, more importantly, will know which is most important or valuable to the client. This presupposes a commitment on the part of the counselor in addition to knowledge about tests. There is no way that certification regulations, training programs, or regulating agencies can insure that this situation exists. The counselor knows when he needs further information and skills.

RELIABILITY

A second concept that test users need to consider is that of reliability. This refers to the consistency of test results over a period of time, or the consistency with which a test continues to measure whatever it purports to measure.

It is obvious to anyone who has worked with a person over a period of time that his performance varies. To assume, for example, that the performance of a major leaguer who hits three home runs on opening day is typical defies all we know about the records which have accumulated over some 70–75 years of baseball. The same can often be demonstrated, though not dramatically, in all types of test performance. Counselor and counselee need repeated measures which provide parameters of performance rather than any assumption about the rightness or wrongness of one performance.

Generally, there are two types of errors which affect test scores and thus affect reliability: compensating and systematic errors. Compensating errors are of concern, since they represent variations in the test condition which result in overestimates and underestimates. These do compensate so that we have an average type of result. We shall speak of this type of error later.

A second type of error is related to a behavior which systematically raises or lowers the test takers' score. Cheating tends to raise scores every time so that there is no averaging out. Misreading instructions on the scoring sheet tends to reduce scores systematically. Again, no averaging out occurs. This type of error demands other methods of resolution. One place that this type of error can be dealt with is in the counseling dyad, since the error is really client behavior.

Variance of Scores

There are two types of variance that occur and relate to a test score's reliability. These are group variance, which deals with the spread of scores, and individual variance, which deals with performance of the individual. Most readers will be familiar with group variance, called standard deviation. This represents the average deviation of all scores, in the group under consideration, from the mean score. This type of variance is important whenever prediction is involved, since it provides the data of a client's placement in a group. He is above or below average, in the upper third or fourth, or in the lowest 10 percent. This is a function of the variance of the group and places the individual along a continuum in relationship to others taking the test.

Individual variance, normally the standard error, is the predicted difference in score for the individual on a particular test. This gives us some idea of the overestimating or underestimating that is possible. Individual variance also provides a range of scores rather than a specific score.

These measures provide an estimate of reliability or consistency of the test. In general the reliability of the test is a function of the error variance —i.e., variance in the individual score as related to the total variance (group or standard deviation). It is represented mathematically as follows:

$$\text{Rel coef} = 1 - \frac{\text{error variance}^2}{\text{total variance}^2}$$

In the formula, 1 represents the highest coefficient possible and the ratio represents the amount to be subtracted from the perfect correlation.

It is impossible and impractical to administer a test a sufficient number of times to obtain an error variance. Mathematical formulae allow us to calculate the coefficient. This eventually evolves into the following formula.

$$SE = SD\sqrt{1 - r_{tt}}$$

in which the r_{tt} equals the relationship of individuals' scores at two separate testings. We may obtain a statistical calculation of the error variance from data obtained at minimal test settings.

Since reliability represents the consistency of the test to measure whatever it measures, the variables which affect the individual's score affect the reliability of the test. Conversely, reliability is computed (as will be shown later) based upon the fluctuations of the individual's scores, error variance. More importantly, the standard error helps us understand that the test score represents a range of scores and gives us the probability of the difference of student scores from theoretical true scores. The general assumption is that chances are two out of three that the obtained score differs from the true score by less than whatever is the standard error. This is predicated on the normal curve concept wherein $2/3$ of the cases involved in the measurement fall within one standard deviation plus or minus the mean.

Whenever two tests are compared, a reliability coefficient rather than a standard error is preferred. There are at least four methods of calculating this coefficient.

The Test-Retest Method

This method provides an estimate of the stability of the test. The test is administered to the same student, but a period of several days elapses between the test administration. A number of factors may enter into the discrepancy that occurs—e.g., examinee motivation or interest. We may be developing a relationship that ignores the factor we are most interested in—namely, the content being measured by the test. The test-retest method is seldom used.

Equivalent Forms Method

This measures the equivalence of two different forms of a test designed to measure a similar factor or context. Since tests only sample behavior and include representative content, more than one test could conceivably be developed to test performance in any given area. By administering the two different tests, it is possible to determine the relationship between the two and thus have an estimate of the tests' reliability. Commercial test companies frequently have two or more forms of the same test. Therefore, equivalent form reliability is readily available. This method is used more often than the test-retest method. However, it does not take into account the temporal fluctuations exhibited by the examinee.

Internal Consistency Method

A third way of calculating reliability is to determine internal consistency of a single test. Sometimes only one test form is available, or students may not be able or willing to take two tests within a short time span. It is possible to compare examinee performance on different samples from the same test. This provides a measure of test equivalence. Although various methods may be used to determine the split of items for the calculation of consistency, perhaps it is easiest to assume that the odd-numbered items are one test "form" while the even-numbered items are a second test "form." Then it is a matter of correlating the examinee's scores on the two forms. As with the previous equivalence forms method, the instability of examinee performance over time is not measured. However, this does provide an adequate method of determining equivalence without involvement in unmanageable factors and is a widely used method.

Equivalent Forms Over Time Method

It is apparent that one could administer two forms of the same test with a time interval between administrations. This would give us an estimate of reliability that takes into account several types of error variance. The estimates obtained by this method are usually lower because of the error variance. Both equivalence and stability are measured. This is the most attractive reliability determination method, but is not used often because of the management problems that exist.

With the above brief account of reliability in mind, the question is, How do we use the information on reliability most rationally? It would appear that selecting the test with the highest reliability factors would be an appropriate method. But, this avoids the real meaning of tests which is to help individuals better understand themselves, make better decisions because better predictive data are available, or reach other personally meaningful goals. We must have some standard or structure to help us examine tests and use the one most meaningful to the client.

Often the following general standard is adopted as reflecting minimally accepted reliability coefficients. If the test is to evaluate a group accomplishment level, then .50 or above is acceptable. If the test is to evaluate differences in group accomplishment over more than one performance, the level increases to .90 or above. When dealing with an individual level of accomplishment we need .94 or above; for individual accomplishment or more than one performance, .98 is suggested.

The reader should note that these are arbitrary and that they are meant only as suggestions. If a test seems to be called for and none can be found with the reliability level suggested above, it is still of possible value to use the tests and keep in mind the less than desirable level of consistency that might exist. There is also a need to deal with the type of reliability that is presented. A .90 determined by the split-half method may be less desirable than a .85 reliability determined by the equivalent forms over time method.

SELECTION OF TESTS

A crucial area of tests and use of tests in counseling is that of proper selection of tests. We must be concerned that tests are selected which measure the content we are concerned with and, at the same time, contribute as much as possible to the growth and development of the client.

There is a continuing interest in the issue of client involvement in test selection. Each counselor will need to develop the plan that is most effective for him to use. We hesitate to develop this point further since it can quickly turn into a discussion of counselor activity to meet only counselor needs. This is not our intention. As with all aspects of counseling, the counselor's own unique characteristics play a part in his counseling style. Trying to be what he cannot be, will lead to client deterioration rather than growth.

Goldman (1961) has summarized the points on both sides of the issue:

Client participation seems to make sense based upon the following general factors. First motivation to complete the test accurately and honestly seems enhanced when the client knows about the purposes of testing as well as some specifics of the various tests that might be used. At the same time, the test itself can be a learning device when the counselee understands the reasons for using the test.

Usually test interpretation can be more readily accepted when previous knowledge and involvement of the client are part of the test selection. He is less likely to need to develop rationalizations for his performance and can be more involved in the reality of the results as related to his needs.

As discussed in another portion of the book, the client often needs experience in decision making. Helping choose a test can be a learning situation for the client in this area. Hopefully, he has a model available—i.e., the counselor may discern the alternatives which exist as well as the reasons for choosing certain tests and rejecting others.

Since the discussion of tests will include some description of test content, we can expect the counselee to be somewhat verbal about his feelings—positive and negative—about the tests. This provides additional information for the counselor's use either at the particular point in time or later on when further counseling occurs.

Other factors should be mentioned. Involving the client whenever possible in any portion of the final test selection process helps avoid the buildup of dependency on the counselor. Although independence is not necessarily a goal of all counseling, certainly anything that fosters increased dependence is questionable. From a more conservationist point of view, involving the client in the selection process could reveal areas where accurate measurement is already available. And, time involved in taking the test can be saved and the delay in counseling normally caused by test administration can be avoided.

Many counselors do not wish to allow their clients to participate in the process of test selection. They take this stand based on one or more of the following reasons.

It is very important that the most appropriate tests be administered and interpreted. The counselor should be skilled in selecting tests. The client is not as skilled and the time necessary to improve the test selection skills could be better spent in counseling or test interpretation.

Often the client cannot be objective about the test, since his major area of interest is the concern he brought to the counseling situation. The counselor can be more objective in selection of appropriate tests.

The types of problems identified in the test selection process often are dependency or inability to make decisions. These may be more appropriately dealt with in other ways.

Conclusion

In attempting to aid the reader in resolution of this issue, we would take the following position. In general, involvement of the client in the selection of tests does not seem to have a deleterious effect upon the relationship. Research evidence does not provide a meaningful guide for the process. It is probable that the counselor is an important variable in the process and this should not be overlooked either in the preparation period of the counselor or in his actual practice as a counselor. It is also probable that some clients are more adequate to the task of participating in the test selection process. The key factor here is the counselor and whether he is sensitive to the needs and characteristics of the client. Based upon his clinical observations, the counselor should be able to identify those clients for whom participation would be unwise. In the remaining cases the counsel ought to encourage as much participation as possible by the client in any activity related to his growth.

Other factors are involved in this process. Key among these are the situation in which the counseling takes place, the characteristics of the client, and the availability of test and/or testing specialists. It should be clearly understood that the structure of the institution must be considered when test selection is undertaken. Some schools, for example, look askance at tests which might be labelled personality inventories. It is unwise for the counselor to try to include these tests in any package offered to the client. In addition, one need only read some of the material on testing from the 1960s— e.g., "The Tyranny of Testing" (Hoffman, 1962), to understand some of the problems and misunderstandings associated with tests.

It is also probably unwise to spend a considerable amount of time with very young clients in test selection, since they are not sufficiently well-informed about many factors of tests. The skill necessary to work with students in the elementary school is of sufficient difficulty that adding additional dimensions to the process often is debilitating.

Finally, the counselor must understand himself well enough to know how much involvement he wants to allow the client. We are not suggesting any sort of manipulative or other negative aspects of the counselor-client relationships. Rather, we suggest that the type of cooperative and sometimes elongated involvement necessary for successful collaborative test selection may not fit into the personality characteristics or the role enactment of the counselor.

TYPES OF TESTS

The selection of tests includes a knowledge of the types of tests which are available as well as the technical data which are discussed under reliability and validity. One distinction can be made between standardized and non-standardized tests. The term *standardized* has generally been used to describe a test, or more specifically, a measuring instrument with the following characteristics.

1. A standard administrative process has been developed for the test. This includes the instructional directions which are to be given as well as specific time limits. The standard process allows for similar administration, and hopefully accurate measurement, regardless of the administrator or place of testing.
2. There is an attempt to provide scoring instructions or keys which will eliminate scorer errors on the test. The goal here is that regardless of who the scorer might be, he would record the same results as any other scorer and not be influenced by any personal bias.

3. Various normative data are made available with the test. These data allow for comparison with a wide variety of groups and provide information beyond that of the actual score, however recorded.
4. A manual that includes technical testing data—e.g., validity and reliability—is included. This manual provides information for realistic test selection, especially in the area where test of aptitude, for example, will provide the most meaningful data. The manual obviously does not speak to the test–non-test issue, since most standardized tests are commercially prepared. Among other reasons for the availability of these standardized tests is to provide income for the publisher and author(s) (Adams, 1964).

Other distinctions exist which help separate tests. There are group or individual tests. As is suggested here, the difference is in the area of how many persons can take the test at one time with one examiner. Generally, group tests require less formal and supervised preparation for administration than do individual tests.

There are pencil-paper tests or performance tests. The latter require the use of objects and physical skills for completion and generally provide more direct data for skill area judgment than pencil-paper tests. The difficulty is similar to the group-individual test situation in that pencil-paper tests are much more economical to administer in both time and cost.

A final distinction is speed tests or power tests. The speed test is designed to measure the examinee's speed of accomplishment. Most are so long that no one can finish in the time provided. A power test measures the level of performance of the examinee. Usually items are arranged in increasing order of difficulty and, since the examinee is given sufficient time to finish, performance depends upon the unsuccessful completion of items to determine the level of performance.

All the above distinctions are important if test selection is to be effective. Some of the aspects have built-in rejection probabilities. For example, the counselor who is forced to be his own psychometrist cannot select a test that he is incapable of administering. Often individual tests are not used because the counselor is not skilled in their administration.

The most familiar way to differentiate tests is on the basis of content. The following types can be identified: mental ability, achievement, aptitude, interest inventories, personality inventories, and special tests—e.g., creativity.

There may not be a clear-cut differentiation between various types of tests. For example, a mental ability test that purports to measure the intellectual functioning of the examinee might actually be an achievement test measuring specifics which the examinee has learned. Although the test might be called mental ability, it may have more relevance to achievement. However, for purposes of the present discussion, we shall separate those into the following categories: mental ability tests, aptitude tests, achievement tests, personality inventories, interest inventories, and special tests.

Mental Ability Tests

These types of tests usually fall under the rubric of intelligence tests which are designed to measure the intellectual functioning of the individual. Several factors can be measured such as spatial relations, abstract reasoning, verbal and mathematical competence, or even performance on certain given tasks. In general, one hopes to obtain an idea of the functional level of the individual taking the test so that he can be afforded the most appropriate educational experiences. The intelligence test should give both examiner and examinee a notion of how the client functions in the norm population. Both individual and group intelligence tests exist. Group tests are most popular since they require less administrative time and fewer specific administrative skills.

Achievement Tests

These tests measure the person's learning of specific content areas. Samples of behavior from a particular amount of materials indicate the amount of material that has been learned by the examinee. Various methods are used to obtain this sample, however; most frequently the test is a multiple choice in which the individual is asked to choose the best response. One of the problems here is that several test-taking skills or lack thereof could affect the outcome significantly. Since we are interested in a "true" measure of achievement, there must be an effort to avoid those tests which penalize certain students or overly reward others and, most significantly, do not measure achievement—i.e., learning—in the content areas that have been described. Achievement tests usually are more teaching oriented than counseling oriented. In some cases, counselors are interested in examining achievement; therefore, the counselor needs to know about these tests.

Aptitude Tests

Aptitude tests are samples of behavior in areas in which the examinee has certain potentials. As such they serve a predictive function for the examinee. It is possible to include mental ability tests in this category. We are usually more concerned with tests relating to some specific task area. As an example, the General Aptitude Test Battery (GATB) used by the employment service includes verbal and numerical tests that are combined to indicate a measure of mental functioning. The remaining sub-tests, however,

are more directly related to skills that might be necessary to do certain tasks
—e.g., clerical, eye-hand coordination, or manual dexterity. These aptitudes
can be related to specific job categories and provide information either
about what field the client may wish to enter or those skill areas where
certain training might increase performance level.

There are specific tests for single aptitudes. These are called special aptitude tests and include such instruments as music or art aptitude tests. These
can be of assistance for specific selection in the particular area described.
The reader is cautioned that he still must investigate the validity and reliability of tests. The mere fact that a test is called an art aptitude test does
not necessarily mean that those who do well on the test will be able to succeed in art. If the test and more artistic talent are not related, then the pre-
dictability is meaningless.

A final type of aptitude test has to do with prognostic tests—e.g., reading
readiness tests or algebra prognostic tests. These can be valuable in helping
place students in the most appropriate learning situation. However, it should
also be remembered that test results ought to be meaningfully reported to
a number of persons, including the test taker. Often we use these types of
tests in a negative way—i.e., to reject certain people—and little or no explanation is ever offered to the examinee.

Interest Tests

While mental ability, achievement, and aptitude tests are designed to
measure some maximum performance of the individual, interest tests are
used to measure typical performance. The examinee's involvement in the
testing situation is crucial because if he has little or no interest in the test,
a typical measure will not be obtained. Likewise it is usually possible for
the examinee to answer in a way more acceptable to someone else—to a
counselor, parent, or teacher—than as close as possible to his own feelings.

There are many interest tests which attempt to measure one of the four
types of interests which Super and Crites (1962) have identified: expressed
interest, manifest interest, tested interest, and inventoried interest. In general, expressed interest is the verbal expression of liking or disliking something. Usually these expressions are related to maturity and experience.

Manifest interest is that which is observable because of participation by
the individual in a given activity. A boy voluntarily playing basketball can
safely be assumed to have an interest in basketball. This type of interest can
also be misleading since participation in a given activity may be necessary
for certain fringe benefits to occur. It is usually valuable to look at the activities related to the event and the individual's participation in these to determine the degree of manifest interest. It is important to remember that

lack of participation may not mean lack of interest. Several factors (cost or time) may affect participation and manifest interest.

Tested interest is that interest which can be ascertained by an objective test measuring the vocabulary or other information which the examinee has in a given interest area. Tested interests are based on an assumption that interests result in accumulation of relevant information as well as a specialized vocabulary.

Inventoried interests are those we normally determine by interest check lists. Usually the examinee is asked to check whether he likes or dislikes certain activities or other categorization. Normally, patterns of high and low interest areas result so that the student, if he is honest, can begin to determine the areas of like or dislike in his life.

The latter type of interest is the basis of most published tests. Two tests have dominated the measurement of interest: the Kuder Personal Preference Inventory and the Strong Vocational Interest Blank. The reader is referred to textbooks such as Anastasi (1961) or Cronbach (1960) to learn more about the philosophy and construction of these instruments. Each has value, with the Kuder Personal Preference and other inventories identifying basic interest groups, while the Strong Vocational Interest Blank relates to specific types of patterns of people in occupations which correspond to the pattern of the student's responses.

Personality Inventories

Personality inventories are used to identify various facets of an individual's personality structure. Since the human personality can be multifaceted, there is no instrument which can do more than touch on a few of the facets. However, it is possible to get a picture of some major areas that are part of the personality. For example, if the examinee responds truthfully on certain inventories, one can begin to see a dominant-assertive type as opposed to a submissive, dependent type.

In other cases the inventory can provide information about how closely the response pattern of the examinee resembles the response pattern of certain personality types. An example of this would be the Minnsota Multiphasic Personality Inventory (MMPI), which provides scores in a number of areas that are associated with specific personality disorders—e.g., paranoia.

In the area of personality inventories above all others, it is essential that caution be exercised in the use and particularly interpretation of results. These types of tests were usually used during the decade of the 1960s as ammunition for the anti-testing people in our society. Because certain items (by themselves somewhat unacceptable) are included for various reasons, this test can be misused for many purposes. The counselor should be completely familiar with the test items, should be selective in its use, and should be certain that it will be properly explained and interpreted prior to and following administration.

The reader should have guessed that the reliability and validity of personality tests is not in the range we would normally like. The possibility of faking and of creating positive or negative images is high. Many inventories attempt to deal with this problem by using faking scales or truth scales to determine whether the examinee is responding to certain items in a significantly different way than the standardizing population did. There is no guarantee that this will eliminate the attempts of the examinee to present a more favorable or less favorable picture. The caution of careful use is necessary once again.

Special Tests

The area of creativity is relatively new in testing areas. In general these tests are designed to measure some sort of creativity which the individual may possess—depending, of course, on how one defines creativity. Usually the creativity test asks the individual to respond to set situations. Those who respond in a way different from many others have, at least, a bit of creativity. Again we are looking for patterns rather than specific instances. An example might be helpful. One test which has been used asks the respondent to list the uses of a brick. Those who list the normal uses such as building a wall or as a doorstop are not considered creative. Those who might say that it could be hollowed out and made into a boat would be considered potentially more creative because they were not restricted by a set of assumed rules and regulations or outcomes. No one said that the use ascribed to the brick had to result in some successful or positive outcome. Thus, even though the brick boat would probably sink, the respondent does show some creative tendencies.

INTERPRETATION OF TEST DATA

Once the tests are administered and scored, the counselor must develop a package of information to present to the client. It is of little value to deluge the client with a large mass of undifferentiated material that is most likely misunderstood. Some sort of meaningful method of presentation is necessary.

There may be several methods that the counselor can use to develop the package. First, he must determine the relevant outcomes of the tests. His skill in examining data and drawing out important factors is intimately involved in the process. If the counselor does not feel competent to do this, he should seek outside assistance so that the results presented to the client are manageable and meaningful.

During the course of the interpretive session, the counselor should exert caution in terms of rapid movement through the test results. He must be assured that the client understands what the test measured, how he did on the test, and what predictions or future activities seem indicated. Very often the counselor makes false assumptions about his client's understanding, and the outcome is an even more confused client. This is especially true if any attempt to use some of the standard interpretive devices such as percentiles or deciles is involved. The counselor's skill in translating the test results into understandable terms will often mean the difference between meaningful use of tests and an extremely unproductive session with the client.

A further caution for the counselor to observe deals with the types of data presented. As an example, it is probably unwise to present actual I.Q. scores since these have too much affect related to them. In fact, the actual presentation of test data is probably best done in such couched terms as "slightly above average." Otherwise the more important predictive or selective use of tests will be lost.

The counselor will be faced with a number of interesting dilemmas when interpreting tests. If all clients score well on tests and one could use very positive statements concerning performance, the situation would be more tolerable. Clients are prone to score below average, to be under the acceptable score for placement in various programs—in short, to perform less adequately than we would like. It is necessary for the counselor to provide the interpretation of these data as objectively as possible. Quite often the client has some idea of his level of performance and is not as put down as the counselor assumes. As we suggest in other portions of this book, a great deal of client behavior is related to the behavior of the counselor. If the counselor conveys something negative about the test performance, the client will probably react in kind. This is of no particular value. Test results, as accurate or inaccurate as they are, are meant to provide additional input into self-understanding, prediction, or client movement. They are not end-alls of the counseling situation. One needs to move from the foundation which test results and other data provide.

Finally, it is probably wise to avoid presenting advice at the same time test data are given. Statements such as, "If I were you with these test scores," tend to promote defensiveness or dependence in the client. Obviously, there is no hard and fast rule in this context since sometimes the counselor must make a placement decision based upon his understanding of the client. The caution is that this should be understood by the counselor and the client should not be thrown into the counseling session when unnecessary.

It should be of value to develop some specifics of interpretation. Goldman (1961) lists four kinds of interpretation: descriptive, genetic, predictive, and evaluative. These he describes in terms of questions related to the particular interpretative type.

For descriptive interpretation, suggested questions are as follows. What kind of person is the client? How well does he do on certain tasks? What does he like to do?

For genetic interpretation the following questions are raised. How did the client evolve and arrive at this point in time with these characteristics? What background (parental, experiential, or academic) does he have?

For predictive interpretation the essential queries deal with the following. How will he do in the particular course, sequence, or college? What differential success patterns can I see as possible?

For evaluative interpretations one might ask, What should he do? Should he become a teacher or tradesman?

The reader will note greater use of hard data in the descriptive area and a decrease from there down to evaluative. Although the counselor will use each of these in his counseling, he should be aware of the specific value of each and plan accordingly in the stage of preparing the test data package.

GENERAL RULES OF TEST INTERPRETATION

It is difficult to justify testing an individual without providing for interpretation of the test results. Although this may occur frequently in school, agency, and other settings, it is a questionable activity. The counselor should work toward a system in which test results are used to aid the client reach the goals of counseling.

Interpreting tests must be handled skillfully. As suggested elsewhere in this book, it is of little value to simply provide raw scores or data. The psychological effects of an I.Q. score for some clients might be worse than whatever prompted them to initiate counseling. The counselor may wish to utilize the following guidelines for interpretation (Shertzer and Peters, 1965).

1. The more the client knows about the purpose of testing, the more meaningful the test can be for him. This suggests that the client should be informed of what the tests are going to measure. The earlier this is done, the better. The counselor should have an understanding of the tests and be able to communicate this to the client.

2. In most cases, the client has not had a formal course in measurement terminology. It is the counselor's task to translate these concepts into understandable language for the client. The counselor should look carefully at the test results before meeting with the client and have a tentative plan for the session. Specific scores are of little value to the client. He needs to know where he stands in relation to a particular group, the general population, or a previous level of operation. The counselor should also avoid premature acceptance of client knowledge. This is especially true when a concept like *percentiles* is explained. The probability of misunderstanding is high on the part of the client because of the similarity of the word to the word *percentage*, even though there is a major difference, and because of the proclivity of the client to want to misinterpret data regarding his own performance. The counselor must be the master communicator in this type of counseling setting.

3. It is essential that the confidentiality of test results be maintained. The counselor must exercise care that each client receives his own test package and that the client makes the final decision about how the test results are to be used and communicated to others.

4. The greater the interval between test administration and interpretation, the less value the test will have. It is important to complete the sequence of administration scoring and interpretation of tests as quickly as possible. Any delay will detract from the value of testing which, in some persons' minds, is extremely low as a general rule.

Using tests in counseling includes at least two distinct types of interaction with the client. First, there should be some understanding of why tests might be meaningful and of the general limitations of tests. This means that the counselor and client have an understanding of the needs of the client and the potential value which tests might have. The excerpt below illustrates this area.

C   Perhaps it would be of value to talk about the kinds of ideas which tests can provide and see if you think these would be helpful to you.

S   Yeah, I'd like to know if I can make it in college.

C   That's asking an ability question. Maybe you're asking whether you can be accepted into college as well as whether you can pass the courses there.

S   I think I'll be accepted, but I'm kinda worried about whether I can do college work.

C   So, it would be helpful if we had an idea of how your ability to learn compares with college students.

S   Yeah.

C   One way of getting at that would be to look at your scores on a college entrance test. Have you taken the college boards?

Following a discussion of the college entrance tests, the conversation turns to interests later in the interview.

C   You know that interests are important to examine before you make very many decisions.

S   Well, I'm interested in college.

C   I was thinking about the kinds of things you like to do. What are you interested in and how might these be related to the curriculum you choose in college?

S   I can tell you that I don't like English and Social Studies.

C   O.K. This helps. Maybe we can spend some time getting a clearer picture of what you might like to do. It might be of some help for you to complete an interest check list. This would give you a chance to respond to a large number of activities.

S   O.K.

C   You should remember one thing though. The check list can only provide an accurate picture if you are honest when you are doing it.

The second area for using tests in counseling is the client's actual interpretation of the test results. We have already described some of the factors which should be considered—e.g., the need to clearly communicate the statistical concepts involved. There are other areas that the counselor needs to consider. These include the psychological impingement of the test results upon the client. The counselor needs to be attuned to those actions of the client which signal a personal reaction to the tests. The counselor needs to maintain a balance between a dry academic reporting of test data and the reactions of the client. The excerpt below illustrates how test interpretation can lead to personal exploration by the client.

The student has completed the tests and returns for interpretation of the interest check list. The results suggest that he is interested in public service and math. He does not appear to be interested in those activities which require selling or aesthetic appreciation.

C   Here are the results of the check list. Remember, this means that you are interested in the activities. You seem to be interested in working with people or in some job which relates to math. You don't seem to want to work as a salesman and you have little interest in music or art. How does that fit into your own ideas about yourself?

S   I guess about right.

C   You're not sure about the results.

S   I don't know. I never really did that well in math.

C   You're questioning whether you would be able to succeed in a job which required math?

S   Yes.

C   That's a good thought. You have been able to differentiate between interest and ability. Although you might like math you have not done as well gradewise as you think would be necessary.

S   I do O.K. in the math part like adding and subtracting, but algebra was really hard.

C   You're questioning whether this is an area we ought to explore.

S   What could I do in math?

Client Involvement

We have spoken about the client's involvement in several areas of testing. The most crucial area is in the interpretative setting, and this demands that the client be deeply involved in the process. Some counselors may wish to hurry through test interpretation to get to more "pertinent" topics. This is not a suggested method for the counselor to operate because it demeans the testing and creates a negative attitude on the part of the client as to why tests were used in the first place.

The counselor can facilitate client self-evaluation and involvement by his method of data presentation and test interpretation. The counselor can make tentative statements such as, "You really did not expect the results which occurred," which help the client to think further about himself, the test results, and the decisions or activities which face him. The client puts these data to use with the aid of the counselor rather than the reverse situation in which the counselor uses the test data to tell the client something.

Devices

For some clients there are several devices that can be of assistance during interpretation. These devices usually provide a graphic presentation of data and, more importantly, a fairly clear-cut idea of the relative position of the individual within one or more tested dimensions. Typical examples of these would be the scattergram, a test profile sheet, or a histogram of scores.·

Each device has a particular contribution to make to test interpretation, and the counselor should be aware of this contribution. In general, these are a bit more meaningful for younger clients because they aid in maintaining interest and presenting the data. In each instance they are designed to help the client clarify his understanding of himself and of his thinking.

There are limitations of these types of devices. First, the "cuteness" of the presentation sometimes takes away from the data to be presented. The counselor must guard against this happening. Second, there may be a tendency to develop these more for presentation to other people. The scattergram has been called a teacher-centered instrument since it can be a valuable tool in aiding the teacher to understand a group of pupils. This does detract from the individualized use of test data.

It is beyond the intent of this book to present a long description of these types of devices. We merely suggest that these devices are available. If used with some caution, they can add another dimension to the test interpretation that is necessary.

Group Interpretation

Although we would favor individualized interpretation of test results, there are instances when group methods can be of value. Caution is necessary in this area, since the confidentiality of test results must be maintained.

In general the following are possibilities for group test data presentation. In terms of the preliminary presentation of reasons for testing, it is probable that a skilled counselor can deal with a small group of people. Since much of this type of information is not personal, the presentation can be fairly straightforward in terms of test objectives, what the test measures, and how the test will be used and interpreted. The counselor may encourage questions from the group so that everyone has a good understanding of the purposes of testing.

It is also possible that preliminary test interpretation following administration can be done on a group basis. This is especially true when a profile sheet or similar device is part of the test score. The counselor may explain what the profile is, develop a notion of how the scores are presented, and might even begin some explanation of the test results. This should be a general approach and must not replace individual interpretation.

In addition to the previous guidelines for individual interpretation, the following relate more specifically to group interpretation (Shertzer and Peters, 1965).

1. Choice of words, always a crucial variable, is even more important in group interpretation. An individual within the group may not exercise the option to clarify any misunderstanding he has. Thus, the "truth" of the presentation is extremely critical.

2. Provide an opportunity for questions from the group. Often the counselor is premature in closing the session and some questions or comments are not presented.

3. The skilled counselor will be alert to the individuals in the group. He will attempt to elicit comments from as many people as possible without putting anyone "on the spot." He will also be careful to transfer the reactions—covert and overt—of the group into a non-threatening individual setting. The client who appears to want to participate in a group should be encouraged to raise his questions or issues during the private individual session.

In closing, the counselor should remember that any group situation increases the involvement, potential problem areas, and misunderstanding at perhaps a geometric rather than arithmetic rate. A degree of hazard is involved in this type of interpretation. This suggests that certain tests are more appropriately dealt with in other types of interpretative settings. Usually, these would be interest or personality inventories which will have a close relationship to the individual personal feelings and are better interpreted on a more personal basis.

Reflection of Feelings

Test interpretation does not differ greatly from other types of counseling. Although some focus is upon the test, this is really an extension of the individual and as such means that the focus must still be on the client. Many counselors forget this when the test interpretation option exists, and the client receives relatively little value from the test.

The counselor must, as we suggest throughout this book, focus on the feelings of the client. This means that during and after whatever technical involvement there is, the counselor helps the client deal with the meaning of the test results within his own life. He listens for the client's personal feelings about the test-taking experience, the outcomes of the test, and future life meanings attached to the results. It is best for the counselor to say something like, "You feel badly about the results on the test," since this is a response to the feeling the client has rather than to the actual scores or results.

Testing from our frame of reference is only an extension of the real core of counseling, which is the aid one person can provide to another for living a more adequate and satisfying life. Although at times the inclination is toward a sterile interpretation of tests, the counselor must be constant in his attempts to help the client focus on meaning and his own feelings about the topic of the session.

Prior Experience of the Client

It is important that the counselor be aware of the potential input which the client's prior experience has for the counseling session. Since we have proposed a cooperative model of test interpretation, the client is deeply involved in the process and his feelings and attitudes are relevant variables. The counselor should be willing to postpone testing or test interpretation if it becomes apparent that the client must first work through some feelings prior to objective and meaningful involvement in testing.

An additional element needs to be mentioned in this regard—namely, the test-taking skills of the individual. In any testing program we are interested in an accurate appraisal of the client's performance in various areas. Any known effect that causes an increase or decrease in performance must be taken into account. This is not a suggestion that we adjust all scores to fit the client's image. Rather it is a suggestion that observation of the test-taking situation and the characteristics of the test taker can provide important information for interpretation. As an example, any physical defect that affects performance should be noted. Obvious defects usually preclude involvement in normal test taking. Minor defects often go unnoticed and yet the obtained score is used as if it were an accurate performance level.

Finally, some persons may not have experienced some of the newer methods of testing and scoring and are not always aware of the differences that can occur from faulty test-taking. Others take the instructions too literally, and the resultant score is below what might be predicted. If the counselor is to set up a testing program for the client, he has an obligation to investigate the various aspects that go with testing.

Other Uses

Although we have suggested that the primary purpose for testing is to provide meaningful data for the client, there are other reasons for using tests. Most of these relate to the needs of the client, but we list them separately to illustrate the specific aspect involved (Shertzer and Peters, 1965).

1. Certain tests can provide assistance in fortifying or eliminating alternatives. The use of aptitude tests may be a good example of this since the performance of the client in one or more categories may either indicate a dislike of the area or the need for extra training in the area. Neither alternative may be positively perceived by the client, and thus continued involvement at that particular time in discussion of the identified areas may not be necessary.

2. Tests can be used to assist in planning courses of action that will evolve into decision making. Again, this is related to the personal

needs of the client; but, using tests in any way is a lower level type of concern than when a crucial decision on a course of action is necessary.

3. Tests can provide information concerning strengths and weaknesses of the individual. This information may then be used by the counselor and client to plan effective ways of dealing with the meaning of the test results.

SUMMARY

The potential uses of tests in the counseling process have been discussed in this chapter. It has been suggested that the counselor needs to understand the technical aspects of tests. In addition, skill in selection and interpretation of tests is necessary. We believe that tests can be a valuable addition to the client's understanding of himself. They can provide information for the client to meet his goals in counseling. Proper use of test data can foster client growth. It is incumbent upon the counselor to provide specialized assistance to the client when tests are included in the counseling process.

REFERENCES

Adams, Georgia Sachs. *Measurement and Evaluation in Education, Psychology and Guidance.* New York: Holt, Rinehart & Winston, 1964.

Anastasi, Anne. *Psychological Testing.* New York: Macmillan, 1961.

Cronbach, L. J. *Essentials of Psychological Testing.* New York: Harper & Row, 1960.

Hoffman, B. *The Tyranny of Testing.* New York: Crowell-Collier, 1962.

Shertzer, B., and Peters, H. J. *Guidance: Techniques for Individual Appraisal and Development.* New York: Macmillan, 1965.

Super, D. E., and Crites, J. O. *Appraising Vocational Fitness.* New York: Harper and Row, 1962.

Tyler, Leona. *The Work of the Counselor* (3rd ed.). New York: Appleton-Century-Crofts, 1969.

13

Vocational Counseling

The values of the vast majority of people in society include the need to work and to be somewhat skillful and happy in a job. It is possible that many positions or jobs fulfill these needs, and to some extent no great degree of vocational adjustment may be necessary. This may be a deterrent to providing better vocational assistance to people, since "success" on the job is an acceptable outcome for most people even though they might not be employed in the most meaningful and relevant job.

Vocational choice plays an important role in most people's lives. The work ethic pervades the lives of most persons, and choosing a job is an important facet of life. The fact that few persons go through a formal process in this area obscures the need for effective vocational counseling.

Since Parsons (1909) became involved with the problems of individuals who were out of work, vocational counseling has been somewhat of a dilemma. On the one hand, many people who need counseling assistance tend to need help in some aspect of vocational decision making. At the same time, practioners have generally downgraded vocational counseling as being a rather low-level type of activity that "trained" counselors avoid. However, vocational choice and satisfaction are aspects of our society, and the process of vocational development has importance.

Several basic ideas must be understood by the counselor in the area of vocational counseling. Among these are vocational development theory, organization and use of occupational information, and the world of work. We shall attempt to develop these themes and relate them to the process of counseling, with specific emphasis upon the use of information in counseling.

VOCATIONAL DEVELOPMENT

Since the end of World War II there has been an increasing interest in the process by which individuals approach, enter, and exit the world of work. A number of theories have been developed, and some testing of them over an extended period of time has taken place. From the authors' frame of reference, it would appear that the most meaningful of these deal with the developmental aspect of vocations—i.e., those theories that postulate a sequence of steps through which individuals pass vocationally (Super, 1957).

It is beyond the scope of this book to deal intensively with vocational theory. It is of value, however, to review the major ideas that are incorporated into developmental vocational theory. First, there is the notion that a sequence or series of steps is involved in the process. These steps may have different titles depending upon the therorist, but usually the following classification suffices.

The earliest stage is often one of unrealistic conceptualization of one's potentials and the world of work. The child often thinks about many glamorous types of work or imagines himself as a multi-talented person. If carried to an extreme, either of these activities might eventually lead to real psychological problems, but such thoughts are desirable during the first four to six years of schooling. In fact, it is probably necessary to encourage a rather wide range of thinking on the part of students in the area of work.

The second phase is one in which a narrowing of choice possibilities occurs. This might be labeled a tentative stage in which the individual begins to move toward a more realistic appraisal of himself and potential jobs. It may take the form of eliminating those jobs that have negative valence, or it may be a more realistic understanding of one's inability or unwillingness to do certain kinds of work. This phase normally extends from about the end of elementary school into high school. Certain counseling activities are called for during this period of time.

The third phase of vocational development might be labeled realistic choice making. In this case the potential field becomes more restricted. The individual is faced with several important decisions that are no longer simply intellectual; rather these will affect his life style. Several factors become important during this phase. There is an interrelatedness of choice. Educational decisions are interrelated with vocational decisions since they represent intermediate steps in the vocational choice process. Individual understanding of the vocation in which one has interest is interrelated with self-understanding. A number of factors about a potential vocation may have more meaning for one person than another. There is an availability of materials in which various aspects of jobs are discussed. There are other equally important aspects that may not be covered but should be. For example, many people fail in jobs for psychological reasons. To merely have the prerequisite skills is not a sufficient condition for success. Choosing the job phase is an extremely important time, and the counselor should be deeply involved in the choice-making activity.

A fourth phase that is often identified is that of maintenance. During this period of time the individual settles into the pattern of his vocational life. He may move from one position to another within his own organizational structure, or he may elect to seek a position in another place. Generally, although not entirely true, this time is quieter and smoother vocationally than other phases. Several potential pitfalls do exist, however.

Economic conditions within the society may restrict or eliminate the smoothness of advancement. While the individual may have the requisite skills if no job is available, ambiguity enters the picture and he may have some difficulty dealing with his personal and vocational life. As one gets older and settled into a position, irreversibility may begin. This may interfere with the upward advancement predictable from the earlier vocational pattern. In completely negative terms the employer may be relatively certain that the employee is in a rut; and, as an employer he is not as concerned with the old time employee as was true earlier. Physical conditions of the worker often force a change in activity. This may be a change in physical activity or relocation. Under either condition the adjustment may be extremely difficult for many persons.

The maintenance period has potential for great trauma or little affectation in the life of the worker. The relationship between counselor and client will be quite different at this point in time than at any other time in vocational development.

The final general phase is the stage in which the worker moves toward termination of his vocational activities and, hopefully into a period of meaningful retirement. We are presently in a transition period in terms of this concept. Retirement is an undesirable prospect for many persons just now completing their formal vocational lives. The prevailing ethic has been the goodness of work, and it is extremely difficult for these people to deal with non-work as a way of life. A pattern of life has also developed, which is difficult to break. Retirement forces disruptions to occur, and the individual often cannot cope with them. He begins to manifest certain personal behaviors that are not pleasant but that may be understandable when examined in the light of his life as a worker.

To summarize this brief review, vocational development can be perceived as a series of phases through which most persons move with relatively little difficulty. The uniqueness of each phase demands that the counselor provide differential assistance and information when counseling assistance is necessary. There are no clear-cut times when one phase ends and the next begins, but the counselor may quickly learn to recognize the referents of each phase and, more particularly, the characteristics of the client.

THE WORLD OF WORK

Menninger (1964) suggests that work in our society provides ways for meeting a number of psychological needs. He lists work as an outlet for the aggressive drive that is a major source of energy. He also suggests that work provides an opportunity for the individual to win approval from others. A third need relates to developing satisfying social relationships. A job "provides the opportunity to make (a person) feel that his life is counting for something—that he is leading or directing or creating or serving or shepherding or teaching in significant ways" (p. xvi).

The array of jobs available to the worker is staggering and, at times, bewildering. He is faced with sorting out the jobs that he can do, the ones in which he has an interest, and those that are available. When he makes a selection he finds that the job itself may have several facets that are important for advancement, promotion, increase in salary, and satisfaction. He may find that the selection he has made is not particularly satisfying and must begin the process again. The whole process suggests that more assistance should be available to help the individual make this important decision.

Prior to a discussion of the process of counseling, several aspects of the world of work and the worker's movement into that world should be examined. One major area is the relationship of various aspects of education to the vocational choice. Another is the utilization of practical work experience as a foundation for more realistic choices.

EDUCATIONAL INFORMATION

In an increasingly complex society, vocational choice demands training or education prior to entry into a particular position. Educational choice becomes one step in the vocational choice process. The counselor can assist the client in several areas of educational counseling. First, he can provide help in planning for educational experiences. The guidance offered by a secondary school counselor would be an example of educational planning. A second type of activity would be educational placement. Many employment counselors are involved in educational placement or, in client terms, selection of educational opportunities. Since this choice often is prerequisite to job placement, it is a very important factor. Third, assistance can be offered by a counselor in the area of remediation of educational deficiencies. In general, this type of activity would occur most often in those institutions specifically designed for education. The counselor would be an instructional staff member who has special skills in the diagnosis and assessment of a student's educational problems, and would understand the institutional offerings to a sufficient degree that the client would be offered the most meaningful remediation possible. A fourth area would include preventive educational assistance. The counselor might be more of a coordinator in this area, as he would identify students who appear to be headed toward some difficulty and would utilize out-of-school personnel and facilities to prevent a continued movement of the client toward inadequate levels of achievement or personal functioning (Brammer and Shostrom, 1968).

A final area would be direct counseling concerning the underlying reasons for inadequate educational performance. In this case the client would be facing some academic difficulties that are rooted in lack of motivation, school phobia, or other psychological and non-intellectual factors. The counselor would provide assistance for the client in helping him to understand his problems and hopefully to begin to function more adequately by eliminating the problem or bypassing the affect of the problem.

Quite often the interview begins as an examination of vocational choice, then evolves into an intermediate type of interview and educational planning; or choice becomes the topic with which the counselor works. The following example shows how client and counselor move from vocational choice to a need for examining both educational and vocational information.

C Hi, _____. Come on in. How are you doing?

S O.K.

C I understand you would like to talk with me about some of your future plans.

S Yeah. Mr. _____ said you might be able to help me decide what to do.

C O.K. Why don't you begin by telling me what you have been thinking about in regard to your future schooling or work.

S   Well, I kind of like education, but I also think I might want to be a dentist. I want to keep myself diversified so I can go into other fields.

C   What kinds of things do you think you would have to find out before you made your decision?

S   Well, I'd like to know what my interests are and how I did in the tests I took—like the National Merit.

C   Right. You need to know how you compare with other people to find out how likely you are to be admitted into college. Do you have questions about dentistry? Do you think you know enough about the job?

S   I don't have much real close contact with a dentist. Maybe I could talk to one sometime.

C   I think that would be valuable, and it's good you thought about it. Is there anything else you have considered to help you find out about being a dentist?

S   No, not really. Maybe you could arrange for me to spend a day with a dentist and see what he really does.

C   The idea of spending a day with a dentist is a good one. Perhaps we can work out something for you. If we could, when would you be able to do it?

S   Well, I'll plan on doing it soon if I can. I've got to get moving on some of these ideas I've been thinking about.

C   Great. Before we work out the arrangements, what have you thought about colleges?

S   I'm interested in a small college, but other than that I don't really know.

C   Well, what kinds of things do you think you want to know about college before you make your applications?

S   I'd like to be sure I'm going to be accepted. What are the requirements for admission?

C   That's like what you said before—about how you stack up compared to other people. Have you thought about any ways this might occur?

S   I suppose I could write to the college and ask them.

C   Good. They should have information about admission and various programs. As you know, we already have some catalogs that you might want to examine. Perhaps after you do that we could talk about any questions you might have.

PLANNING EDUCATIONAL EXPERIENCES

The counselor is probably most comfortable in this area of counseling, since his experience as a student is directly related to the goals and objectives of the client. The counselor may not have experienced the specific things which the client wants to decide, but he does have a general idea of the educational world.

The counselor is called upon to help the client select an educational goal that is attainable and in line with the client's aptitudes and interests. He is also called upon to help the client select the best educational experience to meet this goal. We want to specify that college placement, while important, is not the only type of planning necessary. The need for non-college educational prerequisites in many areas of the occupational world suggests that most clients will need information about various types of educational experiences.

In general, the following factors are important. First, the client needs to understand himself and what he wants to do. This may mean some assessment by the counselor. It will also mean that the counselor should help the client develop alternatives and other choices. The counselor may be called upon to confront the client at certain points along the way if it becomes apparent that the client is moving in an unproductive direction. Nothing can be gained by discussing avenues that have little potential for successful completion by the client. In this respect the counselor should rely on fairly hard data and should be certain that he cites verbatim the sources he is using. For example, it is unfruitful to spend time with a client and explore the possibilities of matriculating at a very selective college if the client does not have the characteristics listed for its student population.

A second factor, alluded to above, is an understanding of the educational institution. For college-planning counseling assistance, much information is available and surprisingly up to date. The case is much different for many other types of educational opportunities. The counselor must develop strategies for meeting the needs of his clients in these areas. Probabilities of successful completion of a given course of study, relationship to job opportunities, and job factors are important matters of information needed by the non-college–bound client (Herr and Cramer, 1968).

EDUCATIONAL PLACEMENT

Many counselors in educational institutions are called upon to provide placement service within the institution. Although one might question the way in which counselors generally go about placement, it does not alter the fact that this is part of the tasks accepted by the counselor.

It is important that the counselor understand the various aspects of the educational situation if he is to be effective in providing meaningful placement assistance. He needs to know what is offered in various areas of the curriculum and what differentiates levels of content. In the secondary school situation the counselor should have a keen awareness of what is offered in the various content areas so that the client can be well-informed as to what is being offered and what will be expected of him.

When done correctly, the counselor's job in the area of educational planning can be a very meaningful involvement. If he is interested only in "getting" students into classes or institutions, he has fallen far short of what educational planning ought to be. The interaction can become a meaningful activity for the client who is in need of placement, but only as a last step in the process of self-understanding intermingled with the institution's potential.

Remediation

The counselor's primary involvement in this area would be in diagnosis and then appropriate recommendation. There are several ways by which diagnosis can occur. Appraisal instruments are available in such areas as achievement, attitude, and general study methods. These provide data concerning areas in which the client may be experiencing some difficulty. The counselor ought to be the most skilled person in using these assessment instruments, but eventually the teacher will have to be involved also. Communication with the teacher concerning these results becomes important.

A second area of diagnosis deals with the client's physical and psychological factors. In the case of the physical aspects the counselor will depend upon those more skilled in the area. He should be able to utilize the information which he receives from the specialists, and then aid his client in understanding the cause as well as some potential remedies. The counselor should be skilled in the use of the clinical process to identify psychological factors. Common factors such as motivation or lack of interest are usually easy to recognize. These types of problems usually demand depth-oriented counseling rather than remedial educational processes.

At the same time the client needs to know how various educational experiences relate to his life and goals. He needs to know the requirements for completion of a specific set of experiences. He must come to an awareness of how he fits into the curricula offerings available to him. He should know how one moves into and out of various experiences so that he can take full advantage of what is offered him.

The above speaks of a panacea that probably does not exist in most educational institutions because it assumes too great a degree of freedom of movement by the client. The counselor should help the client adjust to the limitations or restrictions within the institution. The problem is the general assumption that the client must always adjust to the institution. A recurring theme in many counselor education programs is that the counselor ought to be active in changing those institutional practices that inhibit client growth. This poses a dilemma since the counselor must determine how much student radicalism the institution can tolerate. Yet, it is a part of the counselor's role to identify the institutional strengths and weaknesses and utilize these to the client's greatest benefit.

A final aspect of the placement activities of the counselor deals with the opportunities outside the institution in which he works. Often the need arises for the client to seek specialized education, and the counselor can serve as a resource person to aid in this process. He thus needs to know something of the various agencies which exist and, more importantly, methods by which one may take advantage of the agencies' offerings. In a similar vein the counselor needs to know about other levels of the educational enterprise. He should be familiar with the previous levels of client experience and help the client tie these together with future higher-level experiences (Cramer, 1970).

In short, the counselor's involvement in remediation is to provide assistance in diagnosing the area of concern and assisting the client in understanding the concern, giving the kinds of assistance available, and working with the referral specialist who might most closely meet the needs of the student.

PREVENTION

In general, counseling can be more successful if preventive aspects are involved in the process. Although those concerns or problems that demand remediation are more clearly identified, it is also true that successful counseling is a longer process if indeed success does occur. The medical notion of prevention of certain diseases has relevance in the area of educational and vocational counseling assistance. The counselor's involvement is to identify as early as possible the characteristics that might predict inadequate development or functioning on the part of the client. It is then possible to introduce preventive measures into the life of the individual. The following example might point out a method by which this can work.

If we assume that future success in a subject like reading is tied not only to previous reading accomplishment but also to age, it is important to provide assistance as early as possible so that inadequate development of reading skills can be prevented. Thus the solution would be some sort of emphasis upon providing reading aid to the client so that he can avoid the problems which he might fall into later in his academic career. This concept may be applied to levels of the educational enterprise. The client needs to understand the relationship between what he is doing and not doing presently and how this might affect any future goals he may have. Although the counselor has no magical way of changing the present behavior of the client, he can aid the client in seeing his potential and understanding how prevention can be effected.

Inadequate Performance

The counselor, regardless of educational level, should be available to aid the client in understanding and dealing with inadequate academic performance. Obviously, this is closely related to several of the previous areas since counselors generally do not become involved with students whose academic performance is about where it might be expected to be. These persons might seek assistance for other concerns but, in general, we are usually concerned with underachievers or poor achievers who need to improve. The counselor can provide a relatively safe place for investigating inadequate performance. Since the counselor is not called upon to evaluate performance, the counseling environment ought to be more conducive to exploration and resolution of the problem.

It should be noted that not all clients identified as having inadequate academic performance actually have this problem. Anyone who has looked at achievement and ability test results for students realizes that many persons achieve at about the same level as their ability predicts, even though this might be below the expectations of parents, teachers, or school staff. Students sometimes are not bad achievers, but have problems with the demands put on them by others. This again provides the counselor with an opportunity for working closely with people to better understand their needs and aptitudes.

Practical Experience

It is desirable for the client to have an opportunity to gain experience in various areas of vocations, but impossible to provide tryouts for every client in all areas of interest or aptitude. However, until the person has had some practical involvement with the specifics of the vocation, all choices are probably tentative. It is possible to help the client adjust to the position when he is faced with some negative factors on the job, and many employers are beginning to see job satisfaction—the adjustment of worker and job—as being important to the worker's productiveness.

It is still important to provide assistance to the worker who finds difficulty in adjusting to his job. Follow-up and development of alternatives are important. Assuming that the problem is the job and not an unwillingness to work, the vocational counselor can provide valuable service to the client in this oft-neglected area of follow-up and redirection.

THE PROCESS OF COUNSELING

Generally, vocational or educational counseling follows an orderly process beginning with the development of the relationship and ending with follow-up and potential change of plans. In between these two steps the counselor would be involved in helping the client to develop an understanding of the problem or concern which he had. Data would be gathered from several sources and these data would be presented to the client to help him understand himself and the existing vocational decisions and alternatives. The counselor and client would work toward a synthesis of the appraisal process and individual client study into a plan of action or a choice. These steps provide a basis for a model of counselor-client involvement that we shall attempt to develop throughout the rest of this chapter.

These steps will never be as clearly definable as we shall present them. After the relationship is established, there are six factors in vocational and educational counseling. These are appraisal of the client's characteristics, introduction of outside information, exploration, clarification, integration, and the decision (Brammer and Shostrom, 1968).

APPRAISAL OF CLIENT CHARACTERISTICS

There is a need for the client to examine his personal characteristics. This examination would include interests, aptitudes, achievement, aspiration, skills, and values, among others. Various methods could be used in this process, including check lists, inventories, tests, previous records, interview data, and work history. Such areas as special aptitudes, personality traits, and educational attainment would be potentials for focusing the attention of the client.

One of the first tasks of the counselor is to determine the client's knowledge in some of these areas. What aspirations does he have? What limitations exist in terms of training, skills, educational background, and experience? What special aptitudes or skills does he have? The counselor provides assistance for the client to discover as many "facts" as possible about himself.

The client may have specific reasons for going through this process. He may be simply affirming what he already knew. He is not performing at as high a level as he might, or else he might be doing as well or better than might be expected. Often this type of client presents a different problem for the counselor to handle since motivation, anxiety, and unrealistic self-concept might be the problems rather than an inability to make vocational choices or related vocational questions.

A second problem is the client who seems to have nothing going for him. Under this circumstance the counselor has the problems of providing training and/or placement. The client's characteristics may preclude counselor success, but the counselor is still expected to "deliver."

A third situation is posed in the other direction, though to a significantly different degree. Some clients have so many aptitudes and thus possibilities that decision making is inhibited. The counselor may need to provide a hierarchy for the client so that he sees the various value levels that differentiate positions.

Finally, the client may be aided to broaden his scope by the discovery of new material either about himself or a vocational field. The counselor should be prepared to provide the latitude suggested by this situation. Restriction of choice should be avoided, especially for the client who discovers new facets of himself during counseling (Tyler, 1969).

During the initial contacts with the client, the counselor is involved in developing predictions about the client's probabilities. He is preoccupied with learning about the client—not to force a decision, but to be in a position to provide meaningful assistance later in the process. He is listening to determine where the client is in the process of choice. He learns whether the client has relatively accurate information. He is aware of the interaction that is taking place in the counseling process. In short, he is attempting to determine where the client is, where he wishes to go, what his probabilities of getting there are, and how he as the counselor can be of most assistance.

Client Objectives

The client and counselor need to establish mutually agreed upon objectives for the counseling process. These should flow from the data-gathering and interpretation aspects of the early interviews. The counselor helps the client begin to specify particular possibilities. They establish methods of further exploration of specific possibilities. In the case of behavioral counseling a method of reinforcement or learning is established. At the end of this step the counselor and client should have a clear notion of the alternatives that exist. They should be moving toward establishing some hierarchy of possibilities for further exploration.

In some cases the client will not be able to fit the data and his own wishes together. Many clients are unwilling or unable to accept those data which predict unacceptable outcomes for them. Although our predictive powers are not as good as we would like, the counselor should be willing to confront the client at certain points in the process.

Interests

While it is valuable to know whether one has the aptitude to perform certain tasks, there is a need to know whether an interest in the task area exists. The counselor can help the client to determine whether the potential position or area is within his pattern of interests. Job satisfaction has become an important aspect of vocational adjustment. Interests have a significant bearing upon satisfaction.

The area of personal values is related to interests. The individual should understand how he and the job fit together in terms of the values he holds and the demands of the position. The client may be expected to perform certain tasks that are outside his value system. This type of information is important during the choosing stage.

Obviously, there is a need to relate the physical demands of the job to the characteristics of the client. Again, if these are in opposition, the counselor should provide assistance to the client to avoid what will probably be an unsatisfactory situation.

There will be times when the client is forced into a compromise situation in selecting jobs. He may not have as high an interest as one would like; he may not have all of the prerequisites either as demanded by an employer or from his own personal point of view. He may need the job, and the counselor's role is to help him find the very best situation available.

Outside Information

A second area of counselor involvement is providing information about vocations which the client does not have but needs prior to a meaningful decision. Various types of information are available. Commercial publishers have prepared material that lists the important aspects of a vocation. Included would be entry characteristics, the money situation, structure of the vocation, relationship to other vocational fields and levels, and other factual information. Judicious use of this type of information can be helpful to the client as he attempts to work through a vocational decision.

The counselor should also have some personal information about vocations available to his clients. This would be of a much more specific nature since it would be dealing with a particular position at a specific moment in time. The counselor must be somewhat cautious in this latter area, since the potential for over-personalizing is great. It is not uncommon to see a counselor respond to a chance remark of a client when the counselor has some knowledge about the area. Often it does not really matter that the client does not want to know as much as the counselor wants to tell.

The counselor's responsibility includes keeping informational sources up-to-date and relevant. He should be aware when revisions are made and should spend time clarifying the material in the various sources of information to determine relevance to the local situation.

Exploration, Clarification, and Integration

Occupational information serves the client's purposes by providing avenues for further exploration. It is of some importance to note that the process of exploration best served by the client's personal involvement in the use of material telling is not as meaningful as finding out for one's self.

Quite often the client needs to explore vocational possibilities. He is not sure what is available and needs to begin to identify those areas which might be appropriate for him. The counselor needs to be able to assist him in the process of exploring possibilities in a context which the client can handle.

At the same time the client needs to thoroughly understand the various possibilities available to him. He must become realistic in his choice and thus clearly delineate the various possibilities and their characteristics. The counselor should be active in this process. It is incumbent upon the counselor to deal as factually and neutrally as possible in this area. Often a counselor reveals the decision he has made for the client in the way he presents information and clarifies what the client says. The counselor is making a decision which, in all probabality, is not his to make.

Finally, the client must integrate the material into his decision or choice. After the exploratory and clarification processes have been completed, the ultimate meaning for the client is what happens in his vocational life. Successful counseling should lead to a choice that incorporates as much personal vocational and occupational information as possible. Although compromise is usually part of the process, this should be held at a minimal level.

The Decision

Hopefully, the client is able to make a decision about his vocational future. If not, then the counselor may need to spend some time helping the client understand what has occurred. When more than one possibility exists, the decision is up to the client. The counselor may provide some further assistance during the decision process and as a follow-up.

The process described above could become routine if the counselor is not alert to the occurring interaction. The client is not a set of data to be intermingled with a set of job characteristics. He has values, individuality, needs, and aspirations. Some theorists (Super, 1957) suggest that vocational choice is an implementation of one's self-concept. The closer the occupation to one's conception of himself, the more meaningful that position will be.

A Need for a Decision

The following is a counselor's attempt to help the client move toward a decision about his vocational future. It is obvious that two or three variables are intertwined in any counseling relationship. It is difficult to separate decision-making counseling from vocational counseling, and probably unwise to do so. Most vocational counseling includes implicit educational assistance, since our complex society usually has educational requirements for the vocation the individual might choose.

Cl I'm still lost. I don't know what I want.

Co You're concerned about what's going to be best for you in a job.

Cl Yeah.

Co The idea is that for you you're better off if you have a definite goal.

Cl Yeah. Right. I like several things and I just can't be sure. I'm kinda lost in the middle someplace, you know?

Co You've stated that you have spent a lot of time on art and to throw that away now would kinda bother you.

Cl Yeah. I'm not sure exactly, you know, if the change would stick if I'd stick to it, you know, as far as that goes. If I took law for a career and art for a hobby . . . but it wouldn't work the other way around, you know?

Co   This thing about changing your mind bothers you. You would have to go to college and then to law school. That would take a long time.

Cl   Yeah, seven years. Isn't that right?

Co   It seems like a long time.

Cl   Yeah, especially three years of law school. I'd better pick up on my grades next year, too.

Co   Seems like you're in the middle of a lot of things and don't know which way to go.

Cl   I just want to be sure. I feel more secure with a definite goal in mind.

Co   I kind of sense that you are saying the most important thing is that you want to be happy with your choice. Would money be important to your choice?

Cl   Everyone wants to make as much as he possibly can. How much effort do you put forward and how much do you get out of it? If you didn't have much interest and you didn't work beyond the point of average intensity, then you might stay at the same salary. I think if you wanted to attain the highest financial level, I think you'd have to be pretty well educated.

Co   The interest has to be there.

Cl   Oh yeah. The goal is important, too—interests and self security, for me, are important.

Co   It would be better to have something to point toward. If you really have a goal you'll put more into it when the going is tough. How do you see this goal fitting in with vocational choice? You've talked about this decision several times, but you don't seem to be able to set a goal. You say, "I need a goal but I can't pick one."

Cl   Well I don't know which is best. Should I choose one field and then look at colleges?

Co   You seem to be waiting for something to come along and make you feel sure.

Cl   I just want to make the best choice between these two.

Co   So whatever you eventually pick, you're going to have to stick with.

Cl   I just want to be sure so I don't go halfway through and find out something I didn't know.

Co   You don't want to consider the possibility of change somewhere along the line.

Cl   Right.

Co   Has this been a pattern in your life, starting something and sticking to it?

Cl No, but this seems so big and important that I want to be sure.

Co And you're not sure about the decision. Between now and the time to choose a college, are you going to be able to make the decision?

Cl I just want time to think. I'd just like to work it out now and let you know in the fall so we can work on colleges.

Co Well, what can we do now? Are you going to try to see a lawyer?

Cl Yeah.

Co Do you have any ideas about the type of information you would want to get from him?

Cl Well, yeah. But I guess I'm not as sure as I'd like to be.

Co Perhaps we can spend some time working through some questions you might ask and decide what information you need.

Cl I'd like to do that because I want to be sure about my decision.

BEHAVIORAL COUNSELING IN VOCATIONAL CHOICE

A recent development in the area of vocational counseling relates to the work of the behavioral counselors—especially to those connected with Stanford University. In a series of articles, Krumboltz and many of his students have demonstrated the effectiveness of behavioral counseling in the areas of decision making, vocational exploration, and vocational choice.

In any counseling situation a goal is to have the client change his behavior in his normal life in a manner somewhat similar to his changed mode of behavior with the counselor. This generalization is especially necessary for the behaviorist, since it is possible to elicit certain responses within the counseling setting. Unless these responses lead to changed behavior outside the setting, the counseling has only demonstrated that man can be manipulated by other men.

Several methods have been used by the behaviorist in the area of vocational counseling and choice. It can be demonstrated that the frequency of information-seeking statements as well as information-seeking behavior outside the interview increases when verbal and model reinforcement techniques are used (Krumboltz and Schroeder, 1965). Ryan and Krumboltz (1964) found that verbal reinforcement increased the rate of deliberation responses and that this behavior generalized outside the interview.

It has been shown that the frequency of information-seeking responses during the interview and information-seeking behavior outside the interview were positively associated. A random sampling of participating subjects indicated that there was an increase in the out-of-counseling activity (Krumboltz and Thoresen, 1964; Thoresen and Krumboltz, 1967). In a related study, Michelsen (1970) found that those counselors identified as facilitators on the Carkhuff scale were able to utilize reinforcement to increase the number of information-seeking statements made by the client. They were more efficient in terms of time spent, as well as more effective in terms of number of statements.

Krumboltz and Sheppard (1969) suggest a method for including vocational information in the formal structure of a guidance program. Although primarily aimed at school counseling, there are certain areas of generalization that cut across vocationally oriented counseling, regardless of the level.

They talk about the need for simulation. Generally, the problem should be realistic and representative of problems faced by members of the occupation. The problem should be considered intrinsically interesting by the majority of the target population. The expected outcome is that provision of simulated job experiences will enable persons to better determine for themselves whether a certain kind of work will enable them to receive the kind of reinforcers they seek from life.

ORGANIZATION AND USE OF OCCUPATIONAL INFORMATION

An important area of knowledge and skill deals with the question of occupational information as it relates to counseling. In general, the need is for meaningful delivery of relevant materials for client use.

In many instances, organization of occupational material is already a reality. Many commercial publishing firms have available a wide range of materials that provide information about occupations. Usually these are written on a level at which all but a few clients can read. However, there are always some problems. First, reading does not necessarily mean understanding. The client may have some difficulty in accepting what is said, in clearly understanding the materials, or in blocking out those aspects that interfere with his goals. The counselor may need to spend some time "teaching" clients how to read these materials; although we would support this activity, some counselors and counselor educators do not accept this as a meaningful part of counseling.

A second problem with much professionally published material concerns its datedness. The process of writing a job description, editing, publishing, distributing, and placing it in the client's hand may take up so much time that the information is already out of date. These materials may not be invaluable adjuncts to the client, however; rather, we suggest that some monitoring is necessary. Hoppock (1951), for example, suggests that any material over five years old should be thrown out because of its possible datedness.

Finally, since most available material must of necessity be general in nature to cover a broad spectrum of the potential selling market, its relevance to an individual client could be tenuous. As in test interpretation, group data may not be particularly valuable to an individual. The counselor should provide aid in individualizing the occupational material that is available.

A number of possibilities exist for using mechanical aids to present occupational information. Clients can avail themselves of these aids for exploration activities, and then move to the counseling setting for more specific types of aid.

An example might clarify the above point. It is possible to computerize the various characteristics of jobs or colleges. The simplest way is, most likely, computer assistance in selection of a college. The client can begin to identify areas of interest based upon a number of variables. He begins by making some preliminary choices about the types of courses in which he would like to enroll, characteristics of the student population he thinks would be most compatible to him, cost factors, location, and so on. Once he has indicated the parameters which interest him, the computer can provide specific colleges. In addition, extra data about the college elected can be provided. The client can manipulate his parameters as many times as he likes and continue to receive feedback from the computer. However, the process is incomplete until there is an attempt to examine the output of the computer as it relates to the client. The computer can provide rather instantaneous and up-to-date information, but until this is translated meaningfully into the client's frame of reference, the process is not as valuable as it might be.

This format could be extended to selection of potential job areas (Katz, 1968). In this process the individual client is aided in understanding various characteristics of the job and at the same time can assess some probability of success based upon his own needs, wants, skills, or characteristics. The information gleaned by the client in this process is not sufficient. The counselor helps the individual begin to integrate this into a more meaningful part of his vocational decision making.

The counselor's involvement in the organization of occupational information is threefold. First, he must be aware of and understand the available materials. These materials accessible to the client must be chosen because of their overall relevance to the needs of the clientele being served in the counseling situation. Second, the counselor must be certain that whenever necessary the client receives specialized interpretative and integrative assistance. When questions are raised, the counselor or someone knowledgeable should be available to answer them. Third, the counselor or his surrogate should be aware of the specific local situation in regard to the generalized information that is available. It is of little value to the client to read about some position that simply is not available to him. The local situation should be understood so that whatever is described is also available.

USES OF OCCUPATIONAL INFORMATION

Clients generally have a variety of reasons for seeking out occupational information. Tyler (1969) identifies these as exploratory, understanding, and elaboration. She differentiates these in terms of the types of information that might be used and the sequence in which they generally occur. Exploratory use involves the search for potential alternatives in action. This may be part of the discussion by the counselor with the client in which the task is to list the various alternatives. This may involve the assignment of outside reading. Homework of a specific nature may be helpful in promoting exploration.

When one moves beyond this area, the valuable information can lead to a clearer understanding of the specifics of the occupation or self. Several potential ways might be suggested to aid in this use of information. Talking to a practitioner should aid in the former, although there are some limitations in this area. The worker may have such a negative feeling that no positives are listed. The reverse may be true so that positive characteristics are so meaningful to the worker that he cannot provide any other information. The counselor should act as a balancing agent in these cases. The aspect of self-understanding clearly fits into the counseling setting. The counselor should be skilled in providing assistance to the client by gathering information and relating it to a clearer understanding of self and relationship to occupations.

The final category in the use of information deals with elaboration of whatever plan might be made. This most clearly relates to the need for information about the specifics of a particular position or decision. Once the client has made a decision about his life, he must begin to determine what should be done next. For a client wishing to become a skilled tradesman the necessary information has to do with entry into the job, advancement, working conditions, and so on. Other classifications of using information are possible. For example, Brayfield (1948) lists motivational, informational, and adjustive uses for information. In most cases these classifications are self-explanatory and deal with the type of input and sequencing necessary. Each involves a set of activities by the counselor.

Timing

Timing is of critical importance in the broad category of occupational information. The counselor must be aware of the particular needs of the individual in order to avoid being premature with the introduction of information. Quite often the counselor might hear certain cue phrases that lead him to introduce information into the counseling session. This may be less than meaningful for the client who is not really ready for it. Many clients are noticeably upset when this occurs, because it is an example of the counselor's not hearing what is being said.

We would suggest that the counselor allow the client to take the lead in this kind of situation. The counselor should offer certain bits of information and observe the response of the client. If there seems to be a desire to continue the exploration, the counselor should attempt to aid the client in developing the direction and indicating the amount of information he wishes. Above all, the counselor should avoid overpowering the client with information. It is wiser to say too little and have the client ask for more than to lose the client because too much was said.

Event Versus Developmental

In previous sections we have described some sequential aspects of presenting information. This is predicated on the idea that the vocational decision is developmental in nature rather than a series of discrete events. When viewed in this manner, one assumes a set of unrelated decisions.

The counselor and counselee must know the previous history of the client. Various aspects of his life, important earlier decisions, and background data provide a basis for present and future decisions. This information will be viewed differentially when sequence is assumed. The counselor will be much more concerned about the total relevance and understanding of the material as opposed to large doses of information in some specific area mentioned by the client.

Second, the eventual decisions are viewed as related to future activity and, as such, receive different attention than a decision viewed with some finality. The counselor does not discontinue the possibility of counseling because certain decisions have been made; rather, he aids the client to continue considering the relationships of past decisions to future potentials and alternatives.

Third, any decision may have the potential for limiting the range of behaviors or alternatives available to the client. This paradox can have rather interesting effects upon the client. Some clients see this as a desirable condition. Limiting decision-making possibilities creates a more acceptable world for the client. Some clients probably want a stochastic situation in which the decision rules out all possibilities for any other direction. He has no doubts, nor does he need them, because he has eliminated all alternatives. The opposite is also true. Many clients see so many attractive possibilities that they cannot choose. Regardless, there are limitations engendered by various vocational decisions, and counselor and client should attempt to deal with them to the broadest extent possible.

SUMMARY

Counselors are increasingly being called upon to provide vocational counseling. The changing situation in regard to the number of types of jobs as well as to an increase in the need for education prior to job entry and advancement has created a need for re-emphasizing vocational counseling. In many cases the client's initial contact with a counselor is related to an educational or vocational decision. The counselor can be of considerable assistance to the client if he accepts vocational counseling as part of his role. We have attempted to list some steps in the process, as well as some sources for information and the use thereof. Implicit in our presentation is the importance of the personality of the counselor in the process. His commitment to the client regardless of the client's need is an essential aspect of successful counseling.

REFERENCES

Brammer, L. M., and Shostrom, E. L. *Therapeutic Psychology* (2nd ed.). Englewood Cliffs, N. J.: Prentice-Hall, 1968.

Brayfield, A. H. "Putting Occupational Information Across." *Educational and Psychological Measurement 1948* 8, 493–495.

Cramer, S. H. (Ed.). *Pre-Service and In-Service Preparation of School Counselors for Educational Guidance.* March *1970.*

Herr, E. L., and Cramer, S. H. *Guidance of the College Bound.* New York: Appleton-Century-Crofts, 1968.

Hoppock, R. *Occupational Information.* New York: McGraw-Hill, 1957.

Katz, M. "A Model of Guidance for Career Decision-Making." *Vocational Guidance Quarterly 1966* 15, 2–10.

Krumboltz J.D., and Schroeder, W. W. "Promoting Career Planning Through Reinforcement Models." *Personnel and Guidance Journal 1965* 44, 19–26.

Krumboltz, J. D., and Sheppard, L. E. "Vocational Problem Solving Experiences." In Krumboltz, J. D., and Thoresen, C. E. *Behavioral Counseling.* New York: Holt, Rinehart & Winston, 1969.

Krumboltz, J. D., and Thoresen, C. E. "The Effect of Behavioral Counseling in Group and Individual Settings on Information-Seeking Behavior." *Journal of Counseling Psychology 1964* 11, 324–333.

Menninger, W. C. "The Meaning of Work in Western Society." In Barow, H. (Ed.) *Man in a World at Work.* Boston: Houghton-Mifflin, 1964.

Michekson, D. J. "The Differential Effects of Facilitative and Non-Facilitative Behavioral Counselors Upon Student Verbal Information-Seeking Behavior." Unpublished Doctoral Dissertation, State University of New York at Buffalo, 1970.

Parsons, F. *Choosing a Vocation.* Boston: Houghton-Mifflin, 1969.

Ryan, T. Antoinette, and Krumboltz, J. D. "Effect of Planned Reinforcement Counseling on Client Decision-Making Behavior." *Journal of Counseling Psychology 1964* 11, 315–323.

Super, D. *The Psychology of Careers.* New York: Harper and Row, 1957.

Thoresen, C. E., and Krumboltz, J. D. "Relationship of Counselor Reinforcement of Selected Responses to External Behavior." *Journal of Counseling Psychology 1967* 14, 140–144.

Tyler, Leona. *The Work of the Counselor* (3rd ed.). New York: Appleton-Century-Crofts, 1969.

14

Ethics, Legalities, and Values in Counseling

As counseling becomes a more pervasive aspect of contemporary society, the issues related to ethics, legalities, and values in counseling will become more critical. When great numbers of persons practice a particular profession, the probability of questionable activity is increased. And, when some members of the profession are seen to act in less than desirable ways, the entire profession loses. For this purpose, codes of ethics have been created for the major professional counseling groups—i.e., American Personnel and Guidance Association and American Psychological Association. The counselor must have an understanding of these areas (ethics, legalities, values). We shall attempt to provide foundational information in each area.

Each of these areas will have a different relationship to the process of counseling because of the degree of ambiguity and uncertainty related to each area. One might assume that the general hierarchical downward progression would be from relatively clear-cut ethical considerations to relatively tenuous value considerations. Although this is generally true, there are answered and unanswered questions in all three areas. The reader will also note that interrelationships exist between the areas that may cause even greater difficulty in understanding.

ETHICAL CONSIDERATIONS

Ethics are suggested standards of conduct based upon consensus value that has already been set. A profession attempts to translate as many values as possible into structured expectations of behavior for members as they relate to each other, to the clientele, and to the public. An understanding of ethics can provide the counselor with a method of handling various difficult situations. However, many situations arise for which ethical statements provide little or no assistance.

There are some considerations that need to be discussed in this context. First, there are personal ethics, professional ethics, and institutional ethics. Often these conflict because of the relationship to the value system existing at one of the levels. The school counselor is forced into a decision-making situation when the administration demands certain information about a client—information that was gathered in a confidential manner. The institutional values might be quite clear in terms of the prospective good which could accrue to the student if various data and information would be available, yet the counselor implicitly or explicitly has communicated that a degree of confidentiality does exist. He has an ethical dilemma. The counselor may face an ethical conflict when a client tells the counselor that he is going to do something—e.g., cheat on a test. If one were confident that the cheating would occur or that someone would be hurt by the action, there would be a clear-cut resolution. However, neither of these may be true; therefore, the counselor often does nothing. If, in fact, the cheating does occur, the counselor has another ethical dilemma because he has to decide what, if anything, to do about the situation.

A further consideration is that relatively few counselors know the ethical standards suggested by the professional organizations. Although they might be able to find copies, the need in most situations is for immediate action of an ethical nature. One often does not have time to search through records or literature, and common sense is usually the foundational decision-making principle. This might not be sufficient. The counselor should become knowledgeable about the ethical standards most closely related to his position.

One major specific area of ethical behavior faces many counselors. This is the area of confidentiality. Confidentiality involves the retention of information received in a personal interaction with a client. Sometimes the information or data considered confidential cannot be treated as completely confidential. Confidential information exists at several levels.

The first level might be termed professional use of information. Whatever discussion occurs is done professionally with others who have a degree of understanding as to the meaning of the information. This information is released with the client's consent. Information at this level would be related to test data, records, and other information that might exist about and outside the client. A second level involves information that is transmitted from the client on a personal basis during the counseling interview. The client should be aware of the degree to which confidentiality can exist prior to communication within the counseling situation. The counselor must be able to discern when the information is going to pose a confidentiality problem. He must be able to communicate a structure to the client that will help him understand the consequences (good or bad) that may occur. The counselor also needs to know the constraints under which he works in order to develop a way of dealing with this type of information. We suggest that the plan of handling confidential material should exist in the counselor's mind, but that the implementation comes at the point of introduction of material rather than a structuring speech early in the series of interviews. The latter action will probably preclude any interaction.

The third level of confidentiality is that the counselor simply does not divulge any material given by the client. Two restrictions here would be if clear danger to human life exists or if the client consents to divulging the information. The counselor who assumes this stance may be involved in a legal problem since it is not always clear whether he has privileged communication which is the only legal way to completely avoid some communication of information. This aspect is covered in another part of this chapter.

It is important that the counselor develop a plan for handling the confidentiality issue. Whatever the plan, he needs to be consistent in how he interacts with clients. If he says, "I shall hold confidential whatever you say," he had better be willing and able to follow through.

From the authors' standpoint, confidentiality is such an important facet that it is difficult to conceive of a counselor not accepting the responsibilities and consequences of maintaining confidentiality. If unwilling to do this, then he may wish to reconsider being a counselor.

APGA ETHICAL STANDARDS

The APGA Ethical Standards (1961) lists six specific areas of professional activity: counseling, testing, research and publication, consulting and private practice, personal administration, and preparation for personnel work. In each area general principles are listed, and they are intended to serve as guidelines for the ethical practice of members.

In many cases the easiest way to approach an understanding of the ethical standards is to frame questions that commonly confront the counselor and then develop a statement (to answer the questions) from the Standards. For example, what should a counselor do when he does not feel competent enough to provide professional assistance to the client? (Section B: Counseling Statement 6 provides the answer.)

> The membership shall decline to initiate or shall terminate a counseling relationship when he cannot be of professional assistance to the counselee or client either because of lack of competence or personal limitation. In such instances the member shall refer his counselee or client to an appropriate specialist. In the event the counselee or client declines the suggested referral, the member is not obligated to continue the relationship.

Brammer and Shostrom (1968) summarize ethical behavior nicely when they suggest that "One of the most important safeguards against unethical behavior is knowledge and experience" (p. 154). Wrenn (1958) stated that ethical behavior includes a feeling of responsibility on the part of the counselor to relate his behavior to his ethics as subscribing to a code of ethics.

LEGAL CONSIDERATIONS

The role of the counselor creates several situations that could eventuate in legal action. Although there have been a minimum of such actions, the potential still exists for the counselor to become aware of his legal status. Several areas are identifiable in the legal area: liability, malpractice, libel, slander, and privileged communication. It is beyond the scope of this book to present a legal brief concerning each area, but we shall speak of counselor responsibility in each of these categories.

LIABILITY

Liability is an encompassing term that deals with a person's responsibility in relating to another person with whom he was or is directly involved. Liability can attach to acts of negligence and malpractice, libel and slander.

In general, the counselor is expected to exercise the same care and prudence that any reasonable person would exercise in a similar situation. If he is negligent, he may become liable for any injury or harm that might result. Edwards (1955) suggests that in addition "Courts place emphasis upon the principle of foreseeability: that is a (counselor) will be held guilty of negligence if he pursues a course of action which any reasonably prudent person would have foreseen that some kind of injury might well resolve from the action being taken" (p. 474). (our parentheses)

It is somewhat difficult to develop any firm statement of what the above might mean to counselors at various levels of the profession. An oft cited case used as a precedent is the *Bogust* v. *Iverson* case (Wisconsin, 1958). The counselor was charged with negligently and carelessly failing to perform his duties in three specific ways. First, charges were brought against a college counseling center counselor because his client had committed suicide approximately forty days after counseling with her had been terminated. The parents charged that the counselor failed to secure emergency psychiatric treatment after he was aware, or should have been aware, of her inability to care for her own self. Second, the counselor was charged with failing at all times to advise the parents or contact them concerning her true mental state and emotional condition, thus preventing them from securing proper medical aid. Third, they suggested that the counselor failed to provide proper guidance.

The case was finally resolved in favor of the counselor. The court ruled that before liability can attach there must be found a duty resting upon the person against whom recovery is sought. Since the counselor in this case was qualified as neither a medical doctor nor specialist in mental disorders, the requirement to recognize in the student a condition of the type mentioned was beyond reason. It was said further that the suggested termination of the interviews, which was advanced as a cause for suicide, did not in fact cause the injury or place the girl in a condition worse than that before the interviews began. There was no duty on the counselor's part to continue the interviews; therefore, the termination could not be considered as negligence on his part.

The most substantial reason for denying recovery of mental distress or its physical consequences, however, was that the judicial process is not well adapted to distinguishing valid from fraudulent claims in this area. Causation is difficult to prove, so the court is reluctant to extend recovery for mental distress or even its physical consequences when the defendant is charged with ordinary negligence. Finally, even if the jury had assumed that the counselor had secured psychiatric aid, that the counselor had advised the parents of the girl's emotional condition, or that the counselor had not secured termination, it would require speculation to conclude under these circumstances that she would not have taken her own life. This was beyond the duty and power of the jury or a court (Stevic, 1961).

One can safely assume that counselor liability related to personal injury will attach when the counselor does not act as a reasonably prudent person could be expected to act. The counselor is not generally liable for his client's actions outside the counseling session. Despite the lack of counselor involvement in litigation of this nature, there is a high degree of vulnerability implicit in the counseling relationship. There will probably be an increase in attempts to bring suit for personal injury or harm as a result of counselor negligence.

LIBEL AND SLANDER

Libel is defined as a false written or printed statement that tends to injure the reputation of a living person. With the passage of the open records laws in some states, the potential for libel action has increased. Statements by school personnel that are reflected in the records of students might be used to bring court action against person(s) who wrote them. The same situation may exist in the area of writing statements that might hurt an individual's chances of obtaining a job or getting into a specific educational situation.

Slander is defined in the same manner, but is confined to defamatory words. Slander is more tenuous than libel since the permanancy and thus possibility of examination is considerably less. In each case, malice is an element. Malice may be personal ill-will or a reckless disregard of the rights of others.

Regardless of the extent of malice or any other action related to libel or slander, the victim does have a defense. Basically, these defenses are that the statement is true or that the individual has consented to the statement—in effect, that he has accepted the truth of the matter. There is also a possibility of "qualified privilege," which implies that the communication was made in good faith by one person having an interest or obligation in the matter to a person with a similar interest or duty. The effect here eliminates the presumption of malice.

For required records or subsequent educational or vocational opportunities, the counselor must prepare statements concerning clients. In so doing, he may be faced with the possibility of action for libel. In addition, since feedback to other persons who have some relationship to the client is essential, he may also find that action for slander is possible. The obvious way to avoid losing a court case in either area is to utilize the guidelines of truth and good faith. Increased communication with the client may also have a cooling effect upon potential libel or slander charges.

There are times when the counselor may have to put himself on the line and take the chance that court action might ensue. If the counselor has fairly well-established data concerning a client's physical, mental, moral, or psychological health, he is obliged to report this to various significant persons in the client's life—even though in the process some statement may be construed as slanderous. Thus, if the counselor has good evidence that a female client is pregnant, he should attempt to insure that her health is protected by examination and a doctor's care. If she refuses to voluntarily see a doctor, the counselor may have to involve the parents, although this means telling them that their daughter is unchaste. Since both counselor and parents share an interest in the girl, however, there is qualified privilege.

It must be remembered that counselors have a grave professional and moral responsibility not to needlessly defame and injure the reputation of others. This is true whether the individuals be students, their parents, or other associates. Counselors must take care that communications are related to the needs of the client and that they accurately reflect the truth.

MALPRACTICE

Malpractice generally refers to any professional misconduct, carelessness, or lack of skill in the performance of an established and socially imposed duty (Huckens, 1968). For many counselors the "established and socially imposed duty"—i.e., role—is not clearly delineated, so malpractice is difficult to determine. The case of *Bogus* v. *Iverson* can serve as an example of malpractice as well as negligence. If this counselor had the well-defined and clear-cut social role that we generally assume counselors to have, he probably did not practice his profession admirably. However, the court ruled that the generally accepted counselor role concept was not a reality and that the idea whereby counselors are adequately prepared to furnish services of a therapeutic nature was probably untrue. Although these provide margins of safety in the area of malpractice, they also suggest that there is no profession of counseling.

In many ways this area is most crucial for the counselor. He must deal with his own activity as well as have an awareness of what others are doing. Additionally, he must be willing to involve himself with other counselors. He has several alternatives open to him which need some consideration. First, he needs to clearly understand himself and what he is doing. It is important that the counselor understand the seriousness of the interactions with his clients. It is also important that he have sufficient self-understanding and knowledge of personal limitations to prevent the acceptance of tasks and counseling responsibilities which could lead to charges of malpractice.

Secondly, he may need to be involved with other counselors. Traditionally, counselors have tended to avoid confrontation with other counselors because we are not certain what constitutes good counseling. However, it may be possible to deal with what constitutes bad counseling. Any profession must have internal controls on the behavior of its members. Unless counselors are willing to be involved, internal control will not occur, and the professional status which counselors need and want will not exist.

It should be obvious to the reader that the legal area is a tenuous one, with few, if any, clear-cut statements of legal behavior. There have been few precedent cases to begin determining where counselors stand in the legal area. This tenuity does not excuse behavior detrimental to the client and profession. It suggests that different kinds of behaviors on the part of the counselor and profession are necessary.

PRIVILEGED COMMUNICATION

An area of great concern to most counselors is that of privileged communication. This means, simply, that anything said by a client to a counselor in a counseling interview is privileged and that the counselor will not be called upon to divulge the information regardless of the nature of the information. Privileged communication has long existed for ministers and individual parishioners, lawyers and clients, husbands and wives in legal cases involving one or the other, medical doctors and patients, and, in some cases, counselors and clients. It is not always clear whether counselors, therapists, clinicians, and so on, have privileged communication. There is little consistency across states in this area.

One might assume that, in the absence of legislation, he has privileged communication. However, this assumption may be false and the counselor should clearly have in mind his alternatives before and after the fact.

For purposes of the present discussion, we shall assume that most counselors do not have privileged communication. This suggests several actions for the counselor.

At an appropriate time, the counselor should inform the client of his understanding of privileged communication. This suggests that the counselor is alert to various statements from the client which may have potential for later divulgence. Examples might be statements concerning the client's proclivity to violence, reports of what he had done, and similar statements. Without benefit of privileged communication, the counselor might eventually be asked to repeat, under oath, the statements made by the client.

Any written statement or tape recording of the counseling session could be subpoenaed in a court case. The counselor might have to produce his records on a client. It thus behooves the counselor to keep careful records. He may want to destroy the records regularly so that the client is protected as much as possible.

The counselor should be alert to those statements of the client which might eventuate in testimony by the counselor. At that point, some structuring would be necessary. The protection is for the client who may not be aware of the possible outcomes of his interaction with the counselor. Careful records should be maintained. Care here is intended to insure that the client be protected within the legal interpretations of the counseling process. Records can be and are called for by the courts, and the counselor should be certain that his records are truthful and made in good faith in his client's interest.

With the precautions suggested above, the counselor still may find himself called upon to testify in a court case involving the client. Unless privileged communication exists, several alternatives are available to him. First, he can give the testimony. In effect, he would be saying that the issue is best settled by due process rather than by an individual. He may, on the other hand, refuse to testify and claim violation of confidence, violation of conscience, or infringement of rights. If he does this, he may find himself held in contempt of court and facing a law suit. The counselor may feel compelled to do this, even knowing the potential consequences.

He may develop a compromise kind of activity for his court appearance. Two possibilities exist. First, he is relying on his memory—especially if the records are no longer available—and this can pose a problem for any witness. It is usually difficult to remember the specifics well enough to be of value in any court of law. Secondly, in most cases the material of interest to the court is, from the counselor's point of view, hearsay. He did not actually observe the activities reported by the client. All he knows is that which was told him, and this is usually inadmissible evidence. The counselor can bridge both sides of the question, even after the fact of some court action.

The above should not be misinterpreted to suggest that the counselor play games with client data and the serious problem of any courtroom appearance. This is not intended. The counselor may legitimately deal with the problems within the law. He may face some ethical problems in these areas, but no legal problems.

VALUES IN COUNSELING

Two separate aspects can be examined in the area of values. The first is the degree to which the personal values of the counselor ought to or do affect the relationship with the client. The second is the whole area of counseling wherein values held by the client are part of the counseling topics.

The issue of the value structure of the counselor has always been a part of the professional literature. There has been little disagreement concerning the need for the counselor to understand his value system. The counselor has a value system upon which the important decisions of his life are made. Some counselors seem unaware of the values they espouse, but observation of these people indicates a consistent reflection of their values. The value system of the counselor has critical importance in relating to his interaction with the client.

Although difficult to precisely define values, several principles relating to the construct value can be delineated. Peterson (1970) lists these as follows.

1. "Values are hypothetical constructs." They are inferred; they are criteria by which choice of objects or goals is justified.
2. "Values represent the desirable in the sense of what one 'ought' to do or what he perceives is the 'right' thing to do in any given circumstance." It is necessary to understand the distinction between the "desired" and the "desirable." The desired is tied closely to physiological needs. The desirable seems to transcend mere physiological needs.
3. "Values are motivational forces." Values are related to imitations of action and in direction setting for action.

VALUE ORIENTATIONS

Lowe (1959) identifies four value orientations that compete for the commitment of the counselor or therapist. The dilemma of values is compounded by the demands made by society, organization, client, and counselor himself. Each orientation has merit and a series of followers. Each has critics who disclaim the orientation.

Naturalism

The first system implies that scientific laws account for all phenomena. The things that can be measured or defined operationally constitute naturalism. This has been manifested most clearly in behaviorism, which has become an important factor in counseling. The behaviorist can report striking evidence of successful outcomes in counseling based upon various methods of manipulating behavior to insure effective living for the client and cultural survival. While one may not wish to go to the extent implied by Skinner (1948) in *Walden Two*, it is of some import to note that the manipulation of the client by the counselor can be toward values that are espoused by the majority with less concern over the client's understanding of how his value system meshes with the larger society.

Culturalism

The culturalists develop their value orientation from the social nature of man and the needs resulting from the particular culture in which the person lives. Thus the client is in need of help because he is isolated from other people, unable to relate to others, or unable to adapt to what others in the culture are doing. The value here again is one outside the individual toward which he must move through an adjustment, adaptation, or learning process. The cultural values are clearly delineated, and the therapist's ultimate allegiance is to society. One problem of culturalism is that it disavows the moral responsibility of the individual, allowing instead the substitution of value establishment and perhaps behavior responsibility to reside outside the individual.

Humanism

The humanist moves the locus of concern to the individual. The assumption is made that man can control his own destiny and can realize his own potentialities through rational thought processes. Each person should move toward his highest level of being without particular concern for the values established for him by others. Therapy is designed to create an atmosphere in which the individual's ability to solve his own problems is fostered.

Theism

As is suggested by the word *theism*, the theist believes that loyalty and dependence upon God constitute the major value of life. While the beliefs can be as broadly defined as the religions which contain them, the one central value deals with loving God and finding and accepting the will of God in all of life. Man finds resolution of his problems because of his faith in a God who has a purpose for all men and to whom man must eventually return.

THE COUNSELOR'S VALUES

Each counselor must gain an understanding of his own values as well as the values of others. There does not seem to be one "value" orientation which surpasses the others. However, Lowe (1959) points out that

> as psychologists familiarize themselves with the value orientation under which they operate, . . . they confess their philosophic biases and then turn those biases to fullest advantage by being of professional assistance to the special interest groups with which their values coincide. In such ways . . . the public will receive more of what psychology has to contribute. . . . (p. 692).

This also suggests that the counselor's values are known by all who are affected by him in his professional life.

Values serve as reference points for individuals. They provide a basis for deciding which course of action or choice he should make. Man has always needed these guidelines in order to continue his existence. However, values change and what was prescribed as absolute and final at one point in time becomes tenuous at other points. Man may not be able to adjust to rapidly changing value systems without guilt or anxiety. While some may question the psychologist's involvement in developing value orientations, few would suggest that he can avoid values—his own as well as the client's —in his interaction with the client. Samler (1960) suggests that "values are at the heart of the counseling relationship, are reflected in its content, and affect the process" (p. 35). If this is true, then counseling, which deals with modification of behavior, includes changes in attitudes and values on the part of the client.

The counselor's value system may be viewed in various ways. At the first level the counselor or therapist would simply know his own value system but avoid introducing this into the counseling interview. He would not indicate his own position in any of the moral or value areas which might be raised, even though he might have an idea of what he would do. The key concept is to provide a situation in which the client may move from a position of external evaluation and valuing to an internalized locus of evaluation. Any value input by the counselor would work against this objective.

It can be suggested that in fact the value system of the counselor is intimately involved in the process of counseling. The responses made by the counselor are related to values held by the counselor and toward which, through subtle reinforcement, the client is moving. The counselor may as well be open about the interjection of counselor values into the session.

A second position holds that it is impossible to remain neutral or not have an influence on the client since he has, for the most part, come to a counselor for precisely that type of assistance. A major question is raised by this general position—namely, that if, in fact, values and moral stance are inherent in any relationship, to what degree are they used or abused by the counselor? Most persons who would want to be placed in this category would want to avoid manipulation of values. They would suggest that the individual's philosophy is and must remain his own. There is some question as to whether counselors are superhumans and have a fully developed and adequate value structure. For example, he might ask, "If my values are not completely developed, can I impose them on my client?"

A question often raised in this second position on values is whether the counselor ought to provide instruction to the client in developing a value system, clarifying his values, or any of several related value-learning activities.

Some counselors would reject this teaching function in the counseling session, contending that there are more appropriate things to do and more appropriate ways to learn whatever might be taught in the counseling session. Others suggest the opposite—namely, that for some clients the first and most appropriate objective is learning or developing a more comprehensive and acceptable value system.

It should also be apparent that various types of values or morals are introduced into the counseling setting. The counselor may have some areas in which his own thoughts or development of an acceptable system are incomplete. He simply cannot help the client more because the client may already be beyond the point of the counselor. The whole area of religious values might illustrate this point, since the client may wish to have a strong set of religious values which the therapist might not understand. Even if he were able to understand, he may be still unable to help the client move in the desired direction.

The third position is one of active imposition of values upon the client. Intervention by the counselor is necessary and should be an identifiable part of counseling. The counselor must first deal with the values of the client: values about himself, values about the various prospects available to him, values about life and its interrelationships. Until these are known and accepted by the client, he will not be able to make the decision, move in meaningful directions, escape therapy, or be directed in whatever the more cognitive objectives of counseling might be.

Many people are somewhat appalled by this type of statement. It tends to suggest that the counselor has some greater amount of intelligence, skill, or knowledge than anyone else and can begin to set himself above others.

This is not acceptable to certain counselors who would characterize this as a dehumanizing process.

Regardless, there is some evidence that the type of assistance many clients want and readily accept is of the more directive nature without regard to the topic or area of concern. In effect, it is suggested that the client comes seeking help. He sees in the counselor a potential source of this help and wants the counselor to provide assistance.

In some cases the more cynical observers suggest that these clients are only seeking justification from an outside person for what they have already done or are contemplating. As long as someone agrees with them, the action is a bit more acceptable to their own value system.

In order to contrast the views of value introduction into counseling, Peterson (1970) suggests that if man is basically good, then nothing need be added to the counseling session and thus non-direction is logical. Most value questions can be ignored, because once the obstacles are ignored the client will move toward and arrive at proper values. On the other hand, if one views man as evil or with a potential for evil, the counselor cannot allow the client to move in other than positive directions. Value questions are not self-resolving because the client's proclivity would be toward an even greater manifestation of socially unacceptable behavior.

Value Problems

Another aspect of values deals with how the counselor works with an individual whose counseling concern is a value-oriented problem. How does the counselor help the client deal with this type of concern? Although certain concerns may be more appropriately referred to other specialists, it is fairly common that beliefs or, more specifically, belief conflicts are closely related to client anxiety. Typical value problems that clients bring to counseling might be an understanding of life, interrelatedness, life trauma, and morals.

Understanding Life

Most persons go through a process of questioning the meaning of life in general and individual life specifically. Whether the person attempts to derive his meaning from a theological, rational, intellectual, or human framework, he is attempting to understand the totality of life and where he fits into its picture. Most persons face this problem and are able to work through to some satisfactory solution. They may receive help from a religious leader or from a trusted friend, or they just may mature through the process and one day find an acceptable meaning to life and understand themselves. The person who does not accomplish this often seeks the assistance of a counselor. This can occur during adolescence or continue until much later in life. There are probably predictable times when this problem will occur in the lives of persons in our society.

Certain age groups face the problem. Adolescents find a conflict of what they have been told and what they observe in much of society. They are faced with the dilemma as to what is right and how to handle some guilt that accompanies rejection of a previously accepted set of values. Students often have conflicting situations during their years in college. The freedom that they are given in contrast to their restricted past poses difficulties for them in maintaining a way of life or even understanding the life they live. Adults, too, at certain age levels are subject to this pressure. As one continues to grow older, he may find less and less meaning in his life and begin to search for some other meaning which he thinks he missed along the way.

Various occurrences tend to generate the same type of life-meaning problem. The outward movement of family members causes some problems for adults—e.g., the mother who has devoted her life to raising a family and maintaining a home. The death of someone near often triggers feelings of misunderstanding about life. New experiences within the world often lead people to examine the meaning of life. In contemporary society the drug culture provides a potent reinforcer for all types of people to re-examine what life is all about. The counselor's first job in working with this type of problem is to help the client become aware of his current value system. This suggests that the counselor has some awareness of value systems and can provide a situation in which clarification can occur. He should avoid pontification in this process because the client needs assistance in developing his own system—not implementing some outside system. Eventually, the counselor should help the client deal with beliefs and effectively implementing them. Finally, the client should move into a period of a more acceptable understanding of his own life and the meaning attached to it.

Although this sounds rather simplistic, it is extremely difficult since many factors are interrelated in the process. For example, there may be impeding forces of a physical, psychological, or familial nature which impinge upon the freedom of the individual.

Although it is probably true that one can do most of what he wants to do in life, these factors do play an important role and must be recognized by the counselor and the client. In all cases the counselor should be alert to the possibility that other, more competent assistance may be necessary.

Problems of Interrelatedness

Another area of value counseling has to do with one's relationship to others. Man is basically a social animal and needs to feel wanted and needed by others. When this does not occur, he begins to develop all kinds of methods of handling the situation.

His satisfaction is often gained by belonging to identifiable social groups. Political groups, work groups, and family units all can be helpful in meeting the social needs of the individual. But in certain situations these groups pose problems for the individual. For example, the person who devotes his time and energy to getting ahead in the business world may reach a certain level and find that he, too, was a product and not the significant person he thought. If he did not have a relationship in the most important aspect of his life, where does this occur? How does he handle this—especially if future conquests do not seem as meaningful or available as in the past?

In all probability, the client facing these types of conditions needs to develop a balance in his relationship endeavors. He begins to learn to involve himself in other activities that provide a broader base for the relationship to generate. His need is to learn where other potential relationships exist and how to take advantage of them. The counselor can help in this situation by simply creating a counseling relationship in which the client sees himself as a meaningful person who can change and can be more effective in interrelatedness situations. He is helped to see how his own behavior or personality may be related to the problems he has, and when he is less manipulative, others tend to respond more favorably to him.

Life Traumas

Various life traumas bring the individual into a counseling relationship. Loss of job, retirement, death of a loved one, some physical problem, and change of geographic location are among the crises which can affect the individual. Often the crisis is not as bad as the thoughts one has about it. In all of life many things occur or statements are made which are misinterpreted by the hearer. For example, many students hear about a change in the curriculum in which they are involved and, without checking the truth of the situation, become quite anxious. Eventually learning the truth does not automatically and completely relieve the anxiety which was produced.

The counselor is faced with both dilemmas in the trauma and the words which accompany the trauma. Normally we think that the greater traumas in life are met by earlier experiences with lesser traumas. In some cases the person has neither faced the lesser trauma nor learned from the experience. He enters counseling with a need to learn how to cope with the specific problem he is presently facing.

The counselor provides a counseling relationship in which the doubts and inadequacies which the client feels are replaced by warmth, acceptance, and genuineness. The client then can begin to examine his own life and learn strategies for dealing with the particular event that leads to counseling. One difficulty in this area is that the counselor may not know whether he was instrumental in helping the client change or whether the passage of time was sufficient to block out whatever was related to the dilemma. The counselor should still strive to help the client work through self-understanding and learning effective strategies for dealing with future situations. The counselor's goal is to help alleviate the present condition and provide assistance for generalizing in future situations.

Moral Problems

Moral problems are often causes for a client to seek counseling assistance. Without getting deeply involved into the why of moral problems at this point, we would only point out that whenever the person is behaving in a way contradictory to the mores of his society, he may eventually seek assistance. There is some question as to why he seeks assistance. Some might suggest that the person wants to justify his behavior. Either he wants someone to say "what you're doing is all right," or he wants to find a set of circumstances under which the behavior would be more acceptable. At this point, he is not interested in changing behavior.

On the other hand, the guilt generated by this behavior can be the focus of attention of the counselor and client. Part of the difficulty in contemporary society is that the mores change more rapidly than the client can accept, and yet his behavior may be in line with the new mores. He is torn between doing something quite acceptable in society but living with previous strongly held values.

Two types of guilt may exist. First, a feeling of not doing as well as he would like. Quite often this is related to a value system oriented to outside persons. For example, parents are prone to pick out the negative aspects of the child's behavior and bypass any positive aspects. This tends to generate a feeling of inadequacy or guilt for not doing better. Often this is translated into "I am a bad person."

A second type of guilt is that related to breaking a specific moral law, social rule, or legal law. These activities tend to create an emotional reaction with which the client may not be able to cope. As a result the person turns inward and does nothing so that the guilt feelings can never come again.

Guilt and its accompanying feelings pose a difficult problem for the counselor. He must first help the client reduce the tensions and anxieties that are related to the guilt. This can be accomplished by again creating a relationship environment in which the client is free to express his feelings and begin to deal with these in an objective way. The client can then move toward understanding the motives behind what he has done. He begins to understand his defense mechanisms and to develop sufficient strength to examine his own needs and values. The rest of the process involves the development of responsibility and positive self-regard. He begins to trust his inner feelings and is able to function more effectively. Effective functioning may be a change of the behavior that caused the guilt, or an acceptance of the behavior as appropriate to one's self-understanding. The former is probably more desirable since only one person is affected. For the latter, several people in the life space of the individual might be affected in various ways. This needs to be examined as part of the process, although the counselor should be careful not to interject his own moral position. The outcome of this type might be contrary to the values held by the counselor or the institution he represents.

The whole area of helping clients in areas of value is very tenuous and ambiguous. Although many problems can be clearly delineated, the process for helping the client understand and resolve these problems is not as easily defined. As a result the best advice that can be offered is to develop a relationship environment which allows for client freedom and depth of feeling. This should be the prime goal of the counselor. Once this is created, the resultant steps will be more easily taken—regardless of the theoretical counseling position which the counselor holds.

The following is an outline for dealing with value conflicts or clarification for the client. The model flows from the work of Thomas (1970).

1. *Identify the value conflict.* A conflict occurs when a problem is not solvable within the client's behavior repertoire. A conflict suggests that various equally attractive alternatives exist.

2. *Identify live options to the conflict.* A live option refers to the fact that a portion of the population in the society is dealing with an alternative in a specific identifiable way. The option represents a judgment of value on the part of someone.

3. *Compare and contrast the various options.* When several options are identified, the client and counselor compare and contrast them for

strengths and weaknesses. The question is, usually, What are the consequences associated with this option?

4. *Rank order the various options.* Counselor and client begin to work out a list of options based upon the merits, good outcomes, lack of bad consequences, and so forth. Selection of the best option should be the natural result of this ranking.

5. *Select the most acceptable option.* The selection process includes commitment on the part of the client. Values, in this case, are commitments to standards of what is personally believed desirable. Until selection and commitment occur, the process is largely intellectual.

6. *Live the choice.* Values and thus the selection of the best option are normative. Public commitment is a necessary experience for value clarification.

The counselor can indicate his values within this framework. He should avoid making the decisions or ranking the options for the client. Glasser (1965) speaks on this point when he suggests, "to the best of our ability as responsible human beings, we must help our patients arrive at some decision concerning the moral quality of their behavior."

SUMMARY

It seems impossible to avoid the impingement of values into the counseling situation. The counselor has identifiable values whether presented covertly or overtly. The client has values and value dilemmas. Society supports certain value systems over others and although increased flexibility seems to be occurring, the client who is too far away from the socially held values faces adjustment difficulties for which he will seek counseling help.

In terms of the values of the counselor, Rogers (1957) makes sense.

> One cannot engage in psychotherapy without giving operational evidence of an underlying value orientation and view of human nature. It is definitely preferable, in my estimation, that such underlying views be open and explicit rather than covert and implicit (p. 199).

REFERENCES

Bogust v. *Iverson*, 192 N. E. 2d 228 (Wisconsin, 1960).

Brammer, Lawrence M., and Shostrom, Everett L. *Therapeutic Psychology* (2nd ed.). Englewood Cliffs, N. J.: Prentice-Hall, 1968.

Edwards, Newton. *The Courts and the Public School.* Chicago: University of Chicago Press, 1955.

"Ethical Standards—American Personnel and Guidance Association." *Personnel and Guidance Journal 1961* 40, 206–209.

Huckins, Wesley. *Ethical and Legal Considerations in Guidance.* Boston: Houghton-Mifflin, 1968.

Lowe, C. Marshall. "Value Orientations—An Ethical Dilemma." *American Psychologist 1959*, 14, 687–693.

Peterson, James Allen. *Counseling and Values.* Scranton, Pa.: International Textbook Company, 1970.

Rogers, Carl R. "A Note on the Nature of Man." *Journal of Counseling Psychology 1957* 4, 199–203.

Samler, Joseph. "Change in Values: A Goal in Counseling." *Journal of Counseling Psychology 1960* 7, 32–39.

Skinner, B. F. *Walden Two.* New York: Macmillan, 1948.

Stevic, Richard. "The Legal Status of the Secondary School Counselor." *Guidance 1961* 1, 8–16.

Thomas, Walter L. *Toward a Concept for Affective Education.* Chicago: Combined Motivation Education Systems, 1970.

Wrenn, C. Gilbert. "Psychology, Religion and Values for the Counselor." *Personnel and Guidance Journal 1958* 36, 326–334.

Subject Index

386

Author Index

Abeles, N., 168, 174, 180
Adams, G. S., 320, 329, 342
Adams, J. S., 126, 129
Adler, A., 26, 27, 38, 54, 55, 56, 57, 58, 59, 60, 61, 62, 63, 67, 231, 232, 263
Adler, G., 65, 68
Adler, K. A., 68
Alexander, F., 65, 68, 231, 232, 233, 263
Allen, T. W., 168, 177
Allport, A. W., 152, 153
Anastasi, A., 332, 342
Anderson, S., 152–153, 252–254, 264
Angel, E., 244, 265
Ansbacher, R., 55, 57–60, 65, 67–69
Ansbacher, H., 55, 57–60, 65, 67–69
Antony, N. A., 158, 177
APA Committee on Training and Clinical Psychology, 159, 160, 177
Appell, M. L., 160, 177
Arbuckle, D., 160, 177, 197, 210
Association of Counselor Education and Supervision, 160
Axelrad, S., 315

Baer, C. E., 175, 178
Baer, D. M., 129
Bailey, K. G., 254, 264
Balogh, S., 198, 201–202, 206, 210
Bandura, A., 111, 122, 126–127, 129–130, 135, 169–170, 177
Barbara, D., 260, 264
Barker, E. N., 23, 25, 150, 153, 157, 158, 181
Bassin, F. V., 69
Baum, O. E., 200–201, 210
Beers, C., 10
Berenson, B. G., 95–99, 162, 171–172, 232, 236, 252, 254, 256, 264
Bergman, P., 158, 181–182

Bernard, H., 161, 179
Betz, B., 174, 182
Biddle, B. J., 189, 210
Bijou, S. W., 117, 130
Bird, D., 190, 211
Black, J., 189, 210
Bohn, M. Jr., 157, 168, 178
Bordin, E. S., 48–51, 65, 187, 190–191, 193, 210, 217, 218, 220, 226–227, 239, 241, 249, 250, 264
Boy, A. V., 86, 97
Brammer, L. M., 11, 19, 24, 177–178, 244, 247–248, 250, 264, 268, 271–272, 280–281, 285, 293, 313, 315, 347, 353, 364, 369, 384
Brams, J. M., 169, 178
Brayfield, H. H., 362–364
Brenner, C., 69
Brill, A. A., 69
Brown, D., 166, 180
Buchheimer, A., 198, 201–202, 206, 210
Bufental, J. F. T., 162, 163, 178
Buss, A. H., 126, 130
Byrne, R. H., 218, 227

Callahan, D. M., 172, 174, 180
Callis, R., 215, 218–219, 227
Campbell, R. E., 167, 178
Cannon, H. J., 157, 178
Carkhuff, R. R., 95–99, 152–153, 162, 171–172, 178, 181, 232, 236–237, 252, 254, 256, 264, 360
Carr, A. C., 95, 97
Carson, R., 174–176, 178
Cartwright, D., 173, 179
Caselle, W. K., 126, 130
Chenault, J., 165, 178
Clemes, S., 189, 210
Collier, M. J., 66
Combs, A. W., 75–76, 84, 95, 98, 141, 168, 178
Cowen, E. L., 95, 98

Cox, D., 69–70
Critchton-Miller, H., 70
Cramer, S. H., 349, 351, 364
Crites, J. O., 331
Cronbach, L. J., 332, 342
Cullen, L. F., 262, 264

D'Andrea, V., 189, 210
Darley, J. G., 217, 228
DeLaney, D. J., 262, 264
Demos, G., 168, 178
Deutsch, D., 68
Dewey, J., 19
Dickinson, J., 222, 224–225, 227
Dollard, J., 102, 111, 116, 130, 132, 232–233, 243, 264
Donnan, H. H., 165, 178
Douds, J., 152, 153
Dreikurs, R., 55, 61–63, 65
Dreyfus, E. A., 160, 178, 232, 235, 264
Dulany, D. E., 130
Durkee, A., 126, 130
Dymond, R. F., 95, 99

Edwards, J., 132
Edwards, N., 369–370, 385
Eisenstein, S., 65
Ekman, P., 262, 264
Ellenberger, H., 244, 265
Emerson, R. W., 255
Emery, J. P., 131
English, A. C., 12, 24
English, H. B., 12, 24
Epstein, S., 240, 241, 264
Erikson, E. H., 41, 47, 65, 70

Farson, R., 161, 178
Felzer, S. B., 200–201, 210
Fenichel, O., 70
Ferenczi, S., 65
Fiedler, F. E., 22, 24, 151, 153, 157, 158, 171, 178, 232, 235, 264
Fisher, K. A., 163, 179
Ford, D. H., 19–20, 22, 24,

390

392